Data Structures

FROM RECIPES TO C

Lawrence E. Turner, Jr.
Andrews University

WCB **Wm. C. Brown Publishers**

Dubuque, Iowa•Melbourne, Australia•Oxford, England

Book Team

Editor *Earl McPeek*
Developmental Editor *Jane Parrigin/Paula-Christy Heighton*
Production Editor *Kay Driscoll*

Wm. C. Brown Publishers
A Division of Wm. C. Brown Communications, Inc.

Vice President and General Manager *Beverly Kolz*
Vice President, Director of Sales and Marketing *John W. Calhoun*
Marketing Manager *Julie Keck*
Advertising Manager *Janelle Keeffer*
Director of Production *Colleen A. Yonda*
Publishing Services Manager *Karen J. Slaght*

Wm. C. Brown Communications, Inc.

President and Chief Executive Officer *G. Franklin Lewis*
Corporate Vice President, President of WCB Manufacturing *Roger Meyer*
Vice President and Chief Financial Officer *Robert Chesterman*

Cover design by Design Associates, Inc.

Cover image illustrated by French Studios, Inc.

A Times Mirror Company

Library of Congress Catalog Card Number: 93–70080

ISBN 0–697–17286–4

Printed in the United States of America by Wm. C. Brown Communications, Inc., 2460 Kerper Boulevard, Dubuque, IA 52001

10 9 8 7 6 5 4 3 2 1

dedicated to

Dorothy Anne

my greatest teacher

Contents

Preface

The door led right into a large kitchen, which was full of smoke from one end to the other: the Duchess was sitting on a three-legged stool in the middle, nursing a baby: the cook was leaning over the fire, stirring a large cauldron which seemed to be full of soup.

"There's certainly too much pepper in that soup!" Alice said to herself, as well as she could for sneezing.

There was certainly too much of it in the <u>air</u>. Even the Duchess sneezed occasionally; and as for as the baby, it was sneezing and howling alternatively without a moment's pause.

To the student:

Data structures is an exciting study. You are fortunate to embark on this adventure in C! The ingenuity of the people who developed the algorithms—as evidenced by the elegance of the concepts and the sometimes simple solutions to difficult situations—makes for a most interesting study.

The material in this text is intended for you, a computer science or computer information systems student, taking your second course in computer science using the C language. It is expected that you have already taken a course in C programming, but are not completely proficient in the C language or programming in general; therefore, the experience gained in solving the problems in the text take you far toward achieving expertise in this area.

The general objectives are to:

- Augment practice in the C programming language, especially in the use of a modular, structured program solution that is stylistically consistent and readable.

- Discuss additional C constructs that were covered lightly, if at all, in the first course in C programming—this includes: recursion, pointers, and structures.

- Present important data structures such as simple lists, strings, stacks, queues, files, linked lists, binary trees, heaps, and hash tables.

- Supply a theoretical basis for how data structures may be stored and accessed in computer memory.

- Provide algorithms that are consistent in notation and adapted for the C language, especially with 0 origin for arrays.

- Provide an understanding of how these algorithms work.

- Provide experience in translating an algorithm or procedure into a working C program.

- Provide a basis for comparison of algorithms, and an analysis of the simpler algorithms, so that comparisons between algorithms can be made.

The mathematical concepts presented here are not difficult. They do not require an advanced knowledge of calculus or discrete mathematics, but some mathematical maturity is expected. Typically, it is assumed that you have taken, or are taking, a college-level mathematics course in either beginning calculus or discrete mathematics. However, a good understanding of Algebra II should be sufficient.

You are not expected to memorize the more complicated algorithms; but by the end of the study of this text you should be able to explain the concepts behind them, describe generally how they work, be able to follow them in detail by hand, and develop a working computer program from them. You are not expected to be able to reproduce all of the analyses; however, you should know how the algorithms differ in their effectiveness.

The algorithms presented in the text have been adapted for the C language. The primary change from the typical formulation has been the use of indices beginning with 0 rather than 1. Special care has been taken to ensure that they are consistent in notation and complete in detail. In many cases the algorithms are not "structured." The advantage in this is that in this form, they may be easier to follow by hand. The disadvantage is that you must carefully develop a structured procedure for the C implementation; however, in doing so you gain experience in developing a structured solution to problems.

Each chapter provides a number of questions, exercises, and problems. For the most part, you should be able to answer the questions fairly directly from your understanding of the text material. However, the answers cannot, typically, be simply regurgitated from a statement in the text. Generally, the exercises require more understanding of the material plus, the ability to synthesize, than do the questions. Completing the exercises may require some thought, as well as a calculation, a derivation, or something to be written out. The problems are typically a programming activity; you should expect to spend considerable time with each problem.

The best way to learn the concepts presented here is to take the time to study the material, work through the examples, answer the questions, complete the exercises, and write C programs. The study of data structures is best reinforced by developing a computer program. The feedback that you get when it works correctly is that you do understand what is asked.

There are a number of programs available for an MS-DOS environment that illustrate these concepts. They allow you to explore some of the effects of modifying parameters and provide you with an experiential "feeling" for how some of the algorithms behave.

It is my wish that you experience as much enjoyment and delight in studying these concepts as I did in writing the material. If, when you complete this course, you not only have a better appreciation for the usefulness of data structures and algorithms, but even *like* them, then my task as a teacher has been more than rewarded!

To the teacher:

This material is designed for the computer science or computer information systems student as a second course in their freshman year. There is sufficient material for a four-credit semester or a two three-credit quarter courses.

It is expected that each student has had a previous course in C programming. It is assumed that each will have had experience in writing and debugging simple programs that use arrays, functions, recursion, pointers, and structures. However, it is also anticipated that even though each student has been exposed as a "first pass" to some of these concepts, the majority of the students are not thoroughly proficient and comfortable. Of course, there will be those students for which the concepts presented are quite easy. Hopefully, there exist exercises and problems at the end of most of the chapters that will challenge even the brightest student. At the other end of the spectrum will be students who will struggle with the concepts and even the more simple programming assignments. It is anticipated, and the level of the books is designed, that the majority of the students fall between these extremes.

A course in data structures can be organized in many different ways. The material is logically structured along several different dimensions. It is possible, for example, to organize the material around processes; that is, to group all of the sorting algorithms together, all of the searching algorithms, etc. With a few exceptions, the organization of this text is around the **data structure**. Generally, there is a progression from simpler, less efficient data structures to more complicated and efficient ones.

Chapter 1 is an introduction, discussing algorithms and their behavior.

Chapter 2 presents an overview of simple random-access lists. The concepts introduced are discussed in more detail in *Chapters 3* (searching), *5* (simple sorts), *6* (advanced sorts), *7* (I/O restricted lists), and *9* (Strings).

Chapter 11 focuses on external media and file processes.

Chapter 12 introduces linked lists, which have advantages for insertion and deletion over simple lists, but have worse behavior for searching.

Chapter 13 uses the linked structure concept to discuss binary trees which retain the advantages of linked lists and combine efficient searching.

Following the discussion of the binary tree structure, *Chapter 14* naturally leads to heaps.

Chapter 15 discusses a structure that, while it is a simple list, is even more efficient than a binary tree for insertions, deletions, and searching—a hash structure.

Thus this order also progresses from the simple and less efficient to the more complicated and efficient data structures.

Sprinkled amongst these chapters are several that build concepts that will be used subsequently and, in some cases, are C-dependent. *Chapter 4* discusses recursion. It is assumed that the students have been exposed to this previously. Now, however, a more mature understanding is needed, since recursion becomes an indispensable tool for presenting certain algorithms.

Chapter 8 could logically be positioned before *Chapter 2*. It covers the basis for the storage of arrays. However, I have found that students often have a difficult time with the mathematical reasoning at the beginning of the course. Therefore, in the spirit of the usual order of computer science topics in the first year of study—where high-level programming is taught first, followed by data structures, and, finally, a presentation of assembler, data representation, number representation, and logic (which one could easily argue is fundamental and should be presented first)—I have moved this material to the middle of the course, and found that it improves the students' ability to grasp and use the material.

Chapter 10 is similar to *Chapter 4* in that the concepts should have been introduced in a first course. The material is positioned at this point in the course because it will be needed in subsequent chapters. Again, it is assumed that the student has already been exposed to the concepts of pointers and structures; however, these are more abstract than other constructs of C—especially pointers.

Chapter 16 is included for completeness. Using linked structures with indices is quite complicated for many students. Changing to pointers represents another level of difficulty. Dynamic memory allocation is even more abstract.

Chapter 9, on strings, is also included for completeness. It is quite true that a first course in C programming must discuss strings. However, the primary focus in this chapter is not on the C library functions and how to use them, but on how they and other string processes might be performed.

Because I have chosen to base the primary order of the text on the data structure, it turns out that the more complicated and lengthy programming assignments occur toward the end of the material. The longest programs consist of the linked list and binary tree maintenance procedures. This is consistent with the maturation of the students' programming experience.

With a data structures course, there is not only a choice of organization, but also a choice concerning depth of material. As an example, *Chapter 13* primarily discusses binary trees. There is an introduction to other tree structures, such as AVL trees, b-trees, and tries; however, these are not presented in detail, with algorithms. Presumably, most students will take a subsequent course in data structures that will cover these and other concepts in greater depth. Other such material that could have been included, but was not—topics such as, data compression, sparse arrays, sets, random files, and keyed files.

I also chose not to include, at present, a chapter on formal graph theory. This could be done, but the emphasis in this book is the delicate interaction of the data structures, the algorithms, and the C language. Ultimately, it was a choice to make the material more "practical" and closer to implementation—however, there was also a desire not to make this text a mere cookbook.

If there is too much material for a given course, or for a given set of students, then *Chapters 9* (Strings) and *16* (Dynamic Memory Allocation) could easily be omitted. *Chapter 14* (Heaps) and *11* (External Media and Sorts) could be omitted, but with more difficulty. Parts of several chapters, especially the last sections of many of the chapters, could be omitted or discussed briefly.

It is my hope that you get as much pleasure and delight from teaching these concepts as I do. If, when you have completed a course using this text, you and your students not only have a better appreciation for data structures and algorithms, but even *like* them, then my task as a writer will be successful!

Acknowledgements:

The quotes at the beginning of each chapter are from Lewis Carroll's delightful stories of *Alice's Adventures in Wonderland* and *Through the Looking Glass*. Fabricated on a most wonderful summer day 1862, they are loved by young children and grown-up children yet today.

No book is ever written in isolation. I appreciate the support and encouragement of many individuals. My children, Jason and Sonja, provided continual interest in the progress of the project and personal encouragement to me. Several classes of students, who struggled with early versions, made constructive suggestions and helped debug the material. It was comments from several of those students about the usefulness of the material to them personally, that motivated me to continue. My colleagues in the Computer Science and Information Systems Department at Andrews University in Berrien Springs, Michigan, have been very supportive. Daniel E. Turk contributed valuable input concerning student reaction to some of the ideas. Michele Pezet Evard provided important ideas about computer visualization. During the final "push," Catherine Knarr furnished much needed understanding.

I wish to thank the reviewers who made many valuable suggestions. They are, in alphabetical order, S. I. Ahmad (Eastern Michigan University), Stephen Allen (Utah State University), Chaitanya Baru (IBM Toronto Labs, IBM Canada, LTD), Alex Biliris (Boston University), Michael Dorey (Brazosport College), Sandra Gum (Salen-TEIKYO University), David Hale (Texas Technical University), Paul Higbee (University of North Florida), Judy Ann Hill (Purdue University Calumet), Les Kinsler (Kansas State University-Salina), James E. Larson (Compu-Train, Inc.), Paul Miller (Edgewood College), Paul W. Ross (Millersville University of Pennsylvania), Jack Thompson (The

University of Tennessee at Chattanooga), and Bernhard Weinberg (Michigan State University).

And to Dorothy Anne, a very special person, who, as part of my life for a sadly brief amount of time, taught me more about those things that are important than I had learned over many long years—this book is gratefully dedicated.

Lawrence E. Turner, Jr.

pax et bonum

List of Algorithms

List of C Functions and Programs

Chapter 1

Data Structures, Algorithms, and C Programs

"You may not have lived much under the sea—" ("I haven't," said Alice)—"and perhaps you were never even introduced to a lobster—" (Alice began to say "I once tasted—" but checked herself hastily, and said, "No, never") "—so you can have no idea what a delightful thing a Lobster-Quadrille is!"

"No, indeed," said Alice. "What sort of a dance is it?"

"Why," said the Gryphon, "you first form into a line along the seashore—"

"Two lines!" cried the Mock Turtle. "Seals, turtles, salmon, and so on: then, when you've cleared all the jelly-fish out of the way—"

"That generally takes some time," interrupted the Gryphon.

"—you advance twice—"

"Each with a lobster as a partner!" cried the Gryphon.

"Of course," the Mock Turtle said: "advance twice, set to partners—"

"—change lobsters, and retire in same order," continued the Gryphon.

"Then, you know," the Mock Turtle went on, "you throw the—"

"The lobsters!" shouted the Gryphon with a bound into the air.

"—as far out to sea as you can—"

"Swim after them!" screamed the Gryphon.

"Turn a somersault in the sea!" cried the Mock Turtle, capering wildly about.

"Change lobsters again!" yelled the Gryphon at the top of its voice.

"Back to land again, and—that's all the first figure," said the Mock Turtle, suddenly dropping his voice; and the two creatures, who had been jumping about like mad things all this time, sat down again very sadly and quietly, and looked at Alice.

1.1   OBJECTIVES

The objectives of this chapter are to:

- Introduce the need for a study of data structures.

- Discuss how data structures and algorithms fit together.

- Give examples of how the choice of a data structure affects the program structure.

- Describe the characteristics of an algorithm.

- Provide an example of how the algorithm functions.

- Perform a simple analysis of an algorithm.

- Introduce the "big O" notation.

- Consider alternate algorithms and their efficiency.

- Describe alternative forms of expressing an algorithm.

- Illustrate how an algorithm might be transformed into a C program.

1.2   INTRODUCTION

An understanding of data structures is central to using a computer. The fundamental computer problem is:

In other words, some form of data is entered into the computer information processing resource, and is stored, manipulated, modified, and finally—in a changed form—sent out of the system.

How data is stored and manipulated in the computer is the study of data structures.

In many cases the original data is summarized; that is, the output data contains far fewer values than the input data. An example is the statistical analysis of a set of values where two resultant values—the mean and the standard deviation—are used to characterize a large number of values.

Another illustration of this would be the accounting information for a business; somewhere there exists a record of all of its monetary transactions. The executives of the company cannot examine every entry for each transaction; rather, what is useful and important is a financial summary of the company, perhaps expressed as a balance sheet.

During a typical quarter or semester of study, a student earns points for each assigned problem or test answer; typically these points are added and recorded for each assignment or test. These totals are then combined into a single value—the final grade—to be turned into the records' office. Ultimately, all of the grades for a student are averaged, the grade-point average is computed, and important decisions are made on that single summarizing value.

On the other hand, there are calculations that may take a small number of input values and generate a very large set of output data. A stellar model may be characterized by a handful of parameters that determine an evolutionary sequence of stellar models, each consisting of hundreds or thousands of numbers.

A graphical program might take a few tens or hundreds of data points, representing objects, and generate a million pixels or points to be plotted on a screen where their intensity and colors depict the desired scene.

1.2.1 Data Structures and Algorithms

In order to perform the manipulation functions of data, it is important to pay careful attention to how the data is to be stored—i.e., the *data structure*! In addition, it is impossible to separate the details of the storage of the data and the procedures used to access and manipulate the data—these procedures are called *algorithms*. Therefore, a study of data structures is intimately connected to a study of the algorithms involved. The data structure concepts and their procedures form the foundation of virtually all computer programs. Indeed, Nicklaus Wirth, the developer of Pascal and Modula-2, has suggested:

$$\text{algorithm + data structure = program.}^1$$

---

[1] He uses this as the title of his Data Structures Book: *Algorithms+Data Structures=Programs*, Prentice-Hall, 1

We can differentiate between data and information. Data is the objective representation of information; it carries meaningful content when interpreted by the user. Thus, information is what the data means to a person. Perhaps we can suggest:

data + person = information.

Of course, one can argue about whether a computer actually understands the data or information—or simply follows rules which tell how electrical signals are to be modified. For the material in this book, we will be concerned with data—its representation, storage, and manipulation—and not the philosophical debate about whether computers can think or whether the data means anything. Regardless, the basic concepts and procedures of data structures may be applied to many diverse situations.

1.3   DATA STRUCTURES

How a single datum might be stored in a computer does not require much thought; although the number of bits required for it and its location must be ascertained, the organization of one item is a vacuous issue. However, when there are several items—or a set of data—the organization becomes important.

Data structures is the study of how data is organized for computer processing. This organization suggests both a static storage arrangement as well as a dynamic relationship between data items.

Many different data structures are possible. The appropriate one for a particular situation depends upon many factors, including: the nature of each item, the number of items to be processed, how the items are to be accessed, the computer resources available, and other details.

The material in this text is concerned with an elementary presentation of various data structures and variations; the procedures for using them; simple analysis of the effectiveness of those procedures; and guidelines for choosing the most appropriate one for the given situation.

The kinds of data structures to be studied will include simple lists, linked lists, stacks, queues, binary trees, hash lists, and heaps. These may be implemented internally, as a list, or externally, as a file. Each item in the list may be simple or may contain a complicated internal structure. The procedures to be covered will include accessing, searching, inserting, deleting, sorting, and merging.

1.4   CHOICE OF DATA STRUCTURE

The effectiveness of the program that accesses and manipulates the data is often greatly influenced by the choice of storage for the data. Thus it is important for a programmer to be familiar with a wide variety of ways of organizing data, the various algorithms that are associated with each, and the characteristics and effectiveness of them.

There are numerous examples of where the inappropriate choice of a data structure has resulted in changing an easy implementation to a very difficult one or one that is extremely inefficient.

1.4.1   Tic-Tac-Toe

As a simple example, the game of tic-tac-toe is played on a 3x3 board. Each square may be empty or contain an X or an O. Players alternate in placing a symbol in an empty square and the game continues until one gets "three in a row" or the board is filled.

The most obvious way of representing this structure in the computer is a two-dimensional array:

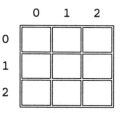

We have used the C convention of using indices that begin with 0.

The array might be an integer array, with the various possibilities for each element chosen arbitrarily as:

empty	0
X	1
O	2

Whenever the computer needs to check for a win, a *series* of expressions that look like this must be used:

```
if (brd[0][0] == 1 && brd[0][1] == 1 && brd[0][2] == 1)
    [process the win for X!]
```

There are eight such expressions. With some clever programming using loops, this might be compressed. However, consider how the computer might select a move. Let us assume that the computer is X or 1. The first thing that one would want to do is find any "line" with two 1's and the third location empty. The move is to place a 1 (or an X) in the empty location and win. The C code to implement this, using only the above structure, is rather complex. Further, if such a move is not possible, then the next best play is to check to see if the opponent has such a position, and play to block it. This is just as messy to program!

A better organization is to consider the "ways of winning." There are exactly eight "lines" of three squares that pass through the board in the various directions. Let us label them as:

0-2	horizontal lines numbered from the top
3-5	vertical lines numbered from the left
6	diagonal line, top left to bottom right
7	diagonal line, bottom left to top right

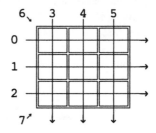

Further, we can number the individual squares sequentially as:

```
        0    1    2

   0 ┌────┬────┬────┐
     │ 0  │ 1  │ 2  │
   1 ├────┼────┼────┤
     │ 3  │ 4  │ 5  │
   2 ├────┼────┼────┤
     │ 6  │ 7  │ 8  │
     └────┴────┴────┘
```

Numbering them this way simplifies the process of locating them and specifying them, since we can use a single number rather than an ordered pair.

A table and its inverse allows an easy translation from one representation to the other:

TIC-TAC-TOE SQUARE AND LINES

Square	Location	Number of Lines	Lines		
0	0,0	3	0	3	6
1	0,1	2	0	4	
2	0,2	3	0	5	7
3	1,0	2	1	3	
4	1,1	4	1	4	6 7
5	1,2	2	1	5	
6	2,0	3	2	3	7
7	2,1	2	2	4	
8	2,2	3	2	5	6

We have also included the "number of lines" and a list of the lines that each square contributes to. As an example, square 0 is located at 0,0. There are three winning lines that use this square: 0 (horizontal, top row), 3 (vertical, left column), and 6 (diagonal, top left to bottom right.)

We can see immediately that some squares are more important than others because they are part of more winning "lines." In particular, the center square is part of four lines, the corner squares contribute to three lines each, and the remaining edge squares only participate in two lines.

It is useful to have an "inverse" table that specifies which squares contribute to each of the eight "lines."

INVERSE TABLE

line	squares		
0	0	1	2
1	3	4	5
2	6	7	8
3	0	3	6
4	1	4	7
5	2	5	8
6	0	4	8
7	6	4	2

These tables make it easy for us to determine which lines are involved with a play at a particular square and which squares contribute to a given line.

Then the primary data structure is a list of "lines":

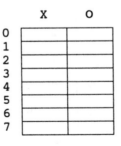

In C we could define this structure as:

```
int line[8][2];
```

The program will record the number of X's and O's that fill a given "line"—initially both lists are set to zero. When a move is made at a particular location; that move is recorded in all "lines" that it could contribute to. It is easy to check for a winning move with a simple list search, such as:

```
for (i=0;  i<8;  i++)
    if (line[i][0] == 2  && line[i][1] == 0)
        {play in line i and win!}
```

Or if such a move is not possible, then:

```
for (i=0;  i<8;  i++)
    if (line[i][0] == 0  && line[i][1] == 2)
        {play in line i and block a certain win!}
```

As an example, consider the following situation with O to play:

	0	1	2
0	X	O	O
1		X	
2	X		

The corresponding list of lines would be:

	X	O
0	1	2
1	1	0
2	1	0
3	2	0
4	1	1
5	0	1
6	2	0
7	2	1

The loops given above would find that no line could produce a win. Line 3 needs to be blocked. (Actually, so does 6, and, unfortunately, both cannot be blocked—X will win regardless!)

Line 3 is the vertical line along the left. Examining the table above, we discover that squares 0, 3, and 6 make up this line. The only one of these squares that contains a 0 is number 3. This, then, is our play.

1.4.2   Anagrams

Consider a much different problem: determining whether an anagram of a given word exists. An *anagram* of a word is another word that consists of a different permutation or arrangement of the same letters. For example:

> alice
> lacie
> celia

are all anagrams. However, "lieac" is not because, even though it is a different permutation of the same letters, it is not a word that exists in normal English. Now if you were given the word "alice" and were asked if another English word exists that is an anagram, how would you proceed? Or more precisely, how would you program a computer to check for you? Assume that you have a dictionary of all English words available.

Probably, the most straightforward scheme would be to generate all of the possible permutations of the letters in the original word and look each one up in the dictionary. Therefore, we would need to try arrangements such as:

> aliec
> alcie
> alcei
> .
> .
> .

Since there are five letters in the word, there are 120 such permutations. (Note that you have five possible choices for the first letter—then, once it is chosen, four for the second, three for the third, etc. The total number is the product $5 \cdot 4 \cdot 3 \cdot 2 \cdot 1 = 5! = 120$.) Looking each word up in a dictionary is not hard, but would take some time. However, if the number of letters in the original word were seven rather than five, there would be 5040 possible "words" to look up!

Is it possible to do better? The answer is "yes," but it requires changing the data structure—in this case an ordered list of English words. What we can do **once** is create a new data structure that consists of pairs of words. The second word in the pair will be the ordinary English word, and the first is its alphabetized version; that is, we rearrange the letters of the word so that they are in alphabetical order. Therefore "alice" becomes:

> (aceil, alice)

A useful thing to note is that all anagrams will have the same alphabetized version. We can then arrange our anagram dictionary into alphabetical order according to the first word in each pair.

When we want to check a new word to see if it has an anagram, we simply rearrange its letters in alphabetical order, then look it up in the anagram dictionary. (If it were originally an English word, we should find it!) We then look for those entries located just before or after it. If there are any with the same alphabetized version, they will be anagrams of the original word.

We could improve upon this even further if we used a different data structure than a simple ordered list. A hash list, given enough memory, could allow us to find an anagram with, on the average, only two or three looks into our dictionary! Even on a very slow computer, this would be fast!

1.5   ALGORITHMS

In addition to the organization of the data, there are the procedures for manipulating the data—these are algorithms.

1.5.1   History

The word "algorithm" comes from "algorism" which in turn comes from the name of a Persian textbook author, Abu Jàfar Mohammed ibn Musâ al-khwârizmî (c. 825 A.D.). He wrote the book *ilm al jabr w'al muqabala* (*The Science of Transposition and Cancellation*) from which we get the word "algebra." The last part of his name (literally "native of [the town] Khwarizmi") was distorted into "algorism," which came to mean "the art of calculation"—now called "arithmetic."

1.5.2   Euclid's Algorithm

By 1950, the word "algorithm" was associated with Euclid's Algorithm (c. 300 B.C.) which first appeared in *Elements, book vii, propositions i and ii.* Stated in modern form this is:

Algorithm E (Find Greatest Common Divisor—Euclid's Algorithm). Given any two positive integers m and n, find their greatest common divisor (GCD); that is, the largest positive integer which evenly divides both m and n.

E1. [find remainder]   Divide m by n, and let r be the remainder.

E2. [is it zero?]   If $r = 0$, then Halt; n is the GCD.

E3. [interchange]   Set $m = n$; $n = r$; Go to step E1.

1.5.3   Characteristics

Euclid's, or any, algorithm expresses a procedure or recipe for performing some action or solving some problem. Formally, an algorithm is a finite set of instructions that has the following characteristics:

1. input (zero or more)

2. output (one or more)

3. unambiguous

4. finite

5. effective

The fourth characteristic, in this list, refers to the time or the number of steps for the algorithm to terminate. Note that a finite set of instructions is not necessarily finite in execution. The simple C construct:

```
while (1)
      ;
```

represents an infinite loop with a very small set of instructions!

The effectiveness of an algorithm involves several similar concepts. An effective algorithm is robust; that is, it handles many different situations without lots of special cases. It is also important that the algorithm performs its action as quickly as possible—that it works efficiently, and ideally, that it takes little computer memory.

These characteristics can also be discerned in most of the recipes found in a typical cookbook. One usually finds a list of ingredients (input), followed by a list or paragraph of instructions (finite in length and hopefully unambiguous). The reputation of the publisher in selecting the particular recipe and testing process ensures that the recipe is a good one (effective); the processes described are usually in terms of time, but, occasionally, are in terms of reaching a particular state (finite); and the end result is described (output). There is at least one non-finite culinary procedure that has been documented and is therefore <u>not</u> an algorithm; this is a procedure concerned with the attempt to boil water while under close observation!

1.5.4   Example Execution

It is not necessary to understand *why* a particular algorithm works as long as one can understand *how* it works. Presumably, one can use Euclid's Algorithm even without understanding the mathematics behind it. Consider the following example:

$$m = 144, n = 60.$$

Clearly, these values satisfy the conditions stated in the algorithm—both are positive integers. Tracing the algorithm:

E1: $r = 24$, since $144/60 = 2$ remainder 24

E2: r is not zero

E3: $m = 60$, $n = 24$

E1: $r = 12$, since $60/24 = 2$ remainder 12

E2: r is not zero

E3: $m = 24$, $n = 12$

E1: $r = 0$, since $24/12 = 2$ remainder 0

E2: r is zero, terminate with GCD $= 12$

Through factoring or inspection you should be able to verify that 12 is indeed the greatest common divisor of 144 and 60. Therefore, the algorithm does produce the desired result—at least for this example!

1.5.5   Format of Formal Algorithms

The format of Euclid's algorithm is typical of what we will be using repeatedly. Each algorithm will be labeled with a one- or two-letter identifier that will remain unique throughout the book. A short title will be provided in parentheses. A phrase will describe what the algorithm attempts to perform and will define the input. Each step is numbered sequentially, using the identifier; the steps are to be performed in order unless otherwise specified. Typically each step will contain a short phrase in brackets that identifies the principal action for that step. Next comes the action to be performed. Finally, the end of the algorithm will be indicated by this heavy vertical line, ▮.[2]

1.5.6   Correctness and Finiteness

The most important aspect of an algorithm is whether or not it is correct; that is, will it produce the desired result in all cases? For the mathematical algorithms—such as Euclid's algorithm—proofs can be devised to show that, indeed, they are correct. In programming it is usually impossible to devise a proof establishing the correctness of the program; rather, programs are tested with a range of input data for which the output is known. If the program passes all of the tests, then the programmer gains some confidence that it is indeed correct. However, no matter how many tests are performed and passed, there is no proof that the program is correct under all circumstances. There have been many examples, unfortunately, where an error—i.e., a bug—was discovered after the program had been in use for many years.

---

[2] This notation is due to Donald Knuth, *The Art of Computer Programming*, Addison-Wesley Publishing Co., 1973.

Euclid's algorithm is finite in its execution. The remainder r is less than n and if initially $n < m$, then at each iteration both m and n are replaced by smaller values, with the new m larger than the new n. Both m and n will remain positive; thus n gets smaller and smaller until the condition that $r = 0$ is met. In the worst case, it will be met when n reaches 1. Unless the two input values are relatively prime, the algorithm will terminate before that condition is met. If initially $n > m$, then the first iteration merely interchanges the values of m and n.

1.6   ANALYSIS OF ALGORITHMS

Euclid's algorithm is also rather effective in that it quickly computes the desired result and terminates. As we study data structures and their associated algorithms, it is important to study the effectiveness of the algorithms. Some algorithms execute quickly and others may take a considerably longer time. Some are good choices for small sets of data but become extremely time consuming for large sets.

There are three possible situations that we might wish to determine for each algorithm:

1. the best case
2. the worst case
3. the average case

Typically, we wish to determine the execution time or some other measure of how long the algorithm takes to execute. In general, the values we find depend upon the size of the data set, n, and the primary problem of algorithm analysis is to determine how these depend upon n. You can determine these precisely by writing a program and timing the execution for a variety of input situations. This, of course, does depend upon not only the steps in the algorithm but hardware factors—such as the clock speed of the CPU. We will attempt to gain a measure of the time by counting the basic operations in the algorithm—operations such as comparisons.

Detailed analysis can be rather messy; thus, we will be content with a rough approximation which gives a general indication of how each algorithm depends upon the data set.

The best case is often the easiest to figure out; in many situations it takes only one operation. The worst case is typically not *as* easy, but is generally not too difficult. The average case is normally the hardest—one must be very careful in deciding exactly what is meant by average. However, it is always true that:

$$\text{best case} \leq \text{average case} \leq \text{worst case.}$$

1.6.1   Euclid's Algorithm

For Euclid's algorithm, a measure of how long the algorithm takes to execute is the number of times step E1 (compute the remainder) is executed. In the above example, it is executed three times. This measure is appropriate since this step is involved in each execution of the loop, and division (or modulo) operations typically take longer than simple comparisons or assignments.

Let us attempt to determine the best, worst, and average quantities as a function of m, since m is typically the largest value. We can then consider all possible relevant values of n; that is, $1 \le n \le m$.

If n is a factor of m, then n divides m evenly, and the "best case" takes 1 execution of step E1.

The worst case is somewhat more difficult to determine, since the detailed behavior of the algorithm is a complicated function of m and n. The worst cases occur when m and n are consecutive values taken from a Fibonacci sequence (see Appendix A).

This conclusion is simplest to observe by writing a computer program that loops over values of m—and for each m, loops over suitable values of n. For each m,n pair, the greatest common divisor is computed and the number of executions of E1 are counted. Finally, the program can print the values of m, n, and counts.

EXECUTION OF EUCLID'S ALGORITHM

m	n	Number of Executions of E1	m	n	Number of Executions of E1
2	1	<u>1</u>	8	1	1
3	1	1		2	1
	2	<u>2</u>		3	3
4	1	1		4	1
	2	1		5	<u>4</u>
	3	2		6	2
5	1	1		7	2
	2	2	9	1	1
	3	<u>3</u>		2	2
	4	2		3	1
6	1	1		4	2
	2	1		5	3
	3	1		6	2
	4	2		7	3
	5	1		8	2
7	1	1	10	1	1
	2	2		2	1
	3	2		3	2
	4	3		4	2
	5	3		5	1
	6	2		6	3
				7	3
				8	2
				9	2

The counts are underlined when a new high value is reached. All possible values of m that are less than 8 require no more than three executions. The first time the algorithm requires four executions is when $m = 8$ and $n = 5$. Continuing, we would discover that a count value of 5 is not required until we reach $m = 13$ and $n = 8$.

When m is large, the table gets very large. Therefore, let us print only the worst case for each value of m; that is, the value of n that takes the maximum number of step E1 executions. In reality, there may be more than one value of n that will take this maximum value. Further, to make our table even smaller and to make the behavior even more obvious, only print values of m, n, and the number of E1 executions whenever that number reaches a new high value. Such a table will give us the smallest worst case; that is, the smallest values of m and n that require more executions of step E1 than the previous ones.

SMALLEST WORST CASE FOR EUCLID'S ALGORITHM

m	n	Number of Executions of E1
2	1	1
3	2	2
5	3	3
8	5	4
13	8	5
21	13	6
34	21	7
55	34	8
89	55	9
144	89	10

For values of m between those in the table (such as 6 or 7), the worst cases are less than that which corresponds to the next higher value of m in the table. For example, the worst case for $m = 6$ or 7 is less than four iterations (it might be 1, 2, or 3, we cannot say for certain, we just know that it is less than 4), the value corresponding to $m = 8$.

For instance, tracing the example of 144 and 89, we obtain:

Step	m	n	Quotient	r	
1	144	89	1	55	
2	89	55	1	34	
3	55	34	1	21	
4	34	21	1	13	
5	21	13	1	8	
6	13	8	1	5	
7	8	5	1	3	
8	5	3	1	2	
9	3	2	1	1	
10	2	1	2	0	GCD = 1

In this case, the decreasing sequence of m's and n's as the algorithm operates is also the Fibonacci sequence. Because the quotient is 1 in all cases except the last, m and n decrease as slowly as possible—hence a "worst" case.

Because of the relationship between the Fibonacci sequence and ϕ, the golden ratio (see Appendix A), for these worst case values, the number of iterations (or executions of step E1) is approximately:

$$(\ln m)/\ln \phi \approx 2.078 \cdot \ln m$$

where

$$\phi = (1+\sqrt{5})/2 \approx 1.618034.$$

In particular, all values of m that are less than 1,000,000 take in the worst case no more than 28 executions of step E1. (The worst case of 28 occurs with $m = 832,040$. The smallest m that requires 29 executions is $m = 1,346,289$.)

The "average case" is usually even more difficult to compute; we also need to know what values of n might occur. The distribution of n's affect the average. Typically one assumes that the possible values of n occur randomly, with a uniform distribution; that is, each value of n occurs the same number of times as any other value. In practice, for a given m, we could count the number of executions of step E1 for each value of n in the range $1 < n < m$, sum them, and divide by the number of n's.

However, for Euclid's algorithm, the worst case grows very slowly. Because the average case is less than, or equal to, the worst case, we can use the worst case as an upper bound on the behavior of the algorithm. Specifically, we would expect that the average case for all possible values of $n < m \approx 1,000,000$ to be somewhat less than 28. It is actually 11.2. However, for a computer program we probably do not need to be terribly concerned about whether the average is 11 or 28. Both are quite small in comparison to the value of m and the execution of the algorithm will be quite fast in any case.

1.6.2   Alternative Greatest Common Divisor Algorithm

As a comparison, consider the following algorithm which also finds the Greatest Common divisor and is considerably less effective!

Algorithm G (Find the Greatest Common Divisor). Given any two positive integers m and n, find their **greatest common divisor** (GCD); that is, the largest positive integer which evenly divides both m and n.

G1. [find minimum]   Set g to the smaller of m and n.

G2. [is it a divisor?]   If g divides both m and n evenly, then Halt; g is the GCD.

G3. [decrement and loop] $g=g-1$; Go to step G2.

This algorithm tries successively smaller values until it finds one which does divide both of the original values evenly. It must terminate, since g will eventually reach 1 if no larger common divisor is found (if the two values are relatively prime). The value 1 does divide any two positive integers evenly, so the algorithm must eventually halt without any special test.

Tracing this algorithm for $m = 144$ and $n = 60$ (the example above) results in:

G1: $g = 60$ which is the smaller of 144 and 60

G2: $144/60 = 2$ remainder 24; $60/60 = 1$ remainder 0

G3: $g = 59$

G2: $144/59 = 2$ remainder 26; $60/59 = 1$ remainder 1

G3: $g = 58$

$\vdots$

G3: $g = 48$

G2: $144/48 = 3$ remainder 0; $60/48 = 1$ remainder 12

G3: $g = 47$

$\vdots$

G3: $g = 12$

G2: $144/12 = 12$ remainder 0; $60/12 = 5$ remainder 0;

since both remainders are 0, Halt with GCD = 12.

This algorithm is correct and has the same input and output as Euclid's Algorithm. It executes in a finite amount of time, but it is certainly less effective—taking 49 iterations with two divisions, for each iteration, as compared to three iterations with only one division (actually a modulo operation, but these are more or less equivalent to a division) for Euclid's Algorithm.

The best case is, again, one execution of step G2. The worst case will be when $n = m-1$ and m is a prime; thus the algorithm will execute step G2 $m-1$ times. Depending upon the particular way the program is written, some of the executions of step G2 will take two divisions which tends to be a time-consuming operation.

Thus for $m \approx 1,000,000$, the worst case is approximately 1,000,000. This algorithm is not particularly effective!

Another, even less effective, algorithm factors each of the two values into their prime factors, then compares the two lists for common numbers and, finally, multiplies those found in both lists together to form the GCD. This procedure is slow and complicated.

The primary purpose of this book is not to give a detailed analysis of algorithms; but some discussion is necessary since the choice between several different algorithms will depend upon their effectiveness.

1.7   *BIG O NOTATION*

The behavior of an algorithm as a function of the size of the data set or some relevant value is what we are usually interested in. In the example of Euclid's algorithm, we wished to determine how long the algorithm takes depending upon m. For operations with lists that we will study later, the important parameter is the number of items in the list.

In most cases a detailed formula for the behavior of an algorithm is unnecessary. Typically, what is more helpful is the general behavior of the algorithm in terms as simple as possible. Indeed, it is often easier to obtain an expression that approximates the behavior, rather than an exact formula.

For example, let us assume that a precise analysis of some procedure gives the result that the number of operations depends upon a parameter n as:

$$N(n) = 3n^2 + 11n - 45.$$

The term that grows most rapidly and dominates the function is the n^2 term. In general, for a polynomial the dominate term will be the one with the highest power.

Therefore, we could write that:

$$n \approx 3n^2, \text{ when } n \text{ gets large.}$$

A table illustrating the value of this expression as n grows illustrates this dominance is given at the top of the next page.

From this table we can observe that the error in using only the n^2 term, rather than the complete formula, becomes a very small percent of the actual value as n gets large. This is because this term grows so much more rapidly than the other two terms that their contribution becomes negligible. We can say that for large values of n, this procedure is basically a $3n^2$ process. We designate this using the "big O" notation:

$$O(3n^2)$$

which we can read "order of $3n^2$".

GROWTH OF A FUNCTION

n	N(n)	$3n^2$	difference	
1	-31	3	-34	-109.68%
2	-11	12	-23	-209.09%
3	15	27	-12	-80.00%
5	85	75	10	11.77%
7	179	147	32	17.88%
10	365	300	65	17.81%
15	795	675	120	15.09%
20	1,375	1,200	175	12.73%
30	2,985	2,700	285	9.55%
50	8,005	7,500	505	6.31%
70	15,425	14,700	725	4.70%
100	31,055	30,000	1,055	3.40%
200	122,155	120,000	2,155	1.76%
500	755,455	750,000	5,455	0.72%
1,000	3,010,955	3,000,000	10,955	0.36%
2,000	12,021,955	12,000,000	21,955	0.18%
5,000	75,054,955	75,000,000	54,955	0.07%
10,000	300,109,955	300,000,000	109,955	0.04%
20,000	1,200,219,955	1,200,000,000	219,955	0.02%
50,000	7,500,549,955	7,500,000,000	549,955	0.01%
100,000	30,001,099,955	30,000,000,000	1,099,955	0.00%

In reality, the factor 3 is relatively unimportant. If we take the ratio of two large values, we discover that the n^2 part is the most significant since the constant factor will cancel. As an example, doubling n from 50,000 to 100,000 results in increasing N by a factor of 4—from 7.5 billion to 30 billion.

Therefore we could write:

$$N \underset{\sim}{\alpha} n^2.$$

where the symbol:

$$\underset{\sim}{\alpha}$$

is read as "approximately proportional to".[3]

We can also characterize this process more simply as $O(n^2)$.

The types of procedures we will be studying include several, like this example, that are $O(n^2)$. Changing n by a factor of 2 results in a factor of 4 change in the result. But there are some others we will encounter. Typically, with data structures, we are interested in a set of n items. Then, it is important to understand the general behavior of the process in terms of the size of the set.

---

[3] In reality, the "big O" notation is defined quite precisely in terms of a limit (see Appendix A). For the purposes of this text, we will use the simpler, and admittedly rather fuzzy concept expressed here. This is sufficient for comparing the behavior of the data structures algorithms presented here.

1.7.1   Various Behaviors

The simplest procedures to analyze are those that are characterized by O(c), read as "order of a constant." (Sometimes, this is also expressed as: O(1).) This means that the execution of the algorithm takes a constant amount of time regardless of the size of the situation. An example would be the time that it takes to access RAM in a computer. It takes the same amount of time to read or write a word in memory, regardless of the total amount of memory. If such an algorithm exists, then we can feel free to use it on any size data set without worrying that the time or number of operations will grow and become prohibitive.

Another important class of algorithms that we will encounter are those characterized by O(n). These are the ones that grow linearly with the size of the data set. An example would be to find the largest element in an unordered set and simply examine each item until we have looked at them all and found the maximum.

We have already examined the O(n²) case. Algorithms that grow quadratically often become impractical, especially when the size of the data set gets large. Examples that we will encounter are the simple sorting procedures.

A function that grows more slowly than a linear procedure, yet more rapidly than the constant case (which does not grow), is O(log n). Euclid's algorithm is one such example. Others that we will encounter include a binary search on an ordered list and tree access algorithms. Logarithms grow very slowly; and an algorithm that behaves this way only increases by a small constant when the size of the data set is doubled (see Appendix A).

A behavior that is intermediate—between a linear and a quadratic growth pattern—is O(n • log n). Some of the more sophisticated sorting algorithms will display this behavior.

We will encounter others, but these five behaviors are the most common for our study of data structures and analysis of their algorithms.

1.7.2   Comparison

Generally, the most important gain in speed is obtained by finding an algorithm that grows more slowly than another. As an example, consider two algorithms that perform the same task:

$$\text{Algorithm 1:} \quad t = 100n$$

$$\text{Algorithm 2:} \quad t = (1/5)n^2.$$

Algorithm 1 takes much longer to perform each of its combined operations, but grows only linearly. Algorithm 2 is quick, but as the size of the data set increases, its execution grows quadratically. For small data sets, Algorithm 2 will outperform Algorithm 1.

TIMES TO PERFORM A TASK

n	Algorithm 1	Algorithm 2
1	100	0.2
3	300	1.8
10	1,000	20
30	3,000	180
100	10,000	2,000
300	30,000	18,000
1,000	100,000	200,000
3,000	300,000	1,800,000
10,000	1,000,000	20,000,000
30,000	3,000,000	180,000,000

From this table we see that Algorithm 2 is faster for small sets; but somewhere between a size of 300 and 1,000, Algorithm 2 begins to take longer.

Changing the constants in either of the two formulas would change the details, but not the essential fact: that for small data sets an algorithm that grows rapidly might be appropriate, but for large data sets it is important to find an algorithm that grows as slowly as possible with increasing size.

The "big O" notation is not only approximate, it is also proportional. As we noted above, the constant factor on the fastest growing term in an expression may be relatively unimportant. We will include such a factor only when it is useful in comparing two similar algorithms.

1.8 ALGORITHM FORMS

Algorithms may be expressed in many different forms. For this text we will typically express the algorithm in the "English" form shown above. For many years, and in some circles even today, the graphical expression of an algorithm, known as a **flowchart** is popular; it uses symbols to indicate various processes. These symbols are connected with lines and arrows to indicate the flow of control.

One disadvantage with conventional flowcharts is the lack of control structures; that is, they naturally can represent a procedure in terms of if () and goto statements, but looping structures such as while (), do/while(), and for (;;) and the switch construct, are much less natural.

However, just as all computer programs may be written in the relatively simple constructs available in machine language, the primitive flowchart constructs can represent all algorithms. On the other hand, it is the control structures of a high-level language that allow efficient programming and debugging; thus it is generally preferred to develop software with a language such as C, rather than an assembly language.

1.8.1   Computer Programs

A working program in some computer language is another important representation of an algorithm. For a number of years the Association for Computing Machinery described algorithms in the ALGOL language. The end result of much of the material in this text is for you to produce a representation of the various algorithms in the form of a C program—indeed, you are expected to be able to follow an algorithm by hand, understand its general characteristics, and translate it into C!

1.8.2   Mathematical Algorithms

Because of their simplicity, mathematical algorithms are very common. One of the advantages of the decimal positional number representation is that we have simple algorithms for manipulating numbers expressed with this representation.

As an example, the problem:

$$\begin{array}{r} 8529 \\ -\ 3274 \\ \hline \end{array}$$

should be able to be solved by any programmer (even without a computer or calculator!). It is unlikely that any individual has seen this particular problem before, since there are approximately 10,000x10,000 = 100,000,000 such problems where a four-digit value is subtracted from a four-digit value. Therefore, no one has memorized the answer; but an algorithm that performs the task has been learned. Indeed, the entire study of arithmetic is basically three steps:

1. learn number facts, i.e., addition and multiplication tables
2. learn algorithms for the basic calculations
3. learn how and when to apply these algorithms

In some sense the algorithm for subtraction is, in reality, non-numerical—it is a symbol manipulating one. It involves comparisons (to determine if "borrowing" is necessary) that may be reduced to determining the position of a given character in a table. The other operation involves subtracting a single digit value from a one- or two-digit value that may be reduced to a lookup table to tell us which symbol to place below each column.

The algorithms that we have considered so far involve numerical processes. However, it is not necessary that the procedure involve any computation at all. The important aspect of an algorithm is that it is a step-by-step procedure to process some information by taking input and producing the desired result.

1.9   C PROGRAMMING

Not only is it important that computer programs work effectively and correctly, but it is critical that they be readable. A well-structured and readable program which pays attention to style as the program is developed, will reduce the number of bugs and hence speed the development process.

Appendix B contains some of the stylistic issues that generally follow conventional C programming. Following stylistic conventions will help you in the programming process and will make it easier for the teacher to help you and grade your product!

1.9.1   Example: Euclid's Algorithm

As an example, let us write a C program to implement Algorithm E, Euclid's Algorithm:

Since the procedure takes two values and returns a single value—and because it might be a useful module—we will write it as a C function. The first step is easy! Write an appropriate header:

```
/*******************************************************
 *
 *      function to compute Greatest Common Divisor
 *          uses Algorithm E, Euclid's Algorithm
 *              params:   m,n    two positive integers
 *
 *              returns:  GCD,  0 < GCD <= min(m,n)
 *
 *******************************************************/
int euclid(int m, int n)
{

}
```

The header is an extended comment; it tells us what the function does, what the parameters are, and what it returns. In short, it tells what the function is and how to use it. The rows of asterisks help to separate visually the module from other functions in the listing. The header also contains the beginnings of the definition of the function.

As presented, the algorithm is not structured in that it contains a "go to" instruction. However, notice that the execution proceeds as:

E1

E2
E3
E1

continuing:

$$E2$$
$$E3$$
$$E1$$

where the test for termination is at step E2. Thus the steps E2, E3, and E1 really constitute a loop that terminates when the remainder is zero; that is, it continues as long as the remainder is not zero. This suggests a control structure as:

```
while (rem != 0) {

}
```

where steps E3 and E1 constitute the interior of the loop, and appear as:

```
while (rem != 0) {
    m = n;
    n = rem;
    rem = m%n;
}
```

This loop requires that *rem* be initialized before the loop executes. Therefore:

```
rem = m%n;

while (rem != 0) {
    m = n;
    n = rem;
    rem = m%n;
}
```

The function terminates with the return to the calling program of the value of the GCD, which is in *n*. The only temporary variable used within the function is *rem*, which must be defined. Therefore, putting everything together, we arrive at:

```
/*******************************************************
 *
 *     function to compute Greatest Common Divisor
 *        uses Algorithm E, Euclid's Algorithm
 *           params:   m,n    two positive integers
 *
 *           returns:  GCD,  0 < GCD <= min(m,n)
 *
 *******************************************************/
int euclid(int m, int n)
{

    int rem;
```

```
    rem = m%n;                /* initial execution of E1 */

    while (rem != 0) {    /* E2 */
        m = n;            /* E3 */
        n = rem;
        rem = m%n;        /* E1 */
    }
    return (n);

}
```

We have added single-line comments grouped toward the right of several of the lines to help associate the C statements with the algorithm. In addition, blank lines between several of the statements help group the lines into readable sets. We have also indented the statements within the braces of the function and, even further, those within the loop. All of these help readability.

There are other ways the loop might be written. In terms of a do while() construct, it might appear as:

```
do {
    rem = m%n;
    m = n;
    n = rem;
} while (rem != 0);

return (m);
```

Here *m* and *n* have been updated before the test is made; therefore, the value of the GCD, which was in *n*, has been stored in *m*, and the function returns *m*. This is less understandable to the programmer who expects the function to return *n*. A comment might help:

```
    return (m);      /* return m because the value of n */
                     /* has been moved to m */
```

However, it is much more obscure when compared to the original algorithm.

Perhaps the neatest C formulation is to use the conditional part of the while loop to perform some of the arithmetic and assignment:

```
while ((rem = m%n) != 0) {
    m = n;
    n = rem;
}
return (n);
```

Because of the precedence of the operations, the assignment must be placed within parentheses in order for it to be performed first. This can be "simplified" by noting that any non-zero value in C is treated as True. Thus, this loop is equivalent to:

```
while (rem = m%n) {
    m = n;
    n = rem;
}
return (n);
```

The disadvantage of this formulation is that it is much less readable and understandable. Many C programmers will spot this, expect a relational operator in the while condition, and guess that it should read:

```
while (rem == m%n) {
```

and "correct" it! Some compilers will spot it and produce a warning since a frequent error is using = in a conditional expression, when == is what is intended.

Which version is better, is an interesting question. Expert C programmers may prefer the last one, since it uses more of the specific knowledge of C constructs. However, most programmers will probably find the more readable version is easier to develop and get working. For the purposes of this text, readability should come before conciseness and cleverness!

In order to test the function we just wrote, a main program that handles the input and output must be developed. By putting the input and output in the main program, we can test a complete module that might be used within another program to compute the GCD for some purpose. If the function printed the GCD, then it could not easily be used as part of another program that simply needs to have the GCD calculated as part of the computation.

Writing the main program and adding our function, we obtain:

```
/*******************************************************
 *
 *      program to compute the Greatest Common Divisor
 *      written by L. Turner, Data Structures, 5 Jan 90
 *
 *******************************************************/
#include <stdio.h>

main()
{
    int euclid(int,int);
    int m,n,g;

    printf("Enter first positive integer:   ");
    scanf("%d",&m);
    printf("Enter second positive integer:  ");
    scanf("%d",&n);
```

```
        g = euclid(m,n);

        printf("\n\nGCD of %d and %d is %d\n",m,n,g);

    }

    /**********************************************************
     *
     *      function to compute Greatest Common Divisor
     *          uses Algorithm E, Euclid's Algorithm
     *              params:   m,n    two positive integers
     *
     *              returns:  GCD,  0 < GCD <= min(m,n)
     *
     **********************************************************/
    int euclid(int m, int n)
    {

        int rem;

        rem = m%n;                  /* initial execution of E1 */

        while (rem != 0) {   /* E2 */
            m = n;           /* E3 */
            n = rem;
            rem = m%n;       /* E1 */
        }
        return (n);

    }
```

The "header," with its comments, helps set the function apart visually from the main program and identifies it as a single entity.

As one might expect, there are many equivalent ways of developing a C program from an algorithm. It is important to realize that for most situations, clarity and readability should not be sacrificed for a marginal gain in speed.

1.10 SUMMARY

The study of data structures is central to the programming process since it focuses on the way data is represented, stored, manipulated, and retrieved in the computer. These are, in practice, the largest uses of computer systems. The efficiency of a program and the ease with which it is developed can depend quite drastically on the choice of a data structure.

Concurrent with a study of data structures is a study of algorithms. These are step-by-step procedures for performing some tasks. They are unambiguous and finite. One of the earliest recognized algorithms was Euclid's algorithm for finding the greatest common divisor of two positive integers. Algorithms will exhibit different behaviors as the size of the problem changes. These behaviors are simply described in terms of the "big O" notation which gives the approximate proportional behavior as the size of the problem gets large. Two algorithms for a given problem may exhibit quite different behaviors—to the point where one is totally impractical to use.

Algorithms may be expressed in different ways; the programmer's task is to translate these into suitable statements and then test the resultant program. It is important that the program be readable in human terms; this will assist in the debugging and documentation processes.

REFERENCES

Carroll, Lewis, *The Annotated Alice, Alice's Adventures in Wonderland & Through the Looking Glass*, introduction and notes by Martin Gardner, Bramhall House, 1960.

Hofstadter, Douglas R., *Gödel, Escher, Bach: An Eternal Golden Braid*, Basic Books, Inc., New York, New York, 1979.

Kernighan, Brian W., and Ritchie, Dennis M., *The C Programming Language*, 2nd ed., Prentice-Hall, Englewood Cliffs, New Jersey, 1988.

Knuth, Donald E., *The Art of Computer Programming*; Fundamental Algorithms, vol. 1., 2nd ed., Addison-Wesley Publishing Co., Reading, Massachusetts, 1973.

Koenig, Andrew, *C Traps and Pitfalls*, Addison-Wesley Publishing Co., Reading, Massachusetts, 1989.

Plum, Thomas, *C Programming Guidelines*, Prentice-Hall, Englewood Cliffs, New Jersey, 1984.

Wirth, Nicklaus, *Algorithms + Data Structures = Programs*, Prentice-Hall, Englewood Cliffs, New Jersey, 1976.

QUESTIONS

Q1.1   Which is correct?

> or   "... data is ..."
>   "... data are ..."

Q1.2   What is the difference between *data* and *information*?

Q1.3   Why is a study of data structures also a study of algorithms?

Q1.4   Given the following tic-tac-toe configuration, write out the appropriate list of "line" data structure with X to play:

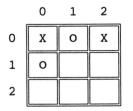

Where should X play?

Q1.5   For the 3x3 tic-tac-toe game, how many different possible configurations are there, assuming that configurations produced by a simple rotation or reflection are different? Can all of these be reached in playing the game?

Q1.6   Are there any other anagrams for 'alice'? If so, what are they?

Q1.7   Values that are powers of 2 are relatively important in computing. It is easy to estimate the power by noting:

$$2^{10} = 1024 \approx 1000 = 10^3.$$

The power of 2 rounded up is the number of bits required to express the values in binary. Thus, every three digits in the decimal expansion needs about 10 bits; 1000 needs 10 bits, 1,000,000 needs 20 bits, etc. Each factor of two requires an additional bit.

Without using a calculator, computer, or table, estimate the power of two (or the number of bits) that corresponds to each of the following:

a.	2000	e.	1,000,000,000
b.	500,000	f.	5,000,000,000
c.	10,000,000	g.	100,000
d.	30,000		

Q1.8   The concept of an algorithm involves a finite value in two distinct aspects. What are these?

Q1.9   Consider the common instruction found on many prescriptions:

"take one tablet three times per day"

Is it ambiguous? How could any ambiguity be reduced or eliminated?

Q1.10   Does an algorithm exist that can compute all the digits of π? Why or why not?

Q1.11   Trace Euclid's algorithm by hand, writing down each step for two values that are divisible, such as 144 and 12. How many times is step E1 executed?

Q1.12   A number of algorithms involve the use of the binary logarithm (base 2), written as:

lg x

Most scientific calculators will have a function key for either (or both) common log or natural log. How can you obtain a binary log from a natural log?

Q1.13   A particular algorithm has been analyzed and its behavior is given by:

$$t = \frac{4n^3 + 2n^2 - 8}{n-3} + 3n - 2$$

What is its "big O" behavior?

Q1.14   A certain process is accomplished via two sub-processes, A and B, each to be executed once. Process A is $O(n)$; process B is $O(n^2)$. What is the "big O" behavior of the combined process? In this case, each sub-process is executed once. Would the "big O" behavior of the combined process change if either one were executed more than once?

Q1.15   For the subtraction algorithm for two integers, what is its "order" in terms of d, the number of digits; that is, what is x in $O(x)$? (Assume that both integers have approximately the same number of digits.)

Q1.16   For the multiplication algorithm for two integers, what is its "order" in terms of d, the number of digits; that is, what is x in $O(x)$? (Assume both integers have approximately the same number of digits.)

Q1.17   The text gave an example of two algorithms with different behavior. The time to perform a task was given by:

```
Algorithm 1:      t = 100n
Algorithm 2:      t = (1/5)n².
```

What value of n will cause these two to take the same amount of time to execute?

Q1.18 A student wrote the following C function as an implementation of Euclid's algorithm—why does it not work properly?

```
int euclid(int m, int n)
{
    int r;
    r = m%n;
    while (r > 0)
        m = n = r = m%n;

    return (n);
}
```

Q1.19 Why is it important for you **initially** to write your C programs with style; that is, with consistent use of white space, comments, etc. rather than "prettying" it up later, after you get it working?

Q1.20 Why is readability of a C program or function stressed over speed and conciseness?

Q1.21 What information should the header of a C function contain? What is the value of a full line of asterisks or some other characters?

Q1.22 Why is it better for the calling program to print the value of the GCD rather than printing the value in the function that computes it?

Q1.23 Consider the following "addition" table:

"+"	X	Y	Z
X	ZZ	X	ZY
Y	X	Y	Z
Z	ZY	Z	X

The two "digits," e.g., ZZ indicate a carry operation.

Using the addition algorithm for ordinary integers, what is the result of:

```
    XZX
+   ZYX
```

EXERCISES

E1.1   In the tic-tac-toe example, we developed a table which gives the number of the square in terms of its location which is an ordered pair:

```
       0   1   2

  0 │ 0 │ 1 │ 2 │

  1 │ 3 │ 4 │ 5 │

  2 │ 6 │ 7 │ 8 │
```

TIC-TAC-TOE SQUARE

Square	Location
0	0,0
1	0,1
2	0,2
3	1,0
4	1,1
5	1,2
6	2,0
7	2,1
8	2,2

a. Write out an algebraic or C function that gives the square number from the row and column number:

```
square(r,c)
```

b. Write out two functions that give the row and column from the square number:

```
row(s)
col(s)
```

For all three of these, there is a simple mathematical expression. Your solution should not use a table lookup or an array, nor does it need any conditional expressions.

E1.2   It is easier to find anagrams for shorter words. Consider the word "stop." How many possible permutations are there? How many of these are actual English words; that is, how many, and what are the anagrams?

E1.3   Assume that an anagram dictionary is composed of a series of word pairs as described in the text:

.
.
.

(aceil, alice)
(aceil, celia)
(aceil, lacie)

.
.
.

Furthermore assume that an algorithm exists that takes a word, such as "celia," and finds its entry in the dictionary. (Assume that the word is in the dictionary!) Write a formal algorithm that looks for and prints out **all** the anagrams for the word.

E1.4   It is easier to find anagrams for shorter words. Consider the word "least." How many possible permutations are there? How many of these are actual English words; that is, how many, and what are the anagrams?

E1.5   By tracing through Euclid's Algorithm by hand, show that the effect of initial values of $n > m$, is to reverse these values. Thus after one pass through the algorithm, we find $n < m$, as we have assumed above.

E1.6   Assume that two integer values are contained in arrays with one digit per location, as:

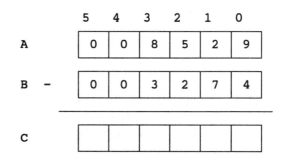

Write a formal algorithm to perform the subtraction of the value in array B from array A. Assume that a value located in array A may become negative so that the "borrowing" from a zero is handled without a special case.

Note that each step involves only arithmetic operations on small values; that is, we compare single digits, add ten, subtract one, and add or subtract two or three values of one or two digits. Hence, this could easily be implemented in a computer where the arithmetic is performed in the CPU's registers and is limited to relatively small integers.

By also developing procedures for addition, multiplication, and division on an array of digits, one can perform the standard arithmetic operations on arbitrarily long integers.

E1.7   There is a closed form expression for the n-th Fibonacci number in terms of the golden ratio:

$$\phi = \frac{1+\sqrt{5}}{2} \approx 1.618033989$$

Thus

$$F_n = \frac{1}{\sqrt{5}}\phi^n - \frac{1}{\sqrt{5}}(-1/\phi)^n.$$

As n gets large, $(-1/\phi)^n$ goes to zero, hence

$$F_n = \frac{1}{\sqrt{5}}\phi^n$$

From the table of the worst cases for Euclid's Algorithm and the table of Fibonacci numbers in Appendix A, observe that x—the number of executions of step E1—is related to the value of m by:

$$m = F_{x+2} \approx \frac{1}{\sqrt{5}}\phi^{x+2}$$

Therefore, solve for x in terms of m and show that

$$x \approx \ln m/\ln \phi + (\ln \sqrt{5}/\ln \phi - 2)$$

$$\approx 2.078 \cdot \ln m$$

E1.8   When one multiplies two values with decimal portions, such as $17.2 \cdot 6.73$, one obtains a sequence of digits 115756. There is a simple algorithm or recipe for placing the decimal point in the proper location in the result, i.e. 115.756.

a. State this "recipe" in the "algorithm" format above.

b. Prove that it does indeed give the proper placement. Hint: write each factor in terms of an integer and a power of 10 (for the example above: $17.2 = 172\text{x}10^{-1}$ and $6.73 = 673\text{x}10^{-2}$); multiply the values and restore to the ordinary notation.

E1.9   The division of an arbitrarily long integer by another arbitrarily long integer is rather complex—especially if each arithmetic operation must be performed with ordinary computer instructions that involve operations only for small integers. A much simpler task is to divide an arbitrarily long integer by a small value, e.g:

$$123 \overline{)5686724519876523092743570467510 0436}$$

If the dividend is contained in an array of digits, then each of the operations of the "long division" process consists of arithmetic operations on small quantities.

Write a formal algorithm to implement this long division process.

E1.10   The simple process to determine if a positive integer, N, is prime is divide it by a sequence of trial factors which are the prime numbers up to the square root of the number to see if any divide it evenly. An easier sequence to generate is: 2, 3, 5, 7, 9, 11, ..., $\sqrt{N}$. (This sequence contains all of the prime numbers as well as several others, but is simple to generate.) Therefore the number of operations is approximately:

$$\frac{\sqrt{N}}{2}$$

However, a more useful way to measure the size of the number—to determine if it is prime—is by the number of digits in the number, n, which is given by:

```
n = ceil[log(N+1)]
```

where log() is the common log, base 10.

From these expressions, show that the order of this process is

$$O(\sqrt{10^n}).$$

E1.11   Even if an algorithm exists, it is not necessarily practical. Consider the "traveling sales person" problem where a person starting from a certain city wishes to travel to each of the others in turn, finally returning to her starting city. She is to visit each city only once (except for the starting city) and the total distance traveled is to be a minimum. The algorithm is easy. If the distance between each two cities is known, then compute the total length of all possible paths.   One of these is a minimum (there might be several). Select it!

To determine the order of this algorithm, consider a set of n cities. Starting with one, there are $n-1$ possible paths, and for each of those there are $n-2$, and so forth, ending with one possible path back to the original. Therefore, how many possible paths are there for n cities?

If $n = 48$ (the capitals of the states of the contiguous United States) and a computer is capable of evaluating 1,000,000 such paths each second, how long would it take to complete the algorithm?

E1.12 Processes which are not arithmetical in nature may also be described in algorithmic form. Write a formal algorithm for calling a friend on the phone. Begin with picking up the phone and end with an "error" condition such as: no dial tone, no answer, busy signal; or with someone answering the phone.

PROBLEMS

P1.1 As a simple example of how the selection of a data structure affects the programming, develop two C programs to compute the day of the year (assuming a non-leap year). Each program should request the number of the month and the day of the month and compute the day of the year.

a. Use:

```
static int dy_mnth[] = {31,28,31,30,31,30,31,31,
                                   30,31,30,31};
```

b. Use:

```
static int dy_mnth[] = {0,0,31,59,90,120,151,181,
                                 212,243,273,304,334};
```

For these two cases the physical data structure is the same; that is, a simple one-dimensional array or list, but the data stored is different. The programming statements reflect this difference.

P1.2 Write a C program to implement Algorithm G. Have it request the two integers, compute the GCD with a function, then print it. Write it with style including appropriate user prompts, internal comments, attention to white space for readability, etc.

Try it on:

a.	144	12	d.	31367	11001
b.	144	13	e.	288	60
c.	5355	34			

P1.3 Write a C program to print a table of the powers of 2; write it with style, including internal comments, attention to white space for readability, etc. Print powers from 0 to 30.

P1.4 Not every procedure that may be described in an "algorithmic" form is actually an algorithm. Consider the following procedure:

Procedure W (Wonder Procedure). Given a positive integer, *n*, determine if the sequence described ends with 1 (the original number is a wondrous number) or continues forever (the original number is unwondrous).

W1. [output]	Output n.
W2. [test]	If n = 1, then Halt; n is Wondrous!
W3. [odd or even]	if n is even, then n=n/2. else n=3n+1.
W4. [loop]	Go to step W1.

Example: 3 10 5 16 8 4 2 1

No known numbers are unwondrous; however, it is not known whether an unwondrous number even exists (see *Gödel, Escher, Bach* by Douglas Hofstadter).

Procedure W is not known to be an algorithm, because it is not known if it will terminate for all possible *n*; that is, is the execution finite in length?

Write a C program that requests a positive integer and prints the values of the sequence generated by Procedure W. Try:

1024, 7, 15, 27, and 29.

P1.5 Write a C program to compute and print the Fibonacci sequence (see Appendix A). The values are given by:

$$F_n = \begin{cases} 1, & n = 1 \text{ and } 2 \\ F_{n-2} + F_{n-1}, & n > 2 \end{cases}$$

Hint, use two variables that are initialized to 1 and contain the values of F_n and F_{n-1}. Add these to obtain the next value and then update them for each iteration.

P1.6   Write a C function to implement Euclid's Algorithm. Use it in a program that reduces a fraction to its lowest terms. Have the program request two integers representing, respectively, the numerator and denominator of the fractions, compute the GCD with a function, then divide the GCD into the numerator and denominator and print the results.

Write it with style, including appropriate user prompts, internal comments, attention to white space for readability, etc.

If you use: `scanf("%d/%d",....);`

then the original fraction may be entered as 4/8.

Try it on:

a. 4/12   c. 34/5355

b. 13/144   d. 3/4

P1.7   One can determine the worst case for Euclid's algorithm by modifying the C function (that implements it) to count the number of times the modulo operation is performed and placing the value in a global variable. Use this in a program that loops over the values of m, and for each m loop over values of n such that $1 \leq n \leq m$. Write the program and have it print the value of m, n, and counts for the worst case for each m.

P1.8   Write a C program that prints the values of logarithms base 2 for the following values of x:

$$
\begin{array}{c}
1 \\
2 \\
5 \\
10 \\
20 \\
50 \\
100 \\
\vdots \\
1,000,000,000
\end{array}
$$

Have it print the exact value of the logarithm as well as the value rounded up to the next integer.

Chapter 2

Simple Random-Access Lists

"Take some more tea," the March Hare said to Alice, very earnestly.

"I've had nothing yet," Alice replied in an offended tone: "so I can't take more."

"You mean you can't take <u>less</u>," said the Hatter: "it's very easy to take <u>more</u> than nothing."

"Nobody asked <u>your</u> opinion," said Alice.

"Who's making personal remarks now?" the Hatter asked triumphantly.

Alice did not quite know what to say to this....

"I want a clean cup," interrupted the Hatter: "let's all move one place on."

He moved as he spoke, and the Dormouse followed him: the March Hare moved into the Dormouse's place, and Alice rather unwittingly took the place of the March Hare. The Hatter was the only one who got any advantage from the change; and Alice was a good deal worse off than before, as the March Hare had just upset the milk-jug into his plate.

2.1   OBJECTIVES

The objectives of this chapter are to:

- Define the simple, random-access list data structure.
- Present typical algorithms for simple list processing.
- Introduce the concept of searching.
- Describe what is meant by sorting.
- Discuss how we might combine lists by catenation and merging.
- Examine the merging algorithm.

2.2   INTRODUCTION

It is relatively easy to access a simple variable and manipulate its value. The instruction set of a computer includes primitives for loading and storing values given an address. In C, or any high-level language, we need only refer to the variable by its name (or symbol) and the compiler will decide where it is to be stored and generate the appropriate address for the executable program.

The next most complicated data structure is a simple sequential list. We can picture the logical or user view of a list as:

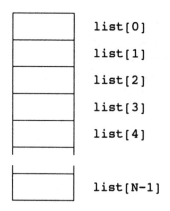

We can define the list to provide sufficient storage (*N* elements) for the items that we wish to store. Besides the list itself we can define an integer variable that holds the actual number of items in the list, n. Initially this will be 0. Of course, in all cases, $n \leq N$.

The C language, as is typical of other high-level languages, allows one to locate the items in the list using an integer index that numbers, sequentially, the locations in the list. C starts with zero; therefore, the locations are ordered with indices 0, 1, 2, ..., $n-1$.

2.2.1   Fundamental Operations

With such a list there are a number of fundamental operations that we might wish to perform:

1. access
2. replace
3. append
4. insert
5. delete
6. search
7. sort

And with two or more lists, we might consider operations that combine the contents:

8. catenate
9. merge

Some of these operations are very simple, others will take a considerable amount of our attention. Indeed, several chapters of this text are devoted to sorting! Depending upon the kind of data, we could add to this list of operations by considering other less frequently needed processes:

1. find minimum (or maximum)
2. find median
3. find mode (the element that occurs most frequently)

These are typically described as modifications of the more fundamental operations. In reality, some data sets do not lend themselves to these. For example, if the list were a list of interstate highway numbers (e.g., **I** 80 or **I** 496), what would be the significance of the largest one?

2.3   ACCESS

To access a given datum given its index, *k*, is a simple operation in most high-level languages, including C:

        list[k]   k=0, 1, ..., n-1.

We can retrieve a value for either comparison or storage as:

        value = list[k];

or

        if (list[k] ....)
            ....;

Such a simple list stored in the memory of a computer is sometimes said to have a random-access property. This means that we can access any item in the list without having to access any other item. Each access takes the same amount of time. There are sequential data structures for which the access is not random. Typically these must be accessed by "reading" or processing items in turn until the desired one is reached—i.e., a serial access scheme. Therefore, the amount of processing it takes to access one given item varies with the logical or physical location of the item in the structure.

2.4   REPLACE

Replacing an item is about as difficult as accessing an item:

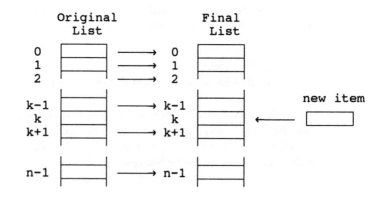

The C code would appear as:

        list[k] = item;   k = 0, 1, ..., n-1.

2.5 APPEND

To **append** to a list means that we will add an item to the list by placing it onto the end of the list.

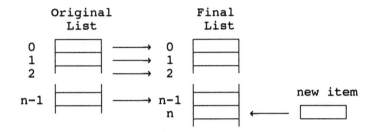

The C code to perform this might appear as:

```
list[n] = item;
n++;
```

Of course, in a real program we might want to check to see that the allocated storage is not exceeded. If the list is defined with *N* elements, then we could precede the above code with a test where we have used a line of "pseudocode" to indicate some action that will depend upon the details of the program:

```
if (n >= N)
      {'list full'}
```

As an example, we might wish to return an error flag or print a message. In any case, we would not want to append the item if there were no place to put it.

The diagram above illustrates the "before" and "after" states; however, in reality this operation is normally performed on a single list.

2.6 INSERT

Adding an item by appending it to the end is relatively easy; however, a more common and potentially useful operation is to add an item by placing it at a specified location in the middle of the list.

To insert a value in the list we want the new item to be placed in the *k*-th location of the list. The old *k*-th item, and all subsequent items, are to be moved in the list to make room.

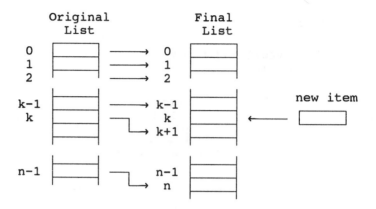

If we copy the old list into a new one, then the process is relatively straightforward.

```
for (i=0; i<k; i++)              /* move items 0 - k-1 */
    new_list[i] = list[i];
new_list[k] = item;             /* insert item at k */
for (i=k+1; i<=n; i++)
    new_list[i] = list[i-1];   /* move remainder */
n++;
```

In order to perform this operation "in place", we get a simplification and a complication. First, it is unnecessary to move the first k items (0 through $k-1$). The complication is that the order in which we perform the operations is important. If we simply delete the first loop in the code above and replace references to new_list[] with list[], we discover that the list from location k onward consists of copies of the new item! We have lost information! The solution is to move the remainder of the list before inserting the new item and to perform the move from the end of the list backwards.

A formal algorithm to perform this process is:

Algorithm IL (Insert in a Simple List). Given a list, LIST, with n items stored and a new item, ITEM, to be stored in location k, move subsequent items to make room, insert ITEM, and update n.

IL1. [move remainder]   Perform step IL2 for i=n,n-1,...,k+1.

IL2. [move item]   LIST[i]=LIST[i-1].

IL3. [store item]   LIST[k]=ITEM.

IL4. [update number]   n=n+1.

This algorithm moves the items in an order that starts with the last item and progresses towards the beginning of the list, moving each item one location:

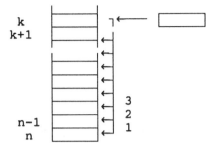

The C code that implements Algorithm IL becomes:

```
for (i=n; i>k; i--)              /* move remainder */
    list[i] = list[i-1];
list[k] = item;                  /* store new item */
n++;                             /* update length */
```

Since the number of operations for this process is $n-k$, it depends upon k. In the best case, where we insert at the end, no movement is necessary—we essentially have an *append* operation. In the worst case, all n items need to be moved if the new item is inserted in location 0. On the average, the insertion is in the middle; and one might expect that on the average this will involve n/2 operations. Thus, this process is an O(n) process. However, these operations involve moving data. If each item is a simple value, then this is fast. In general, each item may involve a large amount of data, and the movement of data is slow.

2.7   DELETE

Deletion from the list involves a process similar to insertion. In general, the unwanted item is to be found somewhere in the middle of the list, and data will need to be moved. However, now we can proceed in a forward order. The old $k+1$ element is moved into the k location, etc. Diagramatically, this appears as the diagram at the top of the next page.

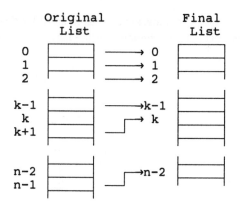

A formal algorithm for performing this is given by:

Algorithm DL (Delete from a Simple List). Given a list, LIST, with n items stored and a location k of an item to be deleted, move subsequent items and update n.

DL1. [move remainder]   Perform step DL2 for i=k,k+1,...,n−2.

DL2. [move item]   LIST[i] = LIST[i+1].

DL3. [update number]   n=n−1.

■

This algorithm moves the items in order starting with the $k+1$ and proceeding toward the end of the list, with each item moved one location:

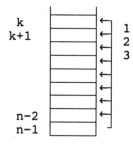

The C code to perform this might be:

```
for (i=k; i<n-1; i++)                    /* move remainder */
    list[i] = list[i+1];
n--;                                      /* update length */
```

Of course, it may be desirable to put in a check to see if the list is presently empty ($n=0$) or if k is out of range ($k<0$ or $k \geq n$).

The number of operations for deletion is similar to insertion. It is O(n) procedure, but these involve movement of data.

2.8 SEARCH

Searching involves looking through the list to see if some desired item, which we shall call the *key*, is present. There are two possibilities: the item is found, or the item is not found. (Such a profound statement!) The simplest searching scheme is to compare sequentially each item in the list with the key—until either the item is found, or the end of the list is reached.

A formal algorithm for performing this is:

Algorithm SU (Serial Search on an Unordered List). Given a list, *LIST*, of *n* elements, find the location of the item, *KEY*.

SU1. [initialize]	i=0.	
SU2. [at end?]	If i >= n, then Halt.	(not found)
SU3. [compare]	If KEY = LIST[i], then Halt.	(found at i)
SU4. [loop]	i=i+1; Go to step SU2.	

∎

And the subsequent C code might be:

```
for (i=0; i<n; i++) {
    if (key == list[i])
        {'found at location i'}
}
{'not found'}
```

Typically, a C function to search for an item will be defined as:

```
int search(list,n, key)
```

and will return the location of *key* if found or a non-valid value, such as −1, if not found. It is then the responsibility of the calling program to use that information—say, print an appropriate message. Thus, a complete C function might appear as:

```
/**********************************************************
 *
 *      function to search for a value in a list
 *         params:      list     list of integers
 *                      n        number stored in the list
 *                      key      value to be searched for
 *
 *      returns:    location (0 thru n-1) if found,
 *                                         else -1
 *
 **********************************************************/
int simple_search(int list[], int n, int key)
{

    int i;

    for (i=0; i<n; i++)
        if (key == list[i])
            return (i);

    return (-1);

}
```

We will examine searching in more detail later. This scheme is one of the simplest, and least effective. The best case is one comparison; and the worst case is *n* comparisons if the key is present. On the average it takes approximately *n*/2 comparisons if the key is present and *n* operations if it is not present in the list. The "big O" behavior is O(n).

2.9   SORT

To **sort** a list means that we will arrange the values into ascending or descending order. There are many different "sort" algorithms—all sorts of assorted sorts—enough to put one out of sorts! In later chapters (5, 6, 12, and 15) we will make several sorties into the topic and describe all of the sordid details! And, as we shall see later, there is no one best sort. Each has different characteristics, and the choice of which one to use depends upon the circumstances.

For the present, let us consider how we might rearrange the items in a list into ascending order. We wish to perform some operations on the entire list—elements 0 through $n-1$—to get the smallest item into the first location of the list (element 0) so that the same values will be in the list when we finish, but in a different order. If we can do this, then we can repeat the procedure on the shortened list—elements 1 through $n-1$. This will put the smallest element in the shortened list into the second location (element 1). We can then repeat with an even shorter list—elements 2 through $n-1$. Finally, we will obtain a list that is only one element long—such a list is, by definition, already sorted, and we can stop with the entire list arranged in ascending order.

The basic procedure that we will use compares the first element with all of the remaining ones, one at a time. If the first element is larger than the other, we will swap them. This means that at the end of each step the smallest item will be in the first location. When we get to the end of the list, the smallest item in the entire list will indeed be in the first location. We can then continue to repeat the procedure, with shorter and shorter lists until a list of only one element is reached. Then the entire list will be sorted!

A formal algorithm to perform this is:

Algorithm W (Simple Swap Sort). Given a list, LIST, of n elements indexed 0 through $n-1$, rearrange these items in place so that they are in increasing order.

W1. [loop over target]   Perform step W2 for $i=0,1,...,n-2$.

W2. [look through rest]   Perform step W3 for $j=i+1,i+2,...,n-1$.

W3. [compare]   If LIST[i] > LIST[j], then Swap(LIST[i], LIST[j]).   ∎

One must be careful in swapping two items. The most obvious approach might produce:

```
list[i] = list[j];
list[j] = list[i];
```

This would work if these two could be done simultaneously, but since the two assignments are performed sequentially, the net result is to store the value that was in *list[j]* in both locations i and j, and lose the original value of *list[i]*. To perform this properly involves an additional variable:

```
temp = list[i];
list[i] = list[j];
list[j] = temp;
```

Algorithm W uses two indices. The first, i, is the index of the location to where we are moving the smallest element. The second, j, allows us to compare the i-th element with the remaining ones in turn. Both of these progress through the list in the same direction.

2.9.1 Example Sort

As an example:

	Original List i = 0	1	2	3	4	Final List
0	34	16	16	16	16	16
1	54	54	28	28	28	28
2	28	34	54	34	34	34
3	16	28	34	54	42	42
4	81	81	81	81	81	54
5	42	42	42	42	54	81

Because we swap items when they are out of order, the list will contain the same values—but in different order—at each step.

2.9.2 Analysis

This sorting algorithm is particularly easy to analyze. For the first value of i, j takes on $n-1$ values and, hence, there are $n-1$ comparisons. For the second value of i, j takes on $n-2$ values, and finally, for the last value of i, j takes on 1 value. Therefore the total number values of j is given by (see also Appendix A):

$$(n-1) + (n-2) + (n-3) +...+ 2 + 1 = n(n-1)/2 \approx n^2/2.$$

Thus, this procedure is an $O(n^2)$ process.

2.9.3 C Implementation

A C function to implement this algorithm is:

```
/*********************************************************
 *
 *          function to perform simple swap sort
 *
 *          params:   list      list of integers
 *                    n         number, indexed 0 - n-1
 *
 *********************************************************/
void swap_sort(int list[], int n)
{

    int i,j,temp;

    for (i=0; i<n-1; i++ ) {
        for (j=i+1; j<n; j++) {
            if (list[i] > list[j]) {  /* if out of   */
                temp = list[i];       /* order, swap */
                list[i] = list[j];
                list[j] = temp;
            }
        }
    }

}
```

As we shall see later, this algorithm is not particularly effective. It is a characteristic of the simple sorting algorithms that the execution time grows as $n^2/2$ for all cases. We will find some sorting algorithms that grow considerably more slowly and hence are suitable for large sets of data. The primary value of Algorithm W is that it is easy to code and visualize.

Algorithm W, the example presented, and the C function all sort the list in place into ascending order. It is a simple modification to produce a sorting into descending order.

W3'. [compare]   If LIST[i] < LIST[j], then Swap(LIST[i], LIST[j]).

2.10 CATENATE

A simple operation that we might wish to perform combines two lists into a single resultant one. One of the simplest ways to combine two lists into one list is through the process of **catenation**. This is performed by copying first one list in order to a third then copying the items from the second list onto the end. The diagram on the top of the next page illustrates this process.

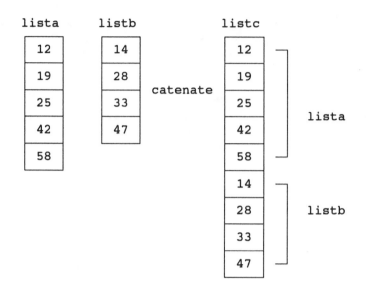

Often, the catenate procedure is used to copy the contents of the second list onto the end of the first one; that is, copy *listb* onto the end of *lista*.
This operation could be performed by using the append operation, one at a time, for each item in the second list.

Rather than repeated calls to an append function, the C code to perform this in one loop could appear as:

```
for (i=0; i<nb; i++)
    lista[i+na] = listb[i];
na += nb;
```

2.11   MERGE

Catenation simply appends the contents of one list onto the end of the other. This is satisfactory if we do not care about the order of the items in the lists. However, if order is important and the original lists are already ordered, then it is possible, and desirable, to combine the two lists in such a way that the resultant list is also ordered. This process is called **merging**, and, fortunately, is quite efficient.

The basic scheme is to use an index that points into each of the two original lists. The items at the indices are compared, and the smaller of the two (assuming ascending order) is copied to the final list; and then the index of the list where the smaller one came from is incremented. This is repeated until the end of one of the lists is reached, then the remainder of the other list is copied.

A formal algorithm to implement the merge procedure is:

Algorithm M (List Merge). Given two lists, *LISTA* and *LISTB*, with lengths *NA* and *NB* respectively, merge them into a single resultant list, *LISTC*, with length NC=NA+NB. If *LISTA* and *LISTB* are originally sorted in ascending order, then *LISTC* will also be sorted.

M1. [initialize indices]	i=0; j=0; k=0.	
M2. [at end of LISTA?]	If i >= NA, then Go to step M7.	
M3. [at end of LISTB?]	If j >= NB, then Go to step M8.	
M4. [find, move smallest]	If LISTA[i] < LISTB[j],	
		then LISTC[k]=LISTA[i]; i=i+1.
		else LISTC[k]=LISTB[j]; j=j+1.
M5. [increment LISTC index]	k=k+1.	
M6. [loop]	Go to step M2.	
M7. [copy rest LISTB]	If j >= NB, then Halt with NC=k.	
		else LISTC[k]=LISTB[j]; j=j+1;
		k=k+1; Go to step M7.
M8. [copy rest LISTA]	If i >= NA, then Halt with NC=k.	
		else LISTC[k]=LISTA[i]; i=i+1;
		k=k+1; Go to step M8.

Executing this algorithm on the following lists, *lista* and *listb*, will produce the resultant list, *listc*. The indices *i* and *j* move down their lists one at a time. Each time either *i* or *j* moves, a value is copied to *listc* and *k* moves. The first few executions of the loop consisting of steps M2 through M6 result in:

	lista		listb		listc
i	12	j	14	k	12
	19		28		
	25		33		
	42		47		
	58				

	lista		listb		listc
	12	j	14		12
i	19		28	k	14
	25		33		
	42		47		
	58				

Continuing:

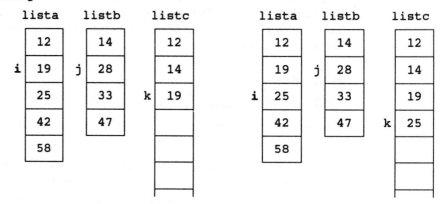

Finally the last element of one of the lists is reached, and the remaining elements of the other is copied to the final list.

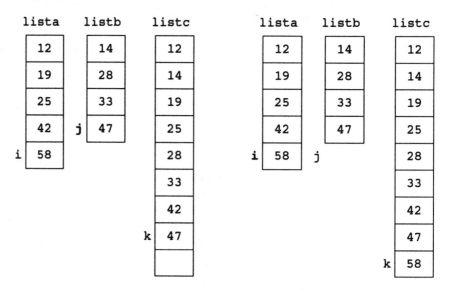

The merge operation is relatively effective. There are at most n_c comparisons since each comparison copies one element to the final list. The indices i and j take on a total of n_c different values, and, of course, k takes on a total of n_c values.

2.11.1 C Implementation

Algorithm M is written in a non-structured way. In order to translate this into a structured C function, it is important to examine the algorithm holistically. We notice that steps M2 through M6 constitute a loop. Since the conditions are at the beginning of steps M2 and M3, it appears to fit the pattern of a while() loop structure. The main difference is that both M2 and M3 terminate the loop by branching to different parts of the algorithm. However, concentrating on the loop structure, it appears that the loop is <u>terminated</u> if:

$$i >= NA \quad \underline{or} \quad j >= NB$$

Therefore the loop <u>continues</u> as long as:

$$i < NA \quad \underline{and} \quad j < NB$$

This last result follows from DeMorgan's Theorem (see Appendix A).

Both statements M7 and M8 follow the pattern of a while() loop structure. However, if we use the condition above to control the main while structure, then we need to be able to determine if we execute step M7 or step M8. This is not difficult. When the while() loop structure terminates it is because either i has reached NA, or j has reached NB. These two conditions cannot occur simultaneously—one must occur first. Therefore, we can test either of these in an if()-else structure to determine which source list still has elements to be copied.

With these we can sketch the control structure of the list merge function:

```
while (i < na && j < nb) {
                                        /* steps M4 and M5 */
}

if (i >= na) {
    while (j < nb) {
                                        /* step M7 */
    }
} else {
    while (i < na) {
                                        /* step M8 */
    }
}
```

2.11.2 Merging and Sorting

One might be tempted to implement a "merge" procedure by catenating the two lists and then sorting the final list; the result should be the same if the original lists are sorted. However, all sorting procedures grow faster than the merging algorithm. As an example, consider two sorted lists of 128 elements. To merge them will take 256 operations. To catenate the second onto the first will take 128 operations (no comparisons, however). To sort the final list of 256 items by the simple swap sort will take approximately $n_c^2/2 = 256 \cdot 256/2 = 32{,}768$ operations. Thus, a single merge procedure is the most effective.

This suggests a possible way to make our simple swap sort more effective. If we have a list of 256 elements, we might divide them into two lists of 128 each. To sort each one takes roughly $128 \cdot 128/2 = 8{,}192$ operations, for a total of 16,384 operations (because there are two lists). A final sorted list may be obtained by merging these two for an additional 256 operations—or a total of 16,640 operations compared to the 32,768 operations it would take to sort the entire list once.

Well if dividing the list into two parts, sorting the two individually, and then merging is helpful, why not try four parts, or eight, or even more! Indeed some of the more sophisticated sorting algorithms that we will consider are based on such a concept. For four sublists of 64 items, it will take about $4(64 \cdot 64/2) = 8{,}192$ sorting operations. To merge these will require 512 operations since merging sublists 1 and 2 requires 128 merging operations, merging sublists 3 and 4 requires 128 merging operations, and, finally, merging these two sublists of 128 items each requires 256 operations, for a total of 512 merging operations. Thus, by doubling the number of sublists, the sorting operations are reduced by half and the merging operations increase by 256.

2.12 NON-ORDERED LISTS

Because insertion and deletion from a simple list involve movement of data which may be time consuming, it is desirable to devise a scheme that reduces these operations. If the list is to be maintained without regard to order, then it is possible to add and remove data without large amounts of data movement.

First, we add items only by the append operation; that is, we simply avoid Algorithm IL with its data movement.

Deletion requires additional thought since the item to be deleted is typically not located conveniently at the end. However, since the ordering of the items in the list is unimportant we can move the last item in the list into the location of the deleted item. This involves the movement of only one item rather than $n-k$ items.

Therefore:

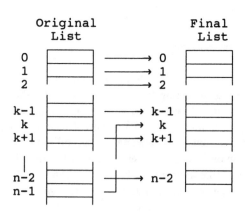

The C code to perform this deletion process is particularly simple and might appear as:

```
n--;
list[k] = list[n];
```

2.13 SUMMARY

A very important data structure is a simple random-access list. There are a number of operations that one might wish to perform on that list. These include: accessing the elements given an index, replacing an item with a new one, appending a new item onto the end, inserting an item into the middle of the list, deleting a selected item, searching the list for the occurrence of a specified item, and arranging the elements of the list into order.

We may wish to combine two lists into a single resultant one. This may be done by two major schemes—catenation and merging. Both are relatively efficient.

REFERENCES

Knuth, Donald E., *The Art of Computer Programming*; Fundamental Algorithms, vol. 1., 2nd ed., Addison-Wesley Publishing Co., Reading, Massachusetts, 1973.

Knuth, Donald E., *The Art of Computer Programming*; Sorting and Searching, vol. 3, Addison-Wesley Publishing Co., Reading, Massachusetts, 1973.

QUESTIONS

Q2.1   It is tempting to write a search function as:

```
void search(int list[], int n, int val)
```

and have the function print out where the value is located or if it is not found, rather than returning the index to the invoking module and letting it handle the output. What are the disadvantages of this method?

Q2.2   If the item that one is searching for is not present in the list, then how many operations will Algorithm SU take?

Q2.3   What are the best, worst, and average cases for deletion from a simple list?

Q2.4   Arrange the following set of items:

42, 32, 67, 9, 12, 15, 45, 17, 31, 53, 5, 27

a. into ascending order.

b. into descending order.

Q2.5   The C code example of deleting from a non-ordered list by copying the last element to the deleted one was written as:

```
n--;
list[k] = list[n];
```

If you wished to write this as one statement, with the reference and decrement of *n* all together, how would it appear?

Q2.6   In inserting into a simple list, we found that we need to move the items forward one location by starting from the end of the list and working backwards. To delete an item we have an algorithm that starts with the item following the deleted item and moves forward to the end of the list. Could we implement the deletion process by starting at the end of the list and working backwards? Why or why not?

Q2.7   Write a formal algorithm for replacement in a simple list using Algorithms IL and DL.

Q2.8   The C code example to append to a list was written as:

```
list[n] = item;
n++;
```

If you wished to write this as one statement, with the reference and decrement of *n* all together, how would it appear?

Q2.9   The text suggested that a search function return a -1 if the search were unsuccessful. What other possible values might we use?

Q2.10   A process that is similar to the search that was considered in the text is one that looks for the largest (or smallest) item in the list rather than one that matches a given value. What is the big O behavior of such a procedure?

Q2.11   In the function that implements the Simple Swap Sort, function swap_sort() as given above, there are four pairs of braces. Which of these are necessary? Why use all four pairs?

Q2.12   If you increase the size of the list to be sorted by Algorithm W by a factor of 10, then how many times longer will it take the algorithm to execute?

Q2.13   Catenation was describe above as taking two lists, *a* and *b*, and producing a third list, *c*, that contains the contents of *a* and *b* in order and one after the other. Write out the C code segment to perform this.

Q2.14   If you had two lists that were not ordered and you wished to combine them into one list, could you use catenate? Merge? Which would you use and why?

Q2.15   What happens in Algorithm M if either of the two initial lists is empty; that is $NA = 0$ or $NB = 0$?

Q2.16   Merge by hand the two following lists:

> lista: 13, 15, 16, 23, 26, 28, 29, 31
>
> listb: 10, 11, 22, 24, 25, 32, 34

Q2.17   The List Merge algorithm (M) used tests such as:

```
If i >= NA, then ....
```

Could these be written as:

```
If i = NA, then ....
```

Why might the $>=$ be preferred to the $=$?

Q2.18   What is the result of performing the List Merge algorithm on two non-ordered lists? As an example, what is the result of merging:

> 4, 5, 1, 2, 9, 12, 7, 6
> 8, 3, 15, 10, 21, 15

Q2.19   Consider two ordered lists 120 and 330 items long, respectively. How many operations would it take to merge these into a final ordered list? How many operations would it take to catenate the second onto the first, then, using the simple swap sort, to sort the resultant into a final ordered list?

Q2.20   What modification(s) would need to be made to the List Merge algorithm so that it would merge two lists, sorted into descending order, into a final sorted (in descending order) list?

Q2.21   In the C implementation of Algorithm M, we controlled the main loop with an "and"; that is, either of two conditions might terminate it (i >= na "or" j >= nb). We then used a single test (i >= na) to control whether we finished with step M7 or step M8. Is it possible for the main loop to terminate with <u>both</u> conditions being false, thereby causing a problem with selecting either step M7 or step M8?

Q2.22   If we had a condition that caused a loop to be terminated as:

```
i > n && list[i] <= k
```

What would be the appropriate condition for the loop to continue to be executed?

Q2.23   Catenation and merging both involve combining two lists into one. With catenation, the final list could be either of the two original lists. Is it possible to merge two lists so that the final list is one of the original lists, without copying the items back? Explain.

Q2.24   The analysis of a certain process involving n items produces:

best	average	worst
14	5n+3	$2n^2-10n+50$

What is the "big O" behavior of this process? Explain.

EXERCISES

E2.1   The search scheme we used, Algorithm SU, is a very simple one. If the item is present, then the best case is 1 comparison (the item is in location 0), and the worst case is n comparisons (the item is in location $n-1$). Determine the exact average case by assuming that you wish to search for each of the items exactly once—count the number of comparisons to find each one, sum these, and divide by the number of items to obtain an average.

E2.2   Rewrite Algorithm DL, to delete from a list, by copying the old list, less the one to be deleted, to a new list.

E2.3   Write a formal algorithm to find the range of the items in a list. The range is defined to be the largest minus the smallest. (Note, this should involve only one pass through the list.)

E2.4   Complete the table that computes the possible operations involved in sorting a list of 256 items by dividing it into sublists, sorting each, and merging them as suggested in the text.

Number of Sublists	Size	Sorting Operations	Merging Operations	Total Operations
1	256	32,768	0	32,768
2	128	16,384	256	16,640
4	64	8,192	512	
8	32	4,096		
16	16			
32				
64				
128				
256				

E2.5   Algorithm W, the simple swap sort, finds the smallest item in the list after its first pass through the list. This item is available to be printed, for example, while the algorithm proceeds to find the next item. Both the indices, *i* and *j*, progress in the same direction, namely, forward through the list; however, there is no reason why they cannot move backwards or in opposite directions.

Rewrite Algorithm W so that **both** of the indices move from the end of the list toward the beginning; which item is found first, the smallest or the largest?

E2.6   An alternative to mathematical induction (see Appendix A) to determine a closed formula for the sum of the first *n* integers is: write the sum from 1 to *n* and also from *n* to 1, adding pieces, counting, etc.

```
S = 1 +  2  +  3  + ... + n
S = n + n-1 + n-2 + ... + 1
```

Use this scheme to derive the closed form:

$$1 + 2 + 3 + \ldots + n = n(n+1)/2$$

E2.7   Rewrite the List Merge Algorithm (Algorithm M) in a structured manner form to avoid the use of a "Go to step xx" statement. Use a construct such as: "Perform steps xx while xxxxx is true" or "Perform steps xx as long as xxxxx condition is met" or "Perform steps xx until xxxxx is reached" or "While xxxxx, Perform steps xx".

E2.8   A process similar to the search that was considered in the text is one that looks for the largest (or smallest) item in the list rather than one that matches a given value. Write a formal algorithm to search for the largest item in a list of *n* elements.

E2.9   Another scheme to implement a non-ordered simple list and avoid the data movement is to use an "EMPTY" indicator. When a record is deleted, it is marked as EMPTY. When a record is to be inserted, the list is scanned and the new record is placed in the first EMPTY location encountered (or if none are found, at the end). When the list is searched, all EMPTY locations are skipped.

   Write out formal algorithms for insertion, deletion, and searching that use this scheme.

E2.10   If we have two lists of length k and $n-k$ items, respectively, what is the total number of operations required to sort each of the two and then merge them? Assume a simple swap sort. Note that the total number of items is *n*. By differentiating this with respect to k and setting the result to zero, show that the minimum number of total operations occurs when k = n/2.

E2.11   A scheme to discover the closed form for the sum of the integers is to guess that the sum is quadratic. That is:

$$1 + 2 + 3 + \ldots + n = an^2 + bn + c$$

   We wish to determine the values of *a*, *b*, and *c*. We can do this by evaluating the sum for the first three integers:

```
n=0:   0 =              c
n=1:   1 =   a +   b +  c
n=2:   3 =  4a +  2b +  c
```

   Solve this set of simultaneous equations for *a*, *b*, and *c*. Show that the solution does agree with the standard closed form expression.

   Note, this does not "prove" the formula. To do this, you need to use mathematical induction. This process allows you to get an idea of what the closed form might be.

PROBLEMS

P2.1   The catenation procedure is an important string operation. A string in C is a list of characters terminated with a NULL character (value 0). Thus, rather than knowing in advance the number of items, the process terminates when the NULL character is encountered. Typically, the catenate function is given two character arrays. The end of the first is determined (by its NULL terminator), then characters from the second are copied to the first until a NULL is encountered, finally a NULL is placed at the end of the combined list.

a. Write a formal algorithm to perform the string catenate procedure.

b. Write a C function to implement this algorithm:

```
void str_cat(first_list, second_list)
char first_list[],second_list[];
```

It may be invoked by:

```
char lista[80],listb[50];

strcpy(lista, "Miss Piggy ");
strcpy(listb, "loves Kermit");

str_cat(lista,listb);

printf("%s\n",lista);
```

Be certain to include: #include <string.h>

P2.2 Write a C function to perform the List Merge Algorithm:

```
void merge(lista,na, listb,nb, listc,nc)
 int lista[],na, listb[],nb, listc[],*nc;
```

The program should follow the algorithm and make no more than one pass through lista[] and listb[].

Write a driver program which assigns values to lista[] and listb[], prints them, invokes merge, then prints the resultant merged list. Hint: you may wish to initialize the original lists as:

```
static int lista[] = {3,7,8,10,...};
```

The original lists should be 10 to 20 elements in length and should both be arranged in non-decreasing order. Your program and merge function should work correctly on any length lists.

Try it on:

a. 2, 3, 5, 7, 8,10,14,16,19,21
    4, 7, 9,11,13,18,23,25,27

b. 5, 7,10,13,22,29,37,42,56
    2, 4, 5, 6,24,26,31,33,42,45,49,52

P2.3   Develop a C program that maintains a simple integer list. The main program should ask for the desired action, then ask for the necessary data, and then invoke the appropriate function to perform the action. The main program should print the appropriate messages stating that the action has occurred, as well as printing the desired values.

Operation	Data Required	Printed Result	Action
initial			set n=0
access	index value		
append	value		
replace	index value		
insert	index value		
delete	index		
search	value	index or not found	
sort			sorts list
print		entire list	
end			end program

The program may be structured as:

```
main()
void access(int list[], int n, int k)
void append(int list[], int *n, int val)
void replace(int list[], int n, int k, int val)
void insert(int list[], int *n, int k, int val)
void delete(int list[], int *n, int k)
int search(int list[], int n, int val)
void sort(int list[], int n)
void print(int list[], int n)
```

For error conditions, such as attempting to append onto a list that is full, to delete from an empty list, or to use an index that is less than zero or greater than $n-1$, have the functions print an appropriate message and perform no action, but simply return.

In order to conserve space or paper when printing the execution, it is suggested that you use a single line prompt:

```
Enter command (T,C,A,R,I,D,F,S,P,Q):
```

At the beginning, or if an incorrect command is entered, you may then wish to print a complete menu:

```
Initial   T      Access   C      Append   A
Replace   R      Insert   I      Delete   D
Search    F      Sort     S      Print    P
End       Q
```

Print a single line message for each action.

Perform the following, in order, on a list that is 7 locations (0 through 6) in length:

```
 1.   initial               11.   append    29
 2.   append    42          12.   access    3
 3.   append    16          13.   delete    2
 4.   append    67          14.   print
 5.   print                 15.   sort
 6.   insert    34 at 1     16.   print
 7.   print                 17.   insert    12 at 3
 8.   search    67          18.   insert    21 at 5
 9.   search    52          19.   insert    17 at 2
10.   append    8           20.   append    78
```

P2.4   Write a C function that prints the contents of an integer list into five columns. It is easy to print this in the order:

```
1 aaaaa   2 bbbbb   3 ccccc   4 ddddd    5 eeeee
6 fffff   7 ggggg   8 hhhhh   9 iiiii   10 jjjjj
```

However, write the function to print as:

```
1 aaaaa   3 ccccc   5 eeeee   7 ggggg    9 iiiii
2 bbbbb   4 ddddd   6 fffff   8 hhhhh   10 jjjjj
```

This is not too difficult if the number of items is a multiple of five. If it is not, then print it with the last column(s) "short." As an example:

```
1 aaaaa   4 ddddd   7 ggggg   10 jjjjj   13 mmmmm
2 bbbbb   5 eeeee   8 hhhhh   11 kkkkk
3 ccccc   6 fffff   9 iiiii   12 lllll
```

Consider the following patterns for small numbers of items:

```
n=1:   1                    n=11:  1    4    7    10
                                   2    5    8    11
n=2:   1    2                      3    6    9
```

```
n=3:  1    2    3                n=12:  1    4    7    10
                                        2    5    8    11
n=4:  1    2    3    4                   3    6    9    12

n=5:  1    2    3    4    5  n=13:  1    4    7    10   13
                                        2    5    8    11
n=6:  1    3    5                        3    6    9    12
      2    4    6
                                 n=14:  1    4    7    10   13
n=7:  1    3    5    7                   2    5    8    11   14
      2    4    6                        3    6    9    12

n=8:  1    3    5    7            n=15:  1    4    7    10   13
      2    4    6    8                   2    5    8    11   14
                                        3    6    9    12   15
n=9:  1    3    5    7    9
      2    4    6    8            n=16:  1    5    9    13
                                        2    6    10   14
n=10: 1    3    5    7    9              3    7    11   15
      2    4    6    8    10             4    8    12   16

                                 n=17:  1    5    9    13   17
                                        2    6    10   14
                                        3    7    11   15
                                        4    8    12   16
```

For any number of items 17 or above, there will always be items printed in all five columns, and only the last column will be short.

Write a C program to test your function and print out lists with a variety of lengths to illustrate that it indeed works as intended.

P2.5   Write a C function that takes an integer list with each item containing one digit and multiplies it by a small positive integer, keeping one digit per item and carrying the rest to the left as it is done in the classical multiplication algorithm.

Use your function to produce a table of the powers of two from 0 through 100. You will also need a function to print the array.

Chapter 3

Searching Algorithms

"Please, your Majesty," said the Knave, "I didn't write it, and they can't prove that I did: there's no name signed at the end."

"If you didn't sign it," said the King, "that only makes the matter worse. You <u>must</u> have meant some mischief, or else you'd have signed your name like an honest man."

There was a general clapping of hands at this: it was the first really clever thing the King had said that day.

"That <u>proves</u> his guilt, of course," said the Queen: "so, off with—."

"It doesn't prove anything of the sort!" said Alice. "Why, you don't even know what they're about!"

"Read them," said the King.

The White Rabbit put on his spectacles. "Where shall I begin, please your Majesty?" he asked.

"Begin at the beginning," the King said, very gravely, "and go on till you come to the end: then stop."

3.1   OBJECTIVES

The objectives of this chapter are to:

- Examine in detail the process of searching a simple list.

- Describe the method of a serial search.

- Present the binary search algorithm.

- Analyze the binary search process.

- Describe the conditions that are necessary and appropriate for a binary search.

- Consider alternatives.

3.2   *INTRODUCTION*

In **Chapter 2** we introduced various list-processing algorithms for a simple random-access list. Now we wish to study a very important set of these in more detail—searching processes.

One of the fundamental operations on any data structure is the retrieval of data that is stored in that data structure. Typically, this involves finding it first. If the exact location were known in advance, it would be a trivial operation to access the value. However, more often we may know the value of the item and need to search for it. You might question why we need to access an item if we already know its value. We might wish to delete it or insert another item. However, in general, there may be many values associated with each item that we wish to retrieve and examine. An example is a list of student names—stored with each name is his or her gender, birthday, class standing, phone number, etc. Given a name, we would like to search the list to find out where that name is stored, so that we could get at the other data associated with it.

If the data structure is being accessed frequently or is large, we need a quick method to search for an item. Searching is often a necessary first step in locating an item to be deleted or in finding an appropriate location to insert a new item.

As we noted previously, there are often two situations that we need to be concerned with:

1. The desired item is present in the data structure.

2. The desired item is NOT present.

We need to be able to handle the second situation gracefully and appropriately. And we must be aware that the best, average, and worst cases for these two situations might be different.

In anticipation of more complicated structures, we will refer to the item that we are searching for as the "search key" or simply the **key**. In general, a key is a field or part of a record that uniquely identifies that record. Therefore, it is appropriate to use this term to represent the item we are looking for.

3.3 SERIAL SEARCHING

The simplest type of search is to examine each location in turn until either the item is found or the end of the list is reached. Algorithm SU, introduced in Chapter 2, is such a scheme. This algorithm is:

Algorithm SU (Serial Search on Unordered List). Given a list, *LIST*, of *n* elements, find the location of the key, *KEY*.

SU1. [initialize]   i=0.

SU2. [at end?]   If i $>$ = n, then Halt.   (not found)

SU3. [compare]   If KEY = LIST[i], then Halt.   (found at i)

SU4. [loop]   i=i+1; Go to step SU2.

                                                                      ■

The process is simply: "Begin at the beginning, and go on till you come to the end: then stop."

3.3.1 Analysis

The effectiveness of this procedure is easy to determine. While the ultimate determination of effectiveness is the time that it takes, we will determine the number of "looks," or number of elements in the list we will need to access, as the measure of its effectiveness.

If the item we are searching for is present, then the best case is for us to find it on the first look (the item is present in location 0). The worst case is to search through the entire list and find it in the last location—hence *n* looks.

The average is somewhat more difficult to determine since it will depend upon the set of items we wish to search for. We will make the assumption that we wish to look for each item in the list the same number of times; that is, they will occur with uniform probability. In reality, this assumption is likely not to be true. Typically, a small number of items are searched for most of the time and many of the items in the list are rarely needed. Indeed, there is a general "law":

20% of the records will require 80% of the activity and the remaining 80% will require the rest of the 20% of the activity.

For the assumption of uniform occurrence, the average may be determined by counting the number of looks for each item, in turn; summing these to get the total count for all; and dividing by the number of items. The first item is found with one look, the second with two, etc. Thus the total looks for the entire set is given by:

$$1 + 2 + 3 + 4 + \ldots + n = n(n+1)/2.$$

Thus the average is this total number of looks required to search for all *n* items divided by *n*:

$$(n+1)/2 \approx n/2.$$

If the item is not present, then (in all cases) the entire list is searched. The best case, worst case, and average case are all *n*.

SUMMARY FOR SERIAL SEARCH ON UNORDERED LIST

	Best	Average	Worst
Present	1	n/2	n
Not Present	n	n	n

In order to specify the "big O" behavior of this algorithm, we must decide which of the above cases should be used. The best case clearly does not reflect the general nature of the algorithm when n gets large. Generally, we will use the average case. Therefore, Algorithm SU is O(n). Of course it does not really matter in this situation, because both the average case and the worst case grow linearly.

3.3.2   Use of a Sentinel

We can make a modification to the algorithm that does not change the number of looks but does make the loop operate faster and hence speeds up the search. There are two comparisons, steps SU2 and SU3, for each iteration of the algorithm. These are typically implemented as part of a C function as:

```
for (i=0; i<n; i++) {
    if (key == list[i])
        return (i);
}

return (-1);
```

While one comparison is obvious—the if () statement—the other is inherent in the for (;;) expression.

The modification consists of placing a copy of the key onto the end of the list and extending the search by one. Under these circumstances, the key will always be found. If it already occurs in the list, it will be found with an index, $i < n$, and the process will halt. If not, then it will be found with $i=n$. The important point is that the test comparing *i* with *n* need not be made at each iteration. A single test when the loop finishes can determine if the key was already present. The C code segment might appear as:

```
    list[n] = key;              /* place key onto end */
    i = 0;

    while (key != list[i])      /* loop until key found */
        i++;

    if (i == n)                 /* decide if at end */
        return (-1);
    else
            return (i);
```

Note that because the desired elements of the list are stored in locations 0 through *n*-1, placing a value in location *n* means that it is not really part of the list—we did not actually append the key to the list by changing the value of *n*. It also means that it is unnecessary to remove it when we are done.

Such a value is called a **sentinel**. It speeds up the execution of the loop; however, the behavior of the algorithm is still O(n).

3.3.3   Ordered Lists

If the list is sorted into ascending (or descending) order, then a slight modification can improve the effectiveness when the item is not present. Basically we take into account the "orderness" of the list, and examine values in the list, until we reach one that is larger than the item we are searching for. Because all of the remaining items are even larger, we can stop looking at that point.

As an example, let us search for the value 36 in the following list that is arranged in ascending order.

```
item
      ┌──────┐
      │  36  │
      └──────┘

   0     1     2     3     4     5     6     7     8     9     10
 ┌─────┬─────┬─────┬─────┬─────┬─────┬─────┬─────┬─────┬─────┬─────┐
 │ 12  │ 16  │ 21  │ 31  │ 34  │ 42  │ 49  │ 51  │ 76  │ 78  │ 93  │
 └─────┴─────┴─────┴─────┴─────┴─────┴─────┴─────┴─────┴─────┴─────┘
                                i
```

When we reach location *i*=5 with a value 42, and have not found the item, then we can stop; the item cannot be found in any of the remaining locations. A formal algorithm to describe the procedure requires a simple addition to Algorithm SU:

Algorithm SO (Serial Search on Ordered List). Given a list, *LIST*, of *n* elements with items arranged in ascending order, find the location of the key, *KEY*.

SO1. [initialize]	$i = 0$.	
SO2. [at end?]	If $i >= n$, then Halt.	(not found)
SO3. [compare]	If KEY = LIST[i], then Halt.	(found at i)
SO4. [gone past?]	If KEY < LIST[i], then Halt.	(not found)
SO5. [loop]	$i = i+1$; Go to step SO2.	

The loop, consisting of steps SO2 through SO4, will execute more slowly than the loop for Algorithm SU because of the extra comparison. However, if we are reading the items from a file, then we need only read the record once for each execution of the loop. In such a case, the read operation may be relatively slow and the extra comparison will add only a negligible time. For the purposes of comparing algorithms, we will count "looks" or accesses of the items in the list. Thus we will treat the two comparisons as one "look."

When we search for an item that is not present in the list, then Algorithm SO may take far fewer looks; of course this will depend upon the distribution of the items we are trying to find in the list. If the majority of the items are less than the first item in the list, the average number of looks will be around 1. If all of the items are larger than the last item, then the average will take *n* looks. For a uniform distribution of items that are roughly in the range of the items in the list, the average number of looks is approximately n/2.

SUMMARY FOR SERIAL SEARCH ON ORDERED LIST

	Best	Average	Worst
Present	1	n/2	n
Not Present	1	n/2	n

The improvement over the Algorithm SU is not significant. Indeed, each loop of Algorithm SO takes three comparisons rather than the two for Algorithm SU. Except in the situations where the key we are searching for is not present, Algorithm SO will execute more slowly than Algorithm SU.

We can modify the algorithm slightly to put only one comparison in the loop, and add one at the end. Essentially, there are three situations that terminate the loop of SO2 through SO5. These are:

1. We have reached the end of the list.

2. We have found the item.

3. We have gone past where the item should be.

These last two may be combined as:

SO3'. [compare]   If KEY $<=$ LIST[i], then Go to step SO6'.

We then eliminate step SO4.
          For SO6' we must differentiate between whether the key was found or not:

SO6'. [found?]   If KEY $=$ LIST[i], then Halt.   (found at i)
                                                  else Halt.   (not found)

This modification makes the execution of the algorithm slightly faster; however, it does not change the "big O" behavior, which is O(n).

3.4   BINARY SEARCHING

A serial search on an ordered list is not very effective, in that it does not use much of the information available from the order of the list. At each look, one item in the list is examined and eliminated. A much more effective way is to make full use of the "order" found in the list. In particular, if we compare the item with the value in the middle of the list, we should be able to eliminate half of the list instead of only one element.

3.4.1   Example

As an example, let us search the following list of 11 elements (indexed 0 through 10) for the item with a value of 34. We begin by comparing this item with the middle element which, in this case, is a 42 located at index 5.

34

0	1	2	3	4	5	6	7	8	9	10
12	16	21	31	34	**42**	49	51	76	78	93

Since 42 is not 34, and 42 is larger than 34, we can eliminate the 42 and all of the higher elements in the list with this one "look." We now have a list that contains only 5 elements to continue to look for the 34.
          Again, we examine the middle element of the remaining list; in this case the 21 located at index 2.

0	1	2	3	4	5	6	7	8	9	10
12	16	21	31	34						

This 21 is not equal to 34 and is less than 34, therefore we can eliminate all values from the beginning through index 2. The remaining list contains only two elements:

0	1	2	3	4	5	6	7	8	9	10
			31	34						

The middle element of a list of 2 elements is ambiguous. We will compute it by adding the lower index and upper index and dividing by 2 (integer divide). Hence, the middle of 3 and 4 is 3.

Examining the 31, we discover that it is less than the 34 we are looking for. Therefore we can eliminate it, which leaves only one element to compare.

0	1	2	3	4	5	6	7	8	9	10
				34						

We have now found the item that we were searching for with only four "looks," including the last one that finds the item. Actually, four looks is sufficient to find any item in this list of eleven.

We can try this procedure with an item that is not in the list. As an example, let us search for 61.

61

0	1	2	3	4	5	6	7	8	9	10
12	16	21	31	34	42	49	51	76	78	93

Because 61 is larger than 42, we now eliminate all of the items in the list up through 42.

0	1	2	3	4	5	6	7	8	9	10
						49	51	76	78	93

It is less than 76, so we have eliminated three more.

0	1	2	3	4	5	6	7	8	9	10
						49	51			

Comparison with the 49 eliminates one item.

0	1	2	3	4	5	6	7	8	9	10
							51			

And finally, the fourth look eliminates all of the items in the list, and the item we are looking for is not found.

0	1	2	3	4	5	6	7	8	9	10

Such a scheme is called a **binary search**. It is quite effective. Since it eliminates roughly half of the list at each look, the number of looks will depend upon the power of 2 that gives the number of items in the list; that is, it behaves as an $O(\lg n)$ search. Consider examining a list of 1,023 elements:

Looks	Items Eliminated	List Remaining
1	512	511
2	256	255
3	128	127
4	64	63
5	32	31
6	16	15
7	8	7
8	4	3
9	2	1
10	1	0

Doubling the size of the list only increases the number of looks by one, which is characteristic of the properties of the lg function (see Appendix A).

3.4.2 Algorithm

A formal algorithm to perform the binary search uses two indices, *lower* and *upper*, to control the portion of the list that has not been eliminated. Initially these are set to 0 and $n-1$, respectively, and hence include the entire list. The index of the item to examined, i (an integer), is computed from these; the value is compared to the item to be searched for; and one of these controlling indices is updated.

Algorithm B (Binary Search). Given a list, *LIST*, of n elements with items arranged in ascending order, find the location of the key, *KEY*.

B1. [initialize]	lower=0; upper=n-1.	
B2. [finished?]	If upper < lower, then Halt.	(not found)
B3. [get midpoint]	i=(lower+upper)/2.	
B4. [compare]	If KEY = LIST[i], then Halt.	(found at i)
B5. [adjust limits]	If KEY < LIST[i], then upper=i-1. else lower=i+1.	
B6. [loop]	Go to Step B2.	

Remember that the arithmetic operations in step B3 are integer operations. This means, for example, that $(0+15)/2 = 15/2 = 7$.

The algorithm terminates if the item is found (step B4) or when the upper index becomes less than the lower index; that is, all of the items have been eliminated (step B2). Each execution of the loop (steps B2 through B6) requires one arithmetic computation of a middle index, two comparisons, and an adjustment of either the lower or upper index.

3.4.3 Conditions for Use

There are two conditions that must be met for a Binary Search to be used:

1. The list must be ordered (either ascending or descending).

2. There must be random access to the list; that is, we must be able to compute and access the middle element of the list or any portion of the list.

This last condition is generally met with the simple lists we are studying. It is generally not met with a list stored in an external medium or a data structure, such as a linked list, where the access is only sequential.

3.4.4 Analysis of the Binary Search

The best case for finding an item that is present in the list is just one look. This would be the case if it happened to be in the middle of the list.

For the worst and average cases, let us diagram the search patterns for a number of small lists. The values on the right-hand side of the following lists are the number of looks that it would take to find the element in that location.

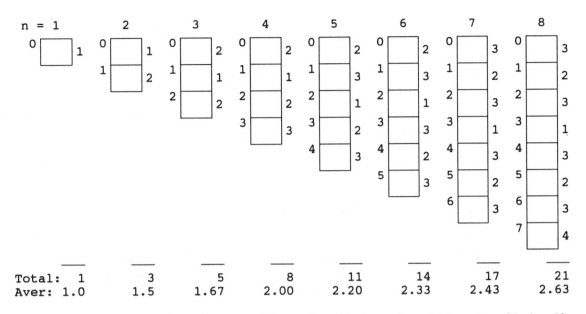

Total:	1	3	5	8	11	14	17	21
Aver:	1.0	1.5	1.67	2.00	2.20	2.33	2.43	2.63

We have also summed the number of looks to give a total number of looks. If we searched for each item in the list once, this would be the total number of looks required to find all items. The average is just the total divided by the number of items.

The last case illustrated, $n=8$, has one element that takes four looks. Each additional value of n up to $n=15$ would add one element that would take four looks. When $n=16$, one element (the last one) would take five looks.

The maximum number of looks for these examples (and others) display the following pattern:

MAXIMUM LOOKS VS N

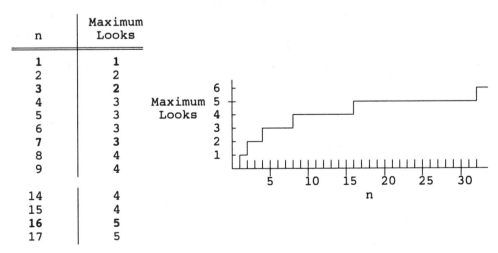

n	Maximum Looks
1	1
2	2
3	2
4	3
5	3
6	3
7	3
8	4
9	4
14	4
15	4
16	5
17	5

Evidently, the maximum number of looks increases at powers of two. An expression that gives the maximum number of looks is:

```
M(n) = ceil(lg(n+1))
```

where the ceil() or "ceiling function" rounds the value of its argument up to the next integer. Formally, the ceil() function returns the smallest integer greater than or equal to its argument.

When *n* gets large, we can simplify this to:

```
M(n) ≈ lg n.
```

This expression agrees with the suggestion above that because the binary search eliminates roughly half the list with each "look", the procedure is O(lgn).

For the average case, we will determine how many looks it takes to search for each item in the list, in turn, and sum these. From the diagram on the previous page, we see that the lists of one, three, and seven elements have a particularly symmetric situation. Let us consider these particular ones for analysis. These lists have:

$$n = 2^m-1, \quad m = 1, 2, 3, \ldots.$$

m	n=2^m-1	total looks
1	1	1
2	3	5
3	7	17
4	15	49
5	31	129
6	63	321

This table is not difficult to compute. We notice that for a list of size one (*m*=1), there is just one look. For a list of size three (*m*=2), there is one item found in the first look, and there are two items to be found with two looks each. For a list of seven (*m*=3), one item takes one look, two items take two looks, and four items require three looks. Therefore, we have the following for the total number of looks to search for each item once, L(m):

```
1:  L(1) = 1
2:  L(2) = 1·1 + 2·2
3:  L(3) = 1·1 + 2·2 + 3·4
4:  L(4) = 1·1 + 2·2 + 3·4 + 4·8
5:  L(5) = 1·1 + 2·2 + 3·4 + 4·8 + 5·16
6:  L(6) = 1·1 + 2·2 + 3·4 + 4·8 + 5·16 + 6·32
```

where each term consists of two factors; the first is the number of looks and the second is the number of items that require that number of looks.

We notice that the first factor in each term increases by one as we move to the right, and the number of terms and last value is just *m*. The second factor in each term is a power of two, but it is a power that is one less than the first factor. That is, as an example, the power that is associated with the factor 5 is 16 which is 2^{5-1}. Therefore:

$$m: \quad L(m) = 1 \cdot 1 + 2 \cdot 2 + 3 \cdot 4 + 4 \cdot 8 + \ldots + (m-1)2^{m-2} + m2^{m-1}$$

Such a pattern leads to a recurrence relation that defines L(m) in terms of L(m−1) since each line is simply the line above it, with one additional term. As an example:

$$L(6) = \underbrace{1 \cdot 1 + 2 \cdot 2 + 3 \cdot 4 + 4 \cdot 8 + 5 \cdot 16} + 6 \cdot 32$$

$$= L(5) + 6 \cdot 32$$

In general, the recurrence relation becomes:

$$L(m) = \begin{cases} 1, & m=1 \\ L(m-1) + m2^{m-1}, & m>1 \end{cases}$$

Unfortunately, a table or a recurrence relation is difficult to work with. What we would like is a simple formula that, given a value of *m*, would allow us to compute the value for L(m) directly. Such a formula is called a **closed form** expression.

We can obtain such a formula by examining the table of values for patterns. First we note that all of the values of *L* are odd. If we remove one from each value, then we end up with even values that appear to be multiples of powers of 2.

m	$n=2^m-1$	Total Looks							
1	1	1	= 1 +	0	=	1 + 0·2	=	1 + $0 \cdot 2^1$
2	3	5	= 1 +	4	=	1 + 1·4	=	1 + $1 \cdot 2^2$
3	7	17	= 1 +	16	=	1 + 2·8	=	1 + $2 \cdot 2^3$
4	15	49	= 1 +	48	=	1 + 3·16	=	1 + $3 \cdot 2^4$
5	31	129	= 1 +	128	=	1 + 4·32	=	1 + $4 \cdot 2^5$
6	63	321	= 1 +	320	=	1 + 5·64	=	1 + $5 \cdot 2^6$
m	2^m-1							1 + $(m-1)2^m$

From this pattern, it is apparent that

$$L(m) = (m-1)2^m + 1.$$

The average number of looks is then given by dividing the total looks by the number of items in the list:

$$A(n) = L(m)/n$$
$$= \frac{(m-1)2^m + 1}{n}.$$

This expression still involves *m*; we would like to express it solely in terms of *n*. This is not difficult, because we have the relationship between *n* and *m*:

$$n = 2^m-1.$$

Thus

$$2^m = n+1$$

and

$$m = lg(n+1).$$

Substituting into the expression for total looks results in:

$$L(n) = [lg(n+1)-1](n+1)+1 = (n+1)lg(n+1) - (n+1) + 1$$
$$= (n+1) \cdot lg(n+1) - n.$$

Therefore, dividing by *n* to get the average, we get:

$$A(n) = (n+1)/n \cdot lg(n+1) - 1, \qquad for \ n = 2^m-1.$$

When *n* gets large this simplifies

$$\approx lg \ n - 1$$

or

$$\approx M(n) - 1.$$

The table on the top of the following page illustrates this, using the exact values for the maximum and average cases. As *n* gets larger, then the average number of looks gets closer to one less than the maximum number of looks.

The expression that we have derived is rigorously correct for values of *n* that are one less than a power of 2; that is:

$$n = 2^m-1, \qquad m = 1, \ 2, \ 3,\ldots.$$

COMPARISON OF MAXIMUM AND AVERAGE FOR THE BINARY SEARCH

m	n=2^m−1	Maximum Looks	Average Looks
1	1	1	1.0000
2	3	2	1.6667
3	7	3	2.4286
4	15	4	3.2667
5	31	5	4.1613
6	63	6	5.0952
7	127	7	6.0551
8	255	8	7.0314
9	511	9	8.0176
10	1,023	10	9.0098
11	2,047	11	10.0054
12	4,095	12	11.0029
15	32,767	15	14.0005
20	1,048,575	20	19.0000

It is an approximation for values of n between these special values. In reality, the exact function for the total number of looks, $L(n)$, is one that is stepwise linear with a slope corresponding to $M(n)$; hence the slope changes abruptly at powers of 2, whereas the function we have derived is a smooth curve. Thus the function for $L(n)$ will underestimate the average number of looks slightly for values of n between the special ones. This is illustrated in the following table.

ACTUAL VERSUS COMPUTED NUMBER OF AVERAGE LOOKS

n	Maximum Looks	Actual Total Looks	Actual Average Looks	Formula Total Looks	Formula Average Looks
125	7	755	6.040	754.1	6.033
126	7	762	6.048	761.6	6.044
127	**7**	**769**	**6.055**	**769**	**6.055**
128	8	777	6.070	776.4	6.066
129	8	785	6.085	783.9	6.077
130	8	793	6.100	791.4	6.088
131	8	801	6.116	798.9	6.098
253	8	1777	7.024	1776.1	7.020
254	8	1785	7.028	1784.6	7.026
255	**8**	**1793**	**7.031**	**1793**	**7.031**
256	9	1802	7.039	1801.4	7.037
257	9	1811	7.047	1809.9	7.042
511	**9**	**4097**	**8.018**	**4097**	**8.018**

Note, for example, that the difference in actual total looks between the consecutive values for 125 (755), 126 (762), and 127 (769) is 7. However, from 127 (769) to 128 (785) the difference is 8, as is the difference that gets us to 785 at 129.

We see that the formulas we derived for the total number of looks, L(n), and the average number of looks, A(n), are indeed less than the actual values except for those special cases that are 1 less than a power of 2.

If the item that we are searching for is not in the list, then Algorithm B will execute the maximum number of times and eliminate half the list with each iteration, until the entire list is eliminated.

The following table summarizes the approximate values for the best, average, and worst cases for a binary search. In all cases, the lg n should be rounded up, and the table is increasingly accurate for large values of *n*.

SUMMARY FOR A BINARY SEARCH ON AN ORDERED LIST

	Best	Average	Worst
Present	1	lg n - 1	lg n
Not Present	lg n	lg n	lg n

The "big O" behavior does not depend upon factors or added constants; hence, for Algorithm B, we have O(lg n).

3.4.5   Short Lists

One last point concerning the analysis of Algorithm B is useful. On short lists, the exact average number of looks for both the binary search and the serial search (Algorithm SU) when the item is present appears as:

	Average Looks	
n	Serial	Binary
1	1	1.000
2	1.5	1.500
3	2	1.667
4	2.5	2.000
5	3	2.200
6	3.5	2.333
7	4	2.429
8	4.5	2.625
9	5	2.778
10	5.5	2.900
11	6	3.000
12	6.5	3.083
13	7	3.154
14	7.5	3.214
15	8	3.267

However, for each look in the binary search there is one calculation of an index, two comparisons, an update of an index, and a test on the indices. For each look of a simple serial search on an unordered list, there is one comparison, an update of an index, and a test on its value. Thus the binary search does more work for each look; indeed, on the surface it appears that it does about twice as much as the simple serial search.

Therefore, from the table, assuming exactly twice the amount of work for each "look," it might be expected that for a list of eleven the two search procedures would take the same time and for shorter lists the serial search might be faster. This is indeed the case. Actual comparisons of execution times show that for lists of ten items or less, it is preferable to use a simple serial search; that is, it is faster, on the average, than the binary search. However, there are two important points: 1.) the binary search is really quite good for short lists; that is, the serial search is only slightly faster, and 2.) the binary search really gains on longer lists. As an example, on a list of 1,000,000 elements, the worst case for the binary search is only 20, with an average around 19. The serial search in this case has a worst case of 1,000,000 and an average of around 500,000.

Therefore, in selecting an appropriate search we can follow the decision tree:

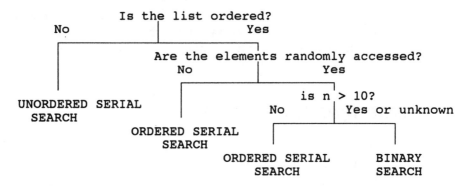

3.4.6 Alternative Formulation

Since Algorithm B does so much work within the loop, it is useful to consider an alternative formulation that simplifies this loop. This is described in Algorithm BA.

Algorithm BA (Binary Search—Alternative Version). Given a list, *LIST*, of *n* elements with items arranged in ascending order, find the location of the key, *KEY*.

BA1. [initialize]   lower=0; upper=n.

BA2. [loop]   While upper-lower > 1, Perform steps BA3 and BA4.

BA3. [get midpoint]   i=(lower+upper)/2.

BA4. [adjust limits]   If KEY >= LIST[i], then lower=i.
                                    else upper=i.

BA5. [compare]   If KEY = LIST[lower], then Halt.   (found at lower)
                                    else Halt.   (not found)
                                                                 ▌

     This algorithm essentially eliminates items in the list until only one element remains. It then checks to see if this is the desired item or not. Notice that the variable *upper* is initially one location past the end of the list. However, it is the *lower* index that is finally tested. Also, the *lower* and *upper* variables are updated slightly differently than they are for Algorithm B.

     Algorithm BA executes the loop (steps BA2-BA4) more times on the average than Algorithm B—it always executes the maximum number of times even in the best case; but, on the average, executes faster because there are fewer comparison operations within the loop.

3.5   SEARCH IMPLEMENTATIONS

For C programming, it is useful to write search (and any other) functions that are reasonably general. Therefore, the search function may be defined as:

```
int search(type list[], int n, type key)
```

where *type* is the appropriate type declaration.

     If found, then return the index of the location, 0 - $n-1$.
     If not found, then return a -1.

     By passing the list[], the number of elements, and the desired item to the function and having it return a "location", this function could work on any simple list of the correct type.

     Algorithm B, the Binary Search, is not written in a structured way. This makes it more challenging to translate into a C function. However, we observe that essentially steps B2 through B6 constitute a loop that is terminated when *upper* < *lower*; that is, the loop is executed as long as *upper* $\geq$ *lower*. When the loop terminates "naturally," then the key is not found and the function returns a -1. The other termination occurs within the loop when the key matches the item, and the function returns the index. Therefore, it is not difficult to implement this algorithm using the structured control structures of C.

3.6   SUMMARY

Searching is an important process. Given a value, we wish to determine if it is present in the list, and if so, where. If the list is unordered, then a **simple serial search** of (O(n) is about the best we can do. If the list is ordered, then we improve the average behavior of the serial search; however, a much more significant improvement comes by using a **binary search**.

The binary search successively divides the list in half, looking for the desired item. Its worst-case behavior is lg n, rounded up. Its average behavior is one less look than the approximate worst case. However, the binary search can only be used on an ordered, random-access list. If the list is sufficiently short, then a serial search can be faster.

By implementing a search function to return information to where the item can be found, we have a module that can be used in a variety of situations.

REFERENCES

Knuth, Donald E., *The Art of Computer Programming*; Fundamental Algorithms, vol. 1., 2nd ed., Addison-Wesley Publishing Co., Reading, Massachusetts, 1973.

Knuth, Donald E., *The Art of Computer Programming*; Sorting and Searching, vol. 3., Addison-Wesley Publishing Co., Reading, Massachusetts, 1973.

Sedgewick, Robert, *Algorithms in C*, Addison-Wesley Publishing Co., Reading, Massachusetts, 1990.

QUESTIONS

Q3.1   What modification in Algorithm SO would be necessary in order to perform a serial search in a list that is arranged in descending order?

Q3.2   Can you use Algorithm SO on an unordered list? Can you use Algorithm SU on an ordered list? Which would you select, if you did not know whether the list were ordered or not?

Q3.3   What is a sentinel and how may it speed up an algorithm? Does it change the "big O" behavior of the process?

Q3.4   A programmer wrote a serial search to match a single letter with the
alphabet, so that she could determine, for example, that an X was the 24th
character. What is the average number of "looks," assuming that the
desired letters were entirely and uniformly random? If she first performed
a single comparison to check if it were greater than M, and if this were true
would start with N, otherwise would start with A, then what is the average
number of looks?

Q3.5   In the text we discussed the possibility of placing the key at the end of the
list (in location *n*) as a sentinel. The code fragment included:

```
if (i == n)          /* decide if key only at end */
       return (-1);
   else
         return (i);
```

Why not simply return *i*? If the key were found earlier, then its
index value would be returned. If not, then *n* would be returned. Since *n*
is not in the valid range of 0 through *n*−1, a value of *n* could signal that
the key was not found in the original list.

Q3.6   The code segment that illustrates the implementation of a sentinel with a
serial search was written with a while () construct. Rewrite it using a for ()
statement.

Q3.7   Why should a C implementation of a search function return the value of the
location, or a special value if not found, rather than printing the appropriate
message internally?

Q3.8   What modification in Algorithm B would be necessary to perform a binary
search in a list that is arranged in descending order?

Q3.9   As an attempt to make the binary search process more efficient, a
programmer suggested:

B4'. [compare]   If KEY > LIST[i], then lower=i+1; Go to step B2'.

B5'. [found?]   If KEY = LIST[i], then Halt.   (found at i)
                           else upper=i−1.

On the average, about how many comparison operations would this
save when searching in a list of *n* elements compared to Algorithm B which
performs two comparisons with each look?

Q3.10 Diagram a list with 15 elements. Beside each location, put the number of looks that Algorithm B would take to locate that item. Sum these and divide by 15 to obtain the average number of looks required to search the list.

Q3.11 State carefully the assumptions made in computing the average number of looks if the key is present for any of the searching algorithms. How is the average case different in principle from the best or worst cases?

Q3.12 How does the "total looks," $L(n)$, that we used in the analysis of the binary search, differ from the worst-case looks?

Q3.13 To search a list of 10,000 elements using a binary search, how many looks would it take? Does it matter much if this is a worst case or an average case? If the item is present or not? Why?

Q3.14 The game of twenty questions allows a total of twenty questions that can be answered with a yes or no response. If the most efficient questions are asked, how many different things may be distinguished?

Q3.15 If you wished to implement a search on an ordered list that could be any length, which search algorithm would you implement?

Q3.16 We have concluded that the average number of looks for a binary search is approximately maximum-1 as the number gets large. This is true for values of n just less than a power of 2. At a power of 2, the maximum increases by one, whereas the average increases by only a small amount. In reality, what is the biggest difference between the average number of looks and the maximum number of looks?

Q3.17 Which would be the preferred binary search algorithm, Algorithm B or Algorithm BA? Why?

Q3.18 Under what conditions can you use a binary search?

Q3.19 Even though the serial search is faster on very short lists, in general, would there be a noticeable slowing if you used a binary search?

Q3.20 If you have list of eight items, how many looks for each one would it take Algorithm B to find each of them? What is the total number of looks? What is the average number of looks?

Q3.21 Which of the three sort algorithms (SU, SO, and B) is the least restrictive? That is, which one will work with the most types of lists?

Q3.22   A programmer, learning that a serial search is faster on short lists, included both functions and invoked them as:

```
if (n <= 10)
    loc = ssearch(list,n, key);
else
    loc = bsearch(list,n, key);
```

Is this a useful thing to do if a number of lists of varying length were to be searched? Comment.

Q3.23   The text suggested several improvements to the searching algorithms such as: use of a sentinel, moving a comparison out of the loop, etc. Do any of these change the "big O" behavior of the algorithm?

Q3.24   We have defined a "ceiling function" as returning the smallest integer greater than or equal to the argument.
     What is ceil(x), where:

a. x = 5   b. x = 12.9

c. x = 13.001   d. x = -1.8

e. x = -42   f. x = -10.1

EXERCISES

E3.1   How could the concept of a sentinel be applied to Algorithm SU? Would it speed up the execution? Write a formal algorithm that uses the key placed at the end of the list as a sentinel.

E3.2   In order to improve the speed of Algorithm SO, one often places a value in location n (thereby creating a list of $n+1$ elements) that is greater than any possible key. Therefore, the loop in Algorithm SO is simplified since the program does not have to test if $i \geq n$ each time; this is called a sentinel. Rewrite Algorithm SO to use such a sentinel.

E3.3   Algorithm SO, Serial Search on an Ordered List, may be rewritten to reduce the three comparisons within the loop to two. One way to do this is to search until you find the first key in the list that is greater than the desired one, or you find the end of the list. Then examine the item just before it to see if it matches the search key. Write a formal algorithm that will do this. Remember the special cases:

1. First item greater than search key.

2. Search key is last item.

3. Search key not present.

E3.4   Consider the following specific example of the 20/80 rule. Assume we have 25 numbers. The first 5 need to be retrieved 80 times each. The remaining 20 are needed 20 times each. If we use a serial search, what is the average number of looks required to search the list? If the order of the items is reversed; that is the last 5 are needed 80 times and first 20 are needed 20 times, what is the average number of looks?

Hint: count the number of looks to get each item using the serial search, multiply by the desired number of times each is needed, total this, and divide by the total number of times searches are made.

E3.5   Another recurrence relation for the total number of looks for Algorithm B may be derived by noting that as we move from one value of *m* to the next, we use the previous set of looks twice (since there are twice as many items plus one additional one), with an additional one look for each element (which is used to determine which half to pursue further):

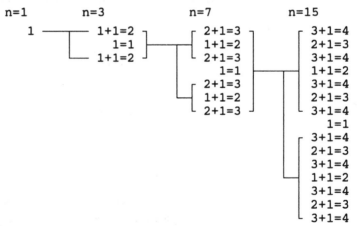

Therefore:

$$L(m) = \begin{cases} 1, & m=1 \\ 2L(m-1)+n, & m>1 \end{cases}$$

From this recurrence relation along with the one presented in the text, solve directly for L(m) by eliminating L(m−1).

E3.6   Write a formal algorithm that implements the modification to Algorithm SU to use a sentinel.

E3.7   Prove that the closed form expression we discovered for the total looks in Algorithm B:

$$L(m) = (m-1)2^m + 1$$

is indeed correct by using mathematical induction and the recurrence relation.

E3.8   Rewrite Algorithm B in a structured form to avoid the use of a "Go to step xx" statement. Use a construct such as: "Perform steps xx while xxxxx is true" or "Perform steps xx as long as xxxxx condition is met" or "Perform steps xx until xxxxx is reached" or "While xxxxx, Perform steps xx" (see Algorithm BA).

E3.9   If you have an ordered list of ten elements, then the discussion above suggests using a serial searching algorithm. Which would be preferred, Algorithm SU or Algorithm SO? Hint: Which is faster for each step? What other conditions might you use or information might you need to decide? What if the majority of items you are looking for do exist in the list? What if most of them are not present?

E3.10   Consider the list:

    3, 6, 7, 10, 13, 14, 18, 21

   Trace Algorithm BA by hand, writing down steps in the algorithm and the values of the indices, lower, upper, and i as you search for:

a.	10	d.	6	g.	3
b.	16	e.	21		
c.	25	f.	1		

E3.11   By writing down lists of one element, two elements, three elements, etc. through at least seven and counting the number of comparisons required to find a given element by Algorithm BA, determine the total number of looks needed to search for all items. Divide this by the number of items to determine the average similar to what was done in the text for Algorithm B. Do lists that are 1, 3, 7, 15, 31, etc. offer some simple patterns? Try to generalize.

E3.12   The searching algorithms presented above generally return the location of the value, if it is found or an indication if the value is not found. This is typically the desired result. However, sometimes a search is not to return a location but a value. Thus, we use the basic search procedure to find a value in an ordered lookup table. The idea is to take an argument, find its location in the table, or—if it is not present—the location of the next smaller item, then return the corresponding value stored with that key. As an example, consider the following lookup table:

x	f(x)
3.0	4.56
3.5	5.78
4.0	7.21
5.0	10.50

If x = 4.0, then the function returns 7.21.
If x = 3.8, then the function returns 5.78.
If x = 2.1, then the function returns 4.56 or error.
If x = 7.2, then the function returns 10.50.

Note that the values of x need to be ordered, but not equally spaced; the values of $f(x)$ may be anything.

Modify the binary search algorithm, Algorithm B, to return the corresponding value in a lookup table.

E3.13   Plot the values of the total looks as one searches a list by Algorithm B:

$$L(n) = (n+1)lg(n+1) - n$$

for values of n = 1 through 31.

On the same plot, graph the exact values of the total number of looks.

PROBLEMS

P3.1   Write a C function to implement the serial search on an ordered list algorithm (Algorithm SO). Have it return the index within the list (return -1 if not found). In addition, have it count the number of looks, which is the number of times step SO3 is executed, and set this value into a global variable.

```
int ssearch(int list[], int n, int key)
```

Write a main() program to initialize the list, request a search key, and print the location if found, or a "not found" message, and the number of looks.

Try it on the list: 2,4,6,8,10,...,1000

For keys of: 500, 1, 121, 704, 8, 371, 1101

P3.2   Write a C function to implement the binary search algorithm (Algorithm B). Have it return the index within the list (return -1 if not found). In addition, have it count the number of looks, which is the number of times step B4 is executed, and set this value into a global variable.

```
int bnsearch(int list[], int n, int key)
```

Write a main() program to initialize the list, request a search key, and print the location if found, or a "not found" message, and the number of looks.

Try it on the list: 2,4,6,8,10,...,1000

For keys of: 500, 1, 121, 704, 8, 371, 1101

P3.3   Write a C function to implement the alternative binary search algorithm (Algorithm BA). Have it return the index within the list (return -1 if not found). In addition, have it count the number of looks, which is the number of times step B4 is executed, and set this value into a global variable.

```
int basearch(int list[], int n, int key)
```

Write a main() program to initialize the list, request a search key, and print the location if found, or a "not found" message, and the number of looks.

Try it on the list: 2,4,6,8,10,...,1000

For keys of: 500, 1, 121, 704, 8, 371, 1101

P3.4   Write a C program that, given n, computes the exact total number of looks and average looks for the binary search algorithm, Algorithm B.

As an example: n = 12, L = 37, average = 3.083

The formula we derived is accurate only for $n = 2^m - 1$. For values of n that are not these, we can use the formula for a value that is the next smallest power of 2 less 1, then add $(m+1)$ for each one until we reach n.   As an example, for $n = 12$, the next smallest value for which the formula is true is 7, which gives 17; we then add $(12-7) \cdot 4$ to get 37.

Try it for:

a. 10	c. 1000	e. 100,000
b. 100	d. 10,000	f. 1,000,000

P3.5   The searching algorithms presented above generally return the location of the value, if found, or an indication if the value is not found. This is typically the desired result. However, sometimes a search is used to return not a location, but a value. Thus we use the basic search procedure to find a value in an ordered lookup table. The idea is to take an argument, find its location in the table or, if not present, the location of the next smaller item, and then return the corresponding value stored with that key. As an example, consider the following lookup table:

x	f(x)
3.0	4.56
3.5	5.78
4.0	7.21
5.0	10.50

If x = 4.0, then the function returns 7.21.
If x = 3.8, then the function returns 5.78.
If x = 2.1, then the function returns 4.56 or error.
If x = 7.2, then the function returns 10.50.

Note that the values of x need to be ordered, but not equally spaced; the values of f(x) may be anything.

Write a C function that, given two lists, an x, and n, will return the value of the item in the second list that corresponds to the closest value to x in the first list.

```
double lookup(double xval[], double fofx[], int n,
              double x)
```

Chapter 4

Recursion

> *"And how many hours a day did you do lessons?"*
> *said Alice, in a hurry to change the subject.*
> *"Ten hours the first day," said the Mock Turtle: "nine the next,*
> *and so on."*
> *"What a curious plan!" exclaimed Alice.*
> *"That's the reason they're called lessons," the Gryphon remarked:*
> *"because they lessen from day to day."*
> *This was quite a new idea to Alice, and she thought it over a little*
> *before she made her next remark. "Then the eleventh day must have*
> *been a holiday?"*
> *"Of course it was," said the Mock Turtle.*
> *"And how did you manage on the twelfth?" Alice went on*
> *eagerly.*
> *"That's enough about lessons," the Gryphon interrupted in a very*
> *decided tone. "Tell her something about games now."*

4.1   OBJECTIVES

The objectives of this chapter are to:

- Introduce the concept of recursion and recursive C functions.

- Give the conditions for a properly determined recursive solution.

- Present examples of recursive algorithms.

- Discuss how recursive algorithms might be applied to data manipulation.

- Explain what tail recursion is and how to eliminate it.

- Provide an comparison between recursive solutions and iterative formulations.

4.2   INTRODUCTION

The simplest computer program is one that executes from top to bottom, with no alternatives or repetition. Most realistic programs have branching and looping. Most of them also have function calls where the execution of the calling module is temporarily suspended and the instructions in the function are followed until they are done; and the execution of the calling module is resumed. Many programs are written with functions calling other functions.

By breaking the program instructions and execution into modules, greater effectiveness in the organization of the program's instructions is realized. The function building blocks may be used in other parts of the same program, or in other programs, resulting in great gains in the programming efficiency. However, a certain amount of overhead time and space will be exacted during execution. Generally speaking, this is considered to be well worth it, since a human's time is more valuable than a computer's time.

An important class of computer functions are those that invoke themselves. These are called **recursive functions**. Most of the high-level languages that permit independent modules also allow the modules to be used recursively.

There are some problems that lend themselves naturally to a recursive solution. Developing a recursive program from the recursive definition is generally much easier than trying to work around the recursion. Shortly, we will consider several important algorithms that manipulate data structures which are inherently recursive.

4.2.1   Recursion and Circular Definitions

There is an important distinction between a recursive definition and a circular definition. If a function calls itself with the same situation (same argument) that it was called, then it probably will execute forever (actually only until the computer's memory is used up through storing the overhead information that is used for the invocation of each function). It is important that the recursive invocation be a different situation than the original one; typically, it will be a slightly smaller or reduced situation. Each recursive call will try to solve a smaller problem. Ultimately, it is hoped that the situation will be small and simple enough that it can be solved directly, without any further function invocations. Then the function can return, and the computer can work itself up out of the chain of calls, until the original invocation terminates and control returns back to the invoking module.

To be a proper **recursive definition** or **function** we must have two conditions:

1. The function invokes itself with a smaller or modified argument.

2. There is a point where the function "bottoms out" and can be evaluated and return a value without invoking itself again.

4.3 RECURSIVE ALGORITHMS

There are a number of algorithms that lend themselves naturally to a recursive formulation. Perhaps the easiest ones to deal with and understand are the mathematical ones. Indeed, we were introduced to one in the previous chapter when we were analyzing the binary search algorithm.

4.3.1 Factorial

One of the simplest recursive definitions is the one for the factorial function. For a non-negative integer value, the factorial, indicated by a !, is the product of the first n positive integers:

$$n! = 1 \cdot 2 \cdot 3 \cdot \ldots \cdot n.$$

By definition $0! \equiv 1$. Of course, $1! = 1$.

The normal recurrence definition in mathematical notation is:

$$n! = \begin{cases} 1, & n \leq 1 \\ n(n-1)!, & n > 1 \end{cases}$$

This is essentially a recursive definition, which may be better seen as:

$$f(n) = \begin{cases} 1, & n \leq 1 \\ n \cdot f(n-1), & n > 1 \end{cases}$$

It fits the pattern of a recursive definition; each value of the function is defined in terms of itself, but the argument is smaller. Finally, there is one value of the argument for which an explicit value is given—this stops the recursion. Essentially, we are stating:

I can know the value of $f(n)$, if I know the value of $f(n-1)$.
I can know the value of $f(n-1)$, if I know the value of $f(n-2)$.
I can know the value of $f(n-2)$, if I know the value of $f(n-3)$.

     ⋮

I can know the value of $f(3)$, if I know the value of $f(2)$.
I can know the value of $f(2)$, if I know the value of $f(1)$.
I do know the value of $f(1)$. Therefore, all of the "if's" are satisfied and I know the value of $f(n)$.

This definition may be translated into a formal algorithm as:

Algorithm F (Factorial). Compute the value of the factorial function of a non-negative integer, *n*.

F1. [finished?]   If n < 2, then return value 1.

F2. [recurse]   Invoke Algorithm F with n−1; Multiply the result by n and return the product.

This algorithm satisfies both requirements for a proper recursive procedure. With each recursive invocation, the size of the argument is reduced. Ultimately it must reach 1. At that point, a value may be obtained and returned without further recursive calls.

This algorithm may be implemented directly into a C function as:

```
/*****************************************************
 *
 *   factorial function
 *
 *   computes n! recursively
 *
 *****************************************************/
long fact(int n)
{

    if (n < 2)
        return (1);

    return (n*fact(n-1));

}
```

The function is defined to return a long int, since the factorial function grows extremely rapidly. Indeed, even 13! exceeds the size of a typical long int in C (see Appendix A).

Executing this function, with an argument of 5, produces an execution chain of function invocations (where the level of operation is indicated by indentation) given on the top of the next page.

Note that we "put on hold" the operation of fact() and recursively call fact() until we find a point that fact() can perform an action and finish (when n=1). Then we can work our way back out—performing the multiplication and finishing each level that we have entered, until we reach the top.

```
level:  1     2     3     4     5
     fact(5)
         fact(4)
             fact(3)
                 fact(2)
                     fact(1) = 1
                  ┌──────────────┘
              2·1 = 2
           ┌──────────┘
       3·2 = 6
    ┌──────────┘
 4·6 = 24
 ┌──────────┘
5·24 = 120
```

Sometimes recursive calls can be confusing. One way to help sort things out is to imagine that we have a series of different functions that call each other. For the factorial case, let us define a series of distinct functions:

```
long fact(int n)
{

    if (n < 2)
        return (1);
    return (n*facta(n-1));

}

long facta(int n)
{

    if (n < 2)
        return (1);
    return (n*factb(n-1));

}

long factb(int n)
{

    if (n < 2)
        return (1);
    return (n*factc(n-1));

}
```

and so forth.

By defining this series, we avoid having any function call itself—each explicitly calls a "look alike" or clone, but not itself.

Now our execution chain looks like:

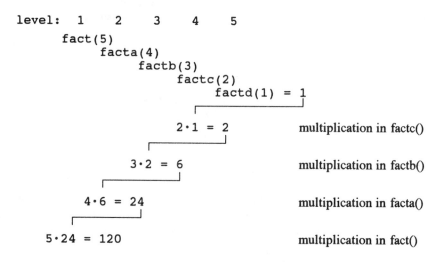

```
level:   1     2     3     4     5
       fact(5)
            facta(4)
                 factb(3)
                      factc(2)
                           factd(1) = 1
```

2·1 = 2	multiplication in factc()
3·2 = 6	multiplication in factb()
4·6 = 24	multiplication in facta()
5·24 = 120	multiplication in fact()

We note that fact() calls facta() and cannot complete its operation until facta() returns a value which can be multiplied by 5; then finally, the result can be returned to the calling program.

When you write recursive C functions, it is important to remember that the function parameters and variables defined within the function are local variables (unless they are declared to be static). Therefore, when the function is invoked, storage is generated for them—and each time they are invoked, additional space is allocated. Thus, the value of a variable within a recursive function will not be affected by a recursive call; it will hold its value until the called function returns and the processing of the original function continues. When a function returns (either explicitly via a return statement, or implicitly by "falling off the end"), the memory that has been allocated for the parameters and local variables is released, to be reused whenever needed.

4.3.2   Sorting

Other non-mathematical problems lend themselves to a recursive approach, as well. In **Chapter 2** we introduced a simple sorting procedure (Algorithm W, Simple Swap Sort). Rewriting this so that the outer index runs "backwards" gives us an alternative algorithm:

Algorithm WA (Simple Swap Sort—Alternative Version). Given a list, *LIST*, of n elements indexed 0 through $n-1$, rearrange these items in place so that they are in increasing order. The algorithm first places the largest element in the last location, then iterates with the shorter list.

WA1. [loop over target]   Perform step WA2 for i=n−1,n−2,...,2,1.

WA2. [look through rest]   Perform step WA3 for j=0,1,...,i−2,i−1.

WA3. [compare]   If LIST[i] < LIST[j], then Swap(LIST[i], LIST[j]). ∎

Algorithm WA is not very much different from Algorithm W. Following it, we obtain this example:

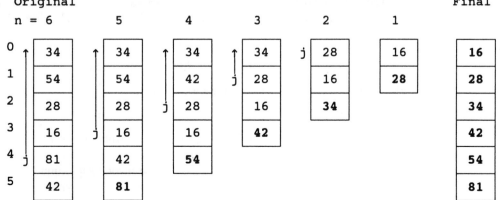

Essentially steps WA2 and WA3 move the *largest* element in the list 0 through $n-1$ into the $n-1$ location (actually 0 through $i-1$ into the $i-1$ location). This complex operation is repeated with a shorter list; therefore, it seems as if a recursive definition might be in order. First, let us see how this might work on the example above. Each time we call the algorithm, the size of the list decreases by one, and we perform its steps on the shorter list. Finally, a list of length 1 is reached. Such a list is already sorted, and we can work ourselves back out; actually, nothing further needs to be done except to return out of the chain of recursive invocations:

The algorithm to implement this is:

Algorithm WR (Simple Swap Sort—Recursive Version). Given a list, LIST, of *n* elements indexed 0 through *n*−1, rearrange these items in place so that they are in increasing order. It is invoked with an argument *n*.

WR1. [are we done?]   If n = 1, then terminate.

WR2. [look through rest]   Perform step WR3 for j=0,1,...,n−1.

WR3. [compare]   If LIST[i] < LIST[j], then Swap(LIST[i], LIST[j]).

WR4. [recurse]   Invoke Algorithm WR with length n−1.

This algorithm satisfies the general requirements for a properly constructed recursive algorithm. It invokes itself with a shorter list each time, and it terminates (returns to the point where it was invoked) when it attempts to operate on a list with one element—such a list is already sorted!

4.3.3   Binary Search

Another algorithm that we have already discussed in some detail is the binary search procedure (Algorithm B). This can also be thought of as a recursive process if one considers that at each step the algorithm examines a list to see if the desired item is in the middle of the list. If it is, then it returns the location; if not, it continues (recurses) to examine a shorter list. When the size of the list is zero elements, the process stops and returns a "Not Found" message.
        Algorithm BR implements this recursive binary search procedure:

Algorithm BR (Binary Search—Recursive Version). Given a list, *LIST*, delineated by a lower index, *LOWER*, and an upper index, *UPPER*, with items arranged in ascending order—find the location of the key, *KEY*. That is, the algorithm is initially invoked with *LOWER*=0 and *UPPER*=*n*−1, where *n* is the number of elements. It recursively examines smaller sublists until either the key is found or the sublist contains no elements (not found).

BR1. [finished?]   If UPPER < LOWER, then Return.   (not found)

BR2. [get midpoint]   i=(LOWER+UPPER)/2.

BR3. [compare]   If KEY = LIST[i], then Return.   (found at i)

BR4. [recurse]   If KEY < LIST[i], then Invoke Algorithm BR
                                        with LOWER and i−1.
                                else Invoke Algorithm BR
                                        with i+1 and UPPER.

Notice that this algorithm is not only given the list to sort and the number of items in the list, but also the appropriate upper and lower indices—we have written these in upper-case just to emphasize that they are provided to the algorithm rather than being set inside as local variables.

Since a C function is typically defined to return a value, we can define the search function to be:

```
int bsearchr(type list[],int lower,int upper, type key)
```

For this recursive algorithm, we must define the function with the limits of the list it is to examine. Thus it is originally invoked as:

```
loc = bsearchr(list, 0,n-1, key);
```

Thus step BR1 might be implemented as:

```
if (upper < lower)
    return (-1);
```

The recursive step, step BR4, must also return a value just like the fact() function. It might be implemented as:

```
if (key < list[i])
    return (bsearchr(list,lower,i-1,key));
else
    return (bsearchr(list,i+1,upper,key));
```

It is important that the function explicitly return a value regardless of how it might terminate (including, "falling off the end").

If this implementation seems obscure, then perhaps the equivalent code appears more reasonable:

```
if (key < list[i])
    loc = bsearchr(list,lower,i-1,key);
else
    loc = bsearchr(list,i+1,upper,key);
return (loc);
```

For all of the examples that we have considered so far, the recursive formulation was just another way of looking at the solution. However, for some problems recursion is the only way, or at least the best way, to consider how the solution might be effected.

4.3.4   Towers of Hanoi

According to an ancient story, somewhere in the far east there is a monastery with a pile of sixty-four disks of increasing size made of pure gold.[1] Once upon a time, these were stacked on each other in a single pile with the largest on the bottom. Each disk is pierced with a hole and they rest on a pin of diamond. They were to be moved from one position to another according to the following rules:

- Only one disk could be moved at a time.

- A larger disk could never be placed on top of a smaller one.

- The pile was moved from one position to another using a single additional temporary position

When this "Tower of Hanoi" is completely moved from one position to another, the end of the world will come!

At the start, a much smaller pile might appear as:

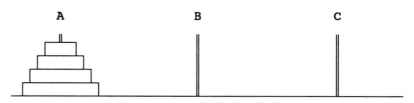

In order to move a pile of n disks from position A to B you must move the top $n-1$ disks to C:

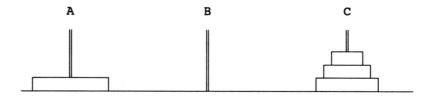

Then move the n-th disk to B:

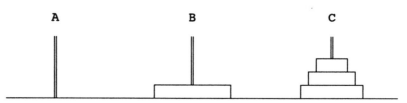

---

[1] For a more complete description, see W.W. Rouse Ball, *Mathematical Recreations and Essays*.

And, finally, move the $n-1$ disks from C to B so they will be on top of the bottom disk:

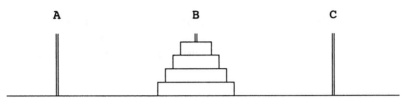

In order to move the pile of $n-1$ disks from A to C, you must first move a pile of $n-2$ from A to B, then move the $(n-1)$th disk to C, and then the pile of $n-2$ from B to C.

Of course, if the pile is only one disk high, then you simply move it from A to B.

Inherent in this description is a recursive procedure. We describe the move of a pile of n disks in terms of moving piles of $n-1$ disks, and there is a simple non-recursive move for the simplest pile of one disk:

Algorithm HT (Towers of Hanoi). Move a pile of n disks from position S (source position) to F (final position) using T (temporary position). The disks are numbered sequentially from top to bottom of the original pile; that is, $1, 2, \ldots, n$.

HT1. [are we done?]   If n = 0, then Return.

HT2. [move top]   Invoke Algorithm HT with n−1 disks from S to T using F.

HT3. [move single]   Move disk n from S to F.

HT4. [move top back] Invoke Algorithm HT with n−1 disks from T to F using S.

This algorithm makes use of the local nature of the parameters of the function. If a C function is defined as:

```
void hanoi(int n, int s,int f, int t)
```

The step HT2 would become:

```
hanoi(n-1, s,t, f);
```

which moves a pile of $n-1$ disks from the source position to the temporary one using the final as an intermediate.

The computation of the number of individual disk moves that it takes to relocate the entire pile follows from this description of the solution process and also involves a recursive definition:

$$M(n) = \begin{cases} 1, & n=1 \\ 2 \cdot M(n-1) + 1, & n>1 \end{cases}$$

Since moving a pile of n disks involves moving a pile of $n-1$ disks, then moving 1, and then moving the pile of $n-1$ disks again.

This recurrence relation generates the sequence:

```
n =   1   2   3   4   5   6
M(n) = 1,  3,  7, 15, 31, 63 ....
```

This is easily recognized as the powers of 2 less one. Evidently, a closed form is: $M(n) = 2^n - 1$.

For a pile of 64 disks, this result evaluates to approximately 1.84×10^{19} moves. At the rate of one move per second, this would take about 585 billion years! If a computer can evaluate one million moves per second, then it would *only* take 585 thousand years!

4.3.5   Printing an Integer

Another simpler example is converting an integer from the internal representation into the characters (digits) for printing. Internally an integer is represented as a pattern of bits. Arithmetic operations are well defined on these values; however, for printing, these need to be converted to the appropriate characters (typically the digits 0 through 9). The most straightforward way of identifying digits is to use the modulo 10 to get the right-most digit and to divide by 10 to get successive digits. The problem is that this procedure extracts the digits that are to be printed in a right-to-left order, whereas we wish to print the digits in a left-to-right sequence. That is, if we use the value of 123 (remember that internally this is represented as a series of bits that has the binary equivalent of one hundred twenty-three), then we obtain the digits (as characters) in order:

> '3'
> '2'
> '1'

However, we wish to print the '1', then the '2', and finally the '3'.

A recursive scheme permits us to do this because we can pass the value to a recursive function that simply divides by 10 and calls itself. If the value is zero, then the recursion is terminated. As the recursive chain unwinds, the digits are printed in succession, with the last one found (in this case, the '1') printed first—which is the order we want for the digits printed in.

A simplistic algorithm to perform this is given by:

Algorithm PI (Print an integer). Given a positive integer, print the digits in base ten, recursively.

PI1. [are we done?]   If n = 0, then Return.

PI2. [get next digit]   Invoke Algorithm PI with n/10.

PI3. [print digit]   Print the digit corresponding to nmod10.

■

Unfortunately, there is one exceptional case that this algorithm will not handle. In general, it will not print leading zeros, which is okay; but there is one value for which we need to have one leading zero printed—the value zero itself! The algorithm also handles only positive integers. If the value is negative, it is also useful to print a leading minus sign. We can implement this algorithm in C with these two "corrections" via two functions:

```c
/*******************************************************
 *
 *        function to perform integer print
 *            params:    num        signed integer
 *
 *        handles single zero and negative values
 *
 *******************************************************/
void printi(int num)
{

    void recurs_prnt(int);

    if (num == 0) {                 /* take care of zero */
        putchar('0');
        return;
    }

    if (num < 0) {                  /* handle negative */
        putchar('-');
        num = -num;
    }

    recurs_prnt(num);               /* process digits */

}

/*******************************************************
 *
 *        function to print recursively the digits of
 *            an integer
 *
 *******************************************************/
void recurs_prnt(int num)
```

```
{
    if (num == 0)            /* reached zero, exit */
        return;

    recurs_prnt(num/10);     /* recurse-smaller value */

    putchar(num%10+'0');     /* print digit */
}
```

The first of our two functions handles the single zero situation, takes care of the sign, and invokes the recursive second function to print the digits. Since all of the individual digits are waiting until the recursive chain is unwound, the '-', if present, is printed first, and the digits are printed in a left-to-right order.

4.3.6   Generating Permutations

One theme that we have discussed, and will return to repeatedly, is the procedure for sorting a list of *n* elements. In general, the original list may be found in any one of its possible n! permutations or rearrangements. That there are indeed n! possible permutations is readily determined by noting that if we have *n* distinct items to be placed in an empty list, then we have *n* choices for the first item. For the second, we have only *n*-1 since that is how many are left. Finally, for the last item, we have only one choice since there is only one item left. Therefore:

n	possible elements for the first choice
n−1	possible elements for the second choice
n−2	possible elements for the third choice
.	
.	
.	
1	possible element for the last choice

The total number of possible orderings is, then, the product of these—which is n!. This function grows extremely rapidly (see Appendix A).

n=1	A
n=2	AB
	BA
n=3	ABC
	ACB
	BAC
	BCA
	CAB
	CBA

A related problem is not simply to count the number of permutations, but to actually produce them.

It is easy to write a C function to generate all of the permutations for a specific number using nested loops. As an example, a function to print all of the permutations for $n=3$ is given by:

```
/*******************************************************
 *
 *      function to produce all permutations of 3 items
 *
 ******************************************************/
void permute3()
{

    int i,j,k;

    for (i=0; i<3; i++ {
        for (j=0; j<3; j++) {
            if (j == i)
                continue;
            for (k=0; k<3; k++) {
                if (k == i || k == j)
                    continue;
                printf("%d %d %d\n",i,j,k);
            }
        }
    }

}
```

The if () statements within the loops are to ensure that the values printed will be unique. There will be eighteen values of k generated out of the possible twenty-seven values if all three loops were allowed to run through their complete ranges. (Only values of k are generated when $j \neq i$.) Out of these, only six lines will be printed.

Such a function is easy to develop. However, if we wished to generate all of the permutations of four items, then we would need to write another function. What would be really clever would be a single C function that takes n as a parameter and generates all of the permutations of the n items.

A recursive algorithm is probably the best way to approach this. We will iteratively generate all of the possible values of the elements for the last position and recursively generate all of the possible permutations of the remaining n-1. Of course, when we get down to one element, there is only one way for it to go and the algorithm will "bottom out."

An algorithm for performing this is:

Algorithm GP (Generate Permutations). Given a list, *LIST*, of k elements (numbered 0 through $k-1$), generate all possible permutations.

GP1. [are we done?]   If k = 1, then Invoke process algorithm; return.

GP2. [loop over items]	Perform steps GP3 through GP5 for i=k−1,k−2,...,1,0.
GP3. [try new value]	Swap(LIST[i],LIST[k−1]).
GP4. [recurse]	Invoke Algorithm GP with k−1.
GP5. [restore list]	Swap(LIST[k−1],LIST[i]).

The loop, steps GP2 and GP3 through GP5, will try all possible elements of the list in position $k-1$. We swap that element with another, recurse on the shorter list, and then restore the original order. The loop then repeats with another possible choice.

Note that for $i = k-1$, the pre-swap and post-swap really do nothing. We could move one recursive call of Algorithm GP before the loop and then run the loop from $k-2$ to 0, gaining a small decrease in execution time. Since the execution of this procedure grows so rapidly, this gain is insignificant. We could also rewrite the algorithm to make the pre- and post-swaps more efficient since there is, in reality, a "three-way" movement of items.

When the size of the list to be permuted reaches one, we can perform whatever task we might choose by invoking some *process* procedure. This might simply print the list out on a line. If so, then invoking Algorithm GP will generate a print-out of all of the permutations of the elements in the list. Note that, most likely, the process procedure will need not only the list but the original size as well.

A possible choice for the process procedure is a C function that checks to see if the list is in sorted order. That is, it gives a True value if the list is indeed sorted and a False value if it is not. If Algorithm GP is modified to recognize this, and terminate, when it has generated a permutation that is sorted, then you have the basis for one of the worst possible sorts—one that will run for thousands of years on even small lists!

Within Algorithm GP, we have run the i index from $k-1$ through 0. This is arbitrary and was chosen so that the order in which the permutations are generated will begin with the initial order. Using a range from 0 to $k-1$ will generate all of the permutations, but in a different order.

4.4   TAIL RECURSION

Each time a computer system invokes another module, there must be certain information that is saved. Specifically, the values of the arguments must be stored so that each may be matched with the appropriate parameter. In addition, the return address must be saved so the execution knows where to go when the function is finished. When the secondary function is finished, then the calling function must be able to be resumed—and all of its information must have been preserved while it was temporarily suspended so the values of the local variables need to be stored. This is true regardless of whether the function recursively invokes itself or calls another function. Thus, there is a certain overhead required in invoking a function that takes both space and time. It takes CPU instructions to set up and store the required data as well as to invoke the secondary process. The data must be stored in a convenient data structure (typically, a Last-In First-Out structure called a stack—see Chapter 7).

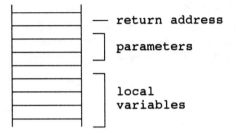

When a function is called from another function (including a recursive call) each function invocation has its own copy of its local variables. This way, the two functions do not interfere with one another. In effect, the calling function is put on hold—its return address, parameters, local variables and any other necessary information saved—while the function it calls is executed. When this secondary one is finished, then the temporary storage associated with it is released and the calling function is once again resumed, with all of its variables intact. It is important when the calling function does resume, that all of its local variables and the return address be present so that it can continue its execution without losing information.

One possible exception arises when a function calls itself recursively in one particular situation. If the last statement in a function is to invoke itself, then there is no need to store all of the current local data for use <u>after</u> the secondary process terminates. When the called process does return to the calling function, the next step is for that function to terminate and return. Therefore, it is possible to invoke the secondary process without having to preserve all of the local information from the first. Indeed, the return address of the first invocation may be applied to the second one.

Such a situation is termed **tail recursion** and, fortunately, occurs frequently. Of the recursive algorithms we have presented above, Algorithms WR (Simple Swap Sort), BR (Recursive Binary Search), and HT (Towers of Hanoi) all display this characteristic (although Algorithm HT also has an "internal" recursive call). Algorithm F (Factorial) does not, because there is an operation (multiplication) that uses local information after the secondary process returns. Algorithm PI does not, because the printing of the digit occurs after the recursive call.

If the compiler is clever enough, it can modify the code generated to eliminate the explicit setup and extra storage for the tail recursive call. However, it is prudent not to trust the implementation of the language if the situation is critical.

Because a recursive formulation is often the simplest, we will, in the future, typically look at an algorithm formulation which may be totally recursive, and then consider how to rewrite it to avoid the tail recursion. So far we have presented (and presented first) the versions of Algorithms WR and BR that remove the tail recursion.

Generally, in the algorithms that exhibit tail recursion, we can rather mechanically modify the parameters to reflect the new values and replace the last recursive call with a "Go to" at the end of the algorithm. In writing a C function, we can achieve the same result by embedding the code in a while ( ) structure. If the conditional clause in the while () statement is the logical *Not* of the "bottoming out" condition, then the function will have a natural exit off the end of the loop.

As an example, consider the alternative Simple Swap Sort, Algorithm WR. Since the last thing the function does is to invoke itself, it exhibits tail recursion.

Normally, we might implement it directly from the recursive algorithm as:

```
void sssort(int list[], int n)
    {
            :                       /* define locals */
            :

        if (n == 1)                 /* bottom condition */
            return;

        for (j=0; j<n; j++) {       /* process list, swap */
            :                       /* where appropriate */
            :
        }

        sssort(list,n-1);           /* recursive call */

    }
```

To eliminate tail recursion, we could simply write it as:

```
void sssort(int list[], int n)
    {
            :
            :

        while (n != 1) {            /* note != to loop */

        for (j=0; j<n; j++ {        /* process list, swap */
            :                       /* where appropriate */
            :
        }
        n--;                        /* modify parameter */
        }

    }
```

Previously, the function halted when n equaled 1; therefore, it must continue as long as n is not equal to 1. (Actually, it is probably best to write this condition as: $n > 1$; this is a more robust condition. It would then handle the situation where originally $n=0$.)

It must be noted that this last version, that eliminates tail recursion, is almost exactly the same as the original iterative version. Both have two nested loops. The

primary difference is that this latest version implements the outer loop using a while ()
structure, whereas the original version used a for (;;) structure!

4.5 ITERATION VERSUS RECURSION

Many processes may be written to be solved either with an iterative, or repeated,
solution or a recursive one. In many cases there is little difference in the efficiency
of the execution. If the recursive program is easier to program, and is not much less
efficient than the iterative one, then the recursive program is preferable. However,
the obvious recursive solution may leave much to be desired in terms of execution
speed and memory use.

4.5.1 Fibonacci Numbers

A Fibonacci Sequence is defined as (see Appendix A):

$$F_n = \begin{cases} 1, & n = 1 \text{ and } 2 \\ F_{n-2} + F_{n-1}, & n > 2 \end{cases}$$

This is a recursive definition. It fits our model better if we think of F_n as F(n).
We can write a recursive C function directly from this definition—the programming is
trivial!

```
/********************************************************
 *
 *       function to compute the n-th Fibonacci number
 *
 *            param:  n
 *
 *       performs the calculation recursively
 *
 ********************************************************/
long fib(int n)
{

    if (n <= 2)
        return (1);

    return (fib(n-2)+fib(n-1));

}
```

Executing this for small values of *n* is quite reasonable. However, one notices
that the execution begins to take a very long time, even for moderate values of *n*, say

$n \approx 10$. This is because of the "double" recursion which is quite inefficient. To illustrate this, consider fib(6) and trace it through the various levels as it executes:

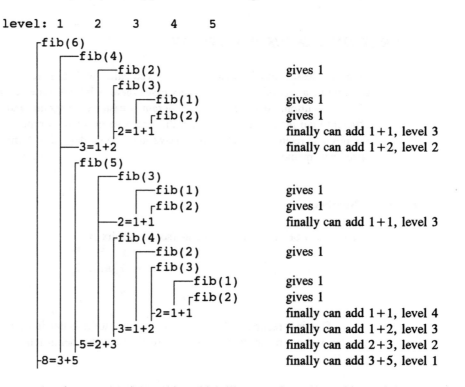

```
level: 1     2     3     4     5
     ┌fib(6)
     │  ┌──fib(4)
     │  │      ┌──fib(2)              gives 1
     │  │      ┌fib(3)
     │  │      │    ┌──fib(1)         gives 1
     │  │      │    ┌fib(2)           gives 1
     │  │      ├2=1+1                 finally can add 1+1, level 3
     │  ├──3=1+2                      finally can add 1+2, level 2
     │  │  ┌fib(5)
     │  │  │  ┌──fib(3)
     │  │  │  │    ┌──fib(1)          gives 1
     │  │  │  │    ┌fib(2)            gives 1
     │  │  │  ├──2=1+1                finally can add 1+1, level 3
     │  │  │  │  ┌fib(4)
     │  │  │  │  │    ┌──fib(2)       gives 1
     │  │  │  │  │    ┌fib(3)
     │  │  │  │  │    │    ┌──fib(1)  gives 1
     │  │  │  │  │    │    ┌fib(2)    gives 1
     │  │  │  │  │    ├2=1+1          finally can add 1+1, level 4
     │  │  │  ├──3=1+2                finally can add 1+2, level 3
     │  ├5=2+3                        finally can add 2+3, level 2
     ├8=3+5                           finally can add 3+5, level 1
```

Another way to picture this, which illustrates how the problem might grow, is:

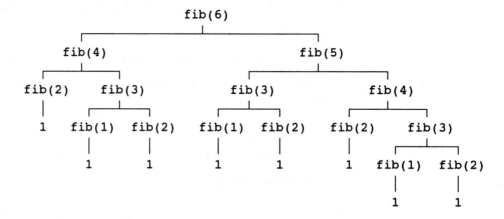

In order to compute fib(6) we needed to compute fib(4) and fib(5). However, fib(5) also needed to compute fib(4) as part of its work. We must work ourselves down until we encounter fib(2) or fib(1), which can be immediately evaluated as 1.

The bottom line is that many values are re-computed during the course of execution. This makes the execution time grow very rapidly. Indeed, by counting the number of times fib(x) is called, we discover that:

Number of
Times Computed

fib(6)	1
fib(5)	1
fib(4)	2
fib(3)	3
fib(2)	5
fib(1)	3
	15 Total Function Invocations

Except for the last value in the list (the number of times fib(1) is evaluated), the number of invocation times obeys a Fibonacci sequence!

If we computed fib(7), we would have to compute fib(5) which would take 9 function invocations, and fib(6) which would take 15 invocations; giving us a total of 25 function invocations (since we also have the original function invocation of fib(7)). Thus, this computation grows very rapidly.

NUMBER OF FUNCTION INVOCATIONS FOR FIB(n)

n	N(n)	n	N(n)
1	1	11	177
2	1	12	287
3	3	13	465
4	5	14	753
5	9	15	1,219
6	15	16	1,973
7	25	17	3,193
8	41	18	5,167
9	67	19	8,361
10	109	20	13,529

The recurrence relation for the number of function invocations is very similar to the ordinary Fibonacci sequence in that each term involves the sum of the two terms immediately preceding it; however, it differs because of an additional constant term:

$$N(n) = \begin{cases} 1, & n = 1 \text{ and } 2 \\ N(n-2) + N(n-1) + 1, & n > 2 \end{cases}$$

Notice that it is easy to write out such a recurrence or recursive relation from the knowledge we have of how the algorithm must operate. Essentially, to compute F_n, we must compute F_{n-2} and F_{n-1}, then add them. If it takes N(n) operations to compute F_n, then clearly $N(n) = N(n-2) + N(n-1) + 1$ operations. (The addition of 1 is from the original operation for F_n.)

With a little insight and writing out a table of values, a closed form for $N(n)$ may be given by:

$$N(n) = 2F_n - 1$$

The Fibonacci sequence grows exponentially, and so does $N(n)$. That is (see Appendix A):

$$F_n \approx \frac{1}{\sqrt{5}}\phi^n \qquad \text{as } n \text{ gets large.}$$

Procedures that grow exponential—$O(x^n)$—are not very useful functions for computation, because even relatively small problems become prohibitive in time. Thus, a recursive solution for computing a Fibonacci number is not a good one. The primary reason is that a given value, such as fib(3), is independently computed several times. This is because of the "double" recursion. F_n is defined not simply in terms of "one copy" of itself, but in terms of two "copies."

The Towers of Hanoi, with its double recursion, also exhibited exponential growth. Later, we will study a sorting procedure, called a Quick Sort, that uses double recursion; however, each time the function calls itself, it is with only about half of the original size problem. The very rapid shrinking of the problem even in the face of the double recursion results in a overall process that grows in a quite slow and reasonable manner. When a function calls itself twice, with only a slightly smaller problem, the execution quickly gets out of hand.

There are two possible solutions for improving this procedure to compute Fibonacci numbers. One is to eliminate the last recursive call. Since this algorithm does not exhibit simple tail recursion, this is not a potentially useful possibility. The second is to attempt to eliminate both calls. Fortunately, it is possible to compute the Fibonacci sequence iteratively. The value of $F(n)$ depends only upon the two previous values. Therefore, it is only necessary to keep these to calculate the next and update them at each iterative step.

Algorithm FB (Fibonacci Sequence—Iterative Version). Given n, a positive integer, compute $F(n)$, the n-th Fibonacci number.

FB1. [do first two]   If n < 2, then return 1.

FB2. [initialize]   fnm1=1; fnm2=1.

FB3. [iterate]   Perform step FB4 for i=2,3,...,n.

FB4. [compute next]   fn=fnm2+fnm1; fnm2=fnm1; fnm1=fn.

FB5. [return result]   Return fn.

Algorithm FB will compute any Fibonacci number very effectively and rapidly. However, it requires more thought to develop, especially in making certain that the upper and lower limits of the loop are correct.

Another way to avoid recursion in this case is to use a list data structure and, hence, some extra storage. We can make an implementation that does, indeed, look very close to the recursive definition. We simply specify a list as *f[]*, fill the first two with ones, then loop, filling the rest until we reach *n*. The notation is similar, since a lookup table—which is essentially what we are generating—and a function are very similar: given a value, they both can return a value. Consider:

```
/*******************************************************
 *
 *        function to compute the n-th Fibonacci number
 *
 *              param:  n
 *
 *              performs the calculation using a list
 *
 *******************************************************/
long fib(int n)
{

    int i;
    long int f[100];

    if (n <= 2)
        return (1);

    f[1] = 1;
    f[2] = 1;

    for (i=3; i<=n; i++)
        f[i] = f[i-2] + f[i-1];

    return (f[n]);

}
```

Finally, consider the following recursive "law."

Hofstadter's Law: *It always takes longer than you expect, even when you take*
                    into account Hofstadter's Law. [2]

---

[2] Attributed to Douglas Hofstadter.

4.6 SUMMARY

A recursive definition defines a process in terms of a simpler example of itself. It will invoke itself until it reaches a "bottoming out" or "basis" case which can be evaluated without further recursion.

A recursive function in C can follow naturally from the mathematical or procedural description of some process. It is a powerful tool in that often one describes how to perform one task that leaves the situation simpler. Recursion then takes care of the rest. An example is to move the largest item in a list to the end. The process is easy to visualize and implement. It is also obvious that a list of one item is already sorted. Therefore, we know how to perform one step—move the largest—and when to stop. Recursion, painlessly, takes care of all the intermediate steps. The programmer does not need to be concerned about what happens—recursion does it all *magically!*

Generally, recursive functions are slower and take more memory than their iterative counterparts; however, they are often easier to develop and write. If the last thing a function does is to invoke itself, then this tail recursion can be easily eliminated which increases the efficiency of the implementation.

Processes which exhibit double recursion tend to grow rapidly.

REFERENCES

Ball, W. W. Rouse, *Mathematical Recreations and Essays*, revised by H. S. M. Coxeter, University of Toronto Press, 1974.

Hofstadter, Douglas R., *Gödel, Escher, Bach: An Eternal Golden Braid*, Basic Books, Inc., New York, New York, 1979.

Kernighan, Brian W., and Ritchie, Dennis M., *The C Programming Language*, 2nd ed., Prentice-Hall, Englewood Cliffs, New Jersey, 1988.

Knuth, Donald E., *The Art of Computer Programming*; Fundamental Algorithms, vol. 1., 2nd ed., Addison-Wesley Publishing Co., Reading, Massachusetts, 1973.

Sedgewick, Robert, *Algorithms in C*, Addison-Wesley Publishing Co., Reading, Massachusetts, 1990.

QUESTIONS

Q4.1 What is the difference between a recursive definition and a circular definition?

Q4.2 It is convenient to think that when a function invokes itself—that is, makes a recursive call—a complete copy of the function is made and executed. Exactly what is duplicated?

Q4.3 What is wrong with the following implementation of a C function to compute a factorial?

```
long fact(int n)
{
    if (n < 2)
        return (1);

    return (n*fact(--n));
}
```

Q4.4 Consider a pile of three disks in the Towers of Hanoi problem numbered from the smallest as 1, 2, and 3. If it is desired to move the pile from A to B using C, then where does the middle move—the one that moves disk #3—take the largest disk to? Where does the very first move take the smallest disk, disk #1? If the number of disks is four, where does the largest disk move to and what is the appropriate first move? Generalize this to apply to any number of disks. Hint, consider whether the pile contains an odd or an even number of disks.

Q4.5 If we number the initial pile of disks in the Towers of Hanoi problem starting with the smallest as 1, the next larger as 2, and the largest as n, then—at any point in the solution—can an even-numbered disk ever sit right on top of another even-numbered disk?

Q4.6 If you wish to compute Fibonacci numbers, what value of n will produce a F_n that will exceed the size of a typical long int (2,147,483,663)?

Q4.7 Besides the total number of function calls required to complete a recursive procedure, an important value to consider is the depth of the recursion. This is the maximum number of recursive functions on hold plus one (the current one); it is important in determining the amount of required temporary storage. For the recursive Fibonacci algorithm, what is the depth required to compute F(n)?

Q4.8 In the text, it was stated that N(n) is $O(x^n)$ because F_n is. Explain why this is the case.

Q4.9 Write all of the permutations of the four characters ABCD.

Q4.10   How long would it take to generate all of the permutations of a 20-element list if a computer could generate 1,000 each second?

Q4.11   In Algorithm GP the loop contained the following steps:

GP3. [try new value]   Swap(LIST[i],LIST[k−1]).

GP4. [recurse]   Invoke Algorithm GP with k−1.

GP5. [restore list]   Swap(LIST[k−1],LIST[i]).

Could the last step, GP5, be written as:

GP5. [restore list]   Swap(LIST[i],LIST[k−1]).

Why, or why not?

Q4.12   Does implementing a recursive version of an iterative algorithm, such as the Binary Search, change the number of operations; that is, the "big O" behavior? Does it change the execution time? How? Does it change the memory required for execution? How?

Q4.13   Why would we wish to write a recursive C function if it is less efficient than an iterative scheme?

Q4.14   We implemented the recursive printing of an integer algorithm as two functions, with the second handling the recursion. We passed the value to the second as a parameter. What would be the effect of we had used a global variable? On readability? On possible side effects? On the overhead for the recursive function call?

Q4.15   Why should we write a program in modules, since a module takes more space and more time to execute?

Q4.16   We have written several mathematical functions as recurrence relations. How are these similar to, or different from, a recursive definition?

Q4.17   What would happen if you implemented the recursive version of the binary search, Algorithm BR, as:

```
if (key < list[i])
    bsearchr(list,lower,i-1,key);
else
    bsearchr(list,i+1,upper,key);
```

Q4.18 The closed form for the number of times the recursive function is invoked to compute F_n is given by:

$$N(n) = 2 \cdot F_n - 1$$

Write out a table for the first ten values of *n* to illustrate that this is a valid form.

Is this really a "closed form" expression?

Q4.19 What are the conditions for tail recursion? If a tail recursion is eliminated, how will the execution time be changed? If tail recursion is eliminated, how will the storage requirements be changed?

Q4.20 Why does the C function, to compute the *n*-th Fibonacci number recursively, not exhibit tail recursion?

Q4.21 In what ways is a list, f[n], like a function, f(n)? How are they different?

Q4.22 A suggestion for a possible sorting scheme is to generate a random permutation of the original list (a mechanical example would be to write the items on slips of paper and put them in a bag, shake it, then draw them out one after another, and lay them in a row); and check it to see if it is in order. If it is, then it is sorted! If it is not, then generate another random permutation and check it. Is it an algorithm? Comment on the scheme suggested in the text of generating all of the permutations of the list and checking each one until the sorted one is found. Is this an algorithm? Are either one of these effective?

EXERCISES

E4.1 Write a recursive formal algorithm for computing the *n*-th Fibonacci number.

E4.2 If you wished to invoke a binary search function from the calling module as:

```
loc = bsearch(list,n,key);
```

yet desired to implement it as a recursive procedure—which requires that a lower and an upper index be given to the function—explain and illustrate how this might be done.

E4.3   Modify Algorithm PI, and the associated C functions that print the digits of a decimal integer, to print the hexadecimal representation (base 16) where: 'A' = 10, 'B' = 11, 'C' = 12, 'D' = 13, 'E' = 14, and 'F' = 15.

E4.4   Consider a small version of the Towers of Hanoi that uses only 5 disks.

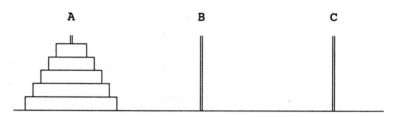

Write down the moves required to transfer the pile from A to B using C. Hint, how many total moves should there be? Where does the top disk go first, B or C?

E4.5   Write a formal algorithm for computing the greatest common divisor (see Algorithm E) recursively. Note that:

$$
gcd(m,n) = \begin{cases} m, & n = 0 \\ gcd(n, rem(m/n)), & \text{otherwise} \end{cases}
$$

This is essentially Algorithm E with the iteration turned into tail recursion.

E4.6   It was easier to rewrite the Simple Swap Sort Algorithm, Algorithm WA, so that the indices went in opposite directions (to find the largest element), then to recurse on a smaller list that "shrank" toward the beginning. Write a formal algorithm that is recursive to find the smallest element first and recurses on a smaller list that shrinks toward the end.

E4.7   The factorial function is a rapidly growing function; however, there is another simple function that also exhibits rapid growth, and that is n^n. Produce a table of $n!$ and n^n for $n=1$ through 10. Which one grows at a faster rate?

E4.8   Algorithm GP, which generates all of the possible permutations of n items, can be modified to generate all possible permutations of n items, taken r at a time, where $1 \le r \le n$. To do this, we halt the recursion when k is 1 or $n-r$ and then print only the right-most r values in the list. Write out the modified algorithm.

E4.9   It is possible to define a "sum of integers" function recursively as:

$$S(n) = \begin{cases} 1, & n = 1 \\ n + S(n-1), & n > 1 \end{cases}$$

a. Write out a C function that would implement this recursively.

b. It is more important to implement this "sum of integers" function iteratively than it was to implement the factorial function iteratively. Why?

    Note, it is possible to write a closed form expression for this problem. This is the "best" way to implement a C function, but for the present we are considering the ramifications of the recursive and iterative versions.

E4.10   Consider the following recurrence relation:

$$G(n) = \begin{cases} 0, & n = 0 \\ n - G(G(n-1)), & n > 0 \end{cases}$$

Write out a table for $G(n)$ for n = 0, 1,..., 10.

E4.11   In solving the n-disk version of the Towers of Hanoi, the full n disks occurred at the beginning and at the end. How many times did a pile of $n-1$ disks occur? Such a pile would consist of all of the $n-1$ smaller disks piled in order; how many times do we get a pile of the $n-2$ smaller ones? n−3? .... 3? 2? 1?

E4.12   The closed form for the number of times the recursive function to compute F_n is invoked is given by:

$$N(n) = 2F_n - 1$$

Prove this formula by mathematical induction.

E4.13   The algorithm to generate all of the permutations, Algorithm GP, has some redundant operations. Initially it attempts to swap the $k-1$ element with the $k-1$ element. Later, it swaps the i-th element with the $k-1$ element then (in the next iteration) swaps the $i-1$ with the $k-1$ element. The net effect is to move the $k-1$ element to i, the element at i to $i-1$, and the item at $i-1$ to k. Rewrite Algorithm GP so that the loop contains only the recursive invocation of Algorithm GP and this movement of data. What happens when $i=1$ or 0?

E4.14   An interesting problem is to determine the sum for the first n Fibonacci numbers. Writing out the first few terms we get:

n	F_n	S_n
1	1	1
2	1	2
3	2	4
4	3	7
5	5	12
6	8	20
7	13	33
8	21	54
9	34	88
10	55	143

From the nature of the problem we can write down the recurrence relation:

$$S_n = \begin{cases} 1, & n=1 \\ S_{n-1} + F_n, & n>1 \end{cases}$$

However, from an inspection of the right-most column above, it appears that this sum is almost a Fibonacci sequence; that is, if we add one to each value, then we get the Fibonacci sequence. Therefore:

$$S_n = F_{n+2} - 1$$

Prove this formula by mathematical induction.

PROBLEMS

P4.1   Write a C function to implement the recursive version of the Simple Swap Sort, Algorithm WR.

Write a main program that initializes a list of 100 items, prints the list, invokes the sort function, and prints the final list.

P4.2   Write a C function to implement the Recursive Binary Search Algorithm. Have it return the index within the list (return -1 if not found).

```
int bsearchr(int list[], int lowr, int uppr, int key)
```

Write a main() program to initialize the list, request a search key, invoke the search function, and print the location if found, or a "not found" message, and the number of looks.

Try it on the list: 2,4,6,8,10,...,100

For keys of: 50, 1, 121, 74, 8, 37

P4.3   In the previous chapter we arrived at a recurrence relation for the total number of looks for Algorithm B (the Binary Search) when each of the elements in the list is searched for once:

$$L(m) = \begin{cases} 1, & m=1 \\ L(m-1) + m2^{m-1}, & m>1 \end{cases}$$

where the size of the list is given by $n = 2^m - 1$.

Write a C function to compute this value recursively. Use it in a program that requests a value for m, then prints m, n, $L(m)$, and the average number of looks.

As an example:

```
Enter m:   3

m = 3 n = 7, total looks = 17 average looks = 2.4286
```

P4.4   Write a C function to compute the recurrence relation we found for the number of calls needed to compute a Fibonacci number recursively:

$$N(n) = \begin{cases} 1, & n = 1 \text{ and } 2 \\ N(n-2) + N(n-1) + 1, & n > 2 \end{cases}$$

While a straightforward solution involves a recursive function, it runs into the same problem as the recursive function that computes F_n.

P4.5   Write a C function that solves the Towers of Hanoi recursively. Have it print out each move as:

```
1.   disk A to B
2.   disk A to C
3.   disk B to C
4.   disk A to B
5.   disk C to A
6.   disk C to B
7.   disk A to B
```

Write a main program that requests the number of disks (in this example, there are 3) and invokes the function.

P4.6   Write a C program to generate all of the permutations of the first n positive integers. That is, implement Algorithm GP as a C function.

```
void permute(int list[], int n, int k)
```

Note that Algorithm GP does not need the value *n*, but that the "process algorithm" it invokes may.

You will also need to write a C function as a "process algorithm" that prints the contents of the list.

```
void process(int list[], int n)
```

Write a main program that requests a small integer, initializes the list with positive integers, and invokes the permutation function.

P4.7   Consider the following recurrence relation:

$$G(n) = \begin{cases} 0, & n = 0 \\ n - G(G(n-1)), & n > 0 \end{cases}$$

Write a C function that computes G(n). Develop a C program that prints a table of G(n) for n = 0, 1,..., 10.

P4.8   The combination of *n* items ($n \geq 0$) taken *r* at a time, C(n,r) may be computed from the recurrence relation:

$$C(n,r) = \begin{cases} 1, & r = 0 \text{ or } r = n \\ C(n-1,r) + C(n-1,r-1), & 0 < r < n \end{cases}$$

a. Write a formal algorithm to implement this recurrence relation.

b. Write a C function that computes C(n,r) recursively and returns the result:

```
long combin(int, int)
```

c.   Test your function on:

   i. C(10,6)   iv. C(5,0)

   ii. C(4,4)   v.   C(6,k), $0 \leq k \leq 6$

   iii. C(8,1)   vi. C(20,10)

Chapter 5

Internal Sorting

At this moment, Five, who had been anxiously looking across the garden, called out "The Queen! The Queen!" and the three gardeners instantly threw themselves flat upon their faces. There was a sound of many footsteps, and Alice looked around, eager to see the Queen.

First came ten soldiers carrying clubs; these were all shaped like the three gardeners, oblong and flat, with their hands and feet at the corners: next the ten courtiers: these were ornamented all over with diamonds, and walked two and two as the soldiers did. After these came...

5.1   OBJECTIVES

The objectives for this chapter are to:

- Explore, in a systematic way, various schemes for sorting.

- Discuss broad categories of sorting.

- Introduce examples of the simpler types of sorts.

- Analyze the sorting algorithms.

- Suggest improvements.

- Give hints on C implementation and how to test whether a sorting function performs correctly.

5.2   INTRODUCTION

In life we are often presented with a random permutation of some set of items. In many of these situations, the items need to be arranged in some sort of order, one that allows us to work with them efficiently. A teacher would typically like to have the students' names arranged in alphabetical order. We find it more convenient to arrange a hand of cards into some sort of order. The index of a book is an alphabetical arrangement of the important words. Returned checks are best stored in numerical order. Protocol dictates the order in which royalty and heads of state appear and are arranged.

The major motivation, of course, is that searching for an item in a sorted list is much more efficient than searching for it in an unsorted list; that is, we may be able to use the binary search of Chapter 3 with its O(lgn) behavior rather than a serial search with an O(n) behavior. As humans, we tend to like things ordered, probably not so much because it looks "neat" but because it is easier to find something in an ordered collection.

The process of sorting is to arrange the items in a list into ascending or descending order; i.e. a sorted list.

For the moment, we will use the data structure of a simple random-access list, although it is possible, and desirable, to consider sorting on more complicated data structures.

As we shall see, there are all sorts of assorted sort algorithms—each with different advantages and disadvantages. There is no one best sort for all possible circumstances, rather there are some simple sorts that generally perform poorly and several sorts that generally do well; however, under some circumstances, a simple sort might outperform one that on the average is much more efficient.

While it is possible to sort into either ascending or descending order, we will consider only the ascending situation. It is relatively easy to modify a sort algorithm for the descending case—typically by changing the "sense" of some comparison operation.

We will also consider lists containing n items, stored in a simple array in locations 0 through $n-1$, to be consistent with the normal practice of the C language.

Generally, we will be concerned with a list that contains distinct items; that is, it will contain no two items with the same value. However, the schemes that we will consider will work—regardless of the uniqueness of the individual values.

Formally, given a list of n items:

$$\{v_0, \ v_1, \ v_2, \ \ldots \ , \ v_{n-1}\}$$

we wish to arrange these so that:

$$v_0 \leq v_1 \leq v_2 \leq \ldots \leq v_{n-1}$$

where the set of values in the original list and the final list are the same. In essence, we wish to find that permutation of the original list so that the items are arranged in order.

5.3   *CATEGORIES AND SCHEMES*

First, we must distinguish between two major categories of sorting algorithms.

External sorts access the data in a serial or sequential fashion. They are suitable for lists that are too large to fit into main memory—hence "external." Typically, the list is read sequentially and one or more lists are generated and written sequentially. The process ends when a final sorted list is written.

Internal sorts are those that may be performed in main memory. They are characterized by random access into the list; we can move around in the list wherever we wish and make swaps or exchanges. The sorts that we will consider in this chapter will be internal sorts.

There are three basic ways in which we can achieve a sort:

1. We can move the items and rearrange the list in place. Typically, this may be implemented without using much extra storage. This is perhaps the most useful and popular scheme. Most of the internal sorts that we consider will fall into this basic method.

2. We can generate another list that is sorted, perhaps retaining the original list. This scheme takes extra storage, since we have both the original and the final sorted list. However, this may be desired especially if the original list is needed.

3. We can generate an index vector that tells how the items are to be rearranged. There are two possible index vectors that might be established:

    a. "from" index vector

        NEWLIST[i] = OLDLIST[INDEX[i]], i=0,1,...,n-1.

    As an example:

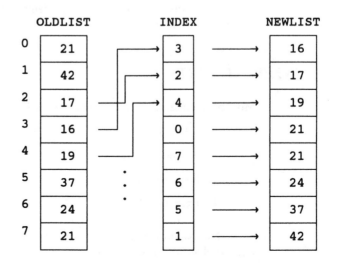

b.   "to" index vector

       `NEWLIST[INDEX'[i]] = OLDLIST[i], i=0,1,...,n-1.`

As an example:

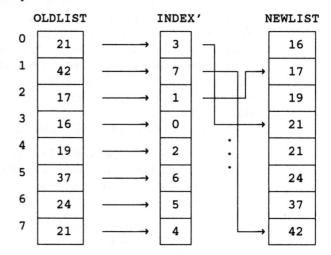

     Once we have an index vector we can, with one simple loop, produce the final sorted list, as long as—in the process of generating the index vector—the original list is left intact. Basically, the problem of sorting is solved once we have the index vector. Index vectors, especially the "from" variety, are useful if we wish to retain the original order of the data yet still be able to access or process the data in a sorted order. Indeed, if each element of the list contains several values, we could produce several index vectors to examine the data in several different ordered arrangements. However, using an index vector takes additional storage.

5.4   INTERNAL SORTS

Most of the internal sorts fall into four major classifications:

     1.   Selection Sorts

     2.   Enumeration Sorts

     3.   Insertion Sorts

     4.   Exchange Sorts

     Selection Sorts generally work by examining the list for the smallest (or largest) element. This item is removed from the list, and the remaining list is scanned for the next smallest (or largest) element, which is then removed. This is continued until all of the items in the list are moved to the final sorted list. In practice, it is possible to perform this sort in place—without physically moving the item from the original list to a second, final list.

Enumeration Sorts compare each item with the other items; the number of items less than a given one is determined. This number tells us where, in the final list, that item will go. As an example, if there are 5 elements less than 42, then 42 will end up at index 5 (indices 0, 1, 2, 3, and 4 hold the 5 smaller values). This sort naturally produces an index vector.

Insertion Sorts add an item to an already sorted list by moving the items in the sorted list until a proper location is found for the new item and it is inserted; when all items have been inserted, the list is sorted.

Exchange Sorts swap or exchange two items that are found out of order. After passing through the lists a sufficient number of times in an orderly fashion, the list is sorted.

These classifications are not perfectly exclusive. Some sorts will use different schemes in different parts of their operation. For example, the implementation of a selection sort that we will be considering uses, in effect, an exchange at the end of each pass; however, the primary process that it uses is a selection of the smallest item in a portion of the list.

There is also another major category that typically is the basis for external sorts where memory limitations are not such a problem. This is a distribution-type procedure, where the items to be sorted are separated into a number of distinct groups which are then reassembled. Typically, more than one copy of the data needs to be present. Each distribution into distinct groups and reassembly creates a more ordered list. This process may be repeated; and when all is done, the items are sorted.

5.5 SELECTION SORT

A **Selection Sort** basically scans the entire list of n items to find the minimum element. When this is found, after looking through the entire list, it can be moved to the beginning of the list. So that we do not lose the first item, we will put it in the same location where we found the minimum; that is, we will exchange the first item (index $=0$) and the smallest item.

After the first pass, the smallest item will be in its final location in the first location (index $=0$) of the list. We can then repeat the process on the shorter list which consists of locations 1 through $n-1$. The second pass will then store the smallest item in this sublist in the second location (index $=1$). This will be the second smallest item in the entire original list. The process is then repeated on the sublist, located at indices 2 through $n-1$, etc. Finally, the last sublist that needs to be scanned is the one consisting of two elements stored at indices $n-2$ and $n-1$. When this "pass" is completed, the smaller of these will be stored at index $n-2$ and the larger, which is the largest in the original list, will be in the last location, index $n-1$.

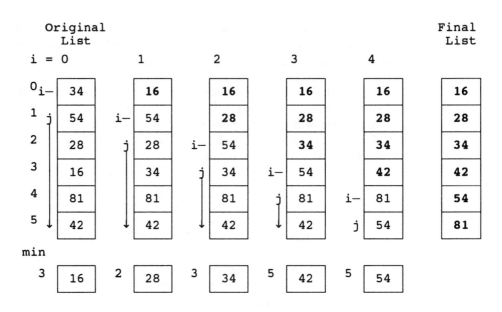

A formal algorithm for performing this is:

Algorithm L (Selection Sort). Given a list, *LIST*, of *n* elements, rearrange these items in place so that they are in increasing order. The algorithm functions by finding the smallest element, then moving it to the target location.

L1. [loop over target] Perform steps L2 through L5 for i=0,1,...,n−2.

L2. [initialize search] min=LIST[i]; loc=i.

L3. [look through rest] Perform step L4 for j=i+1,i+2,...,n−1.

L4. [compare] If min > LIST[j], then min=LIST[j]; loc=j.

L5. [put into place] LIST[loc]=LIST[i]; LIST[i]=min.

■

This sort is rather easy to analyze. For $i=0$, j takes on $n-1$ values ($j=1,2,...,n-1$); for $i=1$, j takes on $n-2$ values ($j=2,3,...,n-1$); hence the total number of comparisons is

$$(n-1)+(n-2)+...+2+1 = n(n-1)/2 \approx n^2/2.$$

This result is the same, regardless of the original ordering of the list or whether the items are all distinct.

Algorithm L selects the minimum each time; hence, the outer loop (the *i* loop) runs forward through the list. The inner loop (the *j* loop) also runs forward; however, it could be written to go from $n-1$ down to $i+1$. The entire algorithm could be rewritten to select the maximum each time and move it to the end of the list. In this case the outer loop would need to run from $n-1$ down to 1.

By selecting the largest item and moving it to the $n-1$ location, it would also be possible to rewrite the algorithm as a recursive one! That is, you would simply recursively invoke the algorithm on the shorter list of $n-1$ items (stored in locations 0 through $n-2$). This recursion is repeated until you reach a list of one element, which is already sorted!

5.6   ENUMERATION SORT

The **enumeration sort** operates by counting. If we count the number of items smaller than a given item, then we know where, in the final list, that item is to go. The most obvious scheme is to compare all of the values with all of the other values:

```
[(compare list[i] with list[j]); j=0,1,...,n-1;
                                  i=0,1,...,n-1.
```

This scheme has two problems:

1. redundant
   no need to compare list[i] with list[i]
   no need to compare list[i] with list[j] and later compare list[j] with list[i]

2. equal items
   both equal items will end up with the same number less than them which suggests they should end up in the same location

We can solve both of these problems by using values of j that are greater than i; that is:

```
[(compare list[i] with list[j]); j=i+1,...,n-1;
                                  i=0,1,...,n-2.
```

We will initially fill the index vector with all zero's. When we compare two values, we will increment the index vector location that corresponds to the *larger* of the two values in the list. If the two values are the same, then we increment the one corresponding to i.

An example showing the list and the index vector at the end of the outer loop is given starting at the top of the next page:

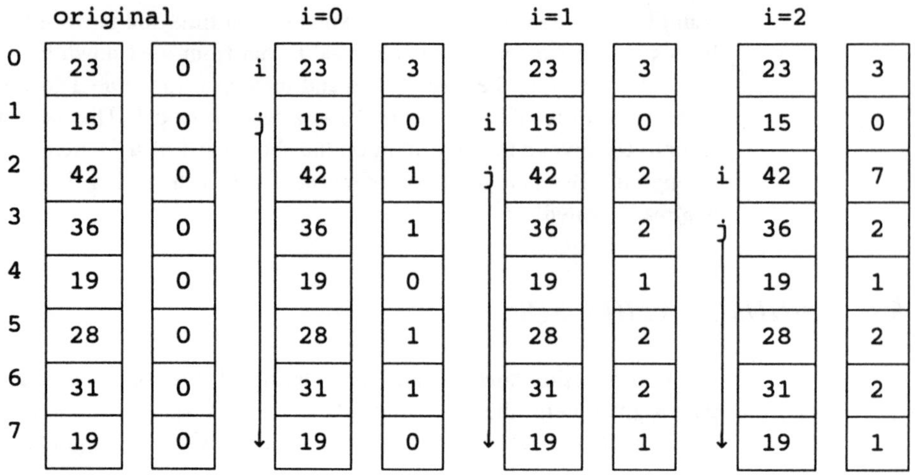

	original		i=0		i=1		i=2	
0	23	0	23	3	23	3	23	3
1	15	0	15	0	15	0	15	0
2	42	0	42	1	42	2	42	7
3	36	0	36	1	36	2	36	2
4	19	0	19	0	19	1	19	1
5	28	0	28	1	28	2	28	2
6	31	0	31	1	31	2	31	2
7	19	0	19	0	19	1	19	1

Continuing this example:

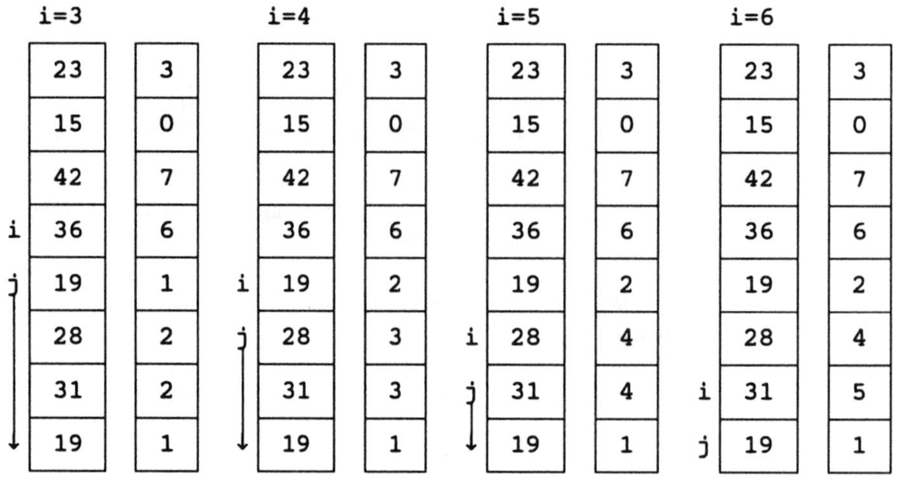

i=3		i=4		i=5		i=6	
23	3	23	3	23	3	23	3
15	0	15	0	15	0	15	0
42	7	42	7	42	7	42	7
36	6	36	6	36	6	36	6
19	1	19	2	19	2	19	2
28	2	28	3	28	4	28	4
31	2	31	3	31	4	31	5
19	1	19	1	19	1	19	1

Once the index vector has been calculated, then we can obtain the sorted list easily, as can be seen in the diagram given on the following page.

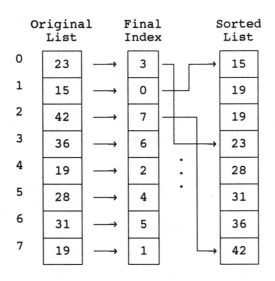

A formal algorithm that implements the enumeration sort is:

Algorithm C (Enumeration Sort). Given a list, *LIST*, of *n* elements, rearrange these items so that they are in increasing order. Establish an index vector, *INDEX*, to count the number of items that are less than each item in the list.

C1. [initialize INDEX]	Perform step C2 for i=0,1,...,n−1.
C2. [set INDEX]	INDEX[i]=0.
C3. [loop over i]	Perform step C4 for i=0,1,...,n−2.
C4. [loop over j]	Perform step C5 for j=i+1,i+2,...,n−1.
C5. [compare & count]	If LIST[i] < LIST[j], then increase INDEX[j] by 1.
	else increase INDEX[i] by 1.

When the Enumeration Sort Algorithm is finished, the sorted list may be obtained by:

NEWLIST[INDEX[i]] = LIST[i];   for i=0,1,...,n-1.

This sort is also rather easy to analyze. For $i=0$, j takes on $n-1$ values ($j=1,2,...,n-1$); for $i=1$, j takes on $n-2$ values ($j=2,3,...,n-1$); hence the total number of comparisons is given by:

$$(n-1)+(n-2)+...+2+1 = n(n-1)/2 \approx n^2/2.$$

This result is the same regardless of the original ordering of the list or if there are repeated items.

5.7   INSERTION SORT

An **insertion sort** takes a new item and inserts it in the proper location in a previously sorted list. It does this by moving each item in the list one at a time until the correct location is found for the new one. This is the procedure that you might use to put a hand of cards in order.

Consider a list of five elements (0 through 4) that are already sorted. We wish to add the next item (element 5, which contains an 8) to this list.

- first, copy the 8 to a temporary variable:

$$3 \quad 5 \quad 9 \quad 12 \quad \underline{15} \quad 8 \qquad 8$$

- 15 is bigger than 8, so copy 15 to the right, duplicating the 15:

$$3 \quad 5 \quad 9 \quad \underline{12} \quad 15 \quad 15 \qquad 8$$

- 12 is bigger than 8, so copy 12 to the right, duplicating the 12, but eliminating the duplicate 15:

$$3 \quad 5 \quad \underline{9} \quad 12 \quad 12 \quad 15 \qquad 8$$

- 9 is bigger than 8, so copy 9 to the right, duplicating the 9, but eliminating the extra 12:

$$3 \quad \underline{5} \quad 9 \quad 9 \quad 12 \quad 15 \qquad 8$$

- 5 is not bigger than 8, so finally insert the 8 after the 5, eliminating the redundant 9:

$$3 \quad 5 \quad 8 \quad 9 \quad 12 \quad 15$$

The list of six elements is now sorted.

Notice that while the process is proceeding, the list contains two copies of one of the items (this item keeps changing); however, when the sort is finished the list contains the same set of items that it originally contained.

The example above illustrates a situation where the new item is inserted somewhere in the middle of the list.

There are two other possibilities that must be considered. If the new element is smaller than the smallest item in the list, then all of the items in the list need to be moved, and the new item is inserted as the first item in the list. In this case, no items in the list will test smaller than the new element, so the test we used above would never be satisfied. This means that either of two conditions will cause the new item to be inserted:

1. the index of the comparison element is less than 0 (we are off the beginning of the list)

or

2. the value of the comparison item is less than the value of the new item.

The other possibility is that the new element is larger than the largest item in the list. In this case, the first comparison will find an element smaller than it, and it will simply be inserted back in its original location. This is taken care of without any special test.

We can begin the process by noting that a list of one element is a sorted list. We insert the second element (index 1) into this list; the process is repeated for the remaining items in the list one at a time.

A formal algorithm to implement this sort procedure is:

Algorithm I (Straight Insertion Sort). Given a list, *LIST*, of *n* elements, rearrange these items in place so that they are in increasing order.

I1. [loop on i]	Perform steps I2 through I7 for $i=1,2,\ldots,n-1$.
I2. [set up values]	$j=i-1$; item=LIST[i].
I3. [reached beginning?]	If $j < 0$, then Go to step I7.
I4. [compare]	If LIST[j] $\leq$ item, then Go to step I7.
I5. [move item]	LIST[j+1]=LIST[j]; $j=j-1$.
I6. [loop]	Go to step I3.
I7. [put into place]	LIST[j+1]=item.

∎

In order to better understand this algorithm, we first note that step I1 suggests a simple counting loop that contains the rest of the steps. Second, note that we get to step I7 if one of two conditions is met—either $k \geq$ LIST[j] or $j < 0$. Thus, steps I3, I4, I5, and I6 constitute a loop. This suggests a while () loop construct to be embedded in a simple for (;;). Further, the condition on the while () can consist of both of the "tests" contained in steps I3 and I4. The "inside" of the while () loop is very easy and fast—move an item and update an index (see step I5).

With these observations of the workings of this algorithm, it can be readily turned into a C function:

```
/******************************************************
 *
 *      function to implement a straight insertion sort
 *
 *          params:   list     list of integers
 *                    n        number, indexed 0 - n-1
 *
 ******************************************************/
```

```
void insert_sort(int list[], int n)
{

    int i,j,item;

    for (i=1; i<n; i++) {
        j = i-1;
        item = list[i];
        while (j >= 0 && list[j] > item) {
            list[j+1] = list[j];
            j--;
        }
        list[j+1] = item;
    }
}
```

Remember that C evaluates only as much of the conditional expression as is required to determine its result. In the while() expression above, **both** conditions must be met. This means that if $j >= 0$ is false (that is, we are off the beginning of the list), then the list is terminated without even an attempt to evaluate list[j] $> k$. Since it is the second condition that fails first for the overwhelming majority of the cases that fail, you might be tempted to reverse the order of the two conditions. This could save a small amount of time at the risk of attempting a comparison with a value that is not in the array. In many cases this probably would not create a problem; however, the program may attempt to address memory outside of the allowed limits.

Another scheme to help speed up the execution is to place at the beginning of the array some value that is smaller than any possible value in the list. Such a value is called a **sentinel**. Because all elements will be inserted to the right of this item, the condition in the while statement may be reduced to (list[j] $> item$). This could easily be done if the values were stored at indices 1 through n, leaving the first location (index=0) empty; however, this is not the usual practice in C. Of course, we might use a selection process to find the smallest element, move this to the first position, then use the insertion process after that—this will allow the inner loop of Algorithm I to run slightly faster, but whether it will reduce the total time is another question.

Another "inefficiency" that we might consider occurs when the new item, originally located immediately after the sorted portion, is larger than any item in the sorted list. In this case, it gets inserted back into its same position. One might be tempted to put in a special test and hence save some time; however, the special comparison itself might take more time than the two storage operations.

Up to this point, all of the sorts that we have considered (including the Simple Swap Sort) have been easy to analyze. They take the same number of comparisons regardless of the original order of the items—generally $\approx n^2/2$. The actual execution times might differ because of the number of swapping operations, but the overall effectiveness of the previous algorithms is about the same.

For the Straight Insertion Sort this situation is different. The number of comparisons does depend upon the original order of the items. If the items are already in ascending order, then step I4 is satisfied on the first comparison, and this "best" case would take only $n-1$ comparisons. On the other hand, if the items were originally ordered in descending order, then each one would have to be moved all the way to the beginning of the list in order to be inserted. This behavior is similar to that of the simple sorts we have considered so far. For $i=1$, 1 comparison; for $i=2$, 2 comparisons, and, hence, for this worst case:

$$1+2+3+\ldots+n-1 \ = \ n \cdot (n-1)/2 \ \approx \ n^2/2.$$

However, for random data one might imagine that, on the average, a particular item might need to be inserted only half-way back into the list and, hence, one might expect $n^2/4$ behavior. Indeed, a careful analysis produces such a result.

Therefore, for the Straight Insertion Sort we have:

best	.	average	worst
n		$n^2/4$	$n^2/2$

Since one typically wishes to sort random data, the average behavior is generally used to characterize this sort. It is considered an $O(n^2/4)$ sort, or, more simply, $O(n^2)$.

5.8   EXCHANGE SORTS

An **exchange sort** is based upon a comparison and the exchange or swap of two elements in the list. The simplest procedure for swapping two elements is:

```
temp = list[i];
list[i] = list[j];
list[j] = temp;
```

Of course, this may be implemented in a function:

```
/*********************************************************
 *
 *       function to swap two values
 *
 *          params:  a,b  addresses of integer values
 *
 *********************************************************/
void swap(int *a, int *b)
{

    int t;

    t = *a;
    *a = *b;
    *b = t;

}
```

This function is then called by:

```
swap(&list[i],&list[j]);
```

Using a function produces more readable code, but executes slightly slower.

5.8.1   Simple Swap Sort

We have already considered an exchange sort with the Simple Swap Sort, which compares all items throughout the remainder of the list with the element in a given location and swaps if the two are out of order. The indices move in the same direction and the comparisons work down the list, comparing items further and further apart in each pass.

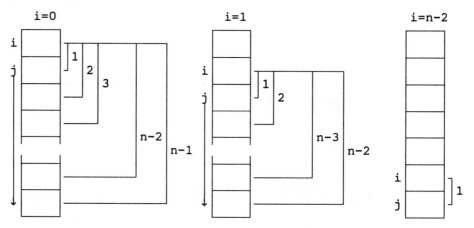

The algorithm for implementing this sort (given previously) is:

Algorithm W (Simple Swap Sort). Given a list, *LIST*, of *n* elements indexed 0 through *n*-1, rearrange these items in place so that they are in increasing order.

W1. [loop over target]   Perform step W2 for $i=0,1,...,n-2$.

W2. [look through rest]   Perform step W3 for $j=i+1,i+2,...,n-1$.

W3. [compare]   If LIST[i] > LIST[j], then Swap(LIST[i], LIST[j]).   ∎

This sort is rather easy to analyze. For $i=0$, j takes on $n-1$ values ($j=1,2,...,n-1$); for $i=1$, j takes on $n-2$ values ($j=2,3,...,n-1$); hence the total number of comparisons is

$$(n-1)+(n-2)+...+2+1 = n(n-1)/2 \approx n^2/2.$$

This result is the same regardless of the original ordering of the list.

5.8.2 Bubble Sort

Another way to compare items and to exchange out of order items is to use the Bubble Sort scheme. Essentially, this sort compares adjacent items and swaps them if they are out-of-order. If we start at the end of the list and proceed toward the beginning, then the smallest item in the list will be moved to location zero. We then repeat the sorting process but stop when the comparisons have reached location 1, which will then hold the next smallest item. We continue until all items are in position.

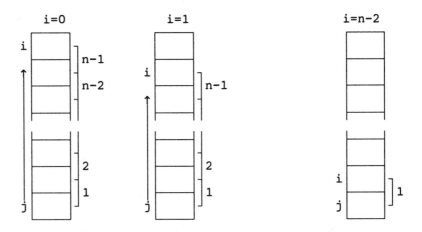

Notice that the two indices that are controlling the sort move in opposite directions—whereas, with the Simple Swap Sort, they moved in the same direction. Actually, the Simple Swap Sort could be set up with the indices moving in the same or opposite directions. The Bubble sort requires that they move in opposite directions.

Because this sort moves the smallest item one location at a time—from its original location to the beginning or top of the list—it is termed a Bubble Up Sort. It is quite possible to run the indices the other way, and move the largest item to the end or the bottom of the list—a Bubble Down Sort.

A formal algorithm for implementing the Bubble Sort is given by:

Algorithm BU (Simple Bubble Up Sort). Given a list, *LIST*, of *n* elements indexed 0 through $n-1$, rearrange these items in place so that they are in increasing order.

BU1. [loop over target]   Perform step BU2 for i=0,1,...,n−2.

BU2. [look through rest]   Perform step BU3 for j=n−2,n−3,...,i.

BU3. [compare]   If LIST[j] > LIST[j+1], then
                    Swap(LIST[j], LIST[j+1]). ∎

This sort is another one that is rather easy to analyze. For $i=0$, j takes on $n-1$ values ($j=n-2$, $n-3$, ..., 1, 0); for $i=1$, j takes on $n-2$ values ($j=n-2$, $n-3$, ..., 2, 1); hence the total number of comparisons is:

$$(n-1)+(n-2)+...+2+1 = n(n-1)/2 \approx n^2/2.$$

This result is the same regardless of the original ordering of the list.

The Bubble Sort, as expressed in Algorithm BU, is no more efficient than the Simple Swap Sort; however, it does lend itself to a slight improvement. If as the j index decrements through the list, no further swaps are required because the elements are already in order, then it is possible to move the i index to the place of the last swap. As an example, consider the following list of 13 items where the first three items have already been bubbled into place ($i=3$):

0	1	2	3	4	5	6	7	8	9	10	11	12
3	5	7	10	12	23	45	31	26	28	42	50	36
			i									

As j moves from the right end (11, 10,..., 4) swapping out of order items we obtain:

3	5	7	10	12	23	26	45	31	28	36	42	50
			i									

where the last swap to be performed occurred with items at location 6. The items from 3 to 6 must already be in the proper place, hence there is no need to perform the j-loop for $i=4$, 5, or 6. Thus, for the next pass we have:

3	5	7	10	12	23	26	45	31	28	36	42	50
							i					

This improvement will reduce the number of comparisons but complicates the algorithm.

Algorithm BI (Improved Bubble Up Sort). Given a list, *LIST*, of n elements indexed 0 through $n-1$, rearrange these items in place so that they are in increasing order.

BI1. [initialize i] $i=0$.

BI2. [set last index] $last=-1$.

BI3. [look through rest]   Perform step BI4 for $j=n-2,n-3,...,i$.

BI4. [compare]   If LIST[j] > LIST[j+1], then
                                  Swap(LIST[j], LIST[j+1]);
                                  $last=j+1$.

BI5. [check if done]   If last > -1, then $i=last$; Go to step BI2.

Algorithm BI replaces a simple counting loop—probably implemented as a for (;;) structure in C, with a more complicated loop. Note that steps BI2 through BI5 still constitute a loop, but now it would probably be more appropriate to implement it as a while () structure in a C function.

The major difference in the performance of this version of the Bubble Sort is that the best case is as good as it can be. If the items are already sorted in order, then there will be no swaps for $i=0$, and the sort is done after one pass through the data! The worst case would occur if the items are in descending order and would take the $\approx n^2/2$ comparisons that the regular Bubble Sort would take. The average case is more difficult. The improvement will help somewhat, but the sort still tends to grow as n^2.

Therefore, for the Bubble Sort we have:

best	average	worst
n	$n^2/2$	$n^2/2$

Another slight improvement might be considered by noting that a small element is moved to the left rather rapidly (for the Bubble Up Sort), even though it is done one location at a time. Large elements move to the right slowly, simply because small elements are removed from the right-end of the list. Therefore, a suggestion is to alternate passes from a Bubble Up Sort and a Bubble Down Sort; that is, two indices are used for i in the Bubble Sort Algorithm and j alternately increments and decrements between these limits that converge upon the center. This Cocktail Shaker Sort does represent a slight improvement over the Improved Bubble Sort, but in reality does not change a poor sort into a good one.

5.9   C IMPLEMENTATION

Ultimately, for the purposes of this text we wish to implement these sorting algorithms as C functions. However, there are also some considerations in writing the "driver" or test program that invokes such a function that we need to consider.

5.9.1   Initial Distributions

There are several distributions that we might like to use to test our C sort functions:

1. ascending
2. descending
3. constant
4. random

This last initial distribution (random) is the typical one that we will want to use. The most convenient way to generate it is to use the appropriate library function:

```
int rand();
```

This function returns a pseudorandom[1] positive integer in the range 0 through 32,767 or whatever is implemented on the specific computer system.

Typically, the function declarations are contained in:

```
<stdlib.h>
```

Because the sequence of integers is computed using a numerical algorithm, it is not truly random, but follows a definite sequence. However, the sequence does satisfy tests of randomness. It is possible to generate the same sequence or different sequences by "seeding" the generator. This is done by using the library function:

```
void srand(int seed);
```

Therefore, a C program segment to generate random values in the range 0-99 (assuming an appropriate range for the pseudorandom values in 36,767 might appear as:

```
#include <stdlib.h>

#define N 200

main()
{
    int list[N],n,i;

    srand(1234);

    n=20;

    for (i=0;i<n;i++)
        list[i] = (double) rand()/32.768; /* random */
       :
```

This segment will always generate the same set of values. If another set is desired, then change the value of the argument to the srand() call.

We can implement other original arrangements by using within the loop the following assignment statements:

```
list[i] = i;                          /* ascending */
list[i] = n-i;                        /* descending */
list[i] = 42;                         /* constant */
```

---

[1]   The set of values generated by the computer are not really random. They are generated by a deterministic routine; however, they "jump" all over the possible range in a seemingly random manner. A good "random" number generating function will produce a set of values that passes a battery of tests for randomness.

```
list[i] = rand();                    /* random */
```

5.9.2   Checking on the Sort

Whenever a sorting algorithm is implemented, it is important that it be tested. There are two possible, rather simple, computerized tests that may help. The first is to add up all the values of the list before sorting it, then add the values after sorting, and compare. This will catch errors that might occur if the final list does not contain the same set of values as the original list. The second test is to check if the final list is indeed in order. Both tests must be passed in order for the sort routine to perform correctly, and they should catch most of the more common errors.

```
pre_sum = list[0];                   /* compute checksum */
for (i=1; i<n; i++)
    pre_sum += list[i];

sort(list, n);                       /* perform sort */

post_sum = list[0];                  /* compute checksum & */
for (i=1; i<n; i++) {                /* for out of order */
    post_sum += list[i];
    if (list[i-1] > list[i])
        printf("ERROR: list[%d] and list[%d] are out
                                of order\n",i-1,i);
}

if (post_sum != pre_sum)
    printf("ERROR: initial and final sums not
                                equal\n");
```

These two tests will not guarantee that your sort routine is working properly, but will catch the most common problems of not ending with a totally sorted list, inadvertently replacing a value with another, and moving a value off either end of the list.

5.10   COMPARISON OF SORTS

We have studied several internal sorts. It is instructive to compare these—not by counting the number of operations or determining their behavior using the "big O" notation—but by timing them. This gives a better indication of their relative behavior in practice. The following tables were constructed using a series of C function implementations of the listed sorting algorithms. They were executed on an 80286 processor with a clock speed of 6 MHz. The items were 16-bit integers to be sorted into ascending order. The timings were determined by using the internal clock and are precise to better than 5% and, typically, better than 1%.

TIMINGS FOR VARIOUS SORT ROUTINES

Times in Seconds for 1,000 Items

Sort	Random	Ascending	Descending	Constant
Simple swap	11.40	8.91	13.95	8.91
Improved bubble	10.67	0.02	13.84	0.02
Insertion	4.65	0.04	9.26	0.04

Times in Seconds for 3,000 Items

Sort	Random	Ascending	Descending	Constant
Simple swap	102.1	80.1	125.6	80.1
Improved bubble	96.4	0.05	124.6	0.04
Insertion	41.7	0.11	83.2	0.11

Times in Seconds for 10,000 Items

Sort	Random	Ascending	Descending	Constant
Simple swap	1118	890	1395	890
Improved bubble	1071	0.15	1384	0.15
Insertion	461	0.35	924	0.35

The four columns are labeled according to the initial ordering of the items. The column labeled "random" is the average for several randomly generated lists. The same lists were used for all the sort executions of different algorithms.

The Simple Swap Sort performs the same number of comparisons, regardless of the original order; however, the number of swapping operations does depend upon the order. Thus, the ascending and constant cases are somewhat faster than the random situation, which in turn is faster than the descending case.

5.11 SUMMARY

Searching through an ordered list is so much more efficient than searching through an unordered list—**sorting** is a common process used to put a list in order.

There are two major classifications of sorting algorithms: those that use random access and hence are suitable for a list contained internally in a computer's main memory, and those that use sequential access which can be used on files that are too large to fit into memory but reside externally.

The internal sorts may be divided into four major categories: selection, enumeration, insertion, and exchange. The **simple sorts** presented as examples all have an $O(n^2)$ behavior. The **insertion sort** does perform somewhat better than the others (including the improved exchange sorts) with a best case of n comparisons and an average case of $n^2/4$ as compared to the others' $n^2/2$ behavior; but it is still essentially an $O(n^2)$ algorithm.

Generally, we would expect a sorting algorithm to operate on a random list, but it should also be able to perform correctly on lists that are already ordered, in either ascending or descending order, as well as on lists with constant data.

It is important to test sorting functions— or indeed, any computer implementation of any algorithm! Simple checks will increase our confidence that the sorting functions are operating correctly and should be used.

REFERENCES

Bentley, Jon L., *"How to Sort,"* *Communications of the ACM*, vol. 27, no. 4, April 1984, Association for Computing Machinery, New York, pp 287-291.

Knuth, Donald E., *The Art of Computer Programming*; Sorting and Searching, vol. 3., Addison-Wesley Publishing Co., Reading, Massachusetts, 1973.

Press, William H., Flannery, Brian P., Teukolsky, Saul A., and Vetterling, William T., *Numerical Recipes in C*, Cambridge University Press, New York, New York, 1988.

Sedgewick, Robert, *Algorithms in C*, Addison-Wesley Publishing Co., Reading, Massachusetts, 1990.

QUESTIONS

Q5.1   How many different arrangements are there of n distinct items?

Q5.2   What modification would be required to cause Algorithm L, Selection Sort, to arrange the items in descending order?

Q5.3   How could you get the items in the list in descending order, from the index vector produced by Algorithm C, Enumeration Sort?

Q5.4   What modification would be required to cause Algorithm I, Insertion Sort, to arrange the items in descending order?

Q5.5   How would you modify the Enumeration Sort, Algorithm C, if the items in the list were stored at indices 1 through n, rather than 0 through $n-1$?

Q5.6   How would you modify the Insertion Sort, Algorithm I, if the items in the list were stored at indices 1 through n, rather than 0 through $n-1$?

Q5.7   Which of the sorts we have discussed depend upon the initial order of the items in the list for determining the number of comparison operations during execution?

Q5.8   Which of the sorts we have discussed will find the first element of the sorted list (the smallest item) in the least amount of time? Which sorts may require the entire procedure to be finished before the smallest item is guaranteed to be found?

Q5.9   The **time** for the execution of the C implementation of the Simple Swap Sort depends upon the initial order of the data, even though the number of comparisons is the same for identical length lists. Why?

Q5.10   Why is Algorithm L, the Selection Sort, termed a "selection sort" and not an "exchange sort" even though effectively an exchange at the end of the inner loop is performed as part of the procedure?

Q5.11   Which of the sorts that we have discussed would be suitable for a recursive formulation; that is, which after some series of operations leave a smaller unsorted list to be processed?

Q5.12   Explain why only checking to see if adjacent items are in order is sufficient to check that the entire list is in order; that is, why does one not have to check each item with all of the others.

Q5.13   The loop to generate a list of random values was written as:

```
for (i=0;i<n;i++)
    list[i] = (double) rand()/32.768;
```

What does the (double) do? Is it necessary? What would happen if you used:

```
list[i] = rand()/33;
```

Q5.14   Why would it be better to write a swap "in-line" as

```
temp = list[i];
list[i] = list[j];
list[j] = temp;
```

rather than calling a function to perform the task as:

```
swap(&list[i], &list[j]);
```

Q5.15 An interesting modification to the C implementation of a sort algorithm is to add a line to count the number of comparisons. That is, we perform something like:

```
void sort(int list[], int n)
{
        count++;
        if (list[i] < list[j])
                ...;
}
```

There are three ways to communicate this back to the calling program:
1. We could modify the routine to return the value explicitly:

```
long sort(int list[], int n)
{

        return (count);
}
```

2. We could pass the value back through the parameter list:

```
void sort(int list[], int n, long *count)
{

        (*count)++;
}
```

3. We could use a global variable:

```
long count;
main()
{

}
void sort(int list[], int n)
{

}
```

Which of these would result in the least number of changes in the sorting function and calling program; and, therefore, is the most unobtrusive?

Q5.16 We have characterized these simple sorts as $O(n^2/2)$ or $O(n^2/4)$. Why did we not simply (and correctly) characterize them as $O(n^2)$?

Q5.17 The Enumeration Sort increments the index vector corresponding to the larger of the two values. Which element is incremented if the values are the same, the one associated with i or with j?

Q5.18 According to the results of actual timings given in the text, the Simple Swap Sort took 11.40 sec to sort a random list of 1,000 items. According to its "big O" behavior, how long would you expect it to take for 3,000 items? for 10,000 items? How do these predictions compare with the values given in the tables?

Q5.19 We have used the sum of the elements of a list as a check on whether the final list contains the same elements as the initial list. This test is not foolproof. How could you be absolutely certain that the final list is a permutation of the initial list; that is, that the two contain the same elements?

Q5.20 We formally defined an ascending sort as:

given a list of n items:

$$\{v_0, v_1, v_2, \ldots, v_{n-1}\}$$

we wish to arrange these so that:

$$v_0 \leq v_1 \leq v_2 \leq \ldots \leq v_{n-1}$$

If the items in the list were distinct, what would the final relation be?

Q5.21 If you wished to print a random list in ascending order, yet still keep the original order of the items, which sort would you use?

Q5.22 In implementing the swap() function, we invoked it as:

```
swap(&list[i],&list[j]);
```

Assuming that list[] is defined as being of int type, then exactly what is:

a. list[i]   b. &list[i]

c. list

Q5.23 If you wished to sort the elements of LIST[m] through LIST[n-1], the end of the list, how could you invoke a C function such as the insert_sort() function given in the text? Hint, this can be done without modifying the function. Hint, what do you pass to the function when you invoke it as:

```
insert_sort(list,n);
```

EXERCISES

E5.1   Given the following set of data, write out the appropriate "to" index vector so that it will arrange the data into ascending order:

23, 42, 15, 5, 8, 19, 34, 11, 28, 37

E5.2   Given the following set of data, write out the appropriate "from" index vector so that it will arrange the data into ascending order:

23, 42, 15, 5, 8, 19, 34, 11, 28, 37

E5.3   Write out a procedure, not necessarily a formal algorithm, that takes a "to" index vector and produces a "from" index vector.

E5.4   Write a formal algorithm for the Selection Sort that is recursive.

E5.5   Write out the formal algorithm for a Bubble Down Sort.

E5.6   Write a formal algorithm for the Cocktail Shaker Sort, where the items are bubbled (alternately) up and down.
   The Cocktail Shaker Sort was described in the text as a Bubble-type Sort with the j index moving between two i indices in alternate directions. The i indices can be implemented as the "last" value in the Improved Bubble Sort; that is, use an *upper_last* and a *lower_last* for the last point where an exchange takes place as the j index increases and decreases, respectively. The sort is finished when these two "last" values come together.

E5.7   One aspect of a sort is whether it is stable. A sort is stable if two of the items are equal—then their final order, when the list is sorted, will be the same as the initial order in the list. A stable sort is useful if you are sorting on more than one part of a complex record. Which of the sorts we have discussed in this chapter are stable?

E5.8   The Insertion Sort may be analyzed using probabilities. Consider a situation where we have a sorted list of one item and are to insert a new item. If these are random, then in half the cases the original item will need to be moved one space. Hence the average number of moves is one-half.

          $(1/2) \cdot 1 = 1/2$

For inserting an item into a list of two, on the average—for one-third of the cases—it will be inserted in the last position, and no items will move; for one-third of the cases, it will be inserted in the second position and one item will move one space, and for one-third of the cases, it will be inserted in the first location and two items will each move one space. Hence the average number of moves is one.

$$(1/3) \cdot 2 + (1/3) \cdot 1 + (1/3) \cdot 0 \; 1$$
$$= 1$$

For the fourth item, the situation is similar:

$$(1/4) \cdot 3 + (1/4) \cdot 2 + (1/4) \cdot 1$$
$$= 3/2$$

Show that for the fifth item, the average number of moves is two.

What is the average number of moves for the n-th item? Therefore, we have the sequence:

$$1/2, \; 1, \; 3/2, \; 2, \; \dots \; , (n-1)/2$$

Note that each of these is a multiple of one-half.

The composite average to sort the entire list is the sum of the individual averages; sum them, and simplify to show that the average number of moves to sort the entire list is:

$$\approx n^2/4.$$

E5.9   The following scheme has been suggested as a selection sort suitable for a list of distinct items. We examine the entire list for the smallest item and copy this to a result list (which is initially empty). To find the smallest item, we place the first item in a variable. Whenever we encounter a new item we check to see if it is smaller than this saved one. If the new item is smaller, we replace the saved item with the new smaller one. We then examine the entire original list, looking for the smallest item that is not in the result list. That is, we compare each item with all of those in the result list. If it is present, we skip and go on to the next in the original list; if not, we see if it the smallest one found so far. At the end of the pass, we append the new smallest item found to the result list.

a. Write out a formal algorithm for this scheme.

b. How much memory does this scheme require if the original list is n elements?

c. What is the "big O" behavior of this algorithm?

d. What happens if the items are not distinct?

A solution to the problem in part d is to count the number of times the minimum item selected at each pass occurs and append that many values to the resultant list.

e. Modify your algorithm to incorporate this improvement.

f. With this improvement, if the list is a constant list, then how many operations are required to sort it?

We can call this sort the Slow Sort!

E5.10   Write out three functions that are useful in implementing and testing sorting routines. The first should return a list of *n* random integers:

```
void rand_fill(int list[], int n, int seed);
```

The second should return the sum of the elements:

```
long listsum(int list[], int n);
```

The third should check the order and return a −1 if all are in order or the index where the first out-of-order pair is found:

```
int check(int list[], int n);
```

Write a program to test these using the C function that was given in the text for the Insertion Sort.

E5.11   The insertion sort that we examined inserted new items into a sorted list that began at location 0. We could also turn it around so that the sorted part was toward the end of the list; that is, start with a list of one contained in location $n-1$, then insert so that the sorted part is contained in locations $n-2$ and $n-1$, etc. Finally, we would insert the item in location 0 in the sorted list contained in locations 0 through $n-1$ to create an entirely sorted list.

a. Rewrite the Insertion Sort Algorithm to perform its sorting in this order.

b. An advantage of this progression is that we can place a sentinel in location *n* that is larger than any item in the list. Therefore, any item will be inserted before it reaches the end, and the condition for termination can be simplified; that is, we do not need to test whether the index is still within range.

Rewrite your algorithm of part a to reflect this use of a sentinel.

E5.12 An interesting way to perform a swap without additional temporary storage makes use of the bit pattern nature of the two values and the properties of the XOR (exclusive or) operation. This is defined as:

A B	A XOR B
0 0	0
0 1	1
1 0	1
1 1	0

If x and y are two values that contain a series of bits, we define the XOR operation on the values to operate on all of the respective pairs of bits taken from each. (This is the C ^ operator.)

The two values may be exchanged by:

```
x = x^y;
y = x^y;
x = x^y;
```

Using the example: $x = 1100$ and $y = 1010$, (this choice gives all possible combinations of bits) show that these three assignments do interchange the values of x and y.

E5.13 In the discussion of the Insertion Sort, the concept of reversing the two conditionals of the while () statement was suggested in the interest of speed but was discarded. Show that in the majority of the cases that fail, it is the present second condition that fails first. However, there is the risk of attempting a comparison with a value that is not in the array. Under what conditions would this last situation occur?

E5.14 The problem of ordering three distinct values in ascending order is the simplest non-trivial sorting situation.

a. How many permutations of the three values are there?

b. What is the maximum number of comparisons that must be made to order three values?

c. Show that two comparisons is the minimum number that could produce an ordered situation, given a particular original ordering; that is, give an example.

d. What is the average number of comparisons; that is, what is the number of comparisons required for each permutation; sum these, and divide by the number of permutations.

E5.15   Finding the minimum and maximum of two values, *a* and *b*, can be done without an explicit comparison, using:

$$\text{min} = \frac{a+b}{2} - \frac{|a-b|}{2} = (a+b - |a-b|)/2$$

$$\text{max} = \frac{a+b}{2} + \frac{|a-b|}{2} = a+b - \text{min}$$

a. The division by two may be moved "outside"; hence, show that even for integers, there will be no truncation error; that is, the division by two will always occur with an even numerator.

b. Using this, write a C function that will "sort" the two arguments in ascending order:

```
void order2(int *a, int *b)
```

c. Develop a scheme to order three values. (Hint, the middle element may be found by summing the three original values and then subtracting the minimum and maximum.)

d. Actually, a single comparison is required to "sort" the two, even though we are performing only arithmetic operations. Where does it occur?

PROBLEMS

P5.1   Enter the C function to implement the Insertion Sort.

```
void insert_sort(int list[], int n)
```

Modify it to count the number of comparisons in the execution, i.e., the number of times step I4 is executed; and store this value in the global variable *numcomp*.

    Write a main() program to initialize a list of at least 100 random elements; print it out, invoke the sort function, print the final list, and print the number of comparisons.

    Include checks in your main program to test whether the sort routine is operating correctly.

P5.2   Enter the C function to implement the Selection Sort.

```
void sel_sort(int list[], int n)
```

Modify it to count the number of comparisons in the execution, i.e., the number of times step L4 is executed; and store this value in the global variable *numcomp*.

Write a main() program to initialize a list of at least 100 random elements; print it out, invoke the sort function, print the final list, and print the number of comparisons. Include checks in your main program to test whether the sort routine is operating correctly.

P5.3   Enter the C function to implement the Enumeration Sort.

```
void enum_sort(int list[], int n, int index[])
```

Write a main() program to initialize a list of at least 100 random elements; print it out, invoke the sort function, and print the final list. Include checks in your main program to test whether the sort routine is operating correctly.

P5.4   Enter the C function to implement the Improved Bubble Sort.

```
void bubble_sort(int list[], int n)
```

Write a main() program to initialize a list of at least 100 random elements; print it out, invoke the sort function, and print the final list. Include checks in your main program to test whether the sort routine is operating correctly.

P5.5   Enter the C function to implement the Slow Sort described in Exercise 5.9.

```
void slow_sort(int list[], int n, int index[])
```

Write a main() program to initialize a list of at least 100 random elements; print it out, invoke the sort function, and print the final list. Include checks in your main program to test whether the sort routine is operating correctly.

Have the sort function count the number of comparisons and the main() program print this value out. Try it for:

a. n = 10   b. n = 50   c. n = 100

P5.6   The Cocktail Shaker Sort is described in the text as a Bubble-type sort that has the *j* index moving between two *i* indices in alternate directions. The *i* indices can be implemented as the "last" value in the Improved Bubble Sort; that is, use an *upper_last* and a *lower_last* as the last point where an exchange takes place as the *j* index increases and decreases, respectively. The sort is finished when these two values come together.

Write a C function that implements the Cocktail Shaker Sort. Have it count the number of comparison.

Write a main() program to initialize a list of at least 200 random elements; print it out, invoke the sort function, and print the final list and the number of comparisons. Include checks in your main program to test whether the sort routine is operating correctly.

Chapter 6

More Internal Sorting

... the royal children: there were ten of them, and the little dears came jumping merrily along, hand in hand, in couples: they were all ornamented with hearts. Next came the guests, mostly Kings and Queens, and among them Alice recognized the White Rabbit: it was talking in a hurried nervous manner, smiling at everything that was said, and went by without noticing her. Then followed the Knave of Hearts, carrying the Kings's crown on a crimson velvet cushion; and, last of all in this grand procession, came THE KING AND THE QUEEN OF HEARTS.

Alice was rather doubtful whether she ought not to lie down on her face like the three gardeners, but she could not remember ever having heard of such a rule at processions: "and besides, what would be the use of a procession," thought she, "if people had all to lie down on their faces, so that they couldn't see it?" So she stood where she was, and waited.

6.1   OBJECTIVES

The objectives for this chapter are to:

- Continue the exploration of sorting algorithms.

- Discuss two schemes built upon simple sorting algorithms that are much more efficient than the originals.

157

- Present the Shell's Sort Algorithm.

- Describe the Quick Sort Algorithm.

- Analyze these algorithms.

6.2   *INTRODUCTION*

In the previous chapter, we examined the four basic types of internal sorts. Each had its own advantages, but, generally speaking, they all exhibited approximately the same growth behavior as the size of the lists changed. They are all $O(n^2)$; thus, doubling the size of a list results in the sort taking four times as long. The **Straight Insertion Sort** improves this bleak situation, on the average, by a factor of 2; and the Straight Insertion Sort and the **Improved Bubble Sort** reduce the best case to $O(n)$. However, sorting a large set of data will take a long time—none of these basic internal sorts are effective except on small data sets.

In order to see the effect of $O(n^2)$ behavior, let us assume that a computer, using one of the simple sorts, can sort a list of ten items in 10 milliseconds. In a program, one would not notice such a delay. Increasing the size of the list to 100 items, still a relatively small list, would take approximately 1 second. (A list of 100 items is 10 times larger than the original list, and hence would take $10 \cdot 10 = 100$ times the amount of time.) Increasing the size of the list to 1,000 items (another increase by a factor of 10) would now take 100 seconds, well over one and a half minutes. A list of 10,000 items would take a very noticeable 10,000 seconds, almost 3 hours!

If these times were appropriate for the Simple Swap Sort or the Bubble Sort, then you might try using a Straight Insertion Sort. Assuming that the speed of each execution of the inner-most loop is the same, then the Straight Insertion Sort would be twice as fast; therefore our original list would take 5 milliseconds, and the list of 10,000 would take "only" 5,000 seconds, or 1.5 hours!

Fortunately, a modification of the Straight Insertion Sort and another scheme, one that is based upon an exchange-type sort, considerably improves the time that it takes to perform a sort by drastically reducing the growth of the number of operations required as the size of the list changes.

6.3   *SHELL'S SORT*

The **Straight Insertion Sort** is an improvement over the other sorts we have considered so far in that its behavior does depend upon the initial ordering of the list. If the list were ordered or almost ordered, then this sort executes quite rapidly. However, it still moves an item essentially one position at a time. If we could initially move out-of-place elements a large distance with one operation, we might gain even more of an improvement.

Such a scheme was proposed by Donald L. Shell in 1959. It is essentially an adaptation of the Straight Insertion Sort, dividing the original list into several overlapping lists so that the items in each sublist are physically spaced apart. Thus, moving an element into place in one of the sublists effectively moves it a large distance. After the sublists are individually sorted by an Insertion Sort they are combined, and the final list is sorted all together by the Straight Insertion Sort. We will need to ascertain whether or not this combination actually increases the performance of the sort, and, equally important, is if it can be programmed easily.

6.3.1   Example

As an example, consider a list of 14 elements. We will separate the list into four sublists. The first sublist consists of elements with indices 0, 4, 8, and 12; the second consists of 1, 5, 9, and 13; etc.

```
original list:
index:      0    1    2    3    4    5    6    7    8    9   10   11   12   13
values:    23   82   45   17   56   12   21   67   42   28   31   35   39   61
separate    |    |    |    |    |    |    |    |    |    |    |    |    |    |
   1       23         |         56         |         42         |         39
   2            82         |         12         |         28         |         61
   3                 45         |         21         |         31         |
   4                      17         |         67         |         35

sort each sublist separately:
   1       23                  39                  42                  56
   2            12                  28                  61                  82
   3                 21                  31                  45
   4                      17                  35                  67
combine
           23   12   21   17   39   28   31   35   42   61   45   67   56   82
and finally sort the combined list:
           12   17   21   23   28   31   35   39   42   45   56   61   67   82
```

Note that the smallest item in the entire list must be in one of the first four positions after separating, sorting each sublist, and then recombining. The second smallest item must be in the second through the eighth locations, regardless of where it was originally located. We would expect that most items will be found within about four locations of their final position.

So far this scheme does not specify how we might sort each of the sublists and the final combined list. However, let us try an insertion sort, since it is more efficient than the other sorts we have encountered.

To compare this scheme of dividing the list into sublists, sorting them, recombining them, and sorting the list again, let us count the number of comparisons of items it takes to sort the list using this scheme with an insertion sort.

```
To sort the 23 56 42 39     takes   6 comparisons.
To sort the 82 12 28 61     takes   4 comparisons.
To sort the 45 21 31        takes   3 comparisons.
To sort the 17 67 35        takes   3 comparisons.
Finally, to finish the sort takes  22 comparisons.
        The total number is thus   38 comparisons.
```

On the other hand, to sort the original list using a Straight Insertion Sort takes 51 comparisons.

In this case, the 16 comparisons required to sort the four sublists—using a "jump" of four to move the elements—drastically reduces the number of straight insertion sort comparisons (from 51 to 22) required to finish the process. Indeed, it reduced the number by 29, more than the 16 comparisons that it took to sorting the four sublists, thus that the combined procedure actually takes <u>fewer</u> comparisons.

6.3.2   Algorithm

In practice, an effective algorithm does not exactly follow the scheme pictured above. First, there is no need physically to separate one list into four separate sublists in order to sort them individually. We can leave them in the same physical list and use an increment; that is, in the example above, an increment of four that takes us from one item to another. The first sublist consists of items with indices of 0, 4, 8, and 12. We can compare the items in the sublist that are logically consecutive, but are located four indices apart, without touching the items in the other three sublists.

Secondly, it is actually easier not to sort each of the sublists in turn, but to insert a new element into each, in turn, as we work through all of the values. That is, we will move through the list, element by element. We note that items 0, 1, 2, and 3 already consist of four sorted lists of one element each. Thus, we first insert item 4 (the fifth item) into the first list, then item 5 into the second list, item 6 into the third list, item 7 into the fourth list, and item 8 into the first list (now consisting of items 0 and 4), etc.

That is, rather than processing the items in the order:

4, 8, 12,   5, 9, 13,   6, 10, 14,   7, 11

we will process them as:

4, 5, 6, 7, 8, 9, 10, 11, 12, 13, 14

It turns out that this scheme is actually easier to program and slightly faster, eliminating an extra loop; however, the number of comparisons will be the same.

We will use the Insertion Sort as the basis for the Shell's Sort although, in principle, it should be possible to base the diminishing increment scheme on any of the sorts in the last chapter. We know that, on the average, the insertion scheme is twice as fast as the others.

The process is then to use the Insertion Sort first—using an increment of four so that we can logically sort four sublists separately—then sort the entire list using an increment of one—the same as the Straight Insertion Sort. We are hoping that the extra work involved in sorting by four will provide a rough order—enough so that the last sorting pass using a one does not take as many comparisons and as much data movement as it would have originally.

The example above uses a sequence of two values of increment to move through the list twice: 4 and 1. In actual practice a moderate to large list will use a longer sequence with more values; the first value will by fairly large, but smaller than *n*, and the last value must be 1. For example, with a list of 100, we might use a sequence of 13, 4, and 1.

The overall efficiency of the sort does depend upon the exact sequence of increments used. Since each value entails one pass through the data, the values in the sequence should decrease rapidly so that there are not too many of them. It is helpful if the sequence is easy to compute. Several possible sequences have been suggested; perhaps the simplest is:

$$n/2, \; n/4, \; n/8, \; ...., \; 1$$

which for a list of 1,000 generates (since the division is integer arithmetic):

$$500, \; 250, \; 125, \; 62, \; 31, \; 15, \; 7, \; 3, \; 1.$$

This sequence is reasonably good for most lists, but if *n* is a power of 2, such as 1,024—then all the values generated for the increments are even except for the last 1. This does not get good mixing between the odd and even sublists and hence the final sort procedure, with an increment of one, is not as effective as it might be. Generally, it is desirable for the elements of the sequence to be relatively prime.

One of the best sequences found uses:

let $h_1 = 1$, $h_{s+1} = 3h_s + 1$, and stop with h_t when $h_{t+2} > n$.

This generates: ..., 9,841, 3,280, 1,093, 364, 121, 40, 13, 4, 1.

Note that we increase *h* until it exceeds *n*, then "backup" twice. As an example for n = 1,000, use:

$$h = 121, \; 40, \; 13 \; ,4 \; ,1.$$

The thought is that sorting the list of 1,000 using an increment of 121 (essentially dividing the list into 121 overlapping sublists) and moving out-of-place items 121 places at a time will reduce the number of times they need to be moved by 40, then by 13, then by 4, and, finally, by 1—greatly reducing the total number of comparison operations.

There is some theoretical basis for using a sequence that increases by a factor of three from term to term. It turns out that for a random list of *n* items, a given element is—on the average—n/3 locations from its final position in the sorted list.

In order to see how this scheme of diminishing increments might work in practice, consider a random list with n = 1,000 elements. According to the scheme above, a Shell's Sort would use the diminishing increments of 121, 40, 13, 4, and 1. In this case, it is also possible to start the sequence with 364. (However, the next possible value in the sequence, 1093, cannot be used.) Let us sort the list several times, using different parts of the sequence.

First let us sort the list using only an increment of one. This effectively reduces the Shell's Sort to a Straight Insertion Sort. The expected number of operations is approximately $n^2/4 = 250,000$, which compares favorably with case A below.

Next, consider sorting the original list with the sequence of 4 and 1. The sequence of four basically divides the original list of 1,000 elements into four lists of 250, to which the Straight Insertion Sort is applied individually. The expected number of operations is $4 \cdot 250 \cdot 250/4 = 62,500$. This compares closely with the number of operations using an increment of four for case B. After sorting these four independent lists and simply putting them back together, the next step is to sort the entire list with an increment of 1—a Straight Insertion Sort, again. If this list of 1,000 elements were randomly ordered it would take about 250,000 operations; however, the list is already highly ordered. Therefore, as we see for case B, it takes only about 10,000 operations for the increment of size 1 to complete the sorting process. The total number of operations from using increments of both the 4 and 1 is then around 72,000.

If we start with an increment of 13—that is, with 13 lists of around 77 elements each—then sorting these takes approximately $13 \cdot 77 \cdot 77/4 = 19,269$. Once the list is somewhat ordered by an increment of 13, the number of operations needed to sort it by 4 is greatly reduced, and the number of operations for the final sort by 1 is decreased. The total number of operations is around 29,000 as we can see in case C.

Continuing this example, we see that the minimum number of total operations of less than 14,000 occurs when we use the sequence 121, 40, 13, 4, and 1. However, there is little difference between beginning the sequence with 121 or with 364 (cases E and F)—and even starting with 40 (case D) the total number of operations is not that much greater than the best case.

NUMBER OF OPERATIONS FOR A SHELL'S SORT

A		B		C	
				13	19,763
		4	62,122	4	6,171
1	246,268	1	9,632	1	2,923
total	246,268		71,754		28,857

D		E		F	
				364	824
		121	2,475	121	1,642
40	6,767	40	2,580	40	2,318
13	3,984	13	2,826	13	2,715
4	4,348	4	3,143	4	3,483
1	2,839	1	2,619	1	2,722
total	17,938		13,643		13,704

Indeed, the total number of comparison operations is dramatically reduced as we increase the number of "passes"—that is, increase the number of values in the diminishing increment sequence. However, we note that starting with 364 (case F) is slightly larger than starting with 121 (case E). If you repeat this with other random lists of 1,000 items, you will find that sometimes starting with 364 will reduce the total number and sometimes it will increase it. In any case, it does not make much difference—both are quite small when compared to case A (Straight Insertion Sort).

If we had a list of 1,100 items—where the largest possible value in the sequence that might be used was 1093—then starting with 1,093 rather than the suggested 384 generally takes slightly more comparison operations. It seems best if the starting value in the sequence is somewhere between 1/3 and 1/2 of the length of the list. On the average, it is suggested that one gets the best results from computing increasing values of the increment until n is reached then "backing up" two values in the sequence to begin.

A formal algorithm to implement this diminishing increment or Shell's Sort is:

Algorithm S (Shell's Sort or Diminishing Increment Sort). Given a list, *LIST*, of n elements, rearrange these items in place so that they are in increasing order.

S1. [loop over increment] Perform step S2 for values of h in the sequence until h=1.

S2. [loop on i]   Perform steps S3 through S7 for i=h,h+1,...,n−1.

S3. [set up values]   j=i−h; item=LIST[i].

S4. [reached beginning?]   If j < 0, then Go to step S8.

S5. [compare]   If item > = LIST[j], then Go to step S8.

S6. [move item]   LIST[j+h]=LIST[j]; j=j−h.

S7. [loop]   Go to step S4.

S8. [put into place]   LIST[j+h]=item.

If we compare Algorithm S with Algorithm I, we discover that steps S2 through S8 are identical to steps I1 through I7, except that the 1's are replaced with h's; these steps are embedded within a loop that uses different values of h.

6.3.3   Increment Sequence

For the diminishing increment sequence use:

$$h_s = \begin{cases} 1, & s = 1 \\ 3h_{s-1} + 1, & s > 1 \end{cases}$$

In practice we start with one, move up the sequence, and stop with h_t when $h_{t+2} > n$. This is easy if we proceed to find a value in the sequence that is larger than n, then start the sorting process with the sequence value that is closer by two values to the beginning of the sequence.

The values generated by this scheme are:

```
s =  1  2    3    4     5     6      7      8      9       10       11
h  = 1,  4,  13,  40,  121,  364,  1093,  3280,  9841,  29524,  88573,  ....
 s
```

For a list of 100 items, the smallest value of the sequence that exceeds 100 is 121 (*s* = 5). Therefore, we begin the sorting process with 13 (*s* = 3), and continue with a "pass" of four, and finally a "pass" with an increment of one.

In C it is quite easy to generate the starting value of the sequence as well as move from the starting value back down to one. We first note that if $h_s = 3h_{s-1}+1$, then $h_{s-1} = (h_s-1)/3$. This allows us to move down the sequence as the sort proceeds (see step S1 in Algorithm S).

```
/*    find initial sequence value   */

      h = 1;
      while (h <= n)       /*   keep moving up the sequence   */
          h = 3*h+1;
      h = (h-4)/9;         /*   backup twice  */
      if (h < 1)           /*   if n < 4, above gives h = 0   */
          h = 1;

/*    loop over sequence values   */

      while (h >= 1) {
          .               /*   insertion sort with h   */
          .
          h = (h-1)/3;
      }
```

Within the while () loop, the code for the Straight Insertion Sort is used with the appropriate substitution of *h* for 1.

6.3.4   Analysis of a Simple Case

A complete analysis of the Shell's Sort is a difficult problem. The best case is clearly for a list that is already sorted in ascending order. For each value in the diminishing increment sequence, it will take approximately *n* comparisons. Therefore, for our example with 1,000 items, there are 5 values used in the sequence (121, 40, 13, 4, 1), hence the algorithm would "pass" through the list five times for a total of $5n$ steps.

The worst case is not easy to find for the general case of *n* items. However, if we restrict ourselves to a two-pass Shell's Sort; that is, increments of four and one only, then we can at least get a handle on its behavior. If we consider a list of 16 elements (integers 1 through 16), working backwards, the worst case for the "one" pass is to put the low elements as far to the right in the final list as possible; thus the four intermediate sorted lists should produce:

```
13              14              15              16
    9               10              11              12
    5           6           7           8
        1           2           3           4
```

When these are combined into one list and sorted by an increment of one, it will take 72 comparisons. Now the worst case for each of the four individually is when they are totally out of order:

```
16              15              14              13
    12              11              10              9
    8           7           6           5
        4           3           2           1
```

It will take 6 comparisons for each of these, for a total of 24 comparison operations. Hence the list

```
16 12   8   4 15 11   7   3 14 10   6   2 13   9   5   1
```

will take a total of 96 comparison operations. Performing this analysis for different lists that are multiples of four in length produces:

$$(5/16)n^2 + (5/4)n - 4 \approx (5/16)n^2.$$

This worst case for the (4,1) Shell's Sort is slightly worse than the average case for the Straight Insertion Sort. For a list of 1,000, the worst case would be 313,746 comparison operations. For the Straight Insertion Sort the average case would be expected to be around 250,000 operations. Of course, for a list of 1,000, we should start with an increment of 121, followed by 40, and then 13 before we get to the increment of four. This makes the analysis much more complicated and, perhaps, should make the worst case even better.

The analysis of the general case of the Shell's Sort is difficult. It can be shown that it is better than $O(n^{3/2})$. Other studies have demonstrated that the average case is between $n^{1.25}$ and $n^{1.30}$.

Using a computer to try empirically random lists of different sizes and counting the number of comparisons, produces this result for the average case:

$$\approx n^{1.25}.$$

Hence, the Shell's sort is $O(n^{1.25})$. This grows considerably less slowly than the simpler $O(n^2)$ sorts. Returning to the example in the Introduction, where we sorted a list of 10 items in 5 milliseconds (using the Straight Insertion Sort) let us assume that the Shell's Sort would also take 5 milliseconds. Now a list of 100 items would take about 89 milliseconds, the list of 1,000 items would take about 1.6 seconds, and the list of 10,000 would take 28 seconds (as compared to 5,000 seconds using the Straight Insertion Sort).

The best case for the Shell's Sort is the situation where the list is already sorted. In this case, the algorithm makes one pass through the data for each value in the sequence; that is, the number of operations is $t \cdot n$, where h_t is the first value in the sequence that is attempted. This process is thus $O(n)$, but is worse than the Straight Insertion Sort by a factor of t.

6.4   PARTITION SORT

We have noted that the simple sorts tend to grow rapidly. If we can divide the list into two halves and sort the pieces independently, we may be able to save considerable operations.

6.4.1   Perfect Partitioning

Let us assume that we do have a separation procedure that takes $n-1$ operations (since to select a specific item may involve comparing one element to all of the other $n-1$ elements) and separates the list into two equal size sublists and a single element:

ssssssssXBBBBBBBB

where all of the elements to the left of X are smaller than X, but not necessarily in order, and all of the elements to the right of X are larger than X, but not necessarily in order. This means each of the two sublists can be sorted independently. It also means that X will be in its final location in the sorted list. Often X is referred to as the **pivot**.

To sort a list, let us use a simple $n(n-1)/2$ sort. Thus, to sort a single list of 1,023 elements would take $1023 \cdot 1022/2 = 522,753$ operations. Assuming that we can separate the list with 1,022 operations ($n-1$ operations) into a single element and two sublists of 511, then it will take $511 \cdot 510/2 = 130,315$ operations to sort each sublist—a total of 260,610 sorting operations to sort both sublists which, when added to the separation operations, would take 261,632 total operations. This is considerably less than the number required to sort the complete list all together!

If this process helps reduce operations and, hence, time, why not further subdivide each of the sublists into a single element and two sublists of 255 elements. To divide the original list took 1,022 operations. To separate each of the two 511-element sublists would take 510 times 2, or 1,020 operations. Thus, the two separation steps would take a total of 2,042 partitioning operations. To sort each of the 255-element lists takes $255 \cdot 254/2 = 32,385$ operations—or a total of 129,540 operations to sort all four. The total number of operations to separate the sublists twice and then sort the four sublists is 131,582 operations.

With three partitioning steps and eight sublists, there are 67,066 total operations. Continuing, we obtain the following table.

THE PERFECT PARTITIONING AND SORTING OF A LIST
n = 1,023

Number Sublists	Length of Sublist	Separation Operations	Sorting Operations	Total Operations
1	1,023		522,753	522,753
2	511	1,022	260,610	261,632
4	255	2,042	129,540	131,582
8	127	3,058	64,008	67,066
16	63	4,066	31,248	35,314
32	31	5,058	14,880	19,938
64	15	6,018	6,720	12,738
128	7	6,914	2,688	9,602
256	3	7,682	768	8,450
512	1	8,194		8,194

By the time we have subdivided the original list enough so that the sublists are one element long, then we need not perform any sorting operations! The sorting of the original list is performed solely by partitioning!

The table above illustrates the effect this has on a list that is originally 1,023 elements long. If we perform the same analysis for lists of other lengths, using the last total operations for each, then we discover the following:

PERFECT PARTITIONING SUMMARY

m	n=2^m−1	Sorting Operations	Partitioning Operations
1	1	0	0
2	3	3	2
3	7	21	10
4	15	105	34
5	31	465	98
6	63	1,953	258
7	127	8,001	642
8	255	32,385	1,538
9	511	130,305	3,586
10	**1,023**	**522,753**	**8,194**
11	2,047	2,094,081	18,434
12	4,095	8,382,465	40,962

The table is constructed with the following assumptions:

separation operations: $n-1$

sorting operations: $n(n-1)/2$

The column labeled "sorting operations" is the number of operations required to sort the entire list without any partitioning.

By examining the values in the last column, it is not difficult to derive the following expression:

$$\text{partitioning operations:} \quad (n+1)[\lg(n+1)-2]+2$$

Therefore, this process is $O(n \cdot \lg n)$. Of course, we must keep in mind that the previous discussion is based upon the existence of a partitioning procedure that can separate the list into two equal sublists and a single element in no more than n operations.

6.5   QUICK SORT

It turns out that there is a partitioning procedure that almost does what we had suggested. This procedure does not guarantee that the two sublists are equal in size, but it does, in $n-1$ operations, perform the partitioning with a single element separating two sublists—the left one composed of elements less than the single element, and the right one made up of bigger elements.

Because of the nature of the procedure—it will be a recursive one—we must specify not only the list, but also the end points that we are to partition. We then invoke the procedure as:

```
quicksort list with 0, n-1.
```

6.5.1   Partition Scheme

The basic scheme is to use two internal indices, one beginning at the top or the left end of the list (in this case, index=0) and the other at the right or the bottom end (in this case, index=$n-1$). The items at these locations are compared and swapped if they are out of order. After a comparison, one of the indices is moved and the other index is left at the same place. After a swap, we change which index moves; when the two indices become equal, the list will be partitioned.

As an example, consider the list of 11 elements:

```
12   3   8   25   42   19   31   7   10    2   15
 i                                            < j
```

Initially we will have j moving. Since list[i] and list[j] are in the correct order, we will decrement j and leave i alone.

```
12   3   8   25   42   19   31   7   10    2   15
 i                                         j
```

Now the two items are out of order, so we will swap them and change the "moving" index to i.

```
2    3    8    25   42   19   31   7    10   12   15
     i >                                      j
```

These items are in order, so we continue moving the *i*.

```
2    3    8    25   42   19   31   7    10   12   15
          i >                                 j
```

These are in order, so we continue moving the *i*.

```
2    3    8    25   42   19   31   7    10   12   15
               i >                            j
```

Out of order, therefore we swap and change the moving index to *j*.

```
2    3    8    12   42   19   31   7    10   25   15
               i                      < j
```

Out of order, therefore we swap and change the moving index to *i*.

```
2    3    8    10   42   19   31   7    12   25   15
                    i >                 j
```

Out of order, therefore we swap and change the moving index to *j*.

```
2    3    8    10   12   19   31   7    42   25   15
                    i               < j
```

Out of order, therefore we swap and change the moving index to *i*.

```
2    3    8    10   7    19   31   12   42   25   15
                         i >    j
```

Out of order, therefore we swap and change the moving index to *j*.

```
2    3    8    10   7    12   31   19   42   25   15
                         i < j
```

These two items are in order, so we continue moving the *j*.

```
2    3    8    10   7    12   31   19   42   25   15
                         i
                         j
```

Since *i* and *j* are equal, we are finished. We note that all of the items to the left of *i* and *j* are smaller than list[i] and all of the items to the right are larger. Further, when the list is completely sorted, the 12 will still be in its present location; and we have taken only 10 comparisons for our list of 11 items.

    This example separates the list into two equal sublists. However, in general this will not be the case. What we would like is to separate the list somewhere in the middle—the closer to the exact middle, the more efficient the process. We can see this if we divide the list once, with the left sublist containing k elements and the right one with $n-k-1$ elements. Sorting these independently will take a total number of comparisons of

$$k^2/2 + (n-k-1)^2/2.$$

Expanding this, taking the derivative with respect to k, setting it to zero to find the minimum, and solving for the k that produces the minimum total number of operations gives:

$$k_m = (n-1)/2.$$

You may have noticed that the item that ended up in the middle was the one originally at the beginning of the list; this is not a coincidence! It is the result of the way we performed the partitioning.

6.5.2   Simple Algorithm

Once we have partitioned the list into the two sublists, then we invoke the partitioning algorithm recursively on the left and the right sublists independently, since no elements in the left sublist will affect the right sublist and vice versa. That is:

      quicksort list with 0,i-1

and

      quicksort list with i+1, n-1.

Each partitioning procedure will place one element in its final location. We can continue the process until a sublist is either zero or one element in length—which means that it is sorted!

This is the essence of a sort developed by C. A. R. Hoare in 1962. It is sometimes called the Partition-Exchange Sort. The simplistic version is:

Algorithm Q' (Quick Sort—Simple Version). Given a list, *LIST*, of n elements, rearrange these items in place so that they are in increasing order. The algorithm is invoked with *LEFT* and *RIGHT* being the indices of the list (or sublist) to be sorted.

Q1'. [are we done?]	If RIGHT-LEFT < 1, then Terminate.
Q2'. [setup]	i=LEFT; j=RIGHT; df='j'.

Q3'. [compare]	If LIST[i] > LIST[j], then Swap(LIST[i],LIST[j]);
	                          If df = 'i', then df='j'.
	                                else df='i'.

Q4'. [increment]	If df = 'i', then i=i+1. else j=j−1.
Q5'. [reached pivot]	If i < j, then Go to step Q3'.
Q6'. [recurse]	Invoke Algorithm Q' with LEFT,i−1; Invoke Algorithm Q' with i+1,RIGHT.

The arguments for the recursive calls are the left and right indices of the left sublist and right sublist respectively:

LEFT				i-1	i	i+1					RIGHT
–	–	–	–	P	–	–	–	–	–	–	–

The recursive process "bottoms out" when a sublist is of length zero or one, which is already sorted! Note that $RIGHT-LEFT+1$ is the number of elements in the sublist.

We notice that this algorithm is "doubly" recursive, with a tail recursion. However, the double recursion cannot be simply eliminated as we did with the Fibonacci calculation, since each of the two sublists are distinct. However, this process does not exhibit the exponential growth that characterized the double recursion of the Fibonacci calculation. The reason for this is that now each recursive call operates on a list that is roughly half the size of the original. Because the size of the list that each recursive call deals with decreases at an exponential rate, the combination produces a reasonably slow overall growth.

6.5.3 Improvements

We can minimize the extra storage required for the recursive calls by two improvements:

1. Eliminate tail recursion.

2. Invoke the algorithm recursively on the shorter sublist; that is, always work on the shortest sublist and get it cleaned up before working on the longer one.

Tail recursion may be eliminated by replacing step Q6' by:

Q6". [recurse]   Invoke Algorithm Q' with LEFT,i−1; LEFT=i+1; Go to step Q1'.

Here we note that the variables *LEFT* and *RIGHT* are the only ones that control the process. By storing a different value in *LEFT* and keeping *RIGHT* the same, we can process the right sublist directly. The recursive call processes the left sublist before the right one is processed, so by the time we get to the right one we can safely reassign *LEFT*.

This step does indeed process both sublists. The recursive call processes the left sublist. Then when it is finished, by setting the variable *LEFT* to $i+1$, we have established the limits for the right sublist, which is then processed iteratively.

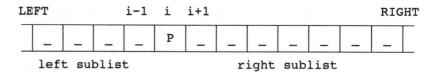

In order to minimize recursion nesting, it is important to invoke the algorithm recursively on the shorter sublist. This will insure that the chain of recursive calls will not go as deep as it would if the longer one is done recursively. The size of the left sublist is given by $i-LEFT$ and the size of the right sublist by $RIGHT-i$; therefore, we test to see which sublist is smaller, recurse for that one, and iterate for the other. That is, we replace step Q6" with:

Q6'". [recurse]   If $i-LEFT < RIGHT-i$, then
                         Invoke Algorithm Q' with LEFT,$i-1$;
                         LEFT=$i+1$; Go to step Q1'.
                              else
                         Invoke Algorithm Q' with $i+1$,RIGHT;
                         RIGHT=$i-1$; Go to step Q1'.

This change does not affect the number of comparisons that the algorithm takes. However, by minimizing the depth of the recursive calls, it does minimize the amount of memory required to store temporary information. By performing the shortest sublist first, we get it cleaned up and release any temporary storage before proceeding on to the longer one which may require more recursive calls. The worst case for storage when processing the shortest sublist first is proportional to lg n. If the largest sublist is consistently processed first, then the storage may be proportional to *n*.

We can replace the if () statements that control which index is to move in steps Q3' and Q4' by a simple calculation scheme. First, we replace the character variable *df* with an integer variable, *dir*, that can take on two values: 0 or 1. The 0 will indicate that *j* is decremented, and the 1 will indicate that *i* is incremented.

To perform this, we initially set it to zero. We then replace step Q4' with:

Q4". [increment]   i=i+dir; j=j+dir−1.

By tracing this through with the two possible values of dir, we note:

When *dir* = 0:   *i* is unchanged, *j* is decremented.
When *dir* = 1:   *i* is incremented, *j* is unchanged.

The value of *dir* is changed in step Q3'; this step is performed whenever the two values of the list are compared, found to be out of order, and are swapped. The process is accomplished by $dir = 1-dir$. When this statement is executed, we get the following:

If *dir* = 1, then *dir* becomes 0
If *dir* = 0, then *dir* becomes 1.

An algorithm that incorporates these improvements is given by:

Algorithm Q (Quick Sort). Given a list, *LIST*, of *n* elements, rearrange these items in place so that they are in increasing order. The algorithm is invoked with *LEFT* and *RIGHT* being the indices of the list (or sublist) to be sorted.

Q1. [are we done?]   If RIGHT−LEFT < 1, then Terminate.

Q2. [setup]   i=LEFT; j=RIGHT; dir=0.

Q3. [compare]   If LIST[i] > LIST[j], then Swap(LIST[i],LIST[j]);
                              dir=1−dir.

Q4. [increment]   i=i+dir; j=j+dir−1.

Q5. [reached pivot]   If i < j, then Go to step Q3.

Q6. [recurse once]   If i−LEFT < RIGHT−i, then
                              Invoke Algorithm Q with LEFT,i−1;
                              LEFT=i+1.
                                      else
                              Invoke Algorithm Q with i+1,RIGHT;
                              RIGHT=i−1.

Q7. [loop]   Go to step Q1.   ∎

This algorithm always uses the first element as the pivot element—that is, the element that is used to separate the list. It is best if the pivot is chosen to be near the middle of the final sorted list. However, we do not know which is the median element until the list is sorted! For random lists the first element is probably as good as any; however, if the list is already sorted in either ascending or descending order, the list will be separated by $n-1$ comparisons into a sublist of length zero, the pivot, and a sublist of $n-1$. The second "pass" of $n-2$ comparisons will produce a sublist of length zero, the pivot, and a sublist of $n-2$. Thus, the number of comparisons is:

$$(n-1) + (n-2) + (n-3) + \dots + 2 + 1 = n(n-1)/2 \approx n^2/2.$$

Unfortunately, this worst case is a rather common one. We can avoid this by employing one of several schemes.

We could swap the element in the middle of the list (the one in location $n/2$) with the first one, before even beginning the algorithm. Another possibility would be to swap a random element with the first one before beginning. A third scheme would be to select the median of the first, middle, and last elements as a separation element—that is, sort these three elements in increasing order: middle, first, last;

then continue with the algorithm. Such a sorting of three items is conveniently done with three comparisons taken from a Simple Swap Sort.

Q1.5 [get pivot]   m = (LEFT + RIGHT)/2;
                        If LIST[m] > LIST[LEFT], then
                                        Swap(LIST[m],LIST[LEFT]).
                        If LIST[m] > LIST[RIGHT], then
                                        Swap(LIST[m],LIST[RIGHT]).
                        If LIST[LEFT] > LIST[RIGHT], then
                                        Swap(LIST[LEFT],LIST[RIGHT]).

The advantage of this scheme is that unless the three elements are equal in value, the pivot element will not be at *exactly* either end of the list (there will be at least one item smaller and one item larger than the pivot). If the list is almost sorted to begin with, then the pivot is generally found near the middle.

This addition to the algorithm tends to make the worst case (which is really bad) less common.

6.5.4   Quick Sort Plus Insertion Sort

To recurse all the way down until a sublist is 0 or 1 in length may take more time than finishing things up with another technique, because of the overhead in setting up the recursive call. We can enhance the overall performance by modifying step Q1 to:

Q1". [are we done?]   If RIGHT-LEFT < 14, then Terminate.

Then finish things up with a Straight Insertion Sort.

The value of 14 is determined empirically to minimize the total time. Note that sublists may be smaller than 14 but, if they are, the algorithm will not recursively continue to partition them.

Algorithm QS (Quick Sort, Insertion Sort). Given a list, *LIST*, of n elements, rearrange these items in place so that they are in increasing order.

QS1. [quick sort]   Invoke Algorithm Q with $0, n-1$.

QS2. [insertion sort]   Invoke Algorithm I with n.

To make certain that the Quick Sort procedure is working before changing the minimum list size to 14 and then finishing with the Insertion Sort, you should always test an implementation of Algorithm QS using a minimum list size of 1 and not follow it with the Insertion Sort. Otherwise, the Quick Sort implementation might not be working correctly but the list gets sorted anyway (rather inefficiently) by the Insertion Sort.

The Quick Sort algorithm is not an easy one to analyze. The worst case, even with choosing the median-of-three to get the partitioning element, is a constant list—one where all of the elements are equal in value. In this case, the sort is proportional to $n^2/2$. In the best case the partitioning element is exactly in the middle of the list; in this case it depends upon $n \cdot \lg n$.

In general for random lists the Quick Sort is one of the fastest sorts—faster than the Shell's Sort. However, its worst case is as bad as the simpler sorts.

6.6   COMPARISON OF SORTS

In the last chapter we presented three tables presenting the timing for the sorting algorithms described there. Let us add to these tables times for the various sorting algorithms that we have just examined. As before, the following tables were constructed using a series of C function implementations of the listed sorting algorithms. They were executed on an 80286 processor with a clock speed of 6 MHz. The items were 16-bit integers to be sorted into ascending order. The timings were determined by using the internal clock and are precise to better than 5% and, typically, better than 1%.

TIMINGS FOR VARIOUS SORT ROUTINES

Times in Seconds for 1,000 Items

Sort	Random	Ascending	Descending	Constant
Simple swap	11.40	8.91	13.95	8.91
Improved bubble	10.67	0.02	13.84	0.02
Insertion	4.65	0.04	9.26	0.04
Shell's	0.37	0.17	0.29	0.17
Quick	0.33	0.26	0.33	11.79
Quick + Insert	0.30	0.20	0.27	11.81

Times in Seconds for 3,000 Items

Sort	Random	Ascending	Descending	Constant
Simple swap	102.1	80.1	125.6	80.1
Improved bubble	96.4	0.05	124.6	0.04
Insertion	41.7	0.11	83.2	0.11
Shell's	1.38	0.62	1.00	0.62
Quick	1.15	0.89	1.15	105.4
Quick + Insert	1.06	0.69	0.99	105.5

Times in Seconds for 10,000 Items

Sort	Random	Ascending	Descending	Constant
Simple swap	1118	890	1395	890
Improved bubble	1071	0.15	1384	0.15
Insertion	461	0.35	924	0.35
Shell's	5.92	2.66	3.74	2.66
Quick	4.47	3.35	4.42	1169
Quick + Insert	4.15	2.78	3.95	1169

The four columns are labeled according to the initial ordering of the items. The column labeled "random" is the average for several randomly generated lists. The same lists were used for all of the sort executions.

The Quick Sorts used a median-of-three to select the pivot element, and the Quick + Insertion used a minimum sublist size of 14.

We can quickly see drastic differences between the $O(n^2)$ sorts, the first four, and the last three algorithms for random and descending data. However, for ascending or constant data, the simplest sorts are the best.

Generally speaking, the Quick plus Insertion Sort is, overall, the fastest except for its worst case, which is very bad. The Shell's Sort is slightly slower, but does not have an extremely bad worst case.

6.7   SUMMARY

The Shell's Sort modification of the Straight Insertion Sort, which breaks the list into sublists, allows out-of-order items to move a large distance during the first passes through the list. This reduces the total number of comparisons and changes the "big O" behavior of the algorithm.

An alterative scheme, producing one of the fastest sorts, is to partition the list into two independent sublists. These sublists are then sorted recursively. The primary disadvantage of the resultant Quick Sort is that its worst case is very bad. By using the median-of-three to select the pivot element, some of the common situations that lead to worst-case executions are eliminated.

REFERENCES

Bentley, Jon L., *"How to Sort," Communications of the ACM*, vol. 27, no. 4, April 1984, Association for Computing Machinery, New York, pp 287-291.

Knuth, Donald E., *The Art of Computer Programming*; Sorting and Searching, vol. 3., Addison-Wesley Publishing Co., Reading, Massachusetts, 1973.

Press, William H., Flannery, Brian P., Teukolsky, Saul A., and Vetterling, William T., *Numerical Recipes in C*, Cambridge University Press, New York, 1988.

Sedgewick, Robert, *"Implementing Quicksort Programs,"* *Communications of the ACM*, Vol 21, No 10, October 1978, Association for Computing Machinery, New York, pp 847-856.

Sedgewick, Robert, *Algorithms in C*, Addison-Wesley Publishing Co., Reading, Massachusetts, 1990.

QUESTIONS

Q6.1 Why must any decreasing increment sequence that we use for the Shell's Sort end with 1?

Q6.2 If you were sorting a list of 100,000 items, what would be the values of the diminishing increment sequence that you would use for the Shell's Sort?

Q6.3 What modification would you need to implement to cause the Shell's Sort Algorithm to sort in descending order?

Q6.4 To find the initial sequence value for the Shell's Sort, the code segment in the text suggested that we use:

```
h = 1;
while (h <= n)        /* keep moving up the sequence */
    h = 3*h+1;
h = (h-4)/9;          /* backup twice */
if (h < 1)
    h = 1;
```

Why is the last if () statement necessary? If it is left out and *n* is small, what initial value of *h* might the function attempt to use?

Q6.5 Which are prime numbers in the standard Shell's Sort diminishing increment sequence: 1, 4, 13, 40, ..., 9841 ? Which are relatively prime to the others in the sequence?

Q6.6 Another sequence that has been proposed for the diminishing increment sequence for the Shell's Sort is:

$$h_s = \left\{ \begin{array}{ll} 1, & s = 1 \\ 2^s - 1, & s > 1 \end{array} \right.$$

Write out the first few terms in this sequence. Are they relatively prime?

Q6.7 Another sequence that has been proposed for the diminishing increment sequence for the Shell's Sort is:

$$h_s = \begin{cases} 1, & s = 1 \\ s! + 1, & s > 1 \end{cases}$$

Write out the first few terms in this sequence. Are they relatively prime?

Q6.8 Why might the Quick Sort Algorithm be called the Partitioning Algorithm rather than Quick Sort?

Q6.9 Using the median-of-three, the worst case for the Quick Sort procedure for distinct items is to partition the list as:

sXBBBBBBBBBBBBBBB

That is, it is partitioned into the three pieces with one element, the pivot, and a sublist with n-2 elements. If this is the consistent picture for all the partitioning processes, how many operations will it take to sort a list of n elements?

Q6.10 What modification would need to be done to cause the Quick Sort Algorithm to sort in descending order?

Q6.11 What modification would need to be done to cause the Quick Sort Algorithm to use the last item as a pivot, instead of the first?

Q6.12 In describing the Shell's Sort algorithm (using the initial example of four sublists on a list of 15 items), the text stated that we would process the elements in the following order:

4, 5, 6, 7, 8, 9, 10, 11, 12, 13, 14

Why did we not need to process elements 0 through 3?

Q6.13 In Algorithm QS it was suggested that the last pass be performed with a Straight Insertion Sort. Why not use a Shell's Sort?

Q6.14 Why is it important when implementing Algorithm QS that you first implement Algorithm Q, and test it, before changing the "1" in step Q1 to "14" and then invoking an implementation of Algorithm I?

Q6.15 According to the results of actual timings given in the text, it took the Quick Sort 0.33 sec to sort a random list of 1,000 items. According to its "big O" behavior, how long would you expect it to take for 3,000 items? For 10,000 items? How do these predictions compare with the values given in the tables?

Q6.16   If you needed to sort a list of 10 items once in a program, would it really matter which sort you used?

Q6.17   By evaluating the expression for the number of partitioning operations:

$$(n+1)[lg(n+1)-2]+2$$

show that it indeed correctly represents the table.

Q6.18   By performing the Insertion Sort by hand and counting the number of comparisons, verify the statement in the text that it takes 51 comparisons to sort the following:

```
index:     0  1  2  3  4  5  6  7  8  9 10 11 12 13
values:   23 82 45 17 56 12 21 67 42 28 31 35 39 61
```

Q6.19   The following list represents the worst case for a (4,1) Shell's Sort with 96 comparisons. How many comparisons would an Insertion Sort take?

```
index:    0  1  2  3  4  5  6  7  8  9 10 11 12 13 14 15
values:  16 12  8  4 15 11  7  3 14 10  6  2 13  9  5  1
```

Q6.20   The following list represents the worst case for an Insertion Sort. How many comparisons would it take to sort it using an Insertion Sort? How many comparisons would a (4,1) Shell's Sort take?

```
index:    0  1  2  3  4  5  6  7  8  9 10 11 12 13 14 15
values:  16 15 14 13 12 11 10  9  8  7  6  5  4  3  2  1
```

Q6.21   It has been suggested that we incorporate the Insertion Sort procedure within the recursive Quick Sort (rather than at the end) as:

Q1". [are we done?]   If RIGHT-LEFT < 1, then Invoke Algorithm I on LIST[LEFT] through LIST[RIGHT]; Terminate.

Comment on whether this would work. Would it result in less operations by the Insertion Sort portion? What about efficiency?

Q6.22   The Shell's Sort is $O(n^{1.25})$ and the Quick Sort is $O(n \cdot lg\ n)$; which is the faster growing?

Q6.23   Of the various sorts we have studied so far, only one, the Enumeration Sort, leaves the original list untouched—yet this is rather inefficient. If you wanted to print a list in ascending order yet keep the original list, which sort would you use? How might you go about this, using one of the more efficient sorts?

EXERCISES

E6.1   In moving up (increasing values of h) the standard sequence for the Shell's Sort, we used the recurrence relation $h_{s+1} = 3h_s + 1$. Show that to "backup" once, we use $(h-1)/3$; in particular, show that the division by 3 leaves no remainder. Therefore, show that to backup up twice, we can use $(h-4)/9$.

E6.2   In analyzing the (4,1) Shell's Sort on 16 items, it was stated that it takes 72 comparisons to sort the following list using the Straight Insertion Sort:

13   9   5   1 14 10   6   2 15 11   7   3 16 12   8   4

Verify this by explicitly counting the number of comparisons required. Note that a simple pattern emerges as you consider blocks of 4: 0,1,2,3 comparisons for the first four; 1,3,5,7 comparisons for the second four; and 1,4,7,10 comparisons for the third four. The pattern is that each block begins with 1 (except for the first one) and increments by 1 for the first block to get the remaining ones; the second block begins with 1 and increments by 2, etc. Therefore, it is easy to generalize.

The "4" operations are even easier. Each group of n/4 items are completely out of order, hence take $0+1+...+n/4-1$ operations.

Indeed, you should be able to determine:

n	"1" oper	"4" oper	Total Operations
8	22	4	26
12	44	12	56
16	72	24	96
20	106	40	146
24	146	60	206
28			

Fill in the next entry in the table (for n = 28).

E6.3   Rewrite the closed formula for the number of partitioning operations derived in the previous exercise in terms of m. Prove this formula, using the recurrence relation derived from the exercise prior to the previous one and mathematical induction.

E6.4   The code segment in the text suggested that to find the initial sequence value for the Shell's Sort, we use:

```
h = 1;
while (h <= n)          /* keep moving up the sequence */
    h = 3*h+1;
h = (h-4)/9;            /* backup twice */
if (h < 1)              /* if n < 4, above gives h = 0 */
    h = 1;
```

Comment on whether the following code performs the same:

```
h = 1;
while (h <= (n-4)/9)
    h = 3*h+1;
```

That is, does it produce the same starting value of *h* for a given *n*? Does it give the appropriate value for small values of *n* (*n* < 4) and, thus, not need the last if() statement in the first segment?

Comment on the efficiency of this scheme; that is, compare the number of operations required to obtain the desired value, especially note the calculations on *n* in the while() condition for each loop execution. Actually, a good compiler would detect that *n* is not changing, and hence move the calculation $(n-4)/9$ outside the loop.

Comment on the readability and understandability of the two formulations.

E6.5　　We have defined the standard diminishing increment sequence for the Shell's Sort in terms of a recurrence relation:

$$h_s = \begin{cases} 1, & s = 1 \\ 3h_{s-1} + 1, & s > 1 \end{cases}$$

By writing the first several of these with the various powers of 3, show that for *s* > 1:

$$h_s = 3^{s-1} + 3^{s-2} + \dots + 3^2 + 3 + 1$$
$$= 3^{s-1} + h_{s-1}.$$

Combining these two recurrence relations, derive a closed form expression for h_s that gives h_s directly in terms of *s*.

E6.6　　In the text, it was stated that the minimum number of sorting operations in the partitioning process occurs when the list is divided into two equal parts. Show that this is the case for one division by dividing the list into two sublists—the left sublist containing *k* elements and the right one with $n-k-1$ elements. Sorting these independently (for the simple $n^2/2$ type of sort) will take a total number of comparisons of:

$$k^2/2 + (n-k-1)^2/2.$$

Expand this, take the derivative with respect to *k*, set it to zero to find the minimum, and solve for the *k* that produces the minimum total number of operations thus demonstrating:

$$k_m = (n-1)/2.$$

E6.7   To show that, on the average, an element in a random list of n items needs to be moved $n/3$ locations to get it to its final position in the sorted list, we can compute the total number of locations distant in terms of the final location 1, 2, ... k, ..., n and divide by the total number. Consider:

```
                 1     2          k

     1           0     1         k-1  ┐
     2           1     0         k-2  │
     3           2     1         k-3  │   sum is
     .                                │   k(k-1)/2
     .                                │
     .                                │
    k-1    k-2   k-3          1       ┘
     k     k-1   k-2          0
    k+1     k    k-1          1   ┐
     .                            │   sum is
     .                            │   (n-k)(n-k+1)/2
     .                            │
     n     n-1   n-2         n-k  ┘
```

Here the table gives the number of locations that the element at the top needs to be moved to get it to the position indicated on the left. As an example, if the 2 is originally located in position 1, then it needs to be moved one location. If, originally, it is in location 2, then it does not need to be moved. The 1 could initially be found in any of the n locations. The total number of locations distant for all these is $n(n-1)/2$. Since there are n such values, the average is $(n-1)/2$. However, 1 is a rather extreme case. A 2 would not need to be moved as far, on the average.

For a particular value of k, the total number of locations to be moved is given by:

$$(n-k)(n-k+1)/2 \; + \; k(k-1)/2$$

where we have summed the two parts that make up the total for the column.

We then wish to sum this over all possible values of k:

$$\sum_{k=1}^{n} [(n-k)(n-k+1)/2 \; + \; k(k-1)/2]$$

By expanding the quantities inside the brackets, combining like terms in k (there should be a constant term, a linear term, and a quadratic term), breaking the summation of the sum of terms into a sum of summations, moving the constant (with respect to k) factors out of the summations, evaluating the summations (see Appendix A), and simplifying—show that this total is:

$$(n-1)n(n+1)/3 \; = \; n^3/3 \; - \; n/3 \; \approx \; n^3/3$$

Since there are n^2 total "distances" contributing to the sum, the average is $n/3$.

E6.8   The perfect partitioning summary led to the following table:

m	n=2^m-1	Partitioning Operations
1	1	0
2	3	2
3	7	10
4	15	34
5	31	98
6	63	258
7	127	642
8	255	1,538
9	511	3,586
10	1,023	8,194
11	2,047	18,434
12	4,095	40,962

We can derive a recurrence relation for the number of partitioning operations by noting that to partition a list, for example, of 1,023 items requires partitioning the list into two pieces with 1,022 operations, then sorting each of the two equal halves using 3,586 operations each. From this observation, write down a recurrence formula of the form:

$$N(m) = \begin{cases} 0, & m = 1 \\ \quad, & m > 1 \end{cases}$$

E6.9   Show that in the standard diminishing increment sequence for the Shell's Sort the values will alternate between odd and even values. Hint: show that an odd value will lead to an even one and vice versa.

E6.10   Show, by examples, that the depth of the recursion and, hence, the amount of temporary storage required for the Quick Sort Algorithm (with tail recursion eliminated) is indeed proportional to lg n in the worst case, if the shortest sublist is processed by the recursive call. If the largest sublist is consistently processed first, then the storage may be proportional to n.

E6.11   In Algorithm Q—with the inclusion of step Q1.5 which selects the median of the first, middle, and last elements as a pivot—what happens if there are less than three items in the sublist? Where is the largest of the three items placed? What is the movement of the indices, i and j, for the first comparison in the partitioning process? Is there any way to take advantage of the initial order of the first and last items to speed up the execution?

E6.12   The perfect partitioning summary led to the following table of partitioning operations as a function of m. We can get a closed formula (as given in the text) in terms of n, by first noting that some of the values from the number of partitioning operations are two more than powers, or multiples of powers, of 2, and that these multiples exhibit a simple pattern as illustrated below.

m	$n=2^m-1$	Partitioning Operations							
1	1	0							
2	3	2	=	2 +	0	=	2 + 0·	4
3	7	10	=	2 +	8	=	2 + 1·	8
4	15	34	=	2 +	32	=	2 + 2·	16
5	31	98	=	2 +	96	=	2 + 3·	32
6	63	258	=	2 +	256	=	2 + 4·	64
7	127	642	=	2 +	640	=	2 + 5·	128
8	255	1,538	=	2 + 1,536				
9	511	3,586	=	2 + 3,584				
10	1,023	8,194	=	2 + 8,192				
11	2,047	18,434	=					
12	4,095	40,962	=					

From these observations, derive the formula for the number of partitioning operations as a function of n.

E6.13   The "big O" behavior of the various sorting algorithms is the behavior as n gets large. However, for very small values of n the behavior is not so simple. Indeed, we cannot use the "big O" behavior to compare algorithms. Consider the various sorting algorithms in this and the preceding chapter. What is the least number of comparisons needed to sort a list of two items? of three items? of four items? of five items? Which of the schemes we have discussed is appropriate? Or are none of them?

E6.14   Assume that you have a list of 1,000 elements, randomly ordered. You need to search this list a number of times during the execution of a program. You may search it sequentially or you may sort it using a Quick Sort, and then search it via a binary search; if you wish to search it once, it is faster to perform a single serial search. If you need to search it many times, then it will take a total of fewer operations to sort once then use the more efficient search. How many searches would it take before it is profitable to sort? (For simplicity, count the number of operations and assume that they all take the same amount of time.)

E6.15   An alternative partitioning scheme operates something like:

Select some value x as the pivot element—this does not have to be in the list.

Starting from the LEFT, increment *i* as long as *i* < RIGHT and LIST[i] < *x*.

Starting from the RIGHT, decrement *j* as long as *j* > LEFT and LIST[i] > *x*.

If i ≤ j, then Swap LIST[i] and LIST[j]; increment *i*;
decrement *j*.

Repeat these last three steps as long as *i* ≤ *j*

This procedure partitions the list into two sublist; partition each recursively to complete the sort.

Give an example showing that this partitioning procedure does indeed partition the list with the left sublist containing items less than *x* and the right sublist containing items greater than *x*. (What about items equal to *x*?)

Write a formal Quick Sort Algorithm based upon this scheme.

PROBLEMS

P6.1   Write a C function to implement the Shell's Sort.

```
void ssort(int list[ ], int n)
```

Have it count the number of comparisons in the execution, i.e., the number of times step S4 is executed and store this value in the global variable *numcomp*.

Write a main() program to initialize a list of at least 100 random elements, print it out, invoke the sort function, and print the final list, as well as the number of comparisons.

Include checks in your main program to test the sort routine.

P6.2   If you initially use *h*=1 in the Shell's Sort routine, then you effectively have a Straight Insertion Sort. Use a list of 1,200 random elements (use the same seed so that you get the same random list for the following), sort it with the Straight Insertion Sort, and print the number of comparisons. (You need not print the list!)

a. How does this compare with $n^2/4$ that you might expect?

b. The Shell's Sort algorithm suggests the sequence of 1, 4, 13, 40, 121, 364, and 1,093 with 364 as the starting increment. How does the total number of comparisons compare if you begin with 1,093 (and use the sequence 1,093, 364, 121, 40, 13, 4, and 1)? Begin with 364 (use only

364, 121, 40, 13, 4, and 1)? Begin with 121? Begin with 40? Begin with 13? etc. (you have already done the "begin with 1" in part a)

P6.3   Some authors suggest that the following sequence be used for the Shell's Sort:

$$n/2, \ n/4, \ n/8, \ldots, \ 1$$

Try this with your program for the same 1,200 element list (see the previous problem). Is it better or worse than the "standard" sequence?

P6.4   Write a C function to implement the Recursive Quick Sort, Algorithm Q.

```
void qksort(int list[], int left,int right)
```

Write a main() program to initialize a list of at least 100 random elements, print it out, invoke the sort function, and print the final list. You need not use the median-of-three for the pivot. Do NOT implement Algorithm QS.
Include checks in your main program to test the sort routine.

P6.5   Write a C function to implement the Recursive Quick Sort, Algorithm Q.

```
void qksort(int list[], int left,int right)
```

Write a main() program to initialize a list of random elements at least 100 long, print it out, invoke the sort function, and print the final list. Use the median-of-three for the pivot. Do NOT implement Algorithm QS. Include checks in your main program to test the sort routine.

P6.6   Implement Algorithm QS using your previously tested Algorithm Q (see previous two problems) and the Straight Insertion Sort function developed previously. Demonstrate its use as in the previous problems. Include checks in your main program to test the sort routine.

P6.7   Using your implementation of the Algorithm QS, modify it to count the number of comparisons in both the partitioning portion (Quick Sort) and the final Insertion Sort cleanup. Set the number of comparisons in a global variable, numcomp. Use a random list of 1,000 elements and build a table varying the size of the minimum sublist; that is, in step Q1, change the size from 1, to 2, to 3, ... What is the value that results in the minimum number of comparisons for the complete sorting process?

Chapter 7

I/O Restricted Lists

"What I was going to say," said the Dodo in an offended tone, "was, that the best thing to get us dry would be a Caucus-race."

"What is a Caucus-race?" said Alice; not that she much wanted to know, but the Dodo had paused as if it thought that somebody ought to speak, and no one else seemed inclined to say anything.

"Why," said the Dodo, "the best way to explain it is to do it." (And, as you might like to try the thing yourself, some winter day, I will tell you how the Dodo managed it.)

First it marked out a race-course, in a sort of circle, ("the exact shape doesn't matter," it said,) and then all the party were placed along the course, here and there. There was no "One, two, three, and away!" but they began running when they liked, and left off when they liked, so that it was not easy to know when the race was over. However, when they had been running half-an-hour or so, and were quite dry again, the Dodo suddenly called out, "The race is over!" and they all crowded round it, panting, and asking, "But who has won?"

This question the Dodo could not answer without a great deal of thought, and it stood for a long time with one finger pressed upon its forehead, (the position in which you usually see Shakespeare, in the pictures of him), while the rest waited in silence. At last the Dodo said, "Everybody has won, and all must have prizes."

7.1   OBJECTIVES

The objectives of this chapter are to:

- Examine the usefulness of lists that have restricted insertions and deletions.
- Discuss stacks and give algorithms.
- Describe queues and give algorithms.
- Consider deques.
- Give examples of the use of these I/O restricted lists.
- Show how they may be implemented in C.
- Demonstrate how to implement a recursive procedure using a stack.

7.2   INTRODUCTION

We have considered the simple random-access list structure and a number of procedures to manipulate the list; these include:

        access
        append
        insert
        delete
        replace

We could perform any of these operations anywhere in the list, and the algorithms that were presented reflected this versatility. We are now going to study a restricted class of lists, one that allows us to perform operations only at the ends—both the normal "end" of the list as well as the "beginning" of the list. This restricts the number of operations on the list as well as access to it. Indeed, the only operations that we will consider will be insertion and deletion; because of this restricted input and output, these lists are termed I/O restricted lists.

At first glance, such restricted lists might appear to have little use; however, they are central to the operation of both computers and society. Whenever we stand in line for some service, we are really using an I/O restricted list that inserts at one and deletes from the other—i.e., a queue. When a computer function is invoked, the parameters, the local variables, and the return address are stored on list that adds and deletes from one end—i.e., a stack. If we are interrupted, say by a phone call, we stop what we are doing, process the call, then return to our original task. Thus a stack can be used to store data and suspend a task temporarily while we process an interruption.

We have already considered insertion at one end of a list—append, which was insertion at the very end of the list. (If the list is indexed 0 through $n-1$ for the n

items in the list, then append adds an element at the $n-1$ end.) This did not require any movement of data that might previously have been in the list. Deletion at this end is also quite simple and does not require any data movement; deletion at the other end is simple as well if we do not insist that the items in the list begin in location 0. By relaxing this requirement, insertion can also be implemented without having to move data, but we have to be careful.

Our logical picture of such a list is:

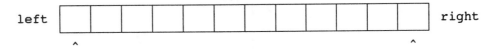

We have only four possible operations to consider:

1. Left insertion 3. Right insertion
2. Left deletion 4. Right deletion

Deletion removes an item from the list, but it must do more; it also must make the value available. Thus, to access an element using just these four operations, we delete it and obtain its value (copy it somewhere) and insert it back into the list in the same place from which we removed it. In practice, such an I/O restricted list is implemented in main memory; therefore, access to a value may be realized rather more directly, without the cumbersome deletion and insertion, and is permitted not only **at** the very ends, but also near the ends.

7.3   STACKS

The first such restricted list we will consider permits insertion at one end and deletion at one end—both processes occur at the same end. It is a LIFO, or Last In—First Out, structure and is termed a **stack**. It gets its name from the physical model of a stack of plates—where plates are added to the top and removed from the top.

Therefore, we have only two of the four possible operations to consider:

1. Left insertion
2. Left deletion

Of course, whether we use the left or the right end of the list really makes no difference!

An old-fashioned spindle for storing paper notes is a good example. Messages are stuck onto the spindle, and are retrieved in the inverse order that they are placed there.

The piles of disks in the Towers of Hanoi problem are also stack structures.

It is customary to depict a stack as a simple list that grows upward, as illustrated at the top of the next page.

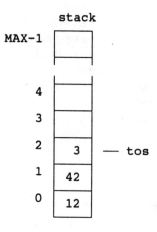

The "top of the stack", where insertions and deletions take place is controlled by the variable, *tos*. This is the index of the top element of the stack. We have depicted the stack as being defined to be *MAX* elements in length.

7.3.1   Algorithms

The operations of insertion and deletion are called **push** and **pop**, respectively. They are quite simple, accessing the top of the stack and updating the *tos* variable. The algorithm for insertion may be defined formally as:

Algorithm SH (Stack Push). Add an item, *ITEM*, to the stack, *STACK*, of physical length *MAX*.

SH1. [check if full]   If tos = MAX-1, then Output 'stack full'; Terminate.

SH2. [increment]   tos=tos+1.

SH3. [store datum]   STACK[tos]=ITEM.

And the complementary algorithm for deletion becomes:

Algorithm SP (Stack Pop). Remove an item, *ITEM*, from the stack, *STACK*.

SP1. [check if empty]   If tos = −1, then Output 'stack empty'; Terminate.

SP2. [get datum]   ITEM=STACK[tos].

SP3. [decrement]   tos=tos−1.

To initialize a stack as empty, we need only set *tos* = −1. Note that setting *tos* to zero will suggest that a value is located in that position. Therefore, the number of items in the stack may be determined as *tos*+1, although, in practice, this value is rarely needed.

7.3.2   C Implementation

Often, a stack is defined with sufficient storage that it is not necessary to check whether the stack is full. The actual use of the stack sometimes ensures that one never tries to pop from an empty stack. These situations are such that we do not need to perform the extra checks and can simplify the implementation. A possible implementation in C might appear as:

```c
int stack[MAX],tos;

/******************************************************
 *
 *       function to perform push to a stack
 *
 ******************************************************/
void push(int item)
{

    tos++;
    stack[tos] = item;

}

/******************************************************
 *
 *       function to perform pop from a stack
 *
 ******************************************************/
int pop()
{

    int item;

    item = stack[tos];
    tos--;

    return (item);

}
```

These two functions would be invoked as:

```c
        push(item);
```

and

```c
        item = pop();
```

We have defined *stack[]* and *tos* as global to the two functions that manipulate them. In general, *stack[]* and *tos* do not need to be global with respect to the programs that use them if the only access to the stack is through these two functions. Indeed, we could pass these via the parameter list as:

```
/*********************************************************
*
*          function to perform push to a stack
*
*********************************************************/
void push(int item, int stack[], int *tos)
{

    (*tos)++;
    stack[*tos] = item;

}

/*********************************************************
*
*          function to perform pop from a stack
*
*********************************************************/
int pop(int stack[], int *tos)
{

    int item;

    item = stack[*tos];
    (*tos)--;

    return (item);

}
```

These two functions would then need to be called as:

```
        push(item, stack,&tos);
```
and
```
        item = pop(stack,&tos);
```

Of course, the variables *stack[]* and *tos* would need to be defined somewhere—most likely in the calling program.

The advantage of this formulation is that these two functions could then be used with a variety of different stacks within the same program. In addition, we have avoided the use of global quantities. Global quantities can produce poor code if they are used excessively and without good reason. There are times when it is appropriate to incorporate them where the focus is upon a particular data structure that has a number of functions operate upon it, but such situations are limited.

The disadvantage in this formulation is that the function invocations are more complicated.

In addition to the above push() and pop(), there does typically need to be some mechanism (perhaps another function) that permits the stack to be initialized to empty; that is, *tos* set to -1.

Using the power of the C language we can "simplify" the push functions as:

```c
void push(int item)
{
    stack[++tos] = item;
}
```

and the pop function as:

```c
int pop()
{
    return (stack[tos--]);
}
```

Because these are essentially one-line definitions, a stack is often implemented "in-line" without the formal definition of external functions. Thus, we have in a single C program or function:

```c
{
    int stack[MAX],tos;         /* define stack */

    tos = -1;                   /* initialize stack */
        :
    stack[++tos] = ...;         /* push to stack */
        :
    ... = stack[tos--];         /* pop from stack */
        :
}
```

Of course, the stack could be defined to be any data type.

It is also possible to implement a stack that grows downward from $MAX-1$, rather than upward from 0.

The stack push and pop procedures (Algorithms SH and SP) are general. They take into account situations where the pushing and popping are performed asynchronously and in random order; that is, they may be invoked from the outside in an intermixed and arbitrary order and at arbitrary times. A simpler situation exists if all of the pushing operations are performed at one time, are finished, and are followed by the popping operations. Indeed, while the number of pushing operations is determined externally (to the push function), the popping operations may be performed until the stack is empty. Thus, we fill the stack with items, then empty it.

The C program segment that reflects this more restricted situation might appear as:

```
{

    int stack[MAX],tos;              /* define stack */

    tos = -1;                        /* initialize stack */

    while ( some external criterion ) {
        stack[++tos] = ...;          /* push to stack */

    }
        .
        .
        .
    while (tos > -1) {
        ... = stack[tos--];          /* pop from stack */

    }
        .
        .
        .
}
```

Assuming that the stack is sufficiently large, this usage does not require all of the power and generality of the complete stack algorithms. There is no need, in this case, to implement the complete and general functions.

The data structure is still a stack in that insertions and deletions are restricted to one end in space; but it is also restricted in time because all insertions are grouped in time, followed by all deletions until the stack is empty. Perhaps we should call it a time-ordered stack!

Stacks are used to store information temporarily where we want to get at the last item that was stored first. This lends itself to nested processes such as function calls. Indeed, in C, the return address for a function, the local variables, and the return value are typically placed on a stack structure. When the function is finished and control returns to the calling module, the stack space is released for future use. If the first function calls a second, then the second function's information is placed on the stack after the first function's information and hence becomes immediately accessible. When the second function returns control to the first function, the storage for the information for the second is released so that the information at the top of the stack is for the first function, where it is needed.

7.3.3   Recursive Procedures—Quick Sort

Recursive procedures can also be implemented using a stack. For example, the Quick Sort procedure, previously described as a recursive procedure, may alternately be rendered a non-recursive procedure using a stack to store information about the sublist that is not currently being processed. After dividing the list into two sublists, the indices for one sublist need to be saved temporarily while the other sublist is being processed.

The stack will need to contain both indices and, hence, will grow and shrink by two at each pass. The pushing and popping of the two indices must be done in the correct order:

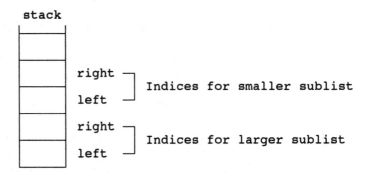

Note that we will consistently push the left index, followed by the right index. This means that when we pop, we have to pop the right index first, followed by the left index.

With this data structure available to hold information temporarily, a formal algorithm that performs the Quick Sort and avoids any recursive calls is:

Algorithm QA (Quick Sort—stack version). Given a list, *LIST*, of *n* elements, rearrange these items in place so that they are in increasing order. The algorithm avoids recursion by using a stack to store the indices of sublists. It is invoked with *n*, number of items to be sorted.

QA1. [set up stack]	Push 0 to empty stack; Push $n-1$.
QA2. [get next sublist]	If stack is empty, then Halt. else Pop RIGHT; Pop LEFT.
QA3. [are we done?]	If RIGHT$-$LEFT < 1, then Go to step QA2.
QA4. [setup]	$i=$LEFT; $j=$RIGHT; dir$=0$.
QA5. [compare]	If LIST[i] $>$ LIST[j], then Swap(LIST[i],LIST[j]); dir$=1-$dir.
QA6. [increment]	$i=i+$dir; $j=j+$dir-1.
QA7. [reached pivot]	If $i < j$, then Go to step QA5.
QA8. [stack sublists]	If $i-$LEFT $<$ RIGHT$-i$,then Push $i+1$; Push RIGHT; Push LEFT; Push $i-1$.

else Push LEFT; Push i−1;
Push i+1; Push RIGHT.

QA9. [continue]   Go to step QA2.

■

When this algorithm is first executed, steps QA1 and QA2 seem to do extra unnecessary work; but pushing the original list limits, and then popping them in the next step actually simplifies the algorithm since we can simply push indices for both sublists and then branch to the beginning. When the stack is empty, the procedure is finished.

In step QA8 we push the indices for the largest sublist onto the stack first followed by the indices for the smallest. This ensures that we will process the shortest sublist first. Processing in this order uses the least possible stack space.

Because of the way the stack is used in this situation, the full general external stack push and pop functions are not needed. The size of the stack is, at most, $2 \cdot \lg n$, hence a stack of 40 is sufficient to sort a list of one million. Thus, it is easy to make the stack large enough and not have to worry that it might become full. On the other hand, the empty stack (*tos* $= -1$) signals the end of the procedure.

7.3.4   Evaluation of Algebraic Expressions

Another typical use of a stack involves the evaluation of algebraic expressions. The use of a stack to store information temporarily allows a simple way to preserve the normal proper order of arithmetic operations, and the order as modified by parentheses.

First, we need to consider a method of evaluating arithmetic expressions, termed Reverse Polish Notation (RPN). This notation was first developed by the Polish logician and mathematician Jan Łukasiewicz (1878-1956). His original notation placed the operator first, followed by the two operands. RPN reverses that so that the two operands appear first, followed by the operation.[1]

The valuable aspect of RPN for our purposes is that it is a scheme for writing an arithmetic expression so that parentheses are unnecessary and the order of the operations is inherent in the notation. This makes it easy for a computer to use. Sometimes this notation is termed **postfix**, since the operator occurs after the operands. For example:

```
3  3  *  4  4  *  +
```

where a space delimits the individual entities. The example is the RPN equivalent to the algebraic expression:

```
3*3  +  4*4
```

---

[1]   As John Ball points out: "Polish" is easier to pronounce than "Łukasiewicz" (wu-ka-sha'-vich), and "reverse Polish" is much easier to pronounce than "Zciweisakuŀ."   John A. Ball, *Algorithms for RPN Calculators*

In ordinary algebra, the operator is placed between the two operands; this can be termed infix.

To evaluate an RPN expression, we use a stack to hold values until it is time to combine them with the arithmetic operations. A formal algorithm for this is:

Algorithm RE (Reverse Polish Notation Evaluation). Given an arithmetic expression that is written in RPN, evaluate it.

RE1. [set up stack]   Initialize the stack to empty.

RE2. [get next item]   While we have not reached the end of the RPN expression, get the next item and perform steps RE3 through RE5.

RE3. [value?]   If item is a value, then push it onto the stack.

RE4. [binary operator?]   If the item is a binary operator, then
          Pop the stack to X,
          Pop the stack to Y,
          Perform Y op X and Push the
             result onto the stack.

RE5. [unary operator?]   If the item is a unary operator, then
          Pop the stack to X,
          Perform op(X) and Push the
             result onto the stack.

RE6. [all done]   The single value on the stack is the desired result.   ■

The typical binary operators in an arithmetic expression are the normal arithmetic operators:

+	addition
−	subtraction
*	multiplication
/	division
^	raise to a power

The unary operators are really simple functions such as:

√	square root
sin	sine
cos	cosine
tan	tangent
log	logarithm
exp	exponential

Therefore, the previous example should give us the following, (reading across with the stack at each step arrayed vertically with the top of the stack at the top!):

```
encountered:   3    3    *    4    4    *    +
stack:                            4
                    3         4    4    16
               3    3    9    9    9    9    25
```

The answer is 25.

A more complicated example, with both binary operations and a unary function, would be:

$$5\ 4\ +\ 5\ *\ 4\ +\ \sqrt{\ }\ 8\ -$$

```
encountered: 5    4    +    5    *    4    +    √    8    -
stack:
                  4         5         4              8
             5    5    9    9    45   45   49   7    7    -1
```

The answer is −1. This RPN expression corresponds to the algebraic expression:

$$\sqrt{[(5+4)*5+4]}\ -\ 8$$

With RPN, not only do we not need parentheses, but the priority order of arithmetic operations no longer needs to be considered (as it is with an ordinary algebraic expression). The position within the RPN expression designates when an operation is to be performed. For example:

```
2+3*4          becomes      2 3 4 * +
(2+3)*4        becomes      2 3 + 4 *
```

In the first example, we would normally perform the multiplication before the addition, because it is higher priority. In the RPN expression, it is performed first because it occurs first in the expression. In the second expression, the addition is performed first because of the parentheses. In the RPN expression, it appears first, so it is executed first.

The evaluation of an RPN expression can also include variables. We need a data structure to store the values of the variables. Whenever we encounter a variable in the RPN expression, we would push the value of the variable. That is, we would modify step RE3 in Algorithm RE. An example might be:

$$X\ 2\ \wedge\ D\ +$$

with

```
X [  5  ]   D [  42  ]
```

becomes as it is evaluated:

```
encountered:  X    2    ^    D    +
stack:
                   2         42
              5    5   25   25   67
```

This RPN expression corresponds to: X^2+D

Evaluating an RPN expression is only half the solution. What we need to do is to evaluate ordinary algebraic expressions; we can do this if we can transform such an expression into an RPN expression.

It turns out that a stack structure is also useful in translating an ordinary algebraic expression, with parentheses, into an RPN expression. For simplicity, let us assume that the infix expression contains only:

> values
> > variable name
> > numeric constant
> arithmetic binary operators
> > ^   high priority
> > / *   medium priority
> > + -   low priority
> parentheses

These items will be termed **tokens**. Each token is a single syntactical entity.

The operations are processed according to the groupings indicated by parentheses, priority, and the left-to-right order. That is, operations inside parentheses are performed first. Multiplication and division are performed before addition and subtraction, and if two operators of the same priority occur, the one on the left is performed first.

The expression can be translated with a single left-to-right scan of the arithmetic expression. The scheme is to use a stack to hold temporarily operators and parentheses. This allows us to treat arithmetic operators of different priority and nested parentheses properly.

Algorithm RC (Conversion of algebraic expression to RPN). Given an algebraic expression, translates it to RPN by scanning the expression once from left to right.

RC1. [initialize]   Initialize the stack to empty and the resultant RPN expression to empty; start at the beginning of the algebraic expression.

RC2. [finished?]   If we have reached the end of the algebraic expression, go to step RC10.

RC3. [get next item]   Get the next token.

RC4. [value?]   If the token is a value, then Move it to the RPN expression; Go to step RC2.

RC5. [(parenthesis?]   If the token is a (, then Push the (to the stack; Go to step RC2.

RC6. [) parenthesis?]   If the token is a), then
>Until a (is at the top of the stack,
>>Pop the stack and move each operator to the RPN expression.
>
>Pop and discard the (; Go to step RC2.

RC7. [stack empty]   If the stack is empty, then the token (which is an operator) is pushed to the stack; Go to step RC2.

RC8. [top (]   If the top of the stack is a (, then the token is pushed to the stack; Go to step RC2.

RC9. [operator]   If the top of the stack contains an operator of higher or equal priority to the token, then
>>the top of the stack is popped and the popped operator is moved to the RPN expression; Go to step RC7.
>
>>>else
>
>the token is pushed to the stack; Go to step RC2.

RC10. [all done]   Until the stack is empty,
>Pop the stack and move each operator to the RPN expression.

Note that when step RC7 is encountered, a binary arithmetic operator has been found on the algebraic string; it is this operator that is pushed to the stack in step RC7 or RC8 and compared with the top of the stack in step RC9.

When we move an item to the RPN expression, we also place a space on the expression to delimit the items. This is necessary to separate numeric values, or variables that might contain more than one character. Without this delimiter, the following creates problems:

$$4 + 23 \quad \text{and} \quad 42 + 3$$

which would become: 423+ without something to separate the numeric values in the RPN expression.

Indeed, for items that contain more than one character some extended procedure may be necessary to identify them and move all of the characters. For unsigned integers; the first character is a digit; all digits that follow, until a non-digit is encountered, are moved. For a variable, the first character is customarily a letter. As an example: 2*(A*(25-2)+X*7)/(M+3)

```
found:   2 * ( A * ( 25 - 2 ) + X * 7 )   / ( M + 3 )
stack:                   - -
                 (   ( (            * *
                 * *   * * * * + + + +           + +
             ( ( ( (   ( ( ( ( ( ( (       ( ( ( (
             * * * * *   * * * * * * * * *   / / / / / /
RPN:     2       A   25  2 - * X   7 * + *   M   3 + /
```

Therefore, the RPN string becomes:

2 A 25 2 - * X 7 * + * M 3 + /

There is one other very useful entity in an algebraic expression that is a bit tricky to handle; this is the unary minus. If we include it, then we can treat all numeric values as unsigned, which simplifies their processing. (There is also a unary plus, but it does nothing useful and can be discarded.) The problem is that ordinarily we use the same character to indicate both the unary minus and the binary operation of subtractions. Therefore, we need to distinguish between these two situations. This is not difficult.

A unary minus, -, can occur only:

> at the beginning of the expression

> after a (

> after a binary operator

A binary subtraction, -, can occur only:

> after a value, either numeric or variable

> after a)

We can keep a flag to tell us what type the previous item was so that when we encounter a -, we know which use it represents.

We could turn all unary minuses into binary subtractions by putting a zero in front of each, except that the unary minus normally has a very high priority. Therefore, we will go ahead and place a 0 value on the RPN expression, but push a special symbol to the stack; a tilde, ~, is convenient. We will include this on our list of operators as highest priority:

$$
\begin{array}{ll}
\sim & 3 \\
{\char`\^} & 2 \\
* \ / & 1 \\
+ \ - & 0
\end{array}
$$

However, when the time comes to move it to the RPN expression, we will change it back to a -.

As an example: -2*(-D^*2-5)

```
found:   - 2 * ( - D ^ 2 - 5 )
stack:
                            ~  ~  ^  ^  -  -
                  (  (  (  (  (  (  (
         ~  ~  *  *  *  *  *  *  *  *  *
RPN:     0  2  -     0  D  -  2  ^  5  -  *
```

Therefore, the RPN string becomes:

$$0 \; 2 \; - \; 0 \; D \; - \; 2 \; \char`^ \; 5 \; - \; *$$

A unary plus would be a + symbol found at a place in the expression where we might expect to find a unary minus. The appropriate way to handle it is to ignore it—simply move to the next token in the algebraic expression.

7.4   QUEUES

A queue is an I/O restricted list that permits insertion **only** at one end and deletion **only** at the opposite end. It is a FIFO, or First In—First Out Structure. A "line" at a ticket window is an example of a queue. (Indeed, in some countries such a linear arrangement of people is called a queue rather than a line.) It is customary to depict a queue as:

```
0    1    2    3    4    5    6    7    8    9      MAX-1
+----+----+----+----+----+----+----+----+----+----+   +----+
|    |    |  D |  A |  T |  A |    |    |    |    |   |    |
+----+----+----+----+----+----+----+----+----+----+   +----+
              ^              ^
              di             ii
```

where now we are using two indices to control the insertions (*ii*) and deletions (*di*); they will indicate the stored elements at either end of the queue.

There is one difference between a line of people waiting in a queue and the computer implementation. Typically, the head of the line (the deletion end) is fixed in position—and the elements of the queue move as deletions occur. This is efficient for humans, since each has its own internal processor, the motion can take place simultaneously—in parallel. For a queue implemented in a computer's memory, it is more efficient not to move data once it is stored in the queue. We use the two indices to indicate the beginning and the end of the stored data. If we picture items being added at the right of the list above and deleted on the left, then the section containing stored data moves to the right. It is tempting to think of the right as the head and the left as the tail. However, this violates our normal view of a "line," where deletions are made at the head of the line, and insertions are made at the "end." Alternatively, we can define the deletion end as the front of the queue and the insertion end as the rear of the queue. The picture, then, is for items to be added to the rear and move up to the front; actually, the front moves back until a given element finds itself at the front.

As with the stack, there are two processes: insertion and deletion. These we could term:

```
insertion:        enqueue or q_in or simply qpush
deletion:         dequeue or q_out or simply qpop
```

The terms qpush and qpop are formulated to be analogous to common terminology for a stack.

For a computer queue, the only insertions and deletions are performed via these two operations. There is no "cutting in line" (insertions in the middle) or "giving up" (deletions from the middle), as might occur in a queue of people.

To insert an item, we perform something like:

```
ii = ii+1
QUEUE[ii] = item
```

And to delete an item we do:

```
x = QUEUE[di]
di = di+1
```

Unfortunately, this simple approach has a number of problems.

0	1	2	3	4	5	6	7	8	9		MAX-1
				S	T	R	U	C	T		E

```
          ^                              ^
          di                             ii
```

Here, the insertion index has reached the right end of the list. We could simply restrict ourselves to a maximum of *MAX* items to be inserted in the queue but, if several have been deleted, it seems such a waste not to use the locations of the deleted items. The answer is to treat the queue as a circular structure—when the indices reach the right end, then they return to the left end and continue.

This is accomplished by:

```
i=i+1
if i = MAX, then i=0
```

where *i* stands for either the insertion or deletion index.

Therefore, after inserting another item in the example above, we have:

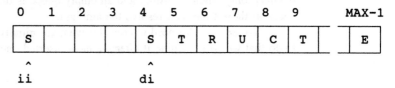

0	1	2	3	4	5	6	7	8	9		MAX-1
S				S	T	R	U	C	T		E

```
  ^                  ^
  ii                 di
```

This allows us to insert more than *MAX* total items into the queue (as long as some have been deleted), until the queue actually is full. The restriction is not *MAX* insertions, but a total of *MAX* items at any one time.

A full queue looks like:

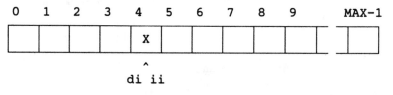

0	1	2	3	4	5	6	7	8	9		MAX−1
T	U	V	W	A	B	C	D	E	F		S

However, this brings up another problem—how to distinguish between a full queue and an empty one. Consider a queue with one item:

0	1	2	3	4	5	6	7	8	9		MAX−1
				X							

According to the scheme that we have been using, *di* and *ii* both have the same value. Now delete that item according to the scheme we have been using:

0	1	2	3	4	5	6	7	8	9		MAX−1

This is exactly the same configuration (as far as the *ii* and *di* indices are concerned) as a full list!

We can solve this ambiguity in a number of ways. The first scheme is to use another variable that keeps track of the number of items in the queue, say *nq*. We increment it when we insert, and decrement it we when delete. If *nq = MAX*, then the list is full. If *nq* = 0, then the queue is empty. However, there is redundant information since for the simple situation:

$$nq = ii - di + 1 \quad \text{or} \quad nq = ii - di + MAX + 1$$

The second scheme and possible solution is to realize that a full queue is obtained only when inserting, and an empty queue is obtained only when deleting. A check at those times can resolve the ambiguity.

To see this, we need to consider what an initially empty queue might look like; to do that we will examine it after we have inserted one item:

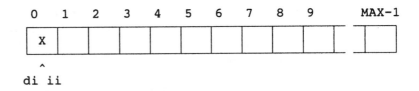

Here both *di* and *ii* are equal to zero. The process of insertion did not change *di*, but it did add one to *ii*. Therefore, before we started, the queue could have looked like:

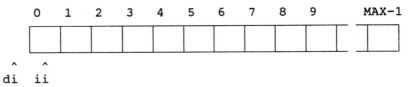

where $di = -1$ and $ii = 0$. Actually, we could have set $di = MAX - 1$, but -1 is more convenient, and $di = -1$ is only possible with an empty queue, since as the queue is used *di* will take on values: 0, 1, ..., $MAX-1$, 0,.... Even though, in this case, $di = ii - 1$, there is no way this could be confused with a full queue. One possible full queue might have $ii = 0$ and $di = MAX - 1$, but it never would have $di = -1$.

Therefore, whenever we delete we check to see if the queue is empty; that is, does *di* equal $ii - 1$ and, if so, then set $di = -1$ and $ii = 0$. This forces all empty queues to look the same.

A third scheme is to use an empty element in the list to resolve the ambiguity; that is, we will allow only $MAX-1$ items to be stored in the queue of length *MAX*. A full queue will thus look like:

```
  0   1   2   3   4   5   6   7   8   9        MAX-1
┌───┬───┬───┬───┬───┬───┬───┬───┬───┬───┐    ┌───┐
│ T │ U │ V │   │ A │ B │ C │ D │ E │ F │    │ S │
└───┴───┴───┴───┴───┴───┴───┴───┴───┴───┘    └───┘
          ^           ^
          ii          di
```

Therefore, for a full queue, $ii = di - 2$. And, for an empty queue, $ii = di - 1$.

It appears that this scheme wastes space. However, the storage requirements of the first two schemes for the extra code to distinguish between a full queue and an empty one is probably more than the memory required for a single item in the queue; and the last scheme is probably faster as well.

7.4.1 Algorithms

It is this last scheme that the complementary formal algorithms implement:

Algorithm QH (Queue Push). Add an item, *ITEM*, to the queue, *QUEUE*, of physical length *MAX*. This algorithm uses tail and head indices, *ii* and *di*, for insertion and deletion, respectively. It reserves one location in the queue to distinguish between an empty and full queue.

QH1. [check if full]   If ii = di−2 or ii = di−2+MAX, then
$$\text{Output 'queue full'; Terminate.}$$

QH2. [increment]   ii=ii+1; If ii = MAX, then ii=0.

QH3. [store datum]   QUEUE[ii]=ITEM.

∎

and:

Algorithm QP (Queue Pop). Remove an item, *ITEM*, from the queue, *QUEUE*, of physical length *MAX*. Uses tail and head indices, *ii* and *di*, for insertion and deletion, respectively.

QP1. [check if empty]   If ii = di−1 or ii = di−1+MAX, then
$$\text{Output 'queue empty'; Terminate.}$$

QP2. [get datum]   ITEM=QUEUE[di].

QP3. [increment]   di=di+1; if di = MAX, then di=0.

∎

To initialize the empty queue, set $ii=-1$ and $di=0$.

Note that the deletion Algorithm QP does not write over the item that is deleted. The data remains on the list, but the index moves on so that the space is available for reuse. Therefore, the value is unaccessible by the ordinary queue procedures, and can be ignored. It is possible to write a zero or blank there, but this is unnecessary and takes extra time and code.

We could have defined our "head" and "tail" indices differently:

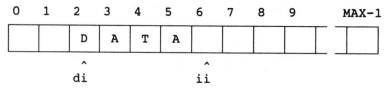

Now they both indicate where the next operation is to take place. The next deletion will take place at location *di* (which is the way we have already defined it), and the next insertion will take place at location *ii*, rather than $ii+1$. This would change the algorithms, but as long as we are consistent this definition will work.

As with the stack data structure, there is a simpler situation for the use of a queue which involves the separation, in time, of all of the insertions followed by all of the deletions. In this case, the number of items in the queue cannot exceed the physical size of the queue, and there is no need to consider the queue as a circular structure. All we need to do is fill the queue, using an insertion index, then empty the queue using a deletion index that takes on successive values from 0 up to the final value of the insertion index.

The C program segment that reflects this more restricted situation might appear as:

```
{
    int queue[MAX],ii,di;          /* define stack */

    ii = -1;                       /* initialize queue */

    while ( some external criterion ) {
        queue[++ii] = ...;         /* push to queue */
    }
       .
       .
       .
    for (di=0; di<=ii; di++) {
        ... = queue[di];           /* pop from queue */
    }
       .
       .
       .
}
```

A queue is an appropriate structure to serve as a temporary storage of data between two devices that may be operating either asynchronously and/or at different speeds. Such a structure is often called a buffer or a circular buffer. A typical example is a keyboard buffer. The letters that come from the keyboard are entered at various times, with random intervals between each. If the computer is busy, then it is best to store these characters in a buffer until the computer can process them.

At the other end of the information flow, the computer may generate output to the printer in bursts that are much faster than the printer can print them; often there is a wait, while the CPU performs additional processing. By placing the information in a buffer, which the printer can access as it prints the information, the CPU can continue to process without having to wait for the printer.

Many CPU's implement a buffer to hold the next few instructions. This allows it to fetch these instructions while another part decodes and executes the current instruction. Such a scheme speeds up the processing greatly. The CPU does not have to wait for a memory access to get the next instruction.

In more biological terms, an animal's stomach is a buffer. The ingestion of food can proceed at a rapid rate, while digestion is performed much more slowly. Of course, with the mixing of eaten goodies and enzymes in the stomach, there is no guarantee that nutrients are removed in the exact order they were entered!

7.5   DEQUES

A deque (pronounced deck) or double-ended queue is the most general of these I/O restricted lists. It may permit any or all of the four operations. Thus, a stack and a queue are special cases of a deque.

Actually, there are not that many different cases that we have to consider. There is one basic deque that permits all four operations:

1.	Left insert	Right insert
	Left delete	Right delete

There are four deques that implement three of the four possible operations:

2.	Left insert	Right insert
	Left delete	
3.	Left insert	Right insert
		Right delete
4.	Left insert	
	Left delete	Right delete
5.		Right insert
	Left delete	Right delete

In reality, cases 2 and 3 are basically the same—just reversed—as are cases 4 and 5. Thus, there are only two such different deques.

There are six deques that use only two of the operations:

6.	Left insert	Right delete	queue
7.	Left delete	Right insert	queue
8.	Left insert		
	Left delete		⌐ stack
9.		Right insert	
		Right delete	⌐ stack
10.	Left delete	Right delete	
11.	Left insert	Right insert	

Cases 6 and 7 are simply queues, and cases 8 and 9 are stacks, which we have examined in detail. These tend to be the most useful of all of the I/O restricted lists.

Case 10 is quite interesting. It allows deletion, but never any insertion. If the deque initially has information, then it might behave somewhat as Top Secret, Read Only Memory (read once information). Why anyone would wish to read from both ends is a bit perplexing! Case 11 is even more curious. It permits insertion, but never any deletion or access. We could call it WOM, or Write Only Memory—anything that goes in is lost forever to the outside world!

Finally, there are four deques that permit only one of the possible operations. Since they cannot allow both insertion and deletion, they are of limited use—as are cases 10 and 11.

Therefore, there really are only five different deques that are of any use. Two of those, which we have studied in detail (stacks and queues), are quite heavily used throughout the hardware and software worlds.

Even though the deque allows other possible operations, it turns out that the queue algorithms are sufficient. We do need to implement the other two similar operations, but the circular buffer, and the way we kept of a full queue and an empty queue, generalize to a deque.

7.5.1 Keyboard Buffer

A simple example of a deque might be a keyboard buffer. Normally, buffers are implemented as queues, with characters from the keyboard being inserted at one end and characters being removed from the other end as the computer processes them. However, it is very useful to implement a special key that deletes from the normal insertion end—the backspace key!

Therefore, we have a deque that looks like:

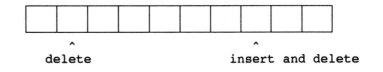

```
         ^                        ^
      delete            insert and delete
```

The action of the backspace key deletes (from the structure) the last character entered, if it is still in the structure (the CPU has not deleted it from the other end yet), and discards it.

7.5.2 Reverse Polish Calculators

Another more complicated example of a deque is the so-called "stack" of Reverse Polish Notation calculators. As far as the user is concerned, the structure is a stack in that the user inserts and deletes from one end and the arithmetic operations take place with the one or two items at this same end of the stack; but, in reality, the circuitry of the calculator inserts and deletes at the other end to maintain a structure that is exactly four elements long.

The "stack" in such a calculator is typically pictured as in the diagram at the top of the next page.

The user enters numbers into the X register, at the bottom of the structure. The X register is also the value that is displayed.

T	−666
Z	1.414
Y	42
X	3.14

Such calculators have an ENTER key which moves items "up" the stack, copying the value in the X register to the Y register, and setting things up so that the next digit key pressed begins to enter a new value into the X register. This process may be diagrammed as:

$$X \rightarrow X, \ X \rightarrow Y, \ Y \rightarrow Z, \ Z \rightarrow T, \ \text{T is lost}$$

Because insertion and deletion are occurring at both ends of the four-element structure, this "stack" is really a deque. We define the four following deque operations:

1. XPUSH   insertion at the bottom in the X register
2. XPOP   deletion at the bottom from the X register
3. TPUSH   insertion at the top in the T register
4. TPOP   deletion at the top from the T register

The ENTER key is then implemented, in terms of these primitive operations, on the original structure with four elements:

V = XPOP	deque length 3
XPUSH V	deque length 4
XPUSH V	deque length 5
V = TPOP	deque length 4

These four deque operations, applied to the structure, in order, maintain the length of the structure at four elements when the series is completed. Intermediately, the "length" of the structure may change. Indeed, each of the calculator's basic operations begins, and ends, with an active deque that is exactly four elements long.

The value *V* that is popped from the top of the "stack" is discarded. For example, after pressing the ENTER key, the "stack" becomes:

T	1.414
Z	42
Y	3.14
X	3.14

If you now press a digit key (or a series of digit keys), then that digit (or series) becomes a new value in the X register:

T	1.414
Z	42
Y	3.14
X	2

Arithmetic operations take place between elements at the bottom of the "stack." Pressing an operation key may be depicted schematically as:

$$Y \text{ op } X \to X, \ Z \to Y, \ T \to Z, \ T \to T$$

The values in the X and Y registers are combined and the result placed in the X register. The values in the Z and T are moved downward, with the value in the T duplicated in the Z and T.

Using our deque operations, the arithmetic keys are implemented as:

V = XPOP	deque length 3
U = XPOP	deque length 2
XPUSH (U op V)	deque length 3
V = TPOP	deque length 2
TPUSH V	deque length 3
TPUSH V	deque length 4

As an example, pressing the x (multiply) key results in:

T	1.414
Z	1.414
Y	42
X	6.28

Note that the bottom two registers have been combined, and the original value in the T register has been replicated.

A function, or unary operation, takes place on the value in the X register only.

V = XPOP	deque length 3
XPUSH f(X)	deque length 4

As an example, pressing the $\sqrt{}$ (square root) key results in:

T	1.414
Z	1.414
Y	42
X	2.506

Other stack manipulation procedures, such as XY exchange, roll up, and roll down, can also be defined in terms of the fundamental deque procedures.

7.6   SUMMARY

I/O restricted lists serve as a very important class of structures in computing.

A stack is a Last In—First Out (LIFO) structure that is used to process function calls and hardware and software interrupts. A recursive function can be rewritten so that it can use a stack to store explicitly temporary information and eliminate the recursion. Algebraic expressions can be translated into a parentheses free notation (RPN) that can be easily evaluated—both processes use stacks.

A queue is a First In—First Out (FIFO) structure that serves as a buffer between two devices. It is typically implemented a logically circular device. Particular attention must be paid to distinguish an empty queue from a full queue.

A deque is a double ended queue, and is the most general I/O restricted structure. However, the algorithms devised for a queue are sufficient for any possible deque.

REFERENCES

Ball, John A., *Algorithms for RPN Calculators*, John Wiley & Sons, New York, 1978.

Kernighan, Brian W. and Ritchie, Dennis M., *The C Programming Language*, 2nd ed., Prentice-Hall, Englewood Cliffs, New Jersey, 1988.

Knuth, Donald E., *The Art of Computer Programming*; Fundamental Algorithms, vol. 1., 2nd ed., Addison-Wesley Publishing Co., Reading, Massachusetts, 1973.

Robertson, J. and Osborne, G., *"Postal System Input Buffer Device,"* Datamation, Sept./Oct. 1960, Vol. 6, No. 5.

Sedgewick, Robert, *Algorithms in C*, Addison-Wesley Publishing Co., Reading, Massachusetts,, 1990.

QUESTIONS

Q7.1   Is a stack of pancakes really a "stack?" That is, are they added and removed one at a time from the top of the pile as would be required for a true stack?

Q7.2   If we have the following situation:

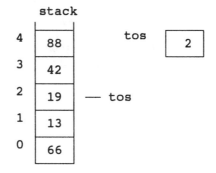

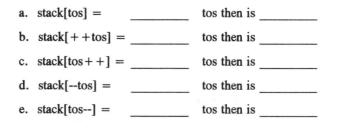

What value is given by each of the following? Assume that each operates independently on the original variables.

    a. stack[tos] = _____   tos then is _____

    b. stack[++tos] = _____   tos then is _____

    c. stack[tos++] = _____   tos then is _____

    d. stack[--tos] = _____   tos then is _____

    e. stack[tos--] = _____   tos then is _____

Q7.3   If we wish to have a stack grow downward from $MAX-1$, then what modifications to Algorithms SH and SP will be necessary? What would be the appropriate value for *tos* for the empty stack situation?

Q7.4   Explain why $2 \cdot \lg n$ integers is the maximum size stack required for Algorithm QA.

Q7.5   The queue operations have what "big O" behavior in terms of the number of items stored; that is, what is x in $O(x)$ if there are n items to be stored in the queue at any one time?

Q7.6   How would the queue algorithms be changed if the ends of the queue were reversed; that is, if the indices were decremented rather than incremented?

Q7.7   In both Algorithms QH and QP we had operations that appeared as:

i=i+1; If i = MAX, then i=0.

Write this as a macro function that may be used in both functions; that is:

#define increment(x) ....

Thus the usage in the C function is simply:

increment(i);

Q7.8   We can define the insertion and deletion indices so that they indicate where the next operation would take place on a queue:

```
        0   1   2   3   4   5   6   7   8   9      MAX-1
      +---+---+---+---+---+---+---+---+---+---+   +---+
      |   |   | D | A | T | A |   |   |   |   |   |   |
      +---+---+---+---+---+---+---+---+---+---+   +---+
                ^               ^
                di              ii
```

Assuming that one "wasted" space is used to distinguish between an empty queue and a full queue, what would be the configuration of a full queue? What would be the configuration of an empty queue?

Q7.9   A standard key on a typical RPN calculator is a XY exchange. Write out the operation for this in terms of the primitive deque operations.

Q7.10   A standard key on a typical RPN calculator is a roll-down; with this key the contents of all of the registers move down except the X, which is shifted to T: $Y \to X$, $Z \to Y$, $T \to Z$, and $X \to T$. Write out the operation for this in terms of the primitive deque operations.

Q7.11   Why is it a simpler situation (compared to the general situation) when the stack or queue insertions all occur first, as a group, and are then followed by a series of deletions until the structure is empty?

Q7.12   What is a buffer and what can it be used for?

Q7.13   If deletions from the interior of a queue are permitted and you do not want to move data, then it is possible to replace the deleted item with some sort of "EMPTY" value. How would you modify the standard insertion and deletion algorithms to handle this?

Q7.14   Write out a formal algorithm that gives the queue status; that is, it returns EMPTY, FULL, or PARTIAL depending upon the values of the insertion and deletion indices.

Q7.15   If two stacks are required for a given program, each one growing and shrinking independently, we could reserve storage for each one independently and restrict each one. This could be wasteful if, for example, one tended to be small when the other was large, and vice versa. How could you implement them so that they could share the available memory? What would happen to the test for a "full stack" situation?

Q7.16   How can you make a variable global to two functions without making it global to other parts of the program?

Q7.17   C permits assignment within expressions. Therefore:

$$... = array[i=i+1];$$

is a valid C construct. What would be the equivalent using the increment operation?

Q7.18   How many different types of deques must we consider? Include stacks and queues in your count.

Q7.19   Classify the following situations as to which type of data structure might be useful in controlling the "state." Explain.

a. You are studying, a friend comes by, the phone rings, the alarm on the oven (cookies are baking) goes off.

b. All of your five teachers give you short homework assignments that are due the next day.

c. The cafeteria is too crowded, as everyone tries to get at the entre serving area.

Q7.20   We frequently implement a stack without checking to see if a push overflows the stack memory. On the other hand, the queue operations almost always check to see if the queue is full or empty. Why?

Q7.21   In the stack version of the Quick Sort, what would be the problem if we replaced step QA8 with the following simpler version?

> QA8'. [stack sublists]   Push LEFT; Push i−1;
> Push i+1; Push RIGHT.

What is the worst possible case size required for the stack?

Q7.22   Why is a stack size of 40 quite sufficient for the stack version of the Quick Sort?

Q7.23   Why are there four possible queues that permit only one operation?

Q7.24   Which of the deque cases presented in the text is a keyboard buffer that permits the use of a "delete" key such as a backspace? Why?

Q7.25   In the examples of converting from an algebraic expression to an RPN expression, the order of the values (variables or numeric constants) were the same in both. Is there ever a situation where the values appear in a different order in the RPN expression than in the algebraic expression?

EXERCISES

E7.1   It is possible to implement a stack with the *tos* variable indicating the location where the next item will be inserted:

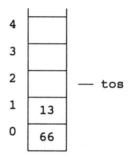

In this example, *tos*=2. Rewrite Algorithms SH and SP to reflect this definition.

E7.2   Rewrite the queue manipulation algorithms (Algorithms QH and QP) using the special situation of $di=-1$ and $ii=0$ to indicate an empty queue (rather than keeping one empty location in the queue to distinguish between a full queue and an empty queue).

E7.3   Write out four formal algorithms for the four general deque operations: left push, left pop, right push, and right pop. Consider carefully how you would handle a full deque and an empty deque.

E7.4   Write a stack version of Algorithm PI.

E7.5   The following expressions are written using RPN. Evaluate them:

   a. 16 4 /

   b. 24 3 2 * −

   c. 144 6 6 * 3 / + −

E7.6   Translate the following arithmetic expressions into RPN:

        a. 3+5*4

        b. 5+3*(9−(4*6+3))/(4/7)

        c. 12/3*2

        d. (6*(3+(5−7*2)/(5−6))+8)/2

E7.7   A stack may be used for temporary storage. Consider a string of characters such as "ABC" and the operation on the string of removing the first item. We wish to move these to an output string where the only operation is to append a character to the end. If these were the only operations and structures, then all we could do is make a copy. However, after removing a character from the input list we have the option of pushing it to a stack— and at any time, we can pop an item from the stack and append it to the output string; then we can rearrange the output string. The three operations are:

    1. Remove character from input string and append it to the output.

    2. Remove character from input string and push it.

    4. Pop a character and append it to the output.

    Using these three operations, how many different arrangements of three elements, "ABC", can you achieve on the output string? How many possible permutations are there? What if there are four items? Five items?

E7.8   A queue may be used for temporary storage. Consider a string of characters such as "ABC" and the operation on the string of removing the first item. We wish to move these to an output string where the only operation is to append a character to the end. If these were the only operations and structures, then all we could do is perform a copy. However, after removing a character from the input list we have the option of placing it in a queue; at any time we can remove an item from the queue and append it to the output string, then we can rearrange the output string. The three operations are:

    1. Remove character from input string and append it to the output.

    2. Remove character from input string and place it in queue.

    3. Take character from queue and append it to the output.

    Using these three operations, how many different arrangements of three elements, "ABC", can you achieve on the output string? How many possible permutations are there? What if there are four items? Five items?

E7.9   Write out a stack version of the recursive algorithm to compute a Fibonacci number.

E7.10   Deletion from the interior of a stack or queue can be implemented without moving data by replacing the item to be deleted with a special value, e.g., NULL or -1.

   a. Write a formal algorithm for searching for an item—use a simple sequential search—and deleting it from the interior of a queue.

   b. Modify the queue manipulation algorithms to ignore such a deleted item when it is encountered.

E7.11   Write out a table that tells which item can follow another in a syntactically correct algebraic expression.

	binary	(	varble	number	unary	)	end
begin							
binary							
(							
variable							
number							
unary							
)							

For each entity at the left of the row, write YES if the entity at the top of the column can follow it.

PROBLEMS

P7.1   Write a C function to implement the Stack Version of the Quick Sort, Algorithm QA.

```
void qksorts(int list[], int n)
```

Write a main() program to initialize a list of at least 100 random elements, print it out, invoke the sort function, and print the final list. You need not use the median-of-three for the pivot. Include in your main program checks to test if the sort routine is working correctly.

P7.2   Write two C functions to implement the queue manipulation algorithms on a buffer of length 8.

```
void qpush(int item)
int qpop()
```

Use the global definition:

```
#define MAX   8
```

The storage for the queue and indices may be implemented as a global or passed as parameters:

```
int buffer[MAX],ii,di;
```

For debugging purposes, implement a DUMP routine that simply prints all values in the queue and the indices:

```
void dump()
{
    int i;

    for (i=0; i<MAX; i++)
        printf("%d  %d   ",i,buffer[i]);

    printf("\n\ninsert at %d delete at %d\n",ii,di);
}
```

Write a main() program to ask for a command:

DUMP	print the buffer and indices	D
QPUSH	and ask for value	I
QPOP	and print value	P
END	end the program	E

You may wish to initialize the buffer by filling it with zeros and initialize the indices to −1 and 0. The only purpose of initializing the list is so that the DUMP routine has something innocuous to print. Normally, only the head and tail indices need be initialized.

Note: It is not necessary to place a zero in the queue whenever an item is deleted; to do so simply wastes time, since the two indices define what is in the active queue.

The qpush() and qpop() functions should print a message for an error condition and do nothing to the queue—simply return.

Try your program, starting with an empty buffer, on the following items, in order:

1.	DUMP	12.	QPUSH 15	23.	QPOP
2.	QPUSH 12	13.	QPUSH 16	24.	QPOP
3.	QPUSH 21	14.	QPUSH 17	25.	QPOP
4.	QPUSH 42	15.	QPOP	26.	QPOP
5.	QPUSH 16	16.	QPOP	27.	QPOP
6.	QPUSH 18	17.	DUMP	28.	QPOP
7.	QPOP	18.	QPUSH 54	29.	QPOP
8.	QPOP	19.	QPUSH 61	30.	QPOP
9.	DUMP	20.	QPUSH 18	31.	DUMP
10.	QPUSH 19	21.	DUMP	32.	QPUSH 85
11.	QPUSH 16	22.	QPOP	33.	DUMP

P7.3   Write a C program to simulate an RPN calculator using a deque with a physical length of eight but a logical length of four. Implement the functions of: ENTER, +, −, *, /. Use the primitive deque operations of XPUSH, XPOP, TPUSH, and TPOP. Note that the four active items in the deque move through the physical locations.

P7.4   Write a C function that, given a string containing an ordinary algebraic expression, will translate into and pass back a string containing the proper RPN equivalent. See Exercise 7.5. For convenience, assume that all values are single letter variable names and that the expression uses only the four binary arithmetic operators and parentheses.

Try your function on:

a.   A+B*C

b.   A+B*(C−(D*E+F))/(G/H)

c.   A/B*C

d.   (A*(B+(C−D*E)/(F−G))+H)/I

P7.5   Write a C function that takes an algebraic expression contained in a string and converts it to an RPN expression contained in a string.

```
void alg_to_rpn(char alg[], char rpn[])
```

For convenience, assume the following:

variables	single upper-case letters
constants	unsigned integers
binary operators	+ − * / ^
unary minus	−
parentheses	( )

The algebraic expression will contain no blanks and can be assumed to be syntactically correct.

Do not forget to terminate the RPN expression with a NULL!

Try your function on the following algebraic expressions:

a. 3+5*4

b. 5+3*(39−(4*6+3))/(4/7)

c. 12/3*2

d. (6*(3+(2*5−7^2)/(5−6))+8)/2

e. −A*(42+B/3^2−C)

P7.6   Develop a stack version of the functions that print an integer (see Algorithm PI and associated C functions). Have it print the integer with commas marking off every group of three digits; i.e., 1,234,567.

P7.7   Write a C function that evaluates an RPN expression contained in a string. Let the RPN expression contain single-letter upper-case integer variables whose values are contained in an array: values[26].

```
int evaluate(char rpn[], int values[])
```

Try your function on the following:

a. 16 4 /

b. 24 3 2 * -

c. 144 6 6 * 3 / + -

d. 4 2 ^ 5 2 ^ +

e. A 3 5 + * F /   where A contains a 7 and F contains a 3

P7.8   Implement C functions for the previous two problems and combine them into a complete program to evaluate an algebraic expression.

Write a main program that will request expressions and a destination variable for the value to be stored in. You might consider each entry in the form:

var = expression

By using, as an example, A = 3, you can store a value in A.

Try it on:

a. A = 3+5*4

b. B = 5+3*(39-(4*6+3))/(4/7)

    c. C = 12/3*2

    d. D = (6*(3+(A*5-7^2)/(B-6))+C)/2

    e. E = -A*(42+B/3^2-C)

At each point, print the values stored in the variables. You probably will want to initialize each variable to zero.

P7.9   The conversion of an algebraic expression to an RPN expression and the evaluation of the RPN expression can use different algebra rules. Consider Boolean algebra:

variables	single-letter upper-case names
constants	0 1
unary negation	~ highest priority

binary operations		
	& and	high priority
	+ or	medium priority
	# xor	medium priority
	> if	low priority
	= iff	low priority

parentheses	()

Write or modify the C functions that translate the algebraic expressions to RPN, and evaluate the RPN expression so that it works on Boolean expressions.

Try your functions on:

    a. 0&1

    b. A+B   where A is 1 and B is 0

    c. ~(A&B)   where A is 1 and B is 1

Chapter 8

Storage of Arrays

"...What's that dish for?"

"It's meant for plum-cake," said Alice.

"We'd better take it with us," the Knight said. "It'll come in handy if we find any plum-cake. Help me to get it into this bag."

This took a long time to manage, though Alice held the bag open very carefully, because the Knight was so very awkward in putting in the dish: the first two or three times that he tried he fell in himself instead. "It's rather a tight fit, you see," he said, as they got it in at last; "there are so many candlesticks in the bag." And he hung it to the saddle, which was already loaded with bunches of carrots, and fire-irons, and many other things.

8.1   OBJECTIVES

The objectives for this chapter are to:

- Discuss ways that lists can be stored in memory.

- Generalize about the index limits of a list.

- Find an expression that relates the index to the actual address of the item.

- Present efficient ways to store two-dimensional structures, tables.

- Generalize the address expressions for higher dimensional arrays.

- Implement general functions in C that handle arrays of various shapes.

223

■ Describe how non-rectangular arrays can be efficiently stored.

8.2   INTRODUCTION

The user or programmer thinks in terms of logical data structures; however, ultimately these must be stored somewhere in the computer's memory. It is important to understand how these data structures can be stored. This is not just an academic issue. The C programming language implements pointers which are addresses. The programmer needs to know how to use these. She needs to know how data structures are stored.

Most high-level computer languages implement rectangular arrays of many dimensions, using indices to access them. However, occasionally it is desirable to store a structure that is not rectangular. Therefore is it important to learn how these are stored in the computer memory.

The C language does not allow us to pass directly to a function the shape of an array as a parameter. However, it is often the case when dealing with matrices that we would want to be able to write a function that handles whatever size array we might wish to define. In order to do so, we must explicitly provide the addressing of the elements.

The C language does implement dynamic arrays where a program can request a chunk of memory to be allocated during execution. If an array is to be stored in this space, then the programmer must know how to convert from an index or indices to actual address. The advantage of dynamic allocation is that the size of the storage need not be specified in advance, but can be determined during the execution of the program. However, additional work must be done by the programmer.

So far we have focused on the algorithms and procedures for using the data structure of an internal list. We have assumed that using an index somehow magically accesses the desired value without worrying about how the computer might actually store the structure and turn the index into an address. Now we will look at storage details of the main memory of a computer to determine how we can efficiently store lists and more complicated structures.

8.3   COMPUTER MEMORY

Main memory in the computer can be viewed as a linear sequence of words. Each word may store some datum and is a "basic" chunk of information. Each word has its unique address. The addresses range from 0 on up to the limit of the machine.

This physical picture is just that—a depiction of how memory is organized. In reality, memory may be scattered across many chips and arranged quite differently; however, it is organized into a single linear sequence according to the addresses. We will refer to this arrangement as the **physical view**.

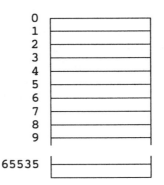

The size of the word (number of bits) varies. We will consider it as the smallest "chunk" of memory that has a unique address. For many microcomputers this is 8 bits or 1 byte. For large supercomputers, it may be on the order of 64 bits. However, the size of the word is often the same as the inherent size of the registers in the CPU. As an example, for machines that are based around the Intel 8088, IBM PC's and compatibles, the word size is taken to 16 bits, even though the memory is addressed in 8-bit units.

A computer with a larger word will process more information in the same amount of time and, hence, has faster throughput, even if the basic clock speed of the CPU is the same.

This type of memory is called Random Access Memory (RAM) because the CPU can access any word of memory in the same amount of time.

The size of the address that the CPU can handle determines the amount of memory that can be accessed. Since more bits can represent more unique patterns, i.e., more addresses, computers using a larger address can access more words of memory. As an example, many microcomputers of the 1970's used a two-byte or 16-bit address. This allowed a total of 65,536 unique addresses (0 - 65,535) and such machines were limited to this amount of memory. The Intel 80x86 has an addressing mode that allows a 20-bit address and hence can access more than one million words (actually 1,048,576). Using an alternative mode, it can utilize a 24-bit address and, hence, can directly access up to 16,777,216 locations. It is fortunate that adding one more bit doubles the potential size of the memory.

Because it is easier to change units than deal with large numbers, a unit of 1 K is common. We note:

$$2^{10} \; = \; 1024 \; \approx \; 1000 \; = \; 10^3$$

In the metric system, 1,000 is 1 kilo (abbreviated k); it is customary to adopt 1 K as 1,024, or approximately one thousand. For the next "prefix" unit the metric system uses 1,000,000 which is 1 Mega (abbreviated M). There is not a good distinction between a desirable "computer" unit and the metric one—both are designated M or Mega. Strictly speaking, 1 Megabyte probably refers to 1024K or 1,048,576, whereas 1 Megabuck means $1,000,000—usually the context will serve to make the distinction. Perhaps when one speaks of numbers of that size, it is unimportant to make a distinction! For a table of powers of 2 see Appendix A.

Logically, we deal with an index when programming with a list. And somehow that index needs to be converted into a memory address for the CPU to access the desired datum. However, before we get there, we need to realize that data comes in different types and, hence, the amount of storage required for each datum varies.

8.4   DATA TYPE

The data type is a designation that provides information about the representation and the size of the datum. You should already be familiar with a number of data types. Examples for C with their typical size include:

integer	int	16 bits
long integer	long	32 bits
character	char	8 bits
floating point	float	32 bits
double precision	double	64 bits

FORTRAN adds a few more possibilities:

complex		complex	2 32-bit quantities
double precision	complex	double complex	2 64-bit quantities

With the **struct** construct in C, we can make even more complicated data types.

In reality the size of each datum will vary with the computer system used. The C programming language defines certain limits—e.g., an int will be at least 16 bits, but if the word size of the CPU is 32 bits, then it is common to implement an int as a 32-bit quantity.[1]

Each datum is represented as a pattern of bits. How the CPU interprets these bit patterns will also depend upon the data type. Characters are represented as an arbitrary pattern, although there are typically one or two standardized patterns that are used. The ASCII set, for example, defines:

A	01000001
B	01000010
.	
.	

---

[1]   C provides an operator, sizeof () that gives the actual size of a given data type. This allows one to write programs that make fewer assumptions about the machine they are to run on and are, hence, more portable.

The non-negative integers are typically stored as the simple binary representation. The negative values are often stored as a 1's or 2's complement in order to simplify the arithmetic processes. Thus 01000001 is a decimal 65.

Floating point quantities are stored in a special representation, similar to scientific notation, that includes a certain number of bits for an exponent, with the rest of the bits for the fraction.

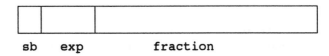

     sb   exp   fraction

The important thing to remember is that the type specifies the internal representation and the **size** of the datum. We will designate the number of words that a given item takes in computer memory as w (for width or words).

8.5 SCALARS

A simple variable is indeed a simple situation. In a high-level language it is accessed by name. The programmer usually does not need to know details of where the value associated with it is stored in memory, its internal representation, or its size. Of course, it is important to know its possible range of values to prevent erroneous results. However, the programmer need only be concerned with the name and, of course, the value stored in the variable.

Each simple variable, called a **scalar**, variable has the following attributes:

name
type   gives representation and size, w
address
value

The *name* and *type* are selected by the programmer. The computer decides where the variable is to be stored (its *address*) during compilation and loading, and the *value* is supplied during execution.

Scalars are easy to deal with and easy for the computer to handle.

As an example, consider the scalar variable x which is defined to be an int (taking two words of memory):

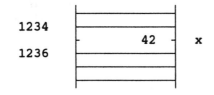

If the programmer wishes to store another value, while retaining the old one, then it is necessary to define another variable with a different name and to write another statement to handle it; this makes it very cumbersome to handle a number of values in a convenient way. Therefore, most high-level languages implement a list structure.

8.6　VECTORS

A vector is a simple linear list of items. It is a one-dimensional array and can contain many values. Logically it can be thought of as:

$$(a_1, a_2, a_3, \ldots, a_n)$$

or

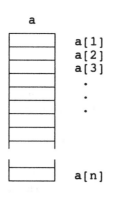

The values in a vector are typically accessed by the use of a subscript or an index. The example above is appropriate for a FORTRAN array, with the indices taking on values 1, 2, ..., n; that is, the indices begin with 1. The C programming language implements arrays with the indices starting with 0; i.e., C uses: 0, 1, 2, ..., n-1. In general, we could specify a lower bound, or an origin, for the set of indices, b, so that the allowed values for the indices would be b, $b+1$, $b+2$, ..., $b+n$-1.

In a general sense, each vector variable has the following attributes:

name	
type	gives representation and size, w
lower index bound, b	
upper index bound, u	
address	depends upon the index
value	depends upon the index

The number of elements is thus:

$$n = u - b + 1,$$

and the total storage required for the vector is $n \cdot w$. Of course, for C vectors, $b=0$.

As far as the programmer is concerned, for most uses it does not matter where in the computer memory the individual elements of the list are stored, as long as the computer provides storage for them and keeps track of where they are stored. The important aspect for the programmer is only to relate a given value with its index—at the computer level, there needs to be some way to relate the actual address of the datum with its index. One could implement some sort of a lookup table; however, a more systematic approach, allowing the address to be computed easily from the index, is more useful. Therefore, we need to decide upon the storage details of how we store the vector in the computer memory and devise a function that gives us the actual address of the i-th item in the list; that is, we want a function:

$$\texttt{address(i).}$$

where i is the value of the index, and the function gives the appropriate address.

A reasonable approach is to store the elements of the list in contiguous memory locations. As an example, consider a vector by the name of *list*, the lower index bound of $b=1$, a total of $n=6$ elements with each taking two memory locations, $w=2$. The computer decides to store the vector beginning at word 7648.

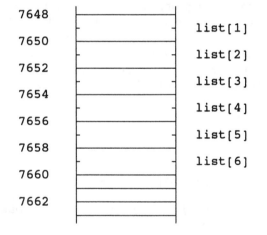

The view of the data as stored in the physical medium—in this case, the computer memory—is termed the **physical view**. The way the programmer views the information via a name and an index is the **logical view**. A primary purpose of the material in a data structures course is to study the physical view rather than simply using the logical view.

By arranging the items of the vector as above, the address becomes quite easy to calculate. A function to perform this is given as:

$$\texttt{address(i) = a + (i-b)} \cdot \texttt{w}$$

where we will take a as the beginning address of the vector. For the example above, this simplifies to:

$$\begin{aligned}
\text{address(i)} &= 7648 + 2(i-1) \\
&= 7648-2 + 2i \\
&= 7646 + 2i.
\end{aligned}$$

Both of the constants in this expression can be determined by the computer before the program is executed. At execution time, the address for a given index can be calculated using only one multiplication and one addition operation.

In general, we can algebraically rearrange our original equation to become:

$$\begin{aligned}
\text{address(i)} &= \text{a-b·w + w·i} \\
&= \text{v + w·i.}
\end{aligned}$$

where the constant *v* is given by:

$$\text{v = a-b·w.}$$

Therefore, if we store a vector in consecutive memory locations, we have a simple linear polynomial expression that gives the address in terms of the index.

Note that in computing the address, we need not know the number of elements of the vector. In C, when the vector is defined, the number of elements is needed; but if a vector appears as a parameter of a function, it only needs to be declared as a vector, and the number of elements is not required. However, a function needs to know where the vector is located and the size of each element. The size is supplied by the declaration. The location, or address, is passed to the function by the calling program.

For example:

```
main()
{

    int list[10];  /* definition */

    fun(list);     /* invocation, passes address */

}

void fun(vec)
int vec[];         /* declaration, gives w */
{

    int i;

    ...vec[i]...    /* access, computes address(i) */


}
```

8.7 TABLES

A table or matrix is a two-dimensional structure arranged in rows and columns:

$$\begin{bmatrix} a_{11} & a_{12} & a_{13} & a_{14} \\ a_{21} & a_{22} & a_{23} & a_{24} \\ a_{31} & a_{32} & a_{33} & a_{34} \end{bmatrix}$$

The first or left-most subscript or index indicates the row, and the second or right-most subscript indicates the column; that is:

$$a_{rc}.$$

Another view of the table is:

column:	1	2	3	4
row: 1	1,1	1,2	1,3	1,4
2	2,1	2,2	2,3	2,4
3	3,1	3,2	3,3	3,4

The above picture is the logical view of the data. In a high-level language we would define such a structure as:

```
DIMENSION IARR(3,4)        FORTRAN
int arr[3][4]              C
```

Of course, the C array would have a lower bound on each index of 0. The first dimension specifies the number of rows and the last dimension specifies the number of columns.

Each table variable has the following attributes:

name
type   gives representation and size, w
lower row index bound, b_r
upper row index bound, u_r
lower column index bound, b_c
upper column index bound, u_c
address   location of first element, a
value   depends upon the indices: i,j

The number of columns is: $\quad n_c = u_c - b_c + 1,$

and the number of rows is: $\quad n_r = u_r - b_r + 1.$

The total storage required for the vector is: $n_r \cdot n_c \cdot w$.

The view of our general table appears according to the indices of each element as:

b_r,b_c	b_r,b_c+1	b_r,b_c+2		b_r,u_c
b_r+1,b_c	b_r+1,b_c+1	b_r+1,b_c+2		b_r+1,u_c
u_r,b_c	u_r,b_c+1	u_r,b_c+2		u_r,u_c

As in the case with vectors, it is unimportant for the programmer to know how the array is stored in the computer. If the programmer consistently accesses each individual element by the two subscripts or indices, then the physical view is irrelevant. However, in our study of data structures, we must be concerned about the physical view. We want an efficient simple scheme for storing the table in the computer's memory so that we can quickly retrieve a value associated with a given pair of indices.

A vector fits naturally into a computer's memory since both are essentially linear structures; however, to store a table it is necessary to perform some rearrangement of the structure. By taking "slices," catenating them end-to-end in order we can get a linear structure; there are two "major" ways to do this.

We can store it row by row:

1,1	1,2	1,3	1,4	→
2,1	2,2	2,3	2,4	→
3,1	3,2	3,3	3,4	→

as:

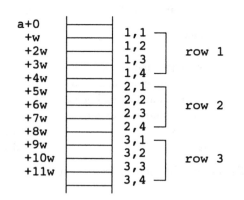

The right-most, or last, subscript varies most rapidly as we progress through memory—this storage will be termed "row-major" storage. (Note that there is the possibility of confusion, because it is the **column** index that varies most rapidly since we store one row at a time.)

Or, we can store our table column by column:

1,1	1,2	1,3	1,4
2,1	2,2	2,3	2,4
3,1	3,2	3,3	3,4

as:

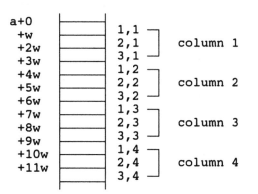

The left-most, or first, subscript varies most rapidly as we progress through memory. This storage will be termed "column-major" storage.

In both cases, we want an expression that allows us to compute the address of the i,j element:

```
address(i,j)
```

8.7.1   Row-Major

For the row-major case note that as we increase j by 1—leaving i constant—the address increases by w. Therefore, our expression will contain a term that appears as: $w \cdot j$. As we increase i by 1, leaving j constant, the address increases by the number of elements in a row (which is the number of columns, $n_c \cdot w$). Therefore, the expression must contain a term that looks like: $n_c \cdot w \cdot i$. The final observation is that when $i = b_r$ and $j = b_c$, then $address(i,j) = a$. Therefore, we obtain:

$$\text{address}(i,j) = a + n_c \cdot w \cdot (i - b_r) + w \cdot (j - b_c), \qquad \text{(row-major)}.$$

where $n_c = u_c - b_c + 1$.

As with the vector case we can simplify this expression:

$$\text{address}(i,j) = v + m_i \cdot i + m_j \cdot j$$

with

$$m_i = n_c \cdot w,$$
$$m_j = w, \text{ and}$$
$$v = a - b_r \cdot n_c \cdot w - b_c \cdot w, \hspace{3em} \text{(row-major)}.$$

This final expression is a simple linear polynomial in the two indices. The constants in the expression may all be computed in advance and each access will involve two multiplications and two additions.

C arrays are stored in row-major form with the lower bound for each index at 0. In this case, v equals a, a particularly simple situation. We note that n_r, the number of rows, is not needed to calculate the address from the indices. Therefore, when a parameter is declared, it is not necessary to specify the left-most size of the array. For example:

```
main()
{

    int table[5][9];    /* definition */

    fun(table);         /* invocation, passes address */

}
void fun(arr)
 int arr[][9];          /* declaration */
{

    int i,j;

    ...arr[i][j]...     /* access */

}
```

As a specific example, consider an array dimensioned 5x3 with the lower bound on the row equal to 1 (thus the rows will be indexed as 1, 2, ..., 5) and the lower bound on the columns equal to -1 (so the columns will be indexed as -1, 0, 1). Each element takes three words.

1,−1	1,0	1,1
2,−1	2,0	2,1
3,−1	3,0	3,1
4,−1	4,0	4,1
5,−1	5,0	5,1

This array is to be stored in memory, in a row-major order, beginning with address 2,148. The physical view would be:

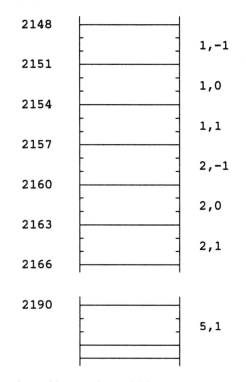

The appropriate address polynomial becomes:

$$\texttt{address(i,j) = v + m}_\texttt{i}\texttt{·i + m}_\texttt{j}\texttt{·j}$$

with

$$\texttt{m}_\texttt{j}\texttt{ = w = 3,}$$
$$\texttt{m}_\texttt{i}\texttt{ = n}_\texttt{c}\texttt{·w = 3·3 = 9, and}$$
$$\texttt{v = a - b}_\texttt{r}\texttt{·n}_\texttt{c}\texttt{·w - b}_\texttt{c}\texttt{·w = 2148 - 1·3·3 - (-1)·3 = 2142.}$$

Thus:

$$\texttt{address(i,j) = 2142 + 9·i + 3·j.}$$

8.7.2 Column-Major

For the **column-major** case, the appropriate polynomial is similar; however, the constants in the address polynomial are different. The only variation is that increasing *j* by 1 results in skipping over an entire column. Therefore:

$$\texttt{address(i,j) = a + w·(i-b}_\texttt{r}\texttt{) + n}_\texttt{r}\texttt{·w·(j-b}_\texttt{c}\texttt{),}\qquad\text{(column-major)}$$

where $n_r = u_r - b_r + 1$.

As with the vector case, we can simplify this expression:

```
address(i,j) = v + mᵢ·i + mⱼ·j
```

with

$$m_i = w,$$
$$m_j = n_r \cdot w, \text{ and}$$
$$v = a - b_r \cdot w - b_c \cdot n_r \cdot w, \hspace{3cm} \text{(column-major)}.$$

Note that this expression for the address does not need the number of columns. Therefore, in a language such as FORTRAN it is not necessary to supply the right-most size. As an example:

```
DIMENSION IARR(8,12)

CALL SUBR(IARR)

END

SUBROUTINE SUBR(ITAB)

DIMENSION ITAB(8, )

... ITAB(I,J) ...

END
```

8.8 BOXES

A box is a three-dimensional rectangular structure. It may be depicted as:

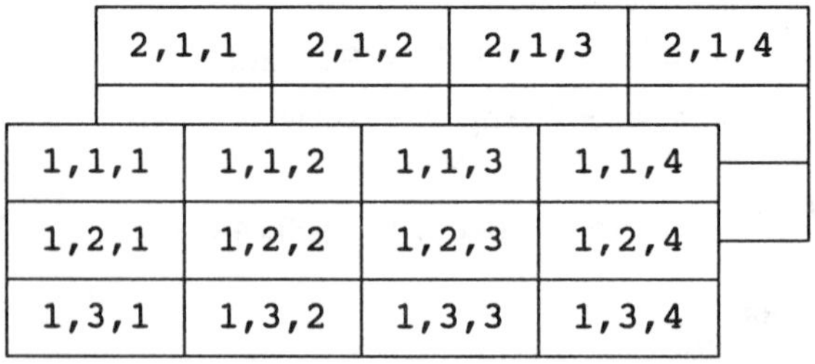

2,1,1	2,1,2	2,1,3	2,1,4
1,1,1	1,1,2	1,1,3	1,1,4
1,2,1	1,2,2	1,2,3	1,2,4
1,3,1	1,3,2	1,3,3	1,3,4

The terminology for describing the box is not as clear as it is with a table. What constitutes a row? A column? Both imply a line segment, but the box consists of planes. We will generalize from the table example and use the term "column" to describe the planes that go across the box (in the example above, numbered 1, 2, 3, and 4), "row" to describe the planes that go down (numbered 1, 2, and three), and "plane" to describe the planes that go back (numbered 1 and 2). Thus, a box with only one plane is simply a table.

```
        s
       e
      n
     a
    l
   p              columns

   r
   o
   w
   s
```

The indices then become:

$$a_{prc}.$$

As with the tables, it is necessary to dissect this in order to fit it into the linear structure of the computer memory. There are a number of ways to do this. A "slice" through the box will produce a plane, which must, in turn, be sliced again into line segments. Even the original slices may be taken in three directions: two orthogonal vertical cuts and one horizontal cut. One possibility is:

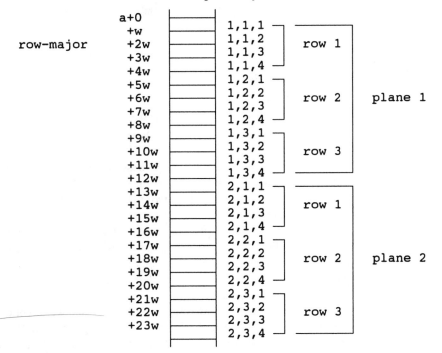

The right-most, or last, subscript varies most rapidly as we progress through memory; the middle one is next, and the left-most, or first, varies the least rapidly. This storage will be termed "row-major" storage even though we recognize that the concept of a row is strange. (At least this terminology is consistent with what we used for a table.)

We now want a function, which we can guess will be a linear polynomial in the three indices i,j,k, to calculate the address. It will be similar to the one for a table, but will have one more term:

```
address(i,j,k) = v + mᵢ·i + mⱼ·j + mₖ·k,
```

where the constants need to be determined.

When k increases by 1, with the other indices constant, the address increases by w. When j increases by one, we skip over a row; that is, the address increases by the number of elements in a row (which is the number of columns) times the size of each. And when i increases by 1, we must skip over an entire plane of rows and columns. Thus, for this "row-major" situation, the address expression becomes:

```
address(i,j,k) = a + nᵣ·n_c·w·(i-b_p) + n_c·w·(j-bᵣ) + w·(k-b_c),
```

where $n_c = u_c - b_c + 1$, $n_r = u_r - b_r + 1$, and b_p is the lower bound on the plane numbering.

As with the case of the vector and the table, we can simplify this expression:

```
address(i,j,k) = v + mᵢ·i + mⱼ·j + mₖ·k,
```

with

$$m_i = n_r \cdot n_c \cdot w,$$
$$m_j = n_c \cdot w,$$
$$m_k = w, \text{ and}$$
$$v = a - b_p \cdot n_r \cdot n_c \cdot w - b_r \cdot n_c \cdot w - b_c \cdot w$$
$$= a - b_p \cdot m_i - b_r \cdot m_j - b_c \cdot m_k, \qquad \text{(row-major)}.$$

This final expression for the address is a simple linear polynomial in the three indices. The constants in the expression may all be computed in advance, and each access of an element will involve two multiplication and two addition operations. There is a pattern here; the multipliers of the indices grow left to right. They are made up of the product of the sizes of the dimensions to the *right* of the index. That is, the multiplier for j, the middle index, consists of the size of only the right dimension—and the multiplier for i consists of the size of the middle dimension and the right dimension. The size of the left dimension, the number of planes, is not needed to compute the address.

This "row-major" ordering is not the only one we might consider; indeed, there are six possible orderings. In this ordering the right-most index varies most rapidly as one moves through memory, the middle varies the next most rapidly, and the left-most varies the slowest.

To picture this, imagine an *indexometer* that moves through memory and displays the indices of each location as it progresses.

The "row-major" scheme would have the right-most or "column" indicator turn the most rapidly. The left-most or "plane" indicator would change the most slowly. Thus, this would behave exactly like an odometer in an automobile except that the "range" of values in each position would be from *b* to *u*, rather than from 0 to 9.

We can imagine storing a box in different orders that will tell how the three individual displays in the indexometer change as we move down through memory.

	Left	Middle	Right		
1	least	mid	most	rapidly	row-major
2	least	most	mid	rapidly	
3	mid	least	most	rapidly	
4	mid	most	least	rapidly	
5	most	least	mid	rapidly	
6	most	mid	least	rapidly	column-major

Only number 1 and number 6 are systematic enough to consider in detail; they can easily generalize to even more dimensions. We will term the "left-to-right" pattern as column-major, just as we termed the "right-to-left" pattern row-major. For the column-major the indexometer would behave like an ordinary odometer that has been reversed right to left.

The diagram on the top of the next page illustrates our example above.

We have not explicitly labeled the pieces that are arranged together (indicated by the line above), as we did for the row-major, because the terminology becomes confused. What is a row? A column? A plane?

For this "column-major" case we obtain, in general:

$$\texttt{address(i,j,k)} = a + w \cdot (i - b_p) + n_p \cdot w \cdot (j - b_r) + n_p \cdot n_r \cdot w \cdot (k - b_c),$$

where $n_p = u_p - b_p + 1$, $n_r = u_r - b_r + 1$, and b_p and u_p are the lower and upper bound on the plane numbering, respectively.

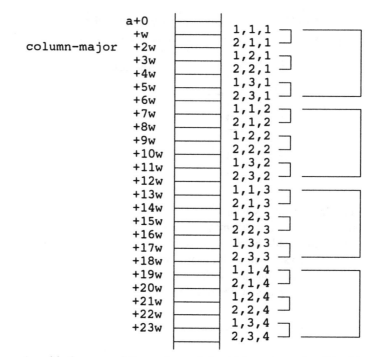

As with the case of the vector and the table we can simplify this expression:

$$\texttt{address(i,j,k)} = \texttt{v} + \texttt{m}_i \cdot \texttt{i} + \texttt{m}_j \cdot \texttt{j} + \texttt{m}_k \cdot \texttt{k,}$$

with

$$\texttt{m}_i = \texttt{w,}$$
$$\texttt{m}_j = \texttt{n}_p \cdot \texttt{w,}$$
$$\texttt{m}_k = \texttt{n}_p \cdot \texttt{n}_r \cdot \texttt{w,} \text{ and}$$
$$\texttt{v} = \texttt{a} - \texttt{b}_p \cdot \texttt{m}_i - \texttt{b}_r \cdot \texttt{m}_j - \texttt{b}_c \cdot \texttt{m}_k, \qquad\qquad \text{(column-major).}$$

This final expression is a simple linear polynomial in the three indices. The constants in the expression may all be computed in advance, and each access will involve three multiplication and three addition operations. There is a pattern here; the multipliers of the indices grow right to left. They are the product, made up of the sizes of the dimensions to the *left* of the index. That is, the multiplier for *j*, the middle index, consists of the size of only the left dimension, and the multiplier for *k* consists of the size of the middle dimension and the left dimension. The size of the right dimension, the number of columns, is not needed to compute the address.

8.9   *HIGHER DIMENSIONAL RECTANGULAR ARRAYS*

We can envision, but perhaps not visualize, a physical picture, of even higher dimensional rectangular arrays. Again, our terminology becomes strained.

8.9.1   Hyperbox

A four-dimensional structure, which we will call a **hyperbox**, consists of a number of boxes. It can be defined with the following relevant bounds in the four indices:

b_b and u_b $\qquad$ $n_b = u_b - b_b + 1$, number of boxes

b_p and u_p $\qquad$ $n_p = u_p - b_p + 1$, number of planes

b_r and u_r $\qquad$ $n_r = u_r - b_r + 1$, number of rows

b_c and u_c $\qquad$ $n_c = u_c - b_c + 1$, number of columns

It will be accessed as:

$$a_{bprc} \quad \text{or} \quad \texttt{array[i][j][k][l]}$$

The "row-major" ordering will again have the right-to-left pattern. The address expression becomes:

```
address(i,j,k,l) = a + np·nr·nc·w·(i-bb) + nr·nc·w·(j-bp) +
                   nc·w·(k-br) + w·(l-bc)
```

As with the previous cases, we can simplify this expression:

```
address(i,j,k,l) = v + mi·i + mj·j + mk·k + ml·l
```

with

$m_i = n_p \cdot n_r \cdot n_c \cdot w,$

$m_j = n_r \cdot n_c \cdot w,$

$m_k = n_c \cdot w,$

$m_l = w,$ and

$v = a - b_b \cdot m_i - b_p \cdot m_j - b_r \cdot m_k - b_c \cdot m_l,$ $\qquad$ (row-major).

Again we note the pattern in computing the multipliers; the size of the right-most dimension, the number of boxes, is not needed.

The "column-major" ordering produces a typical left-to-right pattern and is generalized exactly like the "row-major" case from the appropriate box situation.

8.9.2   Hyperhyperbox

A five-dimensional structure, which we will call a **hyperhyperbox,** consists of a number of hyperboxes. It can be defined with the following relevant bounds in the five indices:

b_h and u_h $n_h = u_h - b_h + 1$, number of hyperboxes

b_b and u_b $n_b = u_b - b_b + 1$, number of boxes

b_p and u_p $n_p = u_p - b_p + 1$, number of planes

b_r and u_r $n_r = u_r - b_r + 1$, number of rows

b_c and u_c $n_c = u_c - b_c + 1$, number of columns

It will be accessed as:

$$a_{hbprc} \quad \text{or} \quad \texttt{array[i][j][k][l][m]}$$

The "row-major" ordering will again have the right-to-left pattern. The address expression becomes:

```
address(i,j,k,l,m) = a + n_b·n_p·n_r·n_c·w·(i-b_h) +
                         n_p·n_r·n_c·w·(j-b_b) + n_r·n_c·w·(k-b_p) +
                         n_c·w·(l-b_r) + w·(m-b_c).
```

As with the previous cases we can simplify this expression:

$$\texttt{address(i,j,k,l,m)} = v + m_i \cdot i + m_j \cdot j + m_k \cdot k + m_l \cdot l + m_m \cdot m,$$

with

$m_i = n_b \cdot n_p \cdot n_r \cdot n_c \cdot w,$

$m_j = n_p \cdot n_r \cdot n_c \cdot w,$

$m_k = n_r \cdot n_c \cdot w,$

$m_l = n_c \cdot w,$

$m_m = w,$ and

$v = a - b_h \cdot m_i - b_b \cdot m_j - b_p \cdot m_k - b_r \cdot m_l - b_c \cdot m_m,$ (row-major).

Again we note the pattern in computing the multipliers. The size of the left-most index, the number of hyperboxes, is not needed.

The address polynomial for the "column-major" case is the same but with different multipliers. The "column-major" ordering is similar except, as noted above, it gives a "left-to-right" pattern to computing the multipliers.

8.10 IMPLEMENTATION IN A VECTOR

Generally, a high-level language will implement rectangular arrays of fairly high dimensions as part of the language structure. Thus, the programmer can simply use what is available without having to be concerned about the addressing of the data structure. However, there may be situations where it is important to perform the addressing explicitly.

So far, we have concentrated on computing the actual address of the desired subscripted item. However, it is possible to implement any multi-dimensional array in a vector. The above address polynomials may be adapted for computing the index into the vector rather than the actual address. For example, consider the two-dimensional table below:

1,1	1,2	1,3	1,4
2,1	2,2	2,3	2,4
3,1	3,2	3,3	3,4

If this is stored in a vector, in C, in a row-major order, the view would be:

vec[0]	1,1
vec[1]	1,2
vec[2]	1,3
vec[3]	1,4
vec[4]	2,1
vec[5]	2,2
vec[6]	2,3
vec[7]	2,4
vec[8]	3,1
vec[9]	3,2
vec[10]	3,3
vec[11]	3,4

We can take our expression for the row-major ordering for a table, and change it, to give the index:

$$\texttt{index(i,j)} = \texttt{a} + n_c \cdot w \cdot (i - b_r) + w \cdot (j - b_c).$$

Note that when $i = b_r$ and $j = b_c$ the index computed should be 0; thus $a = 0$. Further, if the type of the vector and the type of the array are the same, then it takes one element of the vector to store one element of the table, so $w = 1$.

Therefore, we obtain:

$$\texttt{index(i,j)} = n_c \cdot (i - b_r) + (j - b_c).$$

As in the previous cases, we can simplify this expression:

$$\texttt{index(i,j)} = v + m_i \cdot i + m_j \cdot j,$$

with

$$m_j = 1, \quad m_i = n_c, \quad \text{and} \quad v = -b_r \cdot n_c - b_c.$$

For this particular example, $m_j = 1$, $m_i = 4$, and $v = -5$. Thus:

$$\texttt{index(i,j)} = -5 + 4 \cdot i + j.$$

8.10.1   C Implementation

Implementing this in C could consist of a function:

```
int index(int i, int j)
```

that takes the indices of the table and returns the appropriate index into the table. That is:

```
int vec[12];                /* definition */

... vec[index(i,j)] ...     /* access */
```

To illustrate, the following is an example of a C program:

```
/**************************************************************
 *
 *
 *      program to illustrate a function to print tables
 *              of different shapes
 *
 **************************************************************/
#include <stdio.h>

main()
{

    static int a[5][4] = {{1,2,3,4},{6,7,8,9},{2,5,8,4},
                          {7,5,3,9},{5,2,6,0}};
```

```
        static int b[2][3] = {{4,5,6},{7,5,3}};

        void prnt_arr();

        puts("The contents of array A are:\n");
        prnt_arr(a, 5,4);

        puts("The contents of array B are:\n");
        prnt_arr(b, 2,3);

}

/***********************************************************
 *
 *
 *    function to print a two-dimensional array
 *        params:    tble    array, treated as a vector
 *                   nr,nc   actual shape and size
 *
 ***********************************************************/
void prnt_arr(int tble[], int nr, int nc)
{

    void dim();
    int index(),i,j;

    dim(nr,nc);     /* sets values of address polynomial */

    for (i=0; i<nr; i++) {
        for (j=0; j<nc; j++) {
            printf("%2d,%2d = %4d   ",i,j,tble[index(i,j)]);
        }
        printf("\n");
    }
}

/***********************************************************
 *
 *    function to set global variables for addressing a
 *        two-dimensional array
 *
 ***********************************************************/
int origin,imult,jmult;

void dim(int nr, int nc)
{

    jmult = 1;
    imult = jmult*nc;
    origin = 0;

}
```

```
/*************************************************************
 *
 *      function to compute two-dimensional index
 *
 *************************************************************/
int index(int i, int j)
{
    return (origin + i*imult + j*jmult);
}
```

We have included *nr* as a parameter in the dim() function, even though it is not needed. It is easier to simply send both values to the function than to remember which one is needed. By modifying the internal code of dim(), we could store the table in either row-major or column-major depending upon the use.

8.11   NON-RECTANGULAR ARRAYS

The address polynomial, or index polynomial, is a linear polynomial in the indices for a rectangular array. However, it is possible to deal with other shapes. For example, consider a square symmetric table. This is a table of *n* by *n* in size such that:

$$a_{ij} = a_{ji}, \quad i=1,2,\ldots,n; \; j=1,2,\ldots,n.$$

There is much redundant information. For example, the a_{12} element need not be stored explicitly because it is identical in value to the a_{21} element.

$$
\begin{bmatrix}
a_{11} & & & & \\
a_{21} & a_{22} & & & \\
a_{31} & a_{32} & a_{33} & & \\
a_{n1} & a_{n2} & a_{n3} & \cdots & a_{mn}
\end{bmatrix}
$$

Only about half the elements need to be stored since the others are redundant. Let us develop a data structure that stores only the required elements in a vector. We can arrange them in the vector any way we wish, but it is perhaps simplest to use "row-major" ordering:

$$a_{11}; \; a_{21}, \; a_{22}; \; a_{31}, \; a_{32}, \; a_{33}; \; \ldots, \; a_{mn}.$$

Since there is 1 element in the first row, 2 in the second, 3 in the third, etc., the total number of elements is, thus:

$$1 + 2 + 3 + \ldots + n = n(n+1)/2.$$

The logical view will be:

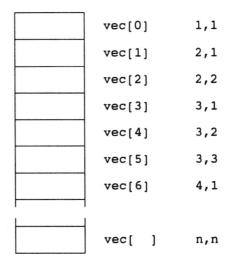

vec[0]	1,1
vec[1]	2,1
vec[2]	2,2
vec[3]	3,1
vec[4]	3,2
vec[5]	3,3
vec[6]	4,1
vec[ ]	n,n

What we want is to specify an index pair, i,j, for the table and compute the correct index into the vector.

First, we notice that for a correct index pair, $i \geq j$; if $i < j$, then we can obtain this condition by interchanging the two indices. Because we are implementing a symmetric matrix, this will not change the desired value.

Second, we note that as we increment j by 1, leaving i constant, the index increases by one. Therefore, the multiplier of j is 1.

Third, in order to get to the section of the vector that stores the i-th row, we must "skip" over $i-1$ rows of length 1, 2, ..., and $i-1$. The total number of elements to be skipped over is, thus:

```
(i-1)(i-1+1)/2 = i(i-1)/2.
```

The appropriate index function then becomes:

```
index(i,j) = v + i·(i-1)/2 + (j-1),
```

where we have subtracted 1 from j because the lower bound is 1.

This formula must produce an index of 0 when $i=1$ and $j=1$; this is achieved for $v=0$.

Therefore our final expression becomes:

```
if i<j, then interchange
index(i,j) = -1 + i·(i-1)/2 + j.
```

Trying some specific values gives the results in the table at the top of the next page.

i	j	Index
1	1	-1 + 1(1-1)/2 + 1 = 0
2	1	-1 + 2(2-1)/2 + 1 = 1
3	1	-1 + 3(3-1)/2 + 1 = 3
2	2	-1 + 2(2-1)/2 + 2 = 2
3	3	-1 + 3(3-1)/2 + 3 = 5

Our final expression seems to be correct. It is not a linear polynomial in the index i (it is actually quadratic in i). This is because the array is not "rectangular," but is "triangular."

8.12   SUMMARY

When programming with an array, the programmer will usually need only be concerned with using an index or indices. However, there are several situations that require an understanding of the way memory is organized and how an array might be stored for efficient access.

Typically, vectors are stored contiguously in the computer's memory. Their linear structure fits the linear structure of the memory. A simple linear expression can calculate an address from a given index—all that is required is the beginning address of the array and the size of each datum.

Tables are two-dimensional and, hence, do not fit directly into linear memory. However, they may be "sliced" apart, either by rows or by columns, and stored contiguously. Both cases produce a simple expression, linear in each index, that can calculate the address.

Addressing schemes for higher-dimensional arrays can be generalized from those used for tables. Both the "row-major" and the "column-major" schemes produce linear expressions in the indices with a simple pattern of determining the multipliers for the indices.

Analogous to actually computing an address is the situation whereby we wish to compute an index into a vector which stores our array.

There are times when we want to conserve memory while storing an array that is not naturally rectangular. Such situations lead to an address expression that is not linear in all of the indices.

REFERENCES

Kernighan, Brian W. and Ritchie, Dennis M., *The C Programming Language*, 2nd ed., Prentice-Hall, Englewood Cliffs, New Jersey, 1988.

Knuth, Donald E., *The Art of Computer Programming*; Fundamental Algorithms, vol. 1., 2nd ed., Addison-Wesley Publishing Co., Reading, Massachusetts, 1973.

Press, William H., Flannery, Brian P., Teukolsky, Saul A., and Vetterling, William T., *Numerical Recipes in C*, Cambridge University Press, New York, 1988.

QUESTIONS

Q8.1   A computer with an address of 17 bits can address how many words of memory?

Q8.2   A supercomputer with a word size of 64 bits can access each word in 100 nanoseconds and add the two 64 bit values in 500 nanoseconds. A desktop computer can access 1 byte in 200 nanoseconds and add two 64-bit quantities in 2,000 nanoseconds. How many times faster is the supercomputer?

Q8.3   What is the difference between 1k and 1K? Is it important or significant?

Q8.4   Integers are typically stored in a format where 1 bit is used to hold the sign information: 0 means that the value is positive, 1 means that it is negative. What is the largest integer that may be represented in a word of:

a.	8 bits	d.	48 bits
b.	16 bits	e.	64 bits
c.	32 bits		

Q8.5   Ultimately all memory references—whether a simple variable name, an indexed array, etc.—must be expressed as what for the CPU?

Q8.6   In most cases, why does it not really matter whether the programmer knows the order in which a table is stored in memory?

Q8.7   Why does a C function not need to be supplied with the left-most "dimension" of a parameter? Why does FORTRAN not need the right-most size of an array?

Q8.8   Why is it useful for the compiler to simplify the address polynomial and compute the constants, rather than leaving it in the more recognizable form?

Q8.9   There is one way to "slice" a vector, two ways to "slice" a table, and six ways to slice a box. How many ways can you "slice" a hyperbox?

Q8.10 When we are implementing an array in a vector of the same type, why is the "width" or size of an item exactly one?

Q8.11   Why is the rectangular three-dimensional structure termed a box rather than a cube?

Q8.12   In a box with row-major ordering, each row is stored contiguously in memory and each plane is stored together. For column-major ordering, which entities are stored contiguously?

Q8.13   In a seven-dimensional rectangular array, which arithmetic operations and how many are required to compute the address of a given element from its indices at execution time?

Q8.14   If the lower bound for each index is 0, then what is the value for v in the address polynomials in terms of the other attributes of the array? (Note, this result is independent of the number of dimensions of the array.)

Q8.15   What are the differences between an address polynomial that computes a physical address and one that computes an index into a C vector?

Q8.16   Will all address polynomials for a rectangular array be linear in the indices, regardless of the number of dimensions of the array?

Q8.17   For a four-dimensional rectangular array that is stored in a column-major order, which index will vary the most rapidly as we move through memory? Which varies the next most rapidly? The least most rapidly?

Q8.18   Why are the terms "row-major" and "column-major" not so well defined for a three-dimensional rectangular array? Why do we use them? How are they consistent with the terminology for tables?

Q8.19   For a table, the number of columns is equivalent to the range of row index numbering and vice versa. What happens with a box?

Q8.20   Do we have to store a vector in contiguous locations in memory? Why is it usually done this way?

Q8.21   What is the basic difference between an address polynomial that gives the actual address in memory and an index polynomial that tells where in a vector, an element of an array is stored?

Q8.22   In our example illustrating the two-dimensional indexing, we implemented two functions that set the values and used them for three global variables:

```
int origin,imult,jmult;
```

How might we have done this without using global variables?

Q8.23 A matrix multiplication of square matrices is defined as:

$$c_{ij} = \sum_{k=1}^{n} a_{ik}b_{kj} \quad \text{for } i=1,2,\ldots,n; \; j=1,2,\ldots,n$$

That is, for a given element in the result we move across the row and down the column forming the sum of the products of those pairs. What is the "big O" behavior of this process?

EXERCISES

E8.1 A two-dimensional array is to be stored in memory in a row-major order. Its dimensions are (6,3), the lower bound on both dimensions is 1, each element takes four words, and it begins at location 4,000.

    a. Draw a picture of how it is stored in memory.

    b. Derive an appropriate address polynomial, reduced to simplest terms (evaluate all factors numerically), that gives the address for the (i,j) element.

E8.2 A two-dimensional array is to be stored in memory in a column-major order. Its dimensions are (5,4), the lower bound on both dimensions is 1, each element takes three words, and it begins at location 2,406.

    a. Draw a picture of how it is stored in memory.

    b. Derive an appropriate address polynomial, reduced to simplest terms (evaluate all factors numerically), that gives the address for the (i,j) element.

E8.3 A three-dimensional array is to be stored in the computer in a row-major order. Its dimensions are:

(2:6,1:4,0:1)

where *x:y* indicates the lower and upper bounds on that dimension, respectively.

    Each element takes two words, and it begins at location 10,400.

    a. Draw a picture of how it is stored in memory.

    b. Derive an appropriate address polynomial, reduced to simplest terms (evaluate all factors numerically), that gives the address for the (i,j,k) element.

E8.4 Consider a six-dimensional array with the appropriate bounds on the indices of $b_f, u_f, b_h, u_h, b_b, u_b, b_p, u_p, b_r, u_r, b_c, u_c$. If each element takes w words, what is the appropriate row-major address polynomial for:

```
array[i][j][k][l][m][n];
```

that is, for the following function?

```
address(i,j,k,l,m,n) = v+mᵢ·i+mⱼ·j+mₖ·k+mₗ·l+mₘ·m+mₙ·n
```

Write expressions for the multipliers $(m_i, m_j, m_k, m_l, m_m, m_n)$ and the constant v.

E8.5 Write a macro for a function A(i,j) that performs the indexing into a vector, vect[], that simulates an n by n matrix where the address of vect[] and n are passed to the function. Thus, we can use the notation A(i,j) inside a function yet it can still operate on matrices of various sizes.

E8.6 Consider a string of bits: 0001001110010101.

In this string there are nine 0's and seven 1's. There are also four 00's, five 01's, four 10's, and two 11's. And there are one 000's, three 001's, three 010's, one 011's, two 100's, two 101's, one 110's, and one 111's. We could continue to analyze this string for occurrences of other bit patterns. To store this data we need:

n_0 n_1

n_{00} n_{01} n_{10} n_{11}

n_{000} n_{001} n_{010} n_{011} n_{100} n_{101} n_{110} n_{111}

n_{0000} n_{0001} $\cdot$ $\cdot$ $\cdot$ n_{1111}

The "row" may be numbered by the number of bits $(1,2,3,...)$ and the values in each row by the decimal value of the bit pattern $(v=0,1,...,2^b-1)$. Thus,

$$n_{bv}$$

will be the number of times a pattern of b bits, corresponding to a value of v, occurs in a given bit string.

That is:

n_{10} n_{11}

n_{20} n_{21} n_{22} n_{23}

n_{30} n_{31} n_{32} n_{33} n_{34} n_{35} n_{36} n_{37}

n_{40} n_{41} $\cdot$ $\cdot$ $\cdot$ $n_{4,15}$

Assume we continue the analysis to store all patterns up to those that are 10 in length.

a. If we store this in a rectangular array, how many elements will there be?

b. How many elements are actually used?

c. If we store them in a one-dimensional array in row-major order; that is:

0	1	2	3	4	5	6	
n_{10}	n_{11}	n_{20}	n_{21}	n_{22}	n_{23}	n_{30}	$\cdots$

what is the appropriate index function of the element:

$$n_{ij}$$

that is:

`index(i,j)`   where `i=1,2,...10` and `j=0,1,...,`2^i-1

Thus:

i	j	Index
1	0	0
1	1	1
2	0	2
2	1	3
2	2	4
2	3	5
3	0	6
4	0	14

Hint: To get to the *i*-th row, we need to skip:

	skip		
1	0		
2	2 =	0+ 2 =	2
3	6 =	2+ 4 =	2+4
4	14 =	6+ 8 =	2+4+8
5	30 =	14+16 =	2+4+8+16

Note: $1+2+4+8+16+\ldots+2^{m-1} = 2^m-1$

E8.7   C stores arrays with 0 starting index; however, often one is given a logical situation where it is easiest to store *N* things that are numbered starting with 1. For a vector, it is tempting to store these in locations 1 through *N* and "waste" location 0; that is, define:

```
        int list[N+1];
```

and use, as an example:

```
        for (i=1; i<=N; i++) {
            ... = list[i];
```

This leaves one location unused or a fraction of unused to usable space given by $1/N$. If N is 100, then 1.0% is unused.

For the two-dimensional situation, we would have:

```
        int table[N+1][M+1];
```

for a N by M situation. How many locations are unused for a table? What percent of the total usable space is taken up by the unused space. If $N=M=10$, what is the specific number of unused locations? The percent of unused as compared to useful locations?

Generalize the situation. Consider the three-dimensional case:

```
        int box[N+1][M+1][P+1];
```

for an N by M by P situation. How many locations are unused for a table? What percent of the total usable space is taken up by the unused space. If $N=M=5$, $P=4$, what is the specific number of unused locations? The percent of unused as compared to useful locations?

Note that for all three of these cases, 100 items are being stored.

E8.8   The simplest entity is a point. If you move a point through some distance, it traces out a line. The line consists of one line and two end points. If you move the line through a distance perpendicular to the first movement, then it traces a square. A square consists of one square, four lines, and four points. Continuing, a cube consists of one cube, six squares, twelve lines, and eight points. This is not difficult to determine. Each line in the square generated a square when a cube was formed, plus the original and final squares make six. Each point in the original square generated a line plus twice the number of points in the square. The number of points simply doubles.

Complete the table that gives the number of entities constituting the given geometric figure.

NUMBER CONTAINED IN THE FIGURE

figure	pnts	lines	sqrs	cubes	hcbs	hhcbs
point	1					
line	2	1				
square	4	4	1			
cube	8	12	6	1		
hypercube					1	
hyperhypercube						1

Hint: Write the recurrence expressions for the number of entities in terms of the number of other entities (in the figure) of one less dimension.

As a matter of information, a hypercube is termed a tesseract.

E8.9   Assume that you want to store a rectangular array in row-major order and all lower bounds are 0. Write out a summary of the address polynomials for the various dimensions from 1 through 7. Notice, particularly, the pattern of the sizes of the array in the various dimensions in computing the multipliers. Repeat for column-major.

E8.10   Consider a pyramidal three-dimensional structure that is analogous to our triangular symmetric matrix. We can picture this in layers as:

```
layer 1:    A
layer 2:    B
            C  D
layer 3:    E
            F  G
            H  I  J
layer 4:    K
            L  M
            N  O  P
            Q  R  S  T
```

Thus each layer is a triangular two-dimensional structure with rows and columns.

Let us assume that all indices begin with 1.

In the layer with index i $(1 \leq i \leq n)$, we have the row index j taking on values $1 \leq j \leq i$ and the column index k taking on values $1 \leq k \leq j$. If we store these as:

```
index:   0  1  2  3  4  5  6  7  8  9
         A  B  C  D  E  F  G  H  I  J ....
i =      1  2  2  2  3  3  3  3  3  3
j =      1  1  2  2  1  2  2  3  3  3
k =      1  1  1  2  1  1  2  1  2  3
```

write out an appropriate index polynomial:

```
index(i,j,k)
```

E8.11   Devise a scheme that would allow a series of numbers to be entered, their average computed, and a list of the values printed out with the deviations from the average. Let the program first ask for the number of values, then loop to request those. To make this interesting, do this using only simple variables; that is, no arrays, no pointers, no dynamic memory allocation!

E8.12   A programmer decided that he wanted to store a 3x5 table in memory in the following order:

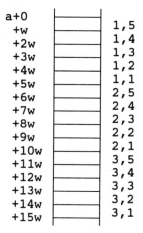

Write out the appropriate (reduced to simplest terms) address polynomial for this situation. Assume a is 1,492 and w is 6.

PROBLEMS

P8.1   Modify the example C functions that implement a two-dimensional table that is to be stored in row-major order in a vector making the dimensions of the table:

1,−1	1,0	1,1
2,−1	2,0	2,1
3,−1	3,0	3,1
4,−1	4,0	4,1

Fill the array, using the modified C functions, with values that correspond to:

$$10 \cdot row + column$$

that is:

```
0        (1,-1)        9
1        (1, 0)       10
2        (1, 1)       11
 .          .           .
 .          .           .
 .          .           .
```

Print out the array in <u>vector</u> form using the ordinary vector indexing, i.e.:

```
for (m=0; m<n; m++)
    printf("%d    %d\n",m,array[m]);
```

```
        0          9
        1          10
        2          11
        ⋮          ⋮
```

P8.2   Write a C program to implement a four-dimensional integer array to be stored in a vector in row-major order. Assume that the lower bound for all dimensions is 1.

```
/* global variables set by dim() and */
/* used by index4() */

    int origin, imult,jmult,kmult,lmult;

/* computes values of the global variables so */
/* index is as simple as possible */

    void dim(nbox,nplane,nrow,ncolumn)
      int nbox,nplane,nrow,ncolumn;

/* used to access the contents of a vector as if */
/* it were a four-dimensional array */

/****************************************************
 *
 *      function to return appropriate index into a
 *          vector for a 4-dimensional rectangular
 *          data structure
 *                  params:     i,j,k,l      indices
 *
 *                  returns:    vector index, 0 origin
 *
 ****************************************************/
int index4(int i,int j,int k,int l)
{
    return (origin+i*imult+j*jmult+k*kmult+l*lmult);
}
```

This minimizes the time during execution by minimizing the arithmetic operations.

The vector: int array[] is then always accessed as

```
array[index4(i,j,k,l)]
```

Write a driver program to use these constructs and perform the following:

a. Fill a 4x5x3x2 with 1000i + 100j + 10k + l using these routines.

b. Print out the array in <u>vector</u> form using the ordinary vector indexing, i.e.:

```
for (m=0; m<n; m++)
    printf("%d    %d\n",m,array[m]);
```

```
    0       1111
    1       1112
    2       1121
    ⋮        ⋮
```

c. For $i=3$, $j=2$, and $l=2$ calculate and print the sum over all possible values of k.

d. For $i=2$, $k=2$, and $l=2$ calculate and print the sum over all possible values of j.

e. For $i=1$ and $j=3$ calculate and print the sum over all possible values of k and l.

f. Repeat parts a, b, c, d, and e for a 3x4x5x2 array. This should involve only changing four constants in your program and recompiling and executing.

P8.3   Write a C program that accepts a string of bits as input, counts the various bit patterns, and then prints the results. Store the data in an array as described in Exercise 8.6. Have it process characters until an 'E' is encountered; that is, it should ignore any characters except '0', '1', or 'E'.

P8.4   Write a C program that will compute the reduced address polynomial and print the first few addresses and indices for a two-dimensional table. The program should request:

a. Size in words of each element

b. Beginning address

c. Lower and upper bounds for row numbering

d. Lower and upper bounds for column numbering

e. Whether row- or column-major ordering is used

It should compute the constants and print a line that looks like:

```
address(i,j) = 1262 + 6i + 2j
```

and a table for the first few (say a maximum of 10) and the last element:

1270	1,1
1272	1,2
1274	1,3
1276	2,1
1298	5,3

Try it for this example and the examples in the chapter:

a. $w = 2$; $a = 1270$; row $= 1,5$; col $= 1,3$; row-major

b. $w = 3$; $a = 1248$; row $= 1,5$; col $= -1,1$; row-major

c. $w = 4$; $a = 4000$; row $= 1,6$; col $= 1,3$; row-major

d. $w = 3$; $a = 2406$; row $= 1,5$; col $= 1,4$; col-major

P8.5 Write a C program much like the one for the previous problem, except have it handle a three-dimensional array.

Try it for:

a. $w = 2$; $a = 14340$; plane $= 1,3$; row $= 1,5$; col $= 1,4$; row-major

b. $w = 3$; $a = 1340$; plane $= 0,2$; row $= 1,5$; col $= 1,4$; column-major

P8.6 Write a C program much like the one for the previous problem, except have it handle a four-dimensional array.

P8.7 Square arrays or matrices are relatively important.

a. Write a C function that takes, as an argument, a square array of size n. The function tests whether the matrix is symmetric or not and returns a 1 or 0,

```
int issymmetric(int mat[], int n)
```

Hint; you will need to treat the matrix as though it were stored in row-major form in a vector.

b. Write a C function that takes, as an argument, a square array of size n, tests whether the matrix is antisymmetric, and returns a 1 or 0, respectively.

```
int isantisymmetric(int mat[], int n)
```

Note: A table is antisymmetric if $a_{ij} = -a_{ij}$ for all possible

values

c. Write a C function that takes, as an argument, a square array of size n, tests whether the matrix is an identity, and returns a 1 or 0, respectively.

```
int isidentity(int mat[], int n)
```

Note: A matrix is an identity if $a_{ii} = 1$ and $a_{ij} = 0$ for $i \neq j$.

Develop a C program that permits the entry of arbitrary-sized square matrices, prints them (using the function illustrated in the chapter), and then tests whether they are symmetric, antisymmetric, or an identity, and prints the results of each test.

Chapter 9

Strings

The twelve jurors were all writing very busily on slates. "What are they doing?" Alice whispered to the Gryphon. "They can't have anything to put down yet, before the trial's begun."

"They're putting down their names," the Gryphon whispered in reply, "for fear they should forget them before the end of the trial."

"Stupid things!" Alice began in a loud indignant voice; but she stopped herself hastily, for the White Rabbit cried out, "Silence in the court!" and the King put on his spectacles and looked anxiously round, to make out who was talking.

Alice could see, as well as if she were looking over their shoulders, that all the jurors were writing down "Stupid things!" on their slates, and she could even make out that one of them didn't know how to spell "stupid," and that he had to ask his neighbour to tell him. "A nice muddle their slates'll be in, before the trial's over!" thought Alice.

One of the jurors had a pencil that squeaked. This, of course, Alice could <u>not</u> stand, and she went round the court and got behind him, and very soon found an opportunity for taking it away. She did it so quickly that the poor little juror (it was Bill, the Lizard) could not make out at all what had become of it; so, after hunting all about for it, he was obliged to write with one finger for the rest of the day; and this was of very little use, as it left no mark on the slate.

9.1   OBJECTIVES

The objectives for this chapter are to:

- Describe what a string is and how C designates a string.

- Discuss string input and output.

- Introduce character operations using C library functions and discuss how these might be implemented.

- Explain string manipulation algorithms and C functions.

- Illustrate sorting with a list of strings.

- Show how string to numeric value processes may be performed.

9.2   INTRODUCTION

The majority of information processing activities involves, not numeric calculations, but the manipulation of characters and sets of contiguous characters termed strings. A **string** behaves as a single logical entity to be manipulated. Unfortunately, the C language does not have a simple string data type as do some other languages, therefore, we need to develop a representation for strings, functions to manipulate strings, and schemes for the input and output of strings.

In practice, strings are represented in a conventional manner. The standard library that is typically supplied with a C compiler contains common routines that manipulate the strings. Hence, the first-time user may simply use these without understanding how they might work. However, a string is an important data structure. Therefore, even though functions are provided in C, we will study the details of how those procedures operate. Indeed, there may be times when we wish to perform some operation with strings for which no standard library function exists.

9.3   STRING REPRESENTATION

A string is stored in the computer in the C language as a **NULL** terminated list of characters. Thus, the "data type" for a string is an array of characters:

```
char strgvar[100];
```

Each element of the array is of **char** type and is usually stored in one byte (8 bits).

Each string is terminated with a NULL character. This character takes on the value of 0; that is, the bit pattern of 00000000. Typically, the identifier NULL is defined in a standard header file as:

```
#define NULL   0   or   #define NULL   '\0'
```

Therefore, in the array *strgvar* there is storage available for a string of 99 characters plus the NULL terminator.

It is important to be able to differentiate between the following entities that appear similar, but are not all equivalent:

0   numeric value 0, generates 00000000

'\0' NULL character, generates 00000000

'0'   character zero, generates 00110000   (using ASCII)

"0"   string constant, generates an address pointing to the two consecutive bytes:

         '0'   00110000
         '\0'   00000000

The first two, of course, are alternative representations of the same value, although the compiler may treat the first, 0, as an integer and treat '\0' as a character. In practice the distinction is generally moot.

Thus, a typical string might be perceived with a "physiological view", halfway between a physical view and a logical view, as:

	0	1	2	3	4	5	6	7	8	9
string	'H'	'e'	'l'	'l'	'o'	'\0'				

We can access individual characters in the string just as we would access individual elements of any list. However, it is often more fruitful to consider the string as a single entity and develop procedures for handling it as such.

We can make a distinction between a list of characters and a string. A string is just a list of characters, but it is NULL terminated. Therefore, all strings are character lists, but not all character lists are strings. The functions that deal with strings generally are given the address of the first character of the string and perform successive operations until a NULL is reached. While the individual characters could be accessed and manipulated by the list above (containing "Hello"), if the NULL were not present, then the string-handling functions would continue until sooner or later a byte with 0 value was encountered or memory limits were reached. The successive characters 'H' 'e' 'l' 'l' 'o', stored in an array of characters, is not a string.

A common error in building a string character-by-character is forgetting to terminate it with a NULL. Strange things then happen if this is used by the string-handling routines! Another common error when defining a string is forgetting to include sufficient space to include the NULL. As an example:

```
char greet[5];
```

which is to store the string "Hello". We need to store six characters, not five!

9.4   STRING I/O

Perhaps the first scheme that might occur to a programmer who is familiar with entering numeric values is to use the scanf() function supplied in the standard C library. The conversion-type specification is simply an *s*. Usage might appear as:

```
char strng[80]

scanf("%s", strng);
```

Since *strng* is an address pointing to the first location of the character array *strng* (&strng[0]), an address operator (&) is not required and should not be used. (We will explore this in greater detail in Chapter 10.)

The scanf() function will append a NULL character to the end of the string.

However, there is a concern and there are problems using the scanf() function for string input. The concern is efficiency. The scanf() function (and the associated printf() function) is a rather powerful function. It converts a series of characters in human-readable form into the appropriate internal binary representation. For numeric data, this may take a rather complicated program. However, for string data the conversion is rather simple—there is no conversion! The function simply stores the characters as they are entered into the appropriate point in memory and stores a NULL character when finished. It would seem that a simpler function might suffice for string input.

The first problem associated with the use of the scanf() function to enter strings is more serious. The scanf() function uses whitespace characters (space, tabs, newline, etc.) in the input string to separate fields that are converted. This is appropriate for numeric data, but it leads to problems with string data where a whitespace character—specifically a space character—might be part of a valid string.

Specifically, the following string "Data structures" typed in for input (without the quotes) and converted by:

```
scanf("%s",str);
```

would result in:

```
'D' 'a' 't' 'a' '\0'
```

being stored in the first five locations (indices 0 through 4) of the character array *str[]*.

The rest of the string, not including the space character, would be left for the next invocation of scanf() or some other string input routine.

The second "problem" is related. The scanf() function will ignore leading whitespace when scanning for a numeric value; however, if you are reading strings, then the whitespace left at the end of one read may be the only thing processed by the next invocation of scanf(). In particular, the newline character used to terminate a keyboard entry will not be part of the first string converted, but will be read by the second invocation. It is awkward to handle strings using scanf().

The simplest and most robust scheme is to use the standard library function of gets(). It would be used as:

```
gets(str);
```

which for the above data would result in:

```
'D' 'a' 't' 'a' ' ' 's' 't' 'r' 'u' 'c' 't' 'u' 'r' 'e' 's'
'\0'
```

being stored in the character array *str[]*.

The function gets() will store the string after stripping off any newline characters (either carriage return or linefeed) and will terminate it with a NULL. This function is also simpler and more efficient than scanf().

Strings may be printed using the standard function printf() and utilizing the conversion type specification of *s*. There is considerable flexibility, using the optional width and justification flag, to place the string where desired. All of the characters of the string, up to, but not including, the terminating NULL, are printed. Unless there is a newline character present in the format specification string, the result of the printf() function will be to keep the cursor on the same line as the printed string at the end of the printed characters.

A simpler function to print a string is the standard function puts(). However, it replaces the NULL character with a newline character '\n'. Therefore, each puts() call will generate a separate line of output.

9.5   *STRING INITIALIZATION*

A string constant may be defined simply by placing the desired characters in quotes. The C language will store the characters with a NULL termination and make the address where the first character is stored available. However, it is often convenient to initialize a string variable. We could, of course, define the string variable, then use string input or the string copy function to store a value in it. A more convenient scheme is to combine the definition and initialization.

First, the character array must be declared to be static, just like its numeric counterpart. (We can initialize a simple variable at the same time it is being defined even though, by default, it is declared to be auto. But an array needs to be declared static.) The simple scheme that is analogous to the integer initialization would be to use:

```
static char string[] = {'H','e','l','l','o','\0'};
```

where we have specified a character for each of the successive locations of the character array *string[]*. It is important to include, explicitly, the terminating NULL. However, since strings are important and useful, it is possible (since it is more convenient) to employ the following:

```
static char string[] = {"Hello"};
```

which results in the storage and initialization as the previous definition. Note that in both cases, the actual storage for *string[]* is computed and set to six characters.

9.6   CHARACTER OPERATIONS

Since a string is simply a sequence of characters stored in a character vector, it is easy to get at individual characters in the string. There are a number of operations and checks that are useful when dealing with characters.

The standard library includes a number of routines that test a character. These are declared in a standard header file and can be "included" in your program via:

```
#include <ctype.h>
```

One example is the function isdigit(). Given a character as an argument, it returns a TRUE value if the character is a decimal digit, 0 through 9, and a FALSE (actually 0) if not. Because the numeric equivalent of the digit characters are arranged consecutively and in order, it is easy to write this logical expression:

```
ch >= '0' && ch <= '9'
```

where the character to be checked is stored in the variable *ch*. The standard library includes a routine called isdigit() that returns this result.

Another standard routine is called isalpha(). This returns a TRUE result if the argument is an upper-case or lower-case alphabetic letter. Because of the numeric equivalent of the letters, this may be simply written as:

```
(ch >= 'A' && ch <= 'Z') || (ch >= 'a' && ch <= 'z')
```

It is much easier to use isdigit(ch) or isalpha(ch) than to write these out.

One single characters operation is to convert a character to upper-case or to lower-case. The standard library includes functions to perform these operations. The function toupper() returns the upper-case version if the argument represents a lower-case letter; if not, it returns the character. We could write such a function as:

```
/*********************************************************
 *
 *     function to convert lower-case letters to
 *               upper-case
 *
 *********************************************************/
char toupper(char ch)
{
    if (ch >= 'a' && ch <= 'z')
        return (ch + 'A'-'a');
    else
        return (ch);

}
```

We have made use of the constant difference between an upper-case letter and a lower-case letter. In ASCII all upper-case letters are 32 (decimal) less than the equivalent lower-case letter. We could use this constant rather than the constant expression 'A' − 'a'; however, it is less to remember if we let the computer compute this value for us. This expression will also work correctly for computers that use EBCDIC as the internal character representation rather than ASCII. In any case, it is the compiler that evaluates the expression; that is, this constant expression will be evaluated at compile time and the appropriate constant used during execution.

Often the standard library will include a simpler and faster routine called _toupper(). This is essentially:

```
ch + 'A'-'a'
```

If the value in *ch* is not a lower-case letter, then the result is rather strange. The use of such a routine should be used only if it is known that *ch* does indeed contains a lower-case letter and speed is important.

There is no standard library function that converts all of the characters in a string to upper-case, although some C library implementations may include such a function. Fortunately, it is easy to write our own function. One simply loops through the characters of the string, replacing each in turn with the result of toupper(). Its heart would be:

```
for (i=0; str[i] != NULL; i++)
    str[i] = toupper(str[i]);
```

The standard library also includes the routines to convert to lower-case: tolower() and _tolower().

9.7   MANIPULATION ALGORITHMS

The kinds of operations used for strings differ from those that would be appropriate for single numeric quantities and even for characters. They also differ from the operations that one would expect are important for lists. As examples: insertion, deletion, sorting, and merging are relatively rare. Catenation is an important operation. Comparison is a major operation but involves the entire string rather than individual elements. Searching the string typically involves looking for the occurrence of one string inside another, rather than looking for a given character.

9.7.1   String Length

Since the string is NULL terminated and no extra quantity is used to record the length of the string, an important function is to determine the number of characters in the string. The standard function that is supplied is declared as:

```
int strlen(char *);
```

The parameter is an address pointing to a string, and the result returned is the number of characters up to, but not including, the NULL.

Keep in mind that a string constant such as `"Hello"` or the name of the character array provides an address to the function.

A C function to perform this might appear simply as:

```
/*********************************************************
 *
 *      function to determine the number of characters
 *      in a string
 *
 *********************************************************/
int strlen(char str[])
{

    int num;

    for (num=0; str[num] != NULL; num++)
        ;

    return (num);

}
```

The example of `"Hello"` contains five characters, not including the NULL. The NULL is stored in location 5 since the indexing begins with 0. Executing:

```
len = strlen("Hello");
```

will result in a value of 5 being returned and stored in len.

This function will perform just like the function supplied in the standard library; however, the library function might be somewhat faster because it would most likely be written to use pointers and generate more efficient code. To use it (or others of the string routines) it is sufficient to include the required function declarations as:

```
#include <string.h>
```

In practice, it is often not necessary to know the length of a string. For example, a loop to access each of the characters might be written as:

```
n = strlen(strg);
for (i=0; i<n; i++)
    ... strg[i] ... ;
```

If this is the only use of the length, then we can substitute:

```
for (i=0; strg[i] != NULL; i++)
    ... strg[i] ... ;
```

Since any non-NULL is treated as True, and assignment not only stores a value but evaluates to that value, this may be written as:

```
for (i=0; ch=strg[i]; i++)
    ... ch ... ;
```

The assignment operation, =, is not a comparison. The "test" portion of the for loop evaluates the *i*-th character of *strg[]*, stores it in *ch*, then checks if it is not a NULL— i.e. True. If it is so, then the loop is executed. When a NULL is encountered, it is stored in *ch*, then the expression is evaluated to False, and the loop terminates. Of course, this makes the code more obscure and a C programmer might expect a == and "correct" it!

Perhaps it really is better to write it as:

```
for (i=0; (ch=strg[i]) != NULL; i++)
    ... ch ... ;
```

9.7.2   String Assignment

Since there is no explicit string assignment operator in C, we must use a function to perform this task. The standard library contains such a function, defined as:

```
char *strcpy(char *, char *)
```

This declaration means that we pass copies of the addresses of the beginning of two strings to the function; that is, we invoke the function using the names of the character arrays that contain the strings. The function returns the address of the first character array.

In practice the return value is discarded, so we will implement the function as a void:

```
/**********************************************************
 *
 *      function to copy one string to another
 *
 *          params:   addresses of the beginning of
 *                    strings
 *
 **********************************************************/
void strcopy(char ds[], char ss[])
{
    int i;

    for (i=0; ss[i] != NULL; i++)
        ds[i] = ss[i];

    ds[i] = NULL;

}
```

The second argument may be the address of a string constant or string variable (a character array). The first argument is an address that generally points to a string variable, although it is possible to point to a string constant. In any case, there needs to be sufficient storage to contain the entire second string.

9.7.3   String Catenation

Catenation is a common operation, and the standard library includes a function that catenates one string onto the end of another. It appears similar to the strcpy() function as:

```
char *strcat(char *, char *)
```

The first string is searched for a terminating NULL, the NULL is then replaced with the first character of the second string (index 0), and the rest of the second string is copied one character at a time, from that point, until the terminal NULL from the second string is found and copied. Therefore, the destination string, now containing all of the characters from both, is properly terminated.

Using our previously defined functions, we might implement this as:

```
char first[50],second[50];

strcpy(&first[strlen(first)], second);
```

Here the strlen() function finds the length of the first string, which is the index of its terminating NULL. The address operator gives the address of this character, and strcopy simply copies the contents of the second string to the first, starting with that address.[1]

As with strcpy() there needs to be sufficient storage in the first character array to hold the combined string.

Occasionally, one wishes to catenate a single character to the end of a string. Since a single character is not a string (it is not NULL terminated), we cannot use the strcat() function. However, it is not difficult to implement such a procedure. The process is to replace the NULL terminating character with the new character and write a new NULL in the next location. In terms of previous functions:

```
len = strlen(string);
string[len] = new;
string[len+1] = NULL;
```

Note that the code on the top of the next page will NOT work correctly:

---

[1]   If we have the definition: char str[20];, then

        str[0]   is a character
       &str[0]   is the address of str[0]
         str   is also the address of str[0]

```
string[strlen(string)] = new;
string[strlen(string)+1] = NULL;
```

The first assignment destroys the string by removing its NULL termination.
Therefore, the second attempt to determine the length of the string fails. However, if
these two statements are reversed, then the procedure does work! Think about it!

9.7.4   String Comparison

The standard C library includes a function to compare two strings:

```
int strcmp(char *, char *)
```

This function returns a value that is:

negative	If first string is less than second
zero	If first string is equal to second
positive	If first string is greater than second

String order is loosely defined as dictionary order; that is, which string occurs
before another in a dictionary. In reality, the rules are simple. We scan the two
strings character by character until either a different character is encountered or the
end of both (a NULL in both) is found. The first different character that is
encountered determines the order of the strings according to the numerical order of
the binary equivalent of the character set. Note that if the end of one string is
encountered before the other, then that string will be "less than" the second, since the
NULL character in the one is less than any other character in the other. If the NULL
is encountered in both strings before any difference is found, then the two strings are
equal. A C function to perform this might appear simply as:

```
/*********************************************************
 *
 *      function to determine the order of two strings
 *
 *          params:   addresses of the beginning of
 *                      strings
 *
 *          returns: negative, string 1 < string 2
 *                   zero,     string 1 = string 2
 *                   positive, string 1 > string 2
 *
 *********************************************************/
int strcmp(char str1[], char str2[])
{
    int k;

    for (k=0; str1[k] != NULL && str1[k] == str2[k]; k++)
        ;

    return (str1[k]-str2[k]);
}
```

The for () loop moves through the string until it finds a NULL in the first one or the first non-equal characters. If these are really different (even if one is a NULL) then it will return a non-zero result. Only if they are both NULL will it return a zero result.

The explicit test for NULL may be omitted in the test within the for (;;) statement since a NULL value is false and any non-NULL is true. We can simply omit the != NULL. Indeed, with pointers, this function may be written even more compactly and efficiently (see Chapter 10).

Another common operation is to search a string for the occurrence of a character or another string. Finding a character in a string is quite easy using a "serial search." Since strings are typically rather short—a few tens of characters—and the characters are not sorted into ascending or descending order, a straightforward serial search is quite satisfactory. The routine can return the index of where the character was found or return an error condition, such as −1, if it is not found.

9.7.5   String Searching

Finding a small string within another string is more complicated. A somewhat brute force scheme is to look first for an occurrence of the first character of the search string in the larger string. Then, when this is found, compare consecutive characters in the two strings until a NULL is found. If the NULL is found first in the search string, then return the index to where the first character was found. If a NULL is found in the large string, then return −1. If a character does not match, then resume looking for the first character of the search string in the larger string. Consider the example:

```
Big pigs like pie after every meal.
```
looking for "pie":

```
0 p
  Big pigs like pie after every meal.        no match

1  p
  Big pigs like pie after every meal.        no match

2   p
  Big pigs like pie after every meal.        no match

3    p
  Big pigs like pie after every meal.        no match

4     p
  Big pigs like pie after every meal.        match

4     pi
  Big pigs like pie after every meal.        try next, match

4     pie
  Big pigs like pie after every meal.        try next, no match
```

```
5         p
    Big pigs like pie after every meal.         no match

          ⋮

14                  p
    Big pigs like pie after every meal.         match

14                  pi
    Big pigs like pie after every meal.         try next, match

14                  pie
    Big pigs like pie after every meal.         try next, match

          next character in search string is NULL, return 14
```

An algorithm to implement this procedure is:

Algorithm SS (String Search) Search a given string, *s2*, for the first occurrence of another string, *s1*. If found, return the index where the match begins. If not found, return −1.

SS1. [initialize]	k=0.	
SS2. [reached end]	If s2[k] = NULL, then Halt.	(not found)
SS3. [first match]	If s1[0] ≠ s2[k], then Go to step SS8.	
SS4. [set index]	j=1.	
SS5. [reached end]	If s1[j] = NULL, then Halt.	(found at k)
SS6. [end of other]	If s2[j+k] = NULL, then Halt.	(not found)
SS7. [compare]	If s1[j] = s2[j+k], then j=j+1; Go to Step SS5.	
SS8. [increment]	k=k+1; Go to Step SS2.	

■

A disadvantage of this procedure is apparent if a partial match is found—then one should be able to use the information gained to reduce the number of comparisons. As an example, when the 'e' was found to be different from 'g' when searching for "pie" (above), then we knew that 'p' was not in "ig"; therefore instead of continuing by comparing the 'p' with the 'i', we could have started with the next character 's'. That is, it should be possible—and it is—never to have to move the index of the second string backwards.

Advanced algorithms that are more efficient than Algorithm SS do exist. However, for the occasional use on relatively small strings, this algorithm may be satisfactory.

9.8   LISTS OF STRINGS

A list of strings may be interpreted as a two-dimensional array of characters. Such a list is defined as:

```
char list[6][10];
```

It may be viewed as:

list

	0	1	2	3	4	5	6	7	8	9
0										
1										
2										
3										
4										
5										

For this example, list[j] is the address of the *j*-th string in the list. Placing the strings `"C"`, `"FORTRAN"`, `"Pascal"`, and `"Ada"` in this list would result in:

list

	0	1	2	3	4	5	6	7	8	9
0	'C'	'\0'								
1	'F'	'O'	'R'	'T'	'R'	'A'	'N'	'\0'		
2	'P'	'a'	's'	'c'	'a'	'l'	'\0'			
3	'A'	'd'	'a'	'\0'						
4										
5										

Since C stores its arrays in row-major order, these would appear in memory (assuming the array is stored with a beginning address of 1,020) as indicated in the diagram at the top of the next page.

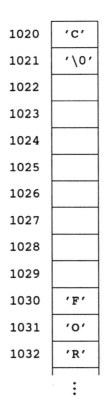

1020	'C'
1021	'\0'
1022	
1023	
1024	
1025	
1026	
1027	
1028	
1029	
1030	'F'
1031	'O'
1032	'R'

Locations 1022 through 1029 would be filled with whatever values might be present before the strings were stored.

A useful situation is to enter a list of strings from the keyboard using a RETURN to signal the end of each line and a RETURN by itself to signal the end of the list. The problem is to perform this efficiently, letting the computer count and store the strings.

The gets() function stores the entered string in the argument. It changes any newline character to a NULL. It also returns a non-zero result until an end of file is encountered. Since we are using a "blank line" to signal the end of the input list, we can exam the first character of the string and terminate the input loop when it is a NULL. Therefore:

```
char str[80];

while (gets(str) != NULL && str[0] != NULL) {
    .
    .
    .
}
```

would test for the end of file and a blank line. Remember that the condition is executed left to right. Therefore, the gets() function retrieves a string and NULL terminates it, checking whether the end-of-file is encountered; if not, it proceeds to check the first character of the string. The loop continues as long as an end-of-file is NOT found and an empty line is NOT entered; that is, it terminates if either the end-of-file is encountered OR an empty string is entered. Within the loop are whatever program statements would be desired to process the contents of the string.

One does not typically encounter an end-of-file when entering strings from the keyboard. In this case, the RETURN on the empty line will signal the termination of the list. If the list has been stored in a file and redirected to the program, then the program may indeed encounter a **real** end-of-file (see Chapter 11). The conditional clause, in the example code segment, will take both cases into account.

The code segment would work for storing a single string, but we wish to enter several into a list and count them. To use a list structure, the code then becomes:

```
char list[50][SIZE];
int n;

n = 0;
while (gets(list[n]) && list[n][0])
    n++;

    ⋮
```

Here, the variable n serves as an index into the list, and counts the strings. Initially $n=0$, and the first string entered is placed into list[0]. If it is an empty string, then the first character is a NULL, and the loop terminates with $n=0$. We have also removed the explicit != NULL since any non-zero or non-NULL value is TRUE anyway.

Note that within the loop no processing of the strings is performed. The loop serves only to input the desired list. The rest of the program then can then do whatever is needed.

To help understand the details of this code segment, keep in mind that:

list	is an address, actually &list[0][0]
list[n]	is an address, actually &list[n][0]
list[n][0]	is a value, character in list[n][0]

9.9   SORTING A LIST OF STRINGS

The algorithms that manipulate a list of strings are identical to those we have presented using integer values (the sorting Algorithms such as: SU, SO, M, and B). However, we must make certain implementation adjustments. If a and b are defined to be int, and u and v are string variables (really character arrays), then

Assignment `a = b;`   becomes   `strcpy(u,v);`

Condition	a < b;	becomes	strcmp(u,v) < 0;
	a == b;	becomes	strcmp(u,v) == 0;

with four other analogous relational expressions.

As an example of a C implementation of one of the algorithms, consider the following implementation of the Straight Insertion Sort (Algorithm I) adapted for a list of strings:

```
/*********************************************************
 *
 *        function to implement a straight insertion sort
 *
 *            params:   list      list of strings
 *                      n         number, indexed 0 - n-1
 *
 *********************************************************/
void insert_sort(char list[][SIZE], int n)
{

    int i,j;
    char item[SIZE];

    for (i=1; i<n; i++) {
        j = i-1;
        strcpy(item,list[i]);
        while (j >= 0 && strcmp(list[j],item) > 0) {
            strcpy(list[j+1],list[j]);
            j--;
        }
        strcpy(list[j+1],item);
    }

}
```

We have made use of the "defined" identifier, SIZE, to specify the shape of the initial list and to provide sufficient temporary storage for any one string in the list.

Remember that to use this sorting function you must:

```
#include <string.h>
```

This will most likely be in your source at the beginning, anyway, if your program is manipulating strings. That way, you have use of the standard library routines throughout your program.

9.10 NUMERIC CONVERSION

Internally, numeric values are represented and stored as bit patterns. However, for input and output they are represented as a series of characters. For most purposes, the standard printf() function handles the complexity of converting the internal value to the appropriate characters that are to be printed, with a variety of chosen options.

In many cases, scanf() performs the inverse for input values, and scanf() does not need to be as complicated as printf(). Generally speaking, it is easier to develop a robust routine that picks a numeric value from a string of characters than it is to write a function that has the flexibility to print a value in a wide range of user chosen formats.

There are several library functions that take a character string and convert the characters that are found to a numeric value. Among these are:

```
int atoi(char *)        converts to a signed integer
long atol(char *)       converts to a long integer
double atof(char *)     converts to a floating point value
```

These may be declared via:

```
#include <math.h>
```

These functions process a sequence of characters that may be interpreted as a numeric value. They terminate with the first character that cannot be recognized as a valid part of a number. As an example, atoi() and atol() recognize an optional sign followed by a sequence of digits. Beginning whitespace characters of *tab* or *space* are skipped, but may terminate the processing.

An algorithm to perform the integer conversion is quite simple:

Algorithm AI (Alphanumeric to Integer) Convert from a sequence of characters representing a valid number to an internal integer value; that is, a string of the form: [white space][sign]digits   where [] indicates an optional quantity.

AI1. [initialize]   value=0; sign='+'.

AI2. [get character]   Set ch to first character in sequence.

AI3. [skip spaces]   If ch is space or tab, then
                         Set ch to next character in sequence;
                         Go to step AI3.

AI4. [get sign]   If ch = '−' or ch = '+', then
                         sign = ch;
                         Set ch to next character in sequence.

AI5. [process digit]   If ch is a digit, then
                         value = 10*value+digit equivalent;
                         Set ch to next character in sequence;
                         Go to step AI5.

AI6. [finish up]   If sign = '−', then value = −value.

The "digit equivalent" is the appropriate numeric value for the character. In C this is obtained by:

```
ch - '0'
```

This algorithm terminates when a non-valid character (including the NULL character signaling the end of the string) is found.

Processing a floating point value is more complicated because there are more optional quantities:

[white space][sign][digits][.digits][E or e[sign][digits]]

Any of the above pieces are individually optional, but there are combinations that must be met. There must be at least one digit in the number portion. If the exponent part is present (an E or e), then at least one digit in the exponent must exist. While each digit processed in the number may result in multiplying the previously extracted value by 10 and adding the digit equivalent as we did with integers, there will need to be a multiplication by a power of 10, one for each digit to the right of the decimal point plus the exponent part, to adjust the final value.

The simplest way to get numeric data into a program is to use the scanf() function. However, the scanf() sometimes does unanticipated things, especially when a string value is also being entered. Therefore, the following is generally more robust; that is, it behaves with fewer problems:

```
char inbuff[20];
int val;

printf("Enter the value:  ");
gets(inbuff);
val = atoi(inbuff);
```

This is, of course, the replacement for:

```
printf("Enter the value:  ");
scanf("%d",&val);
```

The conversion from an internal string to an internal numeric value is performed by the above algorithm and several C library functions. Occasionally, there is the need to convert a numeric value to a string representation. The function printf() performs the conversion but sends the characters to the standard output rather than to an internal string. However, such a function exists! The standard function sprintf() performs the same conversion as printf() but stores the resultant characters in a string. The usage appears as:

```
 sprintf(string, "format specification", list of arguments);
```

The "string" is the address of a character array where the result will be stored. Essentially sprintf() will generate the same characters as does printf(,) except that these are stored as a string; that is, as a sequence of characters that are NULL terminated. An example:

```
char strng[80];

sprintf(strng,"x = %d\n",42);
```

will result in:

	0	1	2	3	4	5	6	7	8
strng	'x'	' '	'='	' '	'4'	'2'	'\0'		

Such a string can be manipulated, additional characters or strings catenated, and printed as desired.

9.11   SUMMARY

A string is an interesting entity. In C, a string is implemented as a NULL terminated character array. The standard C library contains functions to enter and print strings and to manipulate them. It is useful for the programmer to aware of these and to know how to use them; however, it is also valuable to be able to write similar functions.

Generally, changing a function that manipulates a list of integers to one that manipulates a list of strings is a rather mechanical process.

REFERENCES

Kernighan, Brian W., and Ritchie, Dennis M., *The C Programming Language*, 2nd ed., Prentice-Hall, Englewood Cliffs, New Jersey, 1988.

Koenig, Andrew, *C Traps and Pitfalls*, Addison-Wesley Publishing Co., Reading, Massachusetts, 1989.

Sedgewick, Robert, *Algorithms in C*, Addison-Wesley Publishing Co., Reading, Massachusetts, 1990.

QUESTIONS

Q9.1   Write a macro (using a one-line expression) that performs the toupper() function defined in the text.

Q9.2 With an example, show that the following "append a character to a string" operation does not work properly where new is a char variable:

```
string[strlen(string)] = new;
string[strlen(string)+1] = NULL;
```

Why does the following give the proper result?

```
string[strlen(string)+1] = NULL;
string[strlen(string)] = new;
```

Q9.3 In testing the string catenate function (see Problem 9.1) we use:

```
char first[80],second[50];

strcpy(first,"Good ");
strcpy(second,"morning");

strcat(first,second);
```

rather than:

```
static char first[]  = {"Good "},
            second[] = {"morning"};

strcat(first,second);
```

Why would we use the first formulation rather than the second?

Q9.4 Which string is "less than" assuming ASCII representation?

    a. "newspeak" "newsweek"
    b. "newsweek" "news"
    c. "aardvark" "Zebra"
    d. "2"   "10"
    e. "3CPIO"   "R2D2"

Q9.5 In the insertion sort function adapted for a list of strings, why do we need only declare the list as:

```
char list[][SIZE]
```

That is, why do we not need a value in the first set of brackets?

Q9.6 Why would you use ...+'a'−'A' to change a letter to lower-case rather than ...+32?

Q9.7 What would be the appropriate string list array that could be used to store the names of the states of the United States? The names of their capitals?

Q9.8   For a program that deals solely with integers, why might you wish to use gets() and a C function that implements Algorithm AI to input integer values and puts() and an implementation of Algorithm PI to output them rather than using scanf() and printf()?

Q9.9   Why is gets() preferred to using scanf(" %s",) to input a string?

Q9.10   Is there a difference in the result between the following string definitions? If so, what is it?

    a. static char string[] = {'A','l','i','c','e'};

    b. static char string[] = {"Alice"};

Consider the length of the array and what is stored in it.

Q9.11   What is stored in the character array *outbuf* by the following?

    sprintf(outbuf,"%d out of %d girls like C\n", 3,4);

Q9.12   What value is returned by the following?

    atoi(" -42 56 and 21");

Q9.13   What happens if you attempt to use atof() without including <math.h>?

Q9.14   When we are using a library function to deal with strings, what does each require as an argument? For example:

    printf("Last name = %s\n", _____);

What would the printf() function expect to find supplied to it as an argument for the %s specification?
Which of the following would provide this?

    char name[20];

    a. name   d. &name[6]
    b. &name   e. "Alice"
    c. name[3]   f. 'Q'

What about scanf()?

Q9.15   Write a single C statement that would take three int values—hours, minutes, and seconds—and produce a string called *time* that looks like:

    12:34:19 or _9:08:15 or 21:55:02

where a space character is indicated by the underscore.

Q9.16 What is wrong with the following C definition for storing the three-letter abbreviation of the name of a month?

```
char month_name[3];
```

Q9.17 What is the difference in: 'a' and "a"? What happens if you attempt:

```
printf("%s",'a');  or printf("%c","a");
```

Q9.18 What happens if you attempt:

```
printf("%d",'a');  or printf("%d","a");
```

Do you get a 97 (the ASCII equivalent of a) with either? With both? Try it!

Q9.19 In the text, it was suggested that the following would work to append a character onto the end of a string:

```
string[strlen(string)+1] = NULL;
string[strlen(string)] = new;
```

Why is this not a "good" way to perform this operation?

Q9.20 There are several different versions for NULL, namely:

```
NULL   0   '\0'   0x0   etc.
```

In writing your C program how would you choose which to use?

Q9.21 Is it possible to use sets of contiguous characters and manipulate without the NULL terminator? Why or why not? If it is possible, what are the disadvantages?

Q9.22 If a value corresponds to a single digit, 0 through 9, then a single statement call is appropriate to print the digit that corresponds to this digit:

```
putchar(value + '0');
```

If the value corresponded to a single hex digit, 0 through 15, where 10 => 'A', 11 => 'B',...., 15 => 'F', then how could this be written as a single C function call?

Q9.23 How would Algorithm AI need to be modified if the procedure were to detect and print syntax errors in the numeric value—such errors as:

```
−+34  44+34  +      456.34  23Q56
```

EXERCISES

E9.1   Write a formal algorithm to read a string of characters and extract a floating point quantity.

E9.2   Write a C function to convert all of the lower-case letters in a string to upper-case:

```
void string_toupper(char *)
```

It should take, as an example, "R2D2 is a robot" and replace it with: "R2D2 IS A ROBOT" Test it.

E9.3   Using the function in the preceding exercise, also use the Insertion Sort for a list of strings and write a C program to test your routines. It should input a series of strings containing upper- and lower-case letters, change the case, sort them, and print the sorted list with upper-case letters.

E9.4   Write out a C function that performs a binary search on a list of sorted strings. Test it.

E9.5   Write out a C function:

```
int isvowel(char)
```

that returns a True (1) if the character it is given is a lower- or upper-case vowel: {'a','e','i','o','u','y'} otherwise it returns a False (0). Show that it works!

E9.6   Write a formal algorithm that will replace the first occurrence of a string that appears in another larger string with a third string. For example:

replace the word "man" with "person" in:

```
"A dog is a man's best friend!"
```

Use Algorithm SS to find the location of the search string in the larger one.

E9.7   What modifications in Algorithm AI would be required to convert a series of hexadecimal digits into an integer? The hexadecimal digits are: '0', '1',..., '9', 'A', 'B', 'C', 'D', 'E', and 'F'. What would be the change in the "digit equivalent", if both upper- and lower-case letters were recognized as valid hexadecimal digits?

E9.8   What modifications need to be made to the simple list processing algorithms found in Chapter 2 so that they will work with strings? Write them out.

E9.9   A left rotation of a string may be defined as moving all the items in a circular fashion to the left, a desired number of places. As an example, consider the string:

ABCDEFGH

a left rotation of 1 would produce:

BCDEFGHA

a left rotation of 3 (on the original) would result in:

DEFGHABC

It is relatively easy to develop a simple scheme that performs a rotation by one.

a. How many character assignments would be required to perform the rotation by 1?

A rotation by k on a list of n may be implemented by using k rotations of one place.

b. How many character assignments would be required to perform the total rotation by k?

An alternative way is to use a reversal scheme. If we reverse the list containing the first three elements of the above example, we obtain:

CBADEFGH

If we then reverse the list containing the last five elements, we get:

CBAHGFED

Finally, if we reverse the entire list, we obtain:

DEFGHABC

which is just a left rotation by three places.

c. Write out a formal algorithm for rotating a string containing n characters k places to the left.

d. By counting the number of character assignments, determine the exact number to rotate a list of n items k places to the left.

e. Does the result in part d depend upon k?

f. By changing the order of the reversals, we can produce a right rotation. What would be the steps to rotate a list of n items k places to the right?

E9.10 How many different strings of length 10 can be formed from lower-case letters and spaces? If upper-case letters are also allowed, how many are there?

E9.11 Algorithm AI was written in terms of decimal-based numbers. Modify it for changing hexadecimal values represented as a string into an internal numeric value.

E9.12 An interesting problem is to reverse the n characters in a string. This can be done, in place, using one temporary storage location as an $O(n)$ procedure.

a. Write a formal algorithm to perform this.

b. Exactly how many character assignments are needed to do this?

This procedure may be applied to any list of items, not just a string.

PROBLEMS

P9.1 Write a C function to catenate a string onto a second string. You may implement it similar to strcopy() as:

```
void strcatn(char ds[], char ss[])
```

Write it as a complete function; that is, do not use strlen() or strcpy() as was suggested in the text.
   Test it as:

```
char first[50];second[20];

strcpy(first,"Miss Piggy ");   /* fill first */
strcpy(second,"loves Kermit"); /* fill second */

strcatn(first,second);         /* now catenate */

puts(first);
```

P9.2 Write a C function that implements Algorithm AI. Have it return a long integer. Test it on both positive and negative values.

P9.3 Implement the string search algorithm, Algorithm SS, as a C function:

```
int str_search(char str1[], char str2[])
```

It should return the index in str2[] where the string in str1[] is found. If it is not found, then have it return -1.
   Write a driver program to enter two strings, invoke the str_search() function, and print the results.

P9.4   Microsoft BASIC has three functions that return pieces of a string:

LEFT\$(S\$,n)   returns a string consisting of the left *n* characters from the string S\$

RIGHT\$(S\$,n) returns a string consisting of the right *n* characters from the string S\$

MID\$(S\$,k,n) returns a string consisting of *n* characters from string S\$, starting with the *k*-th character

MID\$(S\$,k)   a variant that returns a string consisting of the remaining characters of string S\$, starting with the *k*-th character

Write C functions that perform these actions:

```
void str_left(char dest[], char source[], int num)
void str_right(char dest[], char source[], int num)
void str_mid(char dest[], char source[], int beg,
                                              int num)
void str_remain(char dest[], char source[], int num)
```

where the appropriate characters from source[] are copied to dest[] and NULL terminated.

     If the operation is not possible (for example: str_right("Hello",8)), then dest[0] = NULL. If the operation cannot be totally performed (for example: str_left("Hello",8), then do as much as possible (in this case dest[] contains "Hello").

P9.5   Write a C function that reverses a string in place; that is, the result string is in the same storage area as the original one.

     As an example:

   "When I press this button, time will go backwards."
becomes
   ".sdrawkcab og lliw emit ,nottub siht sserp I nehW"

Write a C program to test this function.

P9.6   For a more interesting problem than simply reversing the characters of a string, reverse the word order. For example:

   "When I press this button, time will go backwards."
becomes
   ".backwards go will time ,button this press I When"

Hint: words consist of letters—these are reversed. Words are separated by non-letters—these are also reversed. You need not attempt to perform this "in place."

P9.7 Write a C function that takes, as a parameter, a string and returns:

0	not a palindrome
1	an ordinary palindrome
2	a perfect palindrome

where a palindrome is a string that is the same forwards and backwards. An ordinary palindrome ignores punctuation and spaces and considers only letters. A perfect palindrome considers all characters. For example:

"Able was I ere I saw Elba"	perfect palindrome
"A man, a plan, a canal, Panama"	ordinary palindrome
"Miss Piggy loves Kermit"	not a palindrome

For simplicity, ignore case for the letters.

Write a C program to test this function. Try the three above as well as:

Never odd or even
Never, ever, ever, even

P9.8 Develop a C program that maintains a simple string list. The main program should ask for the desired action, then ask for the necessary data, then invoke the appropriate function to perform the action.

Operation	Data Required	Printed Result	Action
initial			set n=0
access	index	value	
append	value		
replace	index value		
insert	index value		
delete	index		
search	value	index or not found	
sort			sorts list
print		entire list	
end			end program

Of course, it is appropriate to print messages stating that the action has occurred, that error conditions encountered, etc., as well as printing the desired values.

The program may be structured as:

```
main()
void access(char list[][], int n, int k)
void append(char list[][], int *n, char val[])
void replace(char list[][], int n, int k,
                                    char val[])
void insert(char list[][], int *n, int k,
                                    char val[])
void delete(char list[][], int *n, int k)
int search(char list[][], int n, char val[])
void sort(char list[][], int n)
void print(char list[][], int n)
```

For error conditions, such as the attempt to append onto a list that is full, delete from an empty list, or use an index that is less than zero or greater than n-1, have the functions print an appropriate message and perform no action, but simply return.

Perform the following in order on a list that is 7 locations (0 through 6) in length, each containing the appropriate number of characters needed to store the necessary strings:

1.	initial	11.	append Cat
2.	append Alice	12.	access 3
3.	append Bill	13.	delete 2
4.	append Queen	14.	print
5.	print	15.	sort
6.	insert Duchess at 1	16.	print
7.	print	17.	insert Hatter at 3
8.	search Queen	18.	insert Mouse at 5
9.	search Rabbit	19.	insert King at 2
10.	append Caterpillar	20.	append Dormouse

P9.9   Modify or write a function that performs a Quick Sort on a list of strings. Have it sort the items in ascending order, regardless of the case of the letters. Hint; write a string comparison function that ignores case without actually changing the characters in the strings.

Try it on:

toves
borogoves
raths
Jabberwock
Jubjub bird
Bandersnatch
Tumtum Tree

Chapter 10

C Structures and Pointers

"You are sad," the Knight said in an anxious tone: "let me sing you a song to comfort you."

"Is it very long?" Alice asked, for she had heard a good deal of poetry that day.

"It's long," said the Knight, "but it's very, <u>very</u>, beautiful. Everybody that hears me sing is—either it brings the <u>tears</u> into their eyes, or else—"

"Or else what?" said Alice, for the Knight had made a sudden pause.

"Or else it doesn't, you know. The name of the song is called <u>'Haddocks' Eyes</u>.'"

"Oh, that's the name of the song, is it?" Alice said, trying to feel interested.

"No, you don't understand," the Knight said, looking a little vexed. "That's what the name is <u>called</u>. The name really <u>is</u> '<u>The Aged Aged Man</u>.'"

"Then I ought to have said 'That's what the <u>song</u> is called'?" Alice corrected herself.

"No you oughtn't: that's quite another thing! The <u>song</u> is called <u>'Ways And Means</u>': but that's only what it's <u>called</u>, you know!"

"Well, what <u>is</u> the song, then?" said Alice, who was by this time completely bewildered.

"I was coming to that," the Knight said. "The song really <u>is</u> '<u>A-sitting On A Gate</u>': and the tune's my own invention."

10.1   OBJECTIVES

The objectives of this chapter are to:

- Provide an overview of pointers and pointer manipulation.

- Contrast and compare pointers with array indices.

- Show how pointers can be used within a C program.

- Give examples of how pointers can be used to communicate not only via a parameter list but also as a returned value.

- Demonstrate how list-manipulation algorithms might use a list of pointers.

- Define a C structure.

- Give examples that illustrate how structures are used.

- Present structure operations.

- Discuss pointers and structures.

10.2   INTRODUCTION

One cannot do much programming in C without encountering pointers, pointer variables, and pointer operations. The first introduction is typically the address operator used in the argument to scanf(). Indeed, a pointer is simply an address.

Probably the next situation that you probably came across involved functions that pass values back through their parameter list; the *indirection operator* must be used within the function. However, the use of pointers and pointer manipulation when dealing with arrays gives the programmer considerable freedom and the ability to develop very efficient programs. Here we get to use some of the formulas and concepts developed in Chapter 8!

The mature C programmer will also be familiar with C structures. This is a method whereby the programmer can define record structures. Since functions can return a single value, the use of structures is an obvious choice when several values are to be manipulated.

Combining pointers and structures allows a convenient and efficient implementation of some fairly complex data structures. Stay tuned!

10.3   POINTERS

A pointer is essentially an address. Just as with ordinary values where there are constants and variables, there are pointer values and pointer variables.

For simple variables such as int, double, char, etc., the use of a pointer is limited. However, because C passes information to a function by value—that is, a copy of the original value—such use becomes important if a value must be passed back to the calling procedure via the parameter list. Consider the following function invocation:

```
var = 5;
myfun(var,3);
```

and function definition:

```
void myfun(int x, int y)
{

    x = -1;

}
```

In the calling program the arguments to the function are: *var*, a variable, and 3, a constant. Copies of the values are placed on a stack and it is these copies that are manipulated in the function. They are referenced in the function by the variables x and y. Whatever happens to the values stored in x and y are lost when the function returns to the calling program since these are local to the function and are of storage class auto.

When the function is invoked, the memory might appear as:

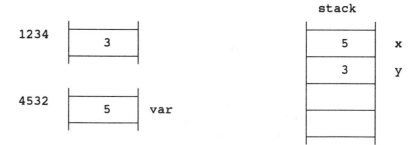

Just before the function returns, these would then appear as:

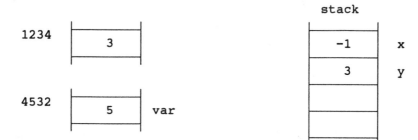

When the control returns to the calling module, the temporary storage allocated on the stack is released for further use.

If we wish to modify a value in the main program, we must explicitly give the function the address of the variable that we wish to modify and, in the function, use the indirect operator. As an example:

```
var = 5;
myfuna(&var,3);

void myfuna(int *x, int y)
{

    *x = -1;

}
```

When myfuna() is invoked, a copy of the address of *var* is placed on the stack. The first line of the function definition includes information that specifies that *x* contains an address; that is, *x* is a pointer. Inside the function the content of *x* is designated by the **x*.

When the function is invoked the memory might appear as:

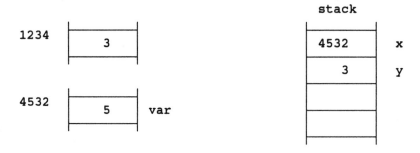

Note that the declaration of *x* is "int *x", which can be read as "x is a pointer to an int" or "the content of x is an int."

Just before the function returns, these would then appear as:

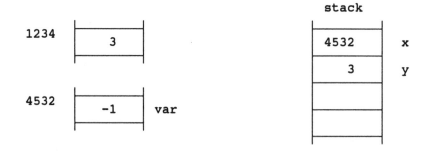

Within the function, assignments to **x* modify the contents of the location that *x* points to. In order to modify *x*, we could use something like: x = 13;.

10.3.1 C Operators

Generally, the indirect operator takes on fairly high precedence; that is, in ordinary expressions *x is evaluated as (*x) before other operations are performed. An important exception is found in the increment and decrement operators, ++ and --.

*x++	means reference the contents of the location pointed to by *x*, then increment the value of *x*; that is, increment the address
(*x)++	means reference the contents of the location pointed to by *x* and then increment; that is, increase the contents by one
*x += 1	has the same result as **(*x)++** as well as ***x = *x+1**
*++x	means increment the value of *x*, the address, then reference the contents of the location pointed to by *x*

The reason for this order of evaluation is to permit the use of pointers in array manipulation without having to use parentheses. In these very common situations, the normal order of operation is to increment the address then reference the contents.

10.3.2 Pointers and Arrays

In C, an array is handled somewhat differently than a simple variable. Generally speaking, it is handled as an address. Consider the following:

```
char strng[80];
```

This definition allocates storage for 80 characters and declares that *strng* is a pointer constant. Let us suppose that this is stored in the computer beginning at address 20180, and that the string "Data Structures" is stored in the array. The physical view would be:

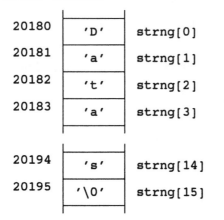

Therefore:

`strng`	an address, it is a constant; in this case, it has the value 20180
`strng[0]`	the first character in the array and in this case has the value `'D'`
`&strng[0]`	the address of the first character in the array, indeed *strng* and *&strng*[0] are identical, with a value of 20180
`strng[3]`	is the fourth character in the string with a value `'a'`
`&strng[3]`	is the address of the fourth character, in this case 20183
`*strng`	is the contents of *strng*, which is `'D'`

We can think of the [] as an operator that acts on an address to give a value just as * acts upon an address to give a value and & acts on a value to give an address. Indeed, there is a simple correspondence between [] and * since both give the contents of a particular address.

$$*(\text{strng}+i) \quad \text{is equivalent to} \quad \text{strng}[i]$$

If all we did was convert one notation into the other, little would be gained. The index notation, *strng[i]*, is probably less abstract and more readable; however, by introducing a pointer variable things can be written in a more compact way.

We can define a pointer to a string (actually a pointer to a character) by:

```
char *cptr;
```

This is now a character pointer variable. Let us assume that it is stored in the computer at address 18920. Most likely, it will be a two-byte quantity.

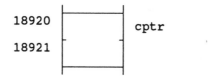

Definition does not initialize it—this may be accomplished by:

```
cptr = strng;
```

Note that both *cptr* and *strng* are pointers. Now,

`*cptr`	gives the first character of *strng*; that is, *strng[0]*, and, in this case, `'D'`

The valuable difference between *cptr* and *strng* is that *strng* is a pointer constant and cannot be changed, whereas *cptr* is a pointer variable and its contents (an address) can be modified.

We cannot get away from using pointers (even though we may be able to remain blissfully unaware) when we use arrays with functions. When an array is used as an argument to a function, C makes a copy of the address and places it on the stack. It is this copy that is passed to the function. By treating arrays in this way, C avoids the overhead of copying the contents of a large array to the stack. Consider the example:

```
{
    int list[20],n;                 /* definition */
        .
        .
    sort(list,n);                   /* invocation */
        .
        .
}

void sort(vector, n)
 int vector[],n;                    /* declaration */
{

    ...vector[i]...;                /* access to list */

}
```

The declaration of the parameters within the function could have equivalently been:

```
void sort(vector, n)
 int *vector,n;
{

}
```

or

```
void sort(int *vector, int n)
{

}
```

The use of the * rather than the [] emphasizes the pointer concept rather than the index concept. In either case, the function only needs to know the address of the beginning of the array and the size and representation of the data (type) in order to access the various elements of the list.

In the calling program, *list* is a pointer constant. In the function, *vector* is a pointer variable. This is analogous to our situation above—i.e., myfun()—with its constant argument and variable parameter.

In either case, the function expects two values: the first is an address and the second is an actual value. In general, whenever a function is expecting an array, it is expecting an address. This is why the scanf() function behaves as:

```
char strng[20];
int x;

scanf("%d", &x);            /* &x is address of x */

scanf("%s", strng);         /* strng is an address */
```

Because scanf() is passing a value back to the calling program, it needs an address of where to store the value. Both &*x* and *strng* are addresses. (Actually, the format string—the "%d"—also passes an address. The "%d" generates storage of three contiguous bytes somewhere in memory, stores '%', 'd', and '\0' in them and places the address of the first byte onto the program stack when scanf() is invoked.)

The use of pointer arithmetic simplifies the use of pointers. Because different data types take different amounts of storage, there needs to be some calculation to adjust for this. When using an index, this is easy to visualize. If array[j] is one item, then array[j+1] is the next item, regardless of the size of the individual items. Similarly, pointer arithmetic automatically takes the size of the item into account. If *aptr* is the address of some element of an array, then *aptr*+1 and *aptr*++ both are the address of the next item in the array, regardless of the size of each element of the array.

In particular, the increment and decrement operators, ++ and −−, allow us to move through a list very efficiently, one item at a time. We do have to be careful about the exact order of execution, since these may be either pre- or post-operations. Remember that ++*k* increments *k*, then evaluates to the new value, whereas *k*++ evaluates to the present value of *k* and then increments.

As an example, assume that in the int array (two bytes per element), array[5] contains a 123, array[6] contains a 42, and *k* contains a 5.

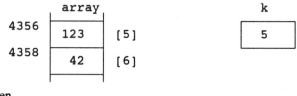

Then

```
array[k++]    evaluates to 123 and k becomes 6

array[++k]    evaluates to 42 and k becomes 6
```

If the pointer variable, *aptr*, is initialized to 4356 (perhaps by `aptr = &array[5]`), then:

`*aptr++`	evaluates to 123 and *aptr* becomes 4358
`*++aptr`	evaluates to 42 and *aptr* becomes 4358

Notice that in both cases the variables that the increment operator apply to—that is, *k* and *aptr*—are changed, regardless of whether the increment is used as a prefix or postfix operator. However, the value of the expression is different. We need to know **which** value the increment operator acts upon and **when** it acts. In the case of **aptr++*, the increment operator acts upon *aptr* because it has higher precedence than does the indirection operator; however, it performs its action <u>after</u> the indirection operator is used to obtain the value of **aptr*. Notice, also, that *aptr* changes by two—the size of the element of the array.

10.4 POINTER USE

The C language defines arrays to begin with an index of zero, with indices taking on values 0 through *n*-1. However, there are times when the problem is more naturally expressed with indices running from 1 through *n*. The classical data structure algorithms are typically written with a "one-origin" array in mind. In our text, they have been carefully rewritten to fit the C language mold. However, it is not difficult to use the power of C and use, in effect, a one-origin list. As you might guess, this involves a pointer!

Consider the list defined as:

```
int list[50];
```

We well understand that the indices take on possible values of:

0, 1, 2, ..., 49.

To this add:

```
int list[50],*lst;
```

where *lst* is a pointer to an integer (exactly like *list*!). We can then include the statement:

```
lst = list-1;
```

Now simply by referencing *lst[i]*, we have an array that has possible indices of 1, 2, 3, ..., 50. In reality, *lst[1]* and *list[0]* are the same. The variable *lst* is, of course, a pointer variable whereas *list* is a pointer constant. If we only use indices to reference values, then it does not make any practical difference.

If an algorithm is written for a "one-origin" vector, the problem naturally fits and it is important to get it working quickly—then this "trick" will work. However, for the programmer who wishes to be proficient in C, it is generally best to work with the C language and become accustomed to thinking in terms of the "zero-origin" arrays that C provides.

We also notice that we can use the pointer scheme and the index scheme for referencing an address interchangeably. That is, even though we defined *lst* as a pointer, we could use an index with it. We could also have utilized **list* to get at a value in *list*, even though it was defined as an array. The only difference is that *list* is a pointer constant and cannot be changed, whereas, *lst* was a pointer variable and could be changed.

10.4.1   String Assignment Example

Using pointers also allows some C programs to be written very succinctly.

Consider an example of a function that copies the contents of one string to another. The typical solution using indices is:

```
void strcopy(char ds[], char ss[])
{

    int i;

    for (i=0; ss[i] != NULL; i++)
        ds[i] = ss[i];

    ds[i] = NULL;

}
```

This function copies characters one at a time from the source string, *ss[]*, to the destination string, *ds[]*, until a NULL is found.

Using pointers, this initially becomes:

```
void strcopy(char *ds, char *ss)
{

    for ( ; *ss != NULL; ss++,ds++)
        *ds = *ss;

    *ds = NULL;

}
```

Since the function receives copies of the actual addresses of *ds[]* and *ss[]*, these may be changed within the function without affecting the values in the calling program. And since these are pointer variables, the declaration *char *ds* and *char ds[]* are equivalent.

We can improve upon this implementation by incorporating the increment and assignment in a while () loop:

```
void strcopy(char *ds, char *ss)
{
    while (*ss != NULL)
        *ds++ = *ss++;

    *ds = NULL;

}
```

The order of the construct *ss++ is, first, to get the contents of the location pointed to by *ss* (*ss), then increment *ss* (a pointer) to point to the next location (ss++). This must be written as is—without parentheses—in order to insure the proper order of the operations. The expression (*ss)++ increments the contents pointed to by *ss*. The expression *(ss++) increments the pointer, then references the value.

We can perform the assignment in the while () conditional:

```
void strcopy(char *ds, char *ss)
{
    while ((*ds++ = *ss++) != NULL)
        ;

}
```

All of the work of the loop is done in the expression of the while () and all that needs to be done within the loop is a null statement.

The assignment of the NULL is made before the while() is terminated, so we do not need the explicit last assignment that used up to this point.

Since a NULL is zero or false and any other character is non-zero or true, this can be simplified as:

```
void strcopy(char *ds, char *ss)
{
    while (*ds++ = *ss++)
        ;

}
```

It should be noted that the library function strcpy() performs a similar process but also returns the address of the destination string. This allows the function to be used as an argument to other functions—if this is helpful. Typical usage simply ignores this return value.

We can add this feature to our function to arrive at the final version:

```
/**********************************************************
 *
 *      function to copy one string to another
 *
 *          paramtrs:    ds    address of destination string
 *                       ss    address of source string
 *
 *          returns:  address of destination string
 *
 **********************************************************/
char *strcopy(char *ds, char *ss)
{

    char *t;

    t = ds;                    /* save address of first */
    while (*ds++ = *ss++)     /* copy second to first */
        ;

    return (t);                /* return address of first */
}
```

Note, that though understanding how the address of an array is passed to a function, there is a simple way to copy only the last part of a string. Consider:

```
        char dest[20],source[30];
```

If the array *source[]* contains the string "Miss Piggy loves Kermit", then

```
        strcopy(dest, &source[5]);
```

would result in "Piggy loves Kermit" being copied to dest[]. This is because *source[5]* is the character ′P′, and thus *&source[5]* is the address of this character. The string copy function simply copies characters from the address it is given until a 0 (or NULL or ′\0′) is encountered.

10.4.2   Date Format Function

The concept of a function returning a pointer is a common one, especially with strings. Consider the example of a date format function, which takes the numerical values of the month, day, and year and returns a pointer to a string with the date neatly formatted. Such a function might appear as:

```
/**********************************************************
 *
 *      function to format a date
 *
 *          params:    m,d,y      month, day, year
 *
 *          returns:  pointer to string;  date as dd MON yy
 *
 **********************************************************/
```

```
char *date_format(int m,int d,int y)
{
    static char mon[][] = {"JAN","FEB","MAR","APR",
                           "MAY","JUN","JUL","AUG",
                           "SEP","OCT","NOV","DEC"};

    static char date[10];

    date[0] = ((d<10) ? ' ' : d/10+'0');   /* set day */
    date[1] = d%10+'0';
    date[2] = ' ';
    date[3] = mon[m-1][0];      /* copy month name */
    date[4] = mon[m-1][1];
    date[5] = mon[m-1][2];
    date[6] = ' ';
    date[7] = (y%100)/10+'0'; /* last 2 digits of yr */
    date[8] = y%10+'0';
    date[9] = '\0';              /* NULL terminate */

    return (date);

}
```

In this function we use string arrays to store a list of the names of the months and a string to store the formatted result. It is important to declare both of these static. In the first instance, *mon*[][], the compiler can only initialize a static array. The reason for the second, *date*[], is more subtle. The compiler will not complain. The function will work correctly, fill the string, and return a pointer to that location in memory where the string is to be found. The problem is that if the string is local, then that memory may be reused before the calling program has a chance to retrieve the desired contents.

Because this function returns a pointer, we could use it wherever a string pointer is expected. For example, the calling program might perform:

```
char date_str[10];

strcpy(date_str, date_format(mnth,day,year));
```

which copies the date string to another string. Or the calling program might print the formatted date as:

```
printf("That date is %s\n", date_format(mnth,day,year));
```

We could have written the function to use standard library functions, such as sprintf(), to fill the string; indeed, the function would contain only one executable line:

```
sprintf(date,"%2d %3s %2d",day,mon[m],y/100);
```

However, the use of a large library function to perform such a simple task might be thought of as overkill. It certainly obscures the details. On the other hand, it is within the spirit of the C programming language to extend the language by using library routines and adding your own functions to a library.

10.4.3 Stacks

While there is generally a simple one-to-one correspondence between an index and a pointer, there are some things that can be done easily with pointers that cannot be conveniently done using indices—generally, the actual machine code that is produced with pointers is more efficient.

Previously, we implemented a stack with a top-of-stack index:

```
{
    int stack[MAX],tos;      /* define stack */

    tos = -1;                /* initialize stack */
    ⋮
    stack[++tos] = ...;      /* push to stack */
    ⋮
    ... = stack[tos--];      /* pop from stack */
    ⋮
}
```

Our picture of this would appear as:

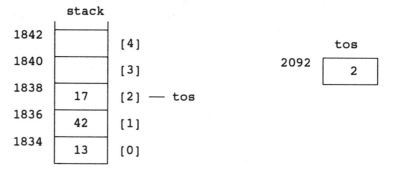

However, it is convenient and more efficient to do this with a stack pointer instead. But first, consider using *tos* slightly differently. Let it be the index of the first element just above the top element of the stack, as is illustrated on the top of the next page.

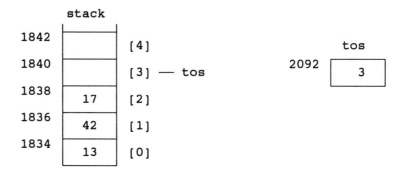

Evidently, an empty stack will occur with *tos*=0. The C code then becomes:

```
{

    int stack[MAX],tos;      /*  define stack   */

    tos = 0;                 /*  initialize stack   */
    .
    .
    stack[tos++] = ...;      /*  push to stack   */
    .
    .
    ... = stack[--tos];      /*  pop from stack   */
    .
    .
}
```

Notice, that we store an item in the location of *tos*, then increment it to the next location. To remove an item, we must first decrement *tos*, then get the value.

This last version can be changed to a pointer version very easily:

```
{

    int stack[MAX],*stk;     /* define stack & top */

    stk = stack;             /* initialize top pointer */
    .
    .
    *stk++ = ...;            /* push to stack */
    .
    .
    ... = *--stk;           /* pop from stack */
    .
    .
}
```

In this implementation, *stk* points to the next available location in the stack, not the element at the top of the stack. As an example, if *stack* is the pointer constant

1834 (this is the address where the *stack* is located in memory) then, after pushing three items onto the stack, we obtain:

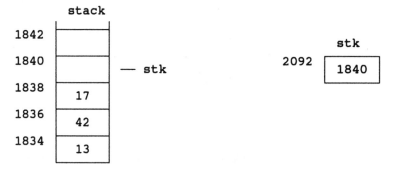

We have diagrammed the stack as we usually picture it, with addresses increasing upwards.

Thus, to push to the stack, we first store the item in the location pointed to by *stk*, then we increment *stk*. This is performed by `*stk++ = ....` When we pop from the stack, we first decrement *stk*, then reference the item: `... = *--stk`.

To expand upon our concept of a simple pointer, just like we expanded upon the concept of a variable, we can declare an array of variables—we can also declare an array of pointers. Of course, this array has an address, which is a pointer!

10.4.4 Sorting a List Using Pointers

The following C program illustrates the use of pointers in sorting a list of items. In this case, the items are strings and the appropriate comparison function is the library function strcmp(char *, char *). The sort function takes as arguments the number of items and a pointer to an array containing a list of pointers to strings. To perform the sort, it rearranges the addresses in the list of pointers without moving the data around.

```
/*********************************************************
 *
 *        driver program for sort using pointers
 *
 *        requests a series of strings from the
 *        keyboard, initializes a vector of pointers
 *        to the vector, calls a sort routine, then
 *        prints the list in order
 *
 *********************************************************/
#include <stdio.h>
#include <string.h>

#define SIZE 100

main()
{
```

```
        void insert_sortp();
        char nlist[SIZE][30],*nptr[SIZE];
        int i,n;

/*      get original list from keyboard  */

        puts("\nEnter list of names\n");
        n = 0;
        while (gets(nlist[n]) && nlist[n][0]) {
            nptr[n] = nlist[n];        /* store string ptr */
            n++;
        }

/*      sort by rearranging pointers  */

        insert_sortp(nptr,n);

/*      print using the list of pointers  */

        for (i=0; i<n; i++)
            printf("%2d    %s\n",i,nptr[i]);

}

/***********************************************************
 *
 *      straight insertion sort function using pointers
 *
 *          params:   *nptr[] pointer to list of pointers
 *                            to strings to be sorted
 *                    n       number of items
 *
 ***********************************************************/
void insert_sortp(char *nptr[], int n)
{

    char *item;
    int i,j;

    for (i=1; i<n; i++) {
        j = i-1;
        item = nptr[i];
        while (j >= 0 && strcmp(item,nptr[j]) < 0) {
            nptr[j+1] = nptr[j];
            j--;
        }
        nptr[j+1] = item;
    }

}
```

The statement in the main program

```
nptr[n] = nlist[n];
```

stores the string pointer constants into a list of string pointer variables so that these values may be modified.

The statement in the function

```
item = nptr[i];
```

is not a string storage assignment, but rather the assignment of an address that points to a string. (Actually, it points to a char.)

The library function strcmp() compares two strings. Since a string in C is a character array that is NULL terminated, the arguments of this function are pointers to strings, just like the strcopy() function we discussed above. The argument *nptr*[j] is the address of the *j*-th string, and *item* contains the address of the item we are trying to insert. Since the actual locations of the strings are not changed, it is not necessary to store the string in a temporary location. The function performs its operation by moving the addresses stored in *nptr*[] so that when the list of strings is printed in the order provided by this index list, they will be printed in order.

It is instructive to compare this function for the Insertion Sort with the one given in Chapter 5 for a list of integers and the one given in Chapter 9 for a list of strings. The basic structure of each is the same. The only differences are the assignment operations, the comparison, and the "type" of the temporary variable *item*.

10.5   COMMAND LINE ARGUMENTS

A C program is executed under UNIX or MS-DOS by entering its name as a "command." When the program is executed it is possible to pass to it information that is included in the same line—the command line.

In reality, a C program, main(), can be thought of as a function that is invoked from the operating system. There are two parameters that allow information to be passed to it:

```
main(int argc, char *argv[])
```

When a program is executed, the operating system parses the command line using spaces as delimiters. It removes the indirection information (that is: < file and > file) for its own use, NULL terminates the other items, and stores pointers to these in *argv*, the argument values. Note that *argv* is a list of pointers to strings. The number of items found is stored in the *argc* variable (the argument count).

The following C program illustrates the use of these:

```
/************************************************************
*
*          program to print command line values
*
************************************************************/
```

```
#include <stdio.h>

main(int argc, char *argv[])
{
    int i;

    for (i=0; i<argc; i++)
        puts(argv[i]);

}
```

The name of the program (including any path information) is the first argument (stored in argv[0]), hence argc is at least 1. It is important to realize that these are strings and need to be converted to numeric values (an internal bit pattern representation), if they indeed represent numeric values.

Using the command line arguments allows us to pass optional information to a program that might control its overall execution. Such optional arguments are sometime called switches. The C compiler is a typical example of a program that uses command line arguments. Other examples might select whether the program is to use color or monochrome display, which files to be use, and the level of sound effects or error messages.

The command line also allows programs to receive information without having to have internal prompts. As an example, consider a program to compute the prime factors of a number.

```
factor 144
 2 2 2 2 3 3
```

is neater than:

```
factor
Enter value:   144
 2 2 2 2 3 3
```

Another useful application is to look for the '?' as an argument and, if found, to generate a short "help" on how to use the program and other information:

```
factor ?
Prime factors, D.A.W., 1990, v 1.0

    factor [value]
```

Of course if the program is executed without any command line arguments, then it should prompt for the value!

Using our example, the factor program might appear as:

```
/**********************************************************
*
*          program to generate prime factors
*               written by D.A.W, 1990, ver 1.0
*
**********************************************************/
#include <stdio.h>
#include <stdlib.h>
#include <math.h>

main(int argc, char *argv[])
{

    long val;

    if (argc == 1) {
        printf("Enter value:   ");
        scanf("%ld",&val);
    } else {
        if (argv[1][0] == '?') {
            puts("Prime factors, D.A.W, 1990, v 1.0") ;
            puts("\nfactor [value]\n");
            exit (0);
        } else
            val = atol(argv[1]);
    }

/*      now process and print prime factors   */

                .
                .
                .

}
```

10.6   *ARRAYS AND POINTERS*

With vectors, the choice of a pointer or an array is arbitrary. That is, parameter declarations of:

```
void fun(int list[])  and  void fun(int *list)
```

are equivalent. However, with two-dimensional arrays there are two alternative ways to implement these tables. The first, the classical method described in Chapter 8, is where the table is stored in consecutive memory locations and an address polynomial is used to compute the address of a given set of indices. As an example, consider a list of strings:

```
char list[6][10]
list
```

	0	1	2	3	4	5	6	7	8	9
0	'C'	'\0'								
1	'F'	'O'	'R'	'T'	'R'	'A'	'N'	'\0'		
2	'P'	'a'	's'	'c'	'a'	'l'	'\0'			
3	'A'	'd'	'a'	'\0'						
4										
5										

Since C stores its arrays in row-major order, these would appear in memory (assuming the array is stored with a beginning address of 1020) as:

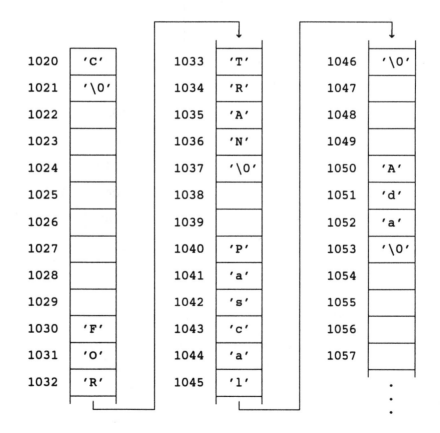

1020	'C'		1033	'T'		1046	'\0'
1021	'\0'		1034	'R'		1047	
1022			1035	'A'		1048	
1023			1036	'N'		1049	
1024			1037	'\0'		1050	'A'
1025			1038			1051	'd'
1026			1039			1052	'a'
1027			1040	'P'		1053	'\0'
1028			1041	'a'		1054	
1029			1042	's'		1055	
1030	'F'		1043	'c'		1056	
1031	'O'		1044	'a'		1057	
1032	'R'		1045	'l'			

The appropriate address polynomial for this situation would be:

```
address(i,j) = 1020 + 10i + j;
```

One way to achieve this via initialization would be:

```
static char list[6][10] = {"C","FORTRAN","Pascal","Ada"};
```

The second possibility is to implement a table using a list of pointers to each row. This allows us to "pack" the strings together and not use the wasted space just to make the array rectangular with all the rows the same length.

Now the addressing behaves like:

```
address(i,j) = list[i] + j.
```

Of course, the list[i] would generate an address polynomial of:

```
address'(i) = a + 2i;
```

One way to produce this structure would be:

```
static char *list[] = {"C","FORTRAN","Pascal","Ada"};
```

The declaration makes it clear that list is a list of pointers to characters.

This second scheme may be faster to execute because it replaces some arithmetic calculations for memory accesses. It generally requires less space (in the first example, there was considerable "wasted" space) even though there is space taken up by the list of pointers. However, it is not convenient to catenate onto one of the strings in the list in the last formulation.

Which one is used is more or less up to the programmer. The declaration of the form:

```
type name[][]
```

suggests a rectangular array, whereas:

```
type *name[]
```

suggests a list of pointers.

We may also build an explicit list of pointers to the rows in our array, as we did in the Insertion Sort example above. In that case, the individual strings were stored in a rectangular array, `char nlist[SIZE][30]`, and we created a list of pointers, `char *nptr[SIZE]`.

Regardless of how the array is implemented, it is important to remember that *list[i][j]* does produce the *j*-th element of the *i*-th row—in this case, a character.

10.7 *STRUCTURES*

Often a simple variable or an array is not sufficient to store a complicated record. Fortunately, C has a construct, called a structure, that allows the user to declare his or her own entity that may be used to store several different items of different type together.

10.7.1 Declaration and Definition

There are certain fundamental data types that are predefined by the C system. Each of these has its own size which, though it does depend upon the system, is predetermined. However, a structure may consist of as many different elements of different types as is desired. We need a way to declare the exact internal structure—one that is as easy as declaring a simple variable or array. This is handled by the **struct** statement. For example:

```
struct time {int hour;
             int minute;
             };
```

This statement defines a new data type called *struct time*. Each element of this type contains two integers—the first is called *hour* and the second is called *minute*.

The word **struct** begins the statement. The name *time* is called the "tag"; it names the structure being defined. It is not a variable name—indeed we are not yet defining a variable—it is more like a type name. This statement may be thought of as the pattern or record structure of something that is called time. However, the names of the variables inside the structure declaration are significant. They become part of the name of a variable that accesses the parts of the structure.

Defining a variable once the structure is declared is simple:

```
struct time now;
```

This defines the variable *now* and allocates space.

Each of the elements of *now* may be individually accessed as:

```
now.hour   and   now.minute
```

where we have used the dot or membership operator. The reference of *now.hour* is an integer.

We can build even more complicated structures. Consider:

```
struct student {char name[20];
                int class;
                double gpa;
                };
```

This structure contains three elements or fields, one of which is an array. Defining a variable is easy:

```
struct student secretary;
```

Thus:

secretary.name	is the address of the array, *name,* in the structure *secretary*
secretary.class	is the value of the *class*
secretary.name[0]	is the value of the first character of the *name*

We also have:

&secretary	which is the address of the structure variable

We can combine the declaration and definition as:

```
struct student {char name[20];
                int class;
                double gpa;
                } secretary,reader;
```

This declares the struct *student* and defines two variables of that type: *secretary* and *reader*.

We can even define a list of structures:

```
struct student classlist[20];
```

which gives us a list of 20 records each looking like struct *student*. Thus:

`classlist`	is the beginning address of the list of structures
`classlist[3]`	is structure number 3 (fourth one) in the list
`&classlist[3]`	is the address of this structure
`classlist[3].name`	is the address of the array, *name*, within the structure number 3 in the list
`classlist[4].name[3]`	references the 4-th (starting with zero) character of the name of the 5-th (starting with zero) student in the class.

10.7.2   C Operations with Structures

An operation that we might want to perform would be to copy the contents of one structure variable to another. We could perform this member-by-member; that is (for the previous example), the assignment operation would take:

```
strcpy(secretary.name, reader.name);
secretary.class = reader.class;
secretary.gpa = reader.gpa;
```

Because this is a common and a rather cumbersome operation which does not lend itself to a generic function, C provides a direct way to perform this:

```
secretary = reader;
```

For this to be possible, the variables on both sides of the assignment must be of the same structure type.

Structures have more in common with a simple variable than the assignment operation. A structure may be passed to a function. Of course, the argument must name a structure and the parameter must be declared to be of that structure tag.

As an example, we could develop a function to print our *student* structure:

```
/*******************************************************
 *
 *      function to print student structure
 *
 *          param:  a       struct student
 *
 *******************************************************/
void print_person(struct student a)
{

    printf("%-30s   %d   %6.2f\n",a.name,a.class, a.gpa);

}
```

As with a simple variable, a copy of the argument structure is placed on the stack and is made accessible to the parameter.

It is important that the declaration of the struct student be accessible to the print_person() function. This means that it should appear outside any function (including main()) exactly analogous to the definition of a global variable. However, the **definition** of a variable of "type" struct student may be within a function block so that the variable is local to that function.

A function can also return a structure. For example, consider a function that adds two time structures where:

```
struct time {int hour;
             int minute;
             };

/**********************************************************
 *
 *    function to add times
 *
 *        params:    t1, t2      structure time
 *
 *          returns:  the sum, with minutes adjusted
 *
 **********************************************************/
struct time add_time(struct time t1, struct time t2)
{
    struct time temp;

    temp.hour = t1.hour+t2.hour;
    temp.minute = t1.minute+t2.minute;

    if (temp.minute >= 60) {
        temp.minute -= 60;
        temp.hour += 1;
    }

    return (temp);

}
```

The function is defined to return a time structure. Its parameters are declared to be of that "type," and an internal variable is defined also to be of this structure.

In the calling program we might invoke this function as:

```
timesum = add_time(span, period);
```

assuming that *timesum*, *span*, and *period* are all defined to be struct *time*!

Therefore, in many cases the use of a structure variable is very similar to the use of a simple variable. If the structure is very large and complicated, it may be better to pass an address pointing to that variable, rather than asking C to make a copy of the entire structure before calling a function.

As you might expect, a list of structures is treated much like a simple list. A copy of the address is passed to the function. Indeed, using a list of structures in a function is very similar to using a list of simple variables.

10.7.3 Sorting a List of Structures

Now we are in position to apply our simple list algorithms to a list of structures. Let us assume that we have a list of students, as we defined previously. We wish to sort these into ascending order by *name*. A C implementation of a Straight Insertion Sort might appear as:

```
/***********************************************************
 *
 *        function to implement a straight insertion sort
 *
 *        params:    list      list of structure student
 *                   n         number, indexed 0 - n-1
 *
 ***********************************************************/
void insert_sort(struct student list[], int n)
{

    int i,j;
    struct student item;

    for (i=1; i<n; i++) {
        j = i-1;
        item = list[i];
        while (j >= 0 && strcmp(list[j].name,
                                        item.name) > 0) {
            list[j+1] = list[j];
            j--;
        }
        list[j+1] = item;
    }

}
```

Note that while we may assign a structure, there is no analogous comparison shortcut. If we wish to determine whether two records are the same, then we must use something like:

```
if (strcmp(secretary.name, reader.name) == 0 &&
        secretary.class == reader.class &&
        secretary.gpa == reader.gpa)
    {action for the two to be equal};
```

Generally, comparison is more useful at the member level; that is, we would probably be more likely to compare two items in a structure variable than the entire contents.

10.8 POINTERS AND STRUCTURES

We can combine the concepts of pointers and structures and define a pointer to a structure. As an example:

```
struct student *sptr;
```

where *sptr* contains an address that points to a **structure** of the "type" **student** once we have initialized it. We can read this definition as: "sptr is a pointer that points to an entity of type struct student."

To access a record using a pointer, we must initialize the pointer to the structure:

```
sptr = &secretary;
```

Then we can use a special operator:

```
sptr->name[0]
```
to access the first character of secretary.name

and

```
sptr->class
```
to access the class datum

These would be equivalent to, respectively:

```
(*sptr).name[0]   and   (*sptr).class
```

The parentheses in this last form are necessary because the member operator is of higher precedence than the indirection operator.

Pointer arithmetic performs properly, even with pointers to a structure. If we have a list of records defined by a struct statement and initialize a pointer variable, *st_ptr*, to contain the address of the first one, then *st_ptr++* or *st_ptr+1* will point to the next one.

It is even possible to include another structure as a member of a structure, as long as the declaration is not done recursively. For example:

```
struct employee {long id;
                 struct student appellation;
                 } clerk;
```

where we have declared the structure *student*, as before.

This construct defines a variable by the name of *clerk* that has data fields of:

```
clerk.id
clerk.appellation.name
clerk.appellation.class
clerk.appellation.gpa
```

Different structures, including those which are nested, may use the same name as a member; there will be no ambiguity since each is a member of a different named structure.

Even though a structure cannot contain itself as a member, it is possible to declare, as a member of a structure, a pointer to that structure; this is quite useful. As an example, we could modify our employee structure to:

```
struct employee {long id;
                 struct student appellation;
                 struct employee *eptr;
                } clerk;
```

Here *eptr*, (actually, *employee.eptr*) contains a pointer to a structure of the "type" *employee*. If it were initialized, then we could access pieces of a structure as:

```
clerk.eptr->id                    or      (*clerk.eptr).id
clerk.eptr->appellation.name
clerk.eptr->appellation.class
clerk.eptr->appellation.gpa
clerk.eptr->eptr
```

The last one is, of course, a pointer value.

It is important to realize that the structure operators, . and ->, the () for function calls, and the [] subscript operator are at the top of the precedence hierarchy. Therefore, if *ptr* is a pointer to a structure with a member *count*, then

`++ptr->count`	increments *count*, *ptr* remains same
`(++ptr)->count`	increments *ptr* before accessing *count*
`(ptr++)->count`	increments *ptr* after accessing *count*

As we have described it, the C structure is basically a record with a fixed number of fixed-length fields. This, of course, is the simplest record structure. As a programmer, one does not have to be aware of the order of the members, since the C compiler references things symbolically through the membership operator. It is possible to set up a more complicated structure through the use of the C union construct. This allows different data types to share the same memory.

10.9 SUMMARY

A pointer is simply an address. When you define an array, you are defining a pointer constant. Pointer variables provide additional flexibility.

Perhaps the simplest use of a pointer is the indirection used within a function that is given an address rather than a value. However, we use a pointer whenever we use an array. An alternative to the standard table is to use a list of pointers to multiple lists. In both cases the use is the same—the compiler produces different code.

C structures are a powerful way of using a more complex "data type"; we can assign structures directly, pass them to functions, and return them from a function. Access to the individual elements of a structure are performed with the membership operator.

As we shall explore shortly, the use of a pointer to a structure provides a convenient way of building linked data structures.

REFERENCES

Kernighan, Brian W., and Ritchie, Dennis M., *The C Programming Language*, 2nd ed., Prentice-Hall, Englewood Cliffs, New Jersey, 1988.

Koenig, Andrew, *C Traps and Pitfalls*, Addison-Wesley Publishing Co., Reading, Massachusetts, 1989.

QUESTIONS

Q10.1   Consider two variables defined as:

```
int x,*p;
```

Assume that x is located at 34210 and p is located at 40200, and the following statements are executed:

```
x = 5;
p = &x;
```

What is the result of the following; that is, what is the value of the expression and what are the values stored in x and p (after executing each of the following, independently)? Assume that an int takes two words of memory.

a. x++   expr = _____   x = _____ p = _____

b. *p   expr = _____   x = _____ p = _____

c. *p++   expr = _____   x = _____ p = _____

d. (*p)++ expr = _____   x = _____ p = _____

e. ++x   expr = _____   x = _____ p = _____

f. ++*p   expr = _____   x = _____ p = _____

Q10.2   What happens if you attempt the following?

a. &42   b. *42

Q10.3   Pointer operations, including indirection, can be rather dangerous if not done carefully. Consider the function defined as:

```
void funny(int *x)
```

   a. What would happen if it were invoked as:

```
funny(3);
```

   b. If an assignment within the function that should have been:

   `*x = 5;`   were written as: `x = 5;`

   what would happen?

Q10.4   A programmer implementing the date format function decided to use the library function strcat() to copy the name of the month as:

```
date[0] = ((d<10) ? ' ' : d/10+'0');   /* set day */
date[1] = d%10+'0';
date[2] = ' ';
strcat(date,mon[m]);    /* copy month name */
date[6] = ' ';
date[7] = (y%100)/10+'0'; /* two digits of year */
date[8] = y%10;
date[9] = '\0';    /* NULL terminate */
```

Why does this not work?

Q10.5   The Straight Insertion Sort function that is given in the chapter sorts a list of student structures in ascending order by name. How would you modify it to sort the same list into descending order by gpa?

Q10.6   In the pointer implementation of a stack, we defined:

```
int stack[MAX],*stk;
```

We then initialized *stk* as: `stk = stack;`

and proceeded to use: `*stk++` and `*--stk.`

Why could we not simply use `*stack++` and `*--stack?`

Q10.7   In the version of the strcopy() function presented in the text, we used a string pointer *t* to store the address of the destination string:

```
char *t;
```

Why did we not use or need?

```
static char *t;
```

Q10.8   Why does C pass a simple variable to a function by value but an array is passed by address?

Q10.9 Consider the following structure and defined variable:

```
struct student {char name[20];
                int class;
                double gpa;
                } classlist[20];
```

Identify each of the following as either an address or a value. Explain, in words, what address or value?

    a. classlist[4].name[5]

    b. classlist[2]

    c. classlist

    d. classlist[6].class

    e. classlist[8].name

Q10.10 What is the difference between *x* and *y* in the following?

```
int x[12], *y;
```

Q10.11 What is the difference between *x* and *y* in the following?

```
void funny(int x[], int *y)
{
    ⋮
}
```

Q10.12 Explain why we cannot define a structure recursively as:

```
struct person {char name[20];
               int age;
               char sex;
               struct person spouse;
               };
```

Q10.13 Why can we define a structure that contains a pointer to that structure as:

```
struct person {char name[20];
               int age;
               char sex;
               struct person *spouse;
               };
```

That is, why is this not recursive?

Q10.14 In the sort that manipulates a list of pointers, the resultant list *nptr* is very similar to an index vector. Is this a "from" or a "to" address vector?

Q10.15 What will be printed if the program to print the command line arguments, called *comline*, is executed with the following?

      a. comline

      b. comline first

      c. comline <comline.c white

      d. comline red >coml.out blue

                (for this one, what are the contents of coml.out)

      e. comline red <comline.c white >coml.out blue

                (for this one, what are the contents of coml.out)

Q10.16 In the declaration of the main program that uses command line arguments, we wrote:

```
main(int argc, char *argv[])
```

Could it have been written as?

```
main(int argc, char **argv)
```

what about?

```
main(int argc, char argv[][])
```

Q10.17 In the standard parameter list for main() to get the command line arguments, exactly what is argv?

```
main(int argc, char *argv[])
```

Q10.18 In a function header, are the following declarations equivalent?

```
void func(int table[N][M])
void func(int *table[M])
```

Q10.19 Consider the following definition and assignments:

```
char ch,*ptr;
ch = 'a';
ptr = &ch;
```

Using *ptr*, how could you access the address of *ch*? The contents of *ch*? The address of *ptr*?

Q10.20 It has been suggested that: "Pointers are the data structures equivalent of "go to" statements." Generally, programmers have learned to avoid using the "go to" statement. Do you think this statement is a valid suggestion? Why should we learn to use pointers?

Q10.21 Why do you think the explicit use of pointers produces faster code than using indexing?

Q10.22 In our example for the initialization of a string array:

```
static char *list[] = {"C","FORTRAN","Pascal",
                                "Ada"};
```

Why did we declare the array as static?

Q10.23 What is the difference between the following definitions?

```
        int *vector[] = {{1,2},{5,7},{8,2}};
```

and

```
        int vector[3][2] = {{1,2},{5,7},{8,2}};
```

Q10.24 In the pointer implementation of a stack, we defined:

```
            int stack[MAX],*stk;
```

What would be the appropriate condition that would tell us if the stack is empty?

Q10.25 Which of the following "defines" and which "declares" *animal*?

a. struct animal {char name[20];
                      int weight;
                      };

b. int animal;

c. void process(int animal[])

d. struct beast {int number;
                      char name[50];
                  } animal;

Q10.26 Why can we perform an operation such as: `list++;` on:

```
        void funct(int list[12])
```

but not on

```
        main()
        {

            int list[12];
```

Q10.27 When C passes a value of a simple variable to a function it makes a copy of that value and places it on the stack. If the entity is an array, what is placed on the stack?

EXERCISES

E10.1   Rewrite the date format function to use:

```
static char mon[] =
        {"JANFEBMARAPRMAYJUNJULAUGSEPOCTNOVDEC"};
```

That is, perform your own indexing into this single string for:

```
date[3] = ....;    /* copy month name */
date[4] = ....;
date[5] = ....;
```

Test it with appropriate input and output.

E10.2   Declare a C structure called *person* that would be suitable for storing a record:

name	20 characters
age	
weight	
height	

Declare a C structure called *address* that would be suitable for storing a record:

street	24 characters
city	16 characters
state	2 characters
zip	5 digits

Declare C structure called *phone* that would be suitable for storing a record:

area code	3 digits
prefix	3 digits
number	4 digits

Use these three structures to declare a C structure that contains:

id	6 digits
name	1 structure of person
local_add	1 structure of address
local_phone	1 structure of phone
mailing_add	1 structure of address
mailing_phone	1 structure of phone

Define appropriate variable names and give the correct C code to access the four-digit number of the local phone.

E10.3   Rewrite the date format function to return a pointer to a string containing the more standard english form of a date:

July 8, 1990

given 7,8,1990.

Use a list of month names defined and initialized as:

```
static char *mname[] = {"January","February",...};
```

Test it with appropriate input and output.

E10.4   What modification would need to be made in the stack C implement outline if we wanted the *stk* variable to point to the element at the top of the stack rather than to the next available location?

E10.5   The C function example that implemented an Insertion Sort on a list of pointers to strings used indexing notation for the elements of the pointer list. Modify it so that it uses pointers to get at this list.

E10.6   Write a string length function that uses pointers; that is, no indices. It should return the number of characters in the string, not including the NULL.

E10.7   Write a string catenate function that uses pointers; that is, no indices. It should return a pointer to the destination string.

E10.8   Consider the structure declaration:

```
struct string {char content[SIZE];
                };
```

and the definitions:

```
struct string s1,s2;
```

Thus we can implement string assignment as:

```
s1 = s2;   instead of   strcpy(s1,s2);
```

What other "string" operations might be implemented directly in C without using functions? Consider the common string operations including initialization, comparison, function arguments, parameters, and return values.

E10.9   A programmer wishes to establish a list of the 50 states of the United States.

a. If these are to be stored in a list of strings as:

```
char states[50][N]
```

what is the appropriate value of *N?* How much total space is required?

b. If these are to be stored with a list of pointers as:

```
char *states[] = {"Alabama","Alaska",...};
```

how much total space is required. Assume each pointer takes two bytes.

E10.10 FORTRAN implements a complex data type; C does not. However, we can define a complex structure:

```
struct complex {double real;
                double imag;
               };
```

In C, we write out functions that perform complex arithmetic. Write out the functions that perform the following complex arithmetic operations:

add
multiply

Each function should take on two arguments, two complex structures, and return a complex structure.

Note: $(a,b)+(c,d) = (a+b,c+d)$
$(a,b)*(c,d) = (ac-bd,ad+bc)$

where (a,b) are the real and imaginary parts, respectively.

PROBLEMS

P10.1 C does not contain a format specification that prints a value with embedded commas. Write a function that returns a pointer to a string that contains the value. Assume an unsigned long int as input. As an example:

```
printf("The value is $ %s\n",commas(1234567));
```

would result in:

```
The value is $ 1,234,567
```

Write a program to test your function.

P10.2 Rewrite the Quick Sort (Algorithm Q) to rearrange a list of pointers to strings. You may use the main() program in the example above, modifying it to print the list before, as well as after, sorting.

P10.3   Write a C function that given (as an argument) a non-negative integer
(unsigned long int) in the range 0 through 10,000,000, will return a pointer
to a string that contains the English equivalent of the number. As an
example:

345,620 would produce:

"three hundred forty-five thousand six hundred twenty"

Write a program to request values, invoke the function, and print the
contents of the resultant string.

Hint, break the value into three parts consisting of up to three digits
each—millions, thousands, and ones. The same function can be used to
generate "three hundred forty-five" as well as "six hundred twenty".

You will need names for the following values:

1, 2, 3, 4, 5, 6, 7, 8, 9, 10, 11, 12, 13, 14, 15
16, 17, 18, 19, 20, 30, 40, 50, 60, 70, 80, and 90

as well as "million," "thousand," and "hundred."

Hint, treat the 0 situation as a special case. (Indeed, it is the only
case where we typically print a leading zero!)

P10.4   C allows us to print a value in a hexadecimal or octal representation with a
standard specification for the printf() function. Write a function that
converts an unsigned 16-bit (or less) value into the binary equivalent. Have
it return a pointer to a string containing the bit pattern. If the original
quantity can fit into 8 bits, then return only an 8 character string otherwise
use all 16 characters. Hint: convert the quantity, then

```
return (strng);     or
return (&strng[8]);
```

As examples: `printf("%d = %s\n",745, itob(745));`

produces: 745 = 0000001011101001

and: `printf("%d = %s\n",65, itob(65));`

produces: 65 = 01000001

Write a program to test and illustrate the use of this function.

P10.5   Rewrite the C function for the Straight Insertion Sort that sorts on the
names of the structure *student* to perform a Shell's Sort.

Write a C program to declare a structure *student*; define a class list
of 20 students; loop and request input to fill the records (three values for

each); print the list; sort the list by name, using the Shell's Sort function; and print the list.

P10.6 The text gives an example where a list of names is sorted by rearranging pointers. It also gives an example where we sorted on a given member of a structure. Combine these two so that you sort on a given member of a structure by rearranging a list of pointers to those structures. Consider the:

```
struct student {char name[20];
                int class;
                double gpa;
                } classlist[20];
```

that we described previously. Write a Shell's Sort function that implements a sort with pointers so that it can sort a list of student records into an alphabetical list. (Hint, modify the Insertion Sort examples.) Enter information for several students, print the original order, sort it, and print the new order. Use one line of output for each record; printing the name, class, and gpa.

Modify the program to sort by gpa in **descending** order. Print the original, sort, and print the final.

Hint: you may wish to set up a file of data that can be read by i/o redirection. This would save having to re-enter the data by hand each time the program is executed.

P10.7 Rewrite the stack version of the Quick Sort, Algorithm QA to use a stack of structures:

```
struct ends {int *left;
             int *rght;
             } stack[N];
```

Store the pointers to the ends of the list to be sorted, and use a pointer to access the stack.

Generate a list of at least 100 random values; print them; sort them; then print them again.

P10.8 Write a program to maintain a simple internal list of records that looks like:

last_name[20]
first_name[20]
birthday
sex

Assume that the records are to be stored in ascending order by last_name.

Hint, define a structure to contain each record.

Implement the following routines:

insert	insert a record
delete	delete a record
print	read and print the file
search	search for desired last name and print contents of record
exit	

Try it with:

1. insert:	Bond	James	2/14/30	M
2. insert:	Fatale	Natasha	5/ 1/36	F
3. insert:	Badenov	Boris	7/21/32	M
4. insert:	Rose	Tokyo	12/ 7/16	F
5. insert:	Leader	Fearless	10/12/22	M
6. insert:	Big	Mr.	5/29/13	M
7. print				
8. search:	Bond			
9. delete:	Fatale			
10. print				

Chapter 11

External Media and Sorts

"The horror of that moment," the King went on, "I shall never, <u>never</u> forget!"

"You will, though," the Queen said, "if you don't make a memorandum of it."

Alice looked on with great interest as the King took an enormous memorandum-book out of his pocket, and began writing. A sudden thought struck her, and she took hold of the end of the pencil, which came some way over his shoulder, and began writing for him.

The poor King looked puzzled and unhappy, and struggled with the pencil for some time without saying anything; but Alice was too strong for him, and at last he panted out "My dear! I really <u>must</u> get a thinner pencil. I can't manage this one a bit: it writes all manner of things that I don't intend—"

"What manner of things?" said the Queen, looking over the book (in which Alice had put '<u>The White Knight is sliding down the poker. He balances very badly</u>') "That's not a memorandum of <u>your</u> feelings."

11.1 OBJECTIVES

The objectives for this chapter are to:

- Present a variety of external media.

- Describe files, records, fields, and their structures.

- Provide algorithms for file operations.

- Give basic information for the C implementation of file structures.

- Discuss properties of external sorts.

- Describe the Radix Sort Algorithm.

- Present the Two-Way Merge Sort Algorithm.

- Analyze these algorithms.

- Show how these external lists can be applied to internal lists.

11.2 INTRODUCTION

The main memory of a computer is generally too small to manipulate large amounts of data. Unfortunately, it is not possible to increase main memory beyond certain limits, even if cost is not a factor. A given computer system is restricted to a limited amount of main memory because of the size of its addresses.

In addition, there is an economic reason for having a balance of different types of data storage in machine-readable form. This balance will include a variety of types of storage media and devices with different characteristics, speeds, and costs.

As we deal with various media, we will discover that their characteristics will constrain the algorithms that manipulate them. One very important characteristic is how we access a given medium. Magnetic tape is the quintessential example of a serial access. One must begin at the beginning and read the data until the desired datum is reached before it may be accessed. Therefore, the time it takes to access an item depends on where it is located. At the other extreme is a random access medium, such as main memory. With this type of access, each datum is directly accessed without having to process any other items. The access time is independent of where is it located. Some devices fall somewhere in the middle. Disks may be randomly accessed by blocks of data. However, the time it takes to access them does depend upon where the data is located, especially where it is relative to the last data accessed. These devices may be termed pseudo-random.

We have studied a number of internal sorts where the information may be stored in main memory. This allows us to access the data randomly. We can move forward and backwards in the data by any amount that we wish, and can swap information with ease.

For large amounts of information stored on an external medium, we must consider procedures that are restricted to reading and writing the data in a serial fashion.

The internal sorts were generally "in-place," requiring little extra storage. External sorts, by their serial access nature, require additional storage. There are typically two copies of the data in existence, at any one time, as the original file is read and a new file is written.

The behavior of the internal sorts could be quantified by the number of comparison operations; however, this is not so relevant for some types of external sorts. Indeed, comparison of keys of large records may be a very fast operation, whereas reading a record from the external medium into memory may be the slow part. Therefore, we will typically characterize the behavior of external sorts by the number of times the file must be read, multiplied by the number of records in the file; that is, the number of read operations.

Since we cannot rearrange elements of a file in place, one might be tempted to sort them by placing them into various "piles" according to their value. These piles would be combined together to produce the final sorted list. Such a procedure is the basis for a distribution type sort. If we had a large enough number of possible piles, then we might end up with one item in each pile, and with many piles empty, then combining these would allow us to sort very quickly. The problem is that setting up and maintaining a large number of piles is generally impractical.

11.3 MEDIA AND DEVICES

Over the years, there have been a number of media that have been used for storing machine readable information. With each, of course, there is a corresponding device. Because the nature of the media and methods of writing and reading have an impact on the algorithms, it is important to understand the limitations of each.

11.3.1 Punched Cards

Punched cards were one of the earliest media used to store data—they were developed and used even before there were computers. The typical punched card measured 3 1/4 by 7 3/8 inches and contained 80 columns—each column consisted of 12 punch positions.[1]

Digits consisted of a single punch per column and upper-case letters were made up of two punches; some other special symbols required three punches in a single column. A space is simply a column with no holes punched.

Punched cards could be randomly accessed by a person with insertion, replacement, and deletion readily performed; however, the cards were serially read and punched by the computer.

Certain computer programming languages reflect their original implementation using punched cards. FORTRAN and COBOL are column oriented, whereas C is much more free formatted. BASIC uses line numbers, which go back to the use of Teletype terminals for entering programs. FORTRAN and COBOL do not use line

---

[1]　The original punched card designed by Herman Hollerith was the same size as the dollar bill at that time. Since then, the size (and value) of the dollar bill has shrunk!

numbers, since editing can be performed manually when the program statements are entered on punched cards.

11.3.2 Magnetic Tape

A fairly old (but still important) method of storing large amounts of information is the use of magnetic tape. This medium is typically on one-half-inch wide 9-track material. The nine tracks accommodate one byte plus an error detection bit (the parity bit) written across the tape.

The surface of the tape is coated with a material that will retain a magnetic field. The data is recorded by a **write** head that produces a magnetic field depending upon the bit to be recorded. This is similar to the analog recording of music on audio tape.

The bytes are written with several different standard densities in bytes per inch (bpi). At 1,600 bpi and a length of 2,400 feet, a tape could hold a maximum of around 44 Mbytes. (Now tapes typically contain much higher densities.) However, tapes are normally not written as a continuous string of bytes. The data is blocked.

A block is the smallest unit of data that is read and written in a single tape operation. That is, an entire block is read at one time. It is normally not possible to read individual bytes. Each block consists of a special byte that indicates the beginning of the block, a special byte that indicates the end of the block, and one or more bytes of error detection. Between each block is a gap in the recorded material—the interblock gap (ibg). This gap is typically around 3/4 inch and is present to allow the tape to stop and start between blocks.

The size of the block is selected with a consideration of the size of the records, the amount of storage available to buffer the block, and the time it takes to read and process the data. Since a block is the smallest unit read or written, there must exist an internal buffer of the size of the block.

As each block is written, a one- or two-byte error detection quantity is calculated and stored with the block. When it is read, this quantity is calculated again and compared to the one on the tape. They must agree. If not, the tape is backed up one record, and the record is read again. Often, an error is a "soft" error and rereading the block will read the data correctly. If the block is too large, this rereading time becomes prohibitive. On the other hand, if the block is too small, a significant fraction of the tape is taken up with the ibg's.

To read an entire tape of 2,400 feet at 120 inch/sec will take about 4 minutes. If the data to be retrieved is, on the average, halfway through a full tape, then the average access time is around 2 minutes. Of course, this is after the tape is mounted. However, once the correct block is reached, then the data may be transferred into the computer at 120 inch/sec * 1600 bytes/inch $\approx$ 190 Kbytes/sec.

A magnetic tape is a totally **serial-access** medium. To reach the data located in the k-th block requires reading all of the previous k-1 blocks; these actually have to be read by the tape drive, and processed, in order to count the blocks and locate the desired one.

The user must also assume that the last block written to the tape is the last physical block on the tape. That is, the only "insertion" operation that is allowed is to append blocks. The reason is that there may be some variation in the actual physical length of a block. If a block is read, the tape backspaced to its beginning, and the block written back onto the tape, then the new block may physically extend past the beginning of the subsequent block.

11.3.3 Disks

With the widespread use of personal computers, the floppy disk or diskette has become quite common. Several years ago, 8-inch disks were customary; then, for some time, the usual was 5.25 inch, but the 3.5-inch diskettes are becoming standard. Not only is the physical size of the disks decreasing, but their storage capacity is increasing. This is primarily the result of more precise and reliable drive technology and more uniform preparation of the magnetic coating on the diskettes.

The diskette stores the data in a series of concentric tracks. A single head on a movable arm slides on the surface of the diskette. The controller and diskette drive cause the head to move to the proper track for reading and writing the data.

Each track is divided into a series of sectors. Each sector is the smallest block of data that may be read or written in a single disk operation. In addition to the data that is stored, there are usually one or more bytes of error detection. These bytes depend upon all the bytes in the block and are computed when the data is written. They are stored with the data. When the data is read, they are computed again and compared with the value read from the disk; if these two are in agreement, it is extremely unlikely that a read error has taken place.

As an example of the capacity of a diskette, the older standard 5.25-inch floppy disk for MS-DOS personal computers (DSDD Double Side, Double Density) consists of 2 sides; each side with 40 tracks, and each track composed of 9 sectors with 512 bytes in each sector. This results in approximately 360 Kbytes of storage. The high-density 5.25-inch disks hold about 1.2 Mbytes of storage. The 3.5-inch disks also come in two varieties: the low-density diskettes hold 720 Kbytes, and the high-density variety can contain 1.4 Mbytes.

Floppy disks typically rotate at 360 rpm. At higher speeds, the flexible surface would vibrate too much and cause problems with the smooth movement of the heads over the surface. Because they are normally not rotating, it takes additional time for the drive to turn on and start rotating, for the head to move to the proper track, and for the correct sector to rotate under the head. Typical access time is, roughly, half a second.

Whereas, magnetic tape is a purely sequential medium, disks do allow some random access to the files. That is, a given sector may be read, modified, and rewritten in the same location. However, a file is typically a sequential structure in that to access the k-th record involves moving through the file until the sector that contains the desired record is found. We can call such an access capability as pseudo-random.

The capacity and speed of a floppy disk are too small and too slow for many applications. The development of a high capacity rigid disk is one of the most significant developments for the computer industry—changing a batch only processing environment to an interactive on-line system.

The technology of a hard disk is very similar to that of a floppy disk. The data is recorded in a series of sectors on concentric tracks. However, because the surface of the disk is rigid, the disk may rotate at a much higher rate of speed, and it rotates continuously. Because of this, it is important that the friction and, hence, the wear on the surface by the head is an absolute minimum. This is achieved by allowing the heads to "fly" over the disk surface on a cushion of air—air that is drawn under the head as the disk spins. The distance between the head and the surface is small compared to the dust or other particles that might settle on the surface if it were exposed to the environment. Hard disks are typically assembled in a clean-room environment and sealed against contamination.

Because they are not easily removed from the computer and transported, they are sometimes called fixed disks.

Hard disks are normally formed with several "platters" connected to a single central axis. Each platter may be prepared on both sides to record data. This increases the capacity without increasing the mechanical complexity. Typical capacities range from a few tens of Mbytes to several hundred Mbytes.

The heads are connected to a single arm that moves them in and out to the desired track. Because a set of tracks forms a three-dimensional structure in space, they may be referred to as a cylinder. There may be several hundred concentric cylinders on a disk, each a designated distance from the central axis.

On the average, the time to access data on a hard disk may range from nearly 100 milliseconds to around 10 milliseconds. This time is taken up in moving the heads to the correct track, as well as in the time it takes for the disk to rotate to bring the correct sector to the read head. However, once the desired sector is under the read heads, the data may be transferred quite rapidly.

11.3.4 Random Access Memory

No discussion of memory is complete without considering random access memory. The heart of any computer's data storage system is main memory. Each word of memory has its own unique address and is randomly accessed. The typical access time is of the order of 0.1 microseconds or less.

During the 1960's and 70's, main memory often consisted of small doughnut-shaped cores of magnetic material (hence the designation of core memory). These cores were strung on an array of tiny wires. Electrical current in the wires could magnetize the cores in either of two magnetic directions—storing a zero or a one. An important feature was that the data was retained even with the power turned off. More recent developments generally use semiconductor memory (RAM or Random Access Memory). While this is volatile—and the data is lost if the power is turned off—it is faster, more compact, and less expensive than core memory.

The limitation on the amount of main memory is determined by the number of bits in the address provided by the design of the CPU and the associated circuitry.

Because of the rapid drop in cost of semiconductor memory, it is becoming increasingly cost effective to use large amounts of the semiconductor memory to replace a magnetic medium device. Of course, one must include the cost of some provision for battery backup in order to keep the memory powered so that it does not lose its contents. However, in this case the semiconductor memory—even though it may be composed of the same components as the main memory—is still secondary storage. Data and programs still need to be transferred into main memory for access by the CPU.

11.4 FILES, RECORDS, AND FIELDS

A **file** is a collection of records. Each record is similar in structure and stores data concerning a single entity.

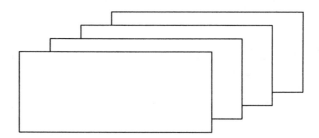

A file is typically stored in a serial or pseudo-random access device.

A **record** is a collection of fields. Each **field** stores some a datum concerning the entity. Typically, each field in a record is different in size and in the type of data stored.

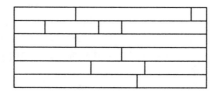

The field that uniquely identifies a record is termed the **key**.

Each field has certain attributes:

    name
    length
    type
    range

granularity
location

The *name* is the logical identifier of the field, like a variable name. Usually it is chosen to be mnemonic. The size or *length* is normally measured in bytes; however, it is possible to have bit fields. The *type* refers to the representation of the data in terms of the bit patterns.

Not all data that appears numeric is, in fact, numeric in nature. Numeric values are data that are subject to arithmetic operations. An example is the height of a person. An appropriate value to compute is the average height of a group of persons. On the other hand, zip codes appear to be numeric, but are really alphanumeric in nature. They are arbitrary identifiers that happen to consist only of digits.

Within a C program, we can represent and declare a record using the C structure; then define variables to hold the record information.

11.5   FILE OPERATIONS

A practical difference between internal lists and external files is that, typically, the length of an internal list is known—we have usually written the algorithms for a list, *LIST*, of length *n*—whereas for an external file, the length is often not known. The last record on the file is marked with an End-of-File (EOF) indicator. The file read routines return a special EOF value if there is an attempt to read beyond the last record. In this way, a file is analogous to a C string with its terminating NULL.

The second difference is that we can access a specific value in an internal list several times, but an external file is accessed by reading a record into an internal buffer. Once the item is read, the record pointer to that position in the file moves to the next item. If we need to access the data several times, we must access the internal copy. When we are finished with that record, we must read the next one into the internal buffer. That is, we must separate the physical accessing of a record and repeated comparisons. This is illustrated by the diagram on the top of the next page.

The combination of the always-moving-forward record pointer and the EOF marker used to signify the end of the file means that when we do read, we must immediately check to see whether the read was successful; that is, if a record was actually read and an EOF was not found.

As an example, consider the Serial Search Algorithm on an ordered list, Algorithm SO. It contains:

SO3. [compare]   If KEY = LIST[i], then Halt.   (found at i)

SO4. [gone past?]   If KEY < LIST[i], then Halt.   (not found)

Here we access *LIST[i]* twice. For a file search, these two need to be modified.

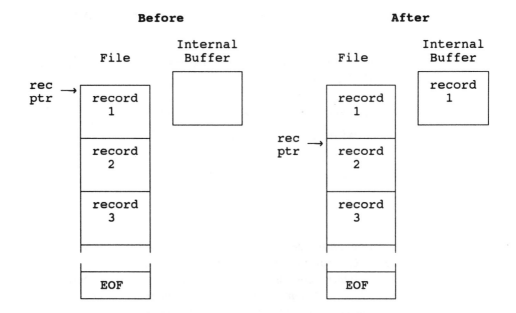

The Serial Search Algorithm for files becomes:

Algorithm FS (Serial Search on Ordered File). Given a file, *FILE*, with items arranged in ascending order, find the record of the key, *KEY*.

FS1. [initialize]   Set file to the beginning.

FS2. [read record]   Read rec from FILE;
                         If EOF, then halt.   (not found)

FS3. [compare]   If KEY = key of rec, then Halt.   (found it)

FS4. [gone past?]   If KEY < key of rec, then Halt.   (not found)

FS5. [loop]   Go to step FS2.

       Generally, we are not so interested in where the record is found in the file, but, rather, would like to have the entire contents of the record that has the desired key field. Therefore, we might return the entire record to the calling module rather than just the index, as we did for an internal list.

       Our algorithms for accessing a file, while very similar to the ones that access an internal list, will differ in their details. They will also differ from those that process strings.

       As an example, consider the operation of copying a file. Because a serial file does not allow random access, the processes of insertion, replacement, and deletion will involve copying the file from one device to another. A file copy algorithm might appear as:

Algorithm FC (File copy). Copies records one at a time from file, *FILE1*, to a second file, *FILE2*.

FC1. [set to beginning]   Set both files to the beginning.

FC2. [read record]   Read rec from FILE1;
If EOF, then Halt.

FC2. [write record]   Write rec to FILE2.

FC3. [loop]   Go to step FC2.

The conditional statement in step FC2 checks to see if the attempt to read a record from *FILE1* failed because of the End-of-File condition.

Similar algorithms would permit insertion, replacement, or deletion. Records would be copied from one file to the other until the appropriate record is reached. Then the new one is copied to the output file—for insertion or replacement. The last one read is then discarded—for replacement or deletion, and the rest of the input file is copied to the second file.

The algorithm for merging two ordered files into a third one is similar to the one for list merging. However, since we must physically read a record and then use that for comparison until it is finally written to the output file, there are some complications that do not appear in the List Merge Algorithm.

In particular, we have to be very careful to keep track of whether a record has been read or not and whether the internal copy is up to date. Once we have read a record, the position in the file moves to the next record. We cannot back up and reread a record.

A straightforward implementation starting with Algorithm M yields:

Algorithm FM' (File Merge). Given two files, *FILEA* and *FILEB*, merge them into a single resultant file, *FILEC*. It is assumed that each file ends with an EOF, which is detected upon a read attempt, and that initially all files are positioned at their beginning.

FM1'. [get record from A]   Read recA from FILEA;
If EOF, then Go to step FM6'.

FM2'. [get record from B]   Read recB from FILEB;
If EOF, then Go to step FM7'.

FM3'. [compare and write]

If recA < recB,
    then Write recA to FILEC;
        Read recA from FILEA;
        If EOF, then Go to step FM5'.
    else Write recB to FILEC;
        Read recB from FILEB;
        If EOF, then Go to step FM7'.

FM4'. [loop]

Go to step FM3'.

FM5'. [EOF on FILEA]

Write recB to FILEC.

FM6'. [get next from B]

Read recB from FILEB;
If EOF, then Halt.
    else Go to step FM5'.

FM7'. [EOF on FILEB]

Write recA to FILEC.

FM8'. [get next from A]

Read recA from FILEA;
If EOF, then Halt.
    else Go to step FM7'.

We reach step FM5' only from within the loop consisting of steps FM3' and FM4'. When we get there, we have read a record into memory from *FILEB* and are ready to write it. The first test for EOF on *FILEA* (step FM1') thus branches to FM6' because we have not yet read a record from *FILEB* and do not have one ready to be written. On the other hand, we get to step FM7' whenever we encounter an EOF on *FILEB*; either because the file is empty or we have found the end within the processing loop. In both cases, we have read a record from *FILEA* into memory, and are ready to write it to the output file, *FILEC*.

    Algorithm FM' is particularly difficult to implement in a structured manner. The problem is that steps FM1' and FM2' branch to different places in the ending portion. It is probably simplest to introduce some redundant instructions as:

FM1". [get record from A]

Read recA from FILEA;
If not EOF, then Go to step FM2".

FM1.5". [get next from B]

Read recB from FILEB;
If EOF, then Halt.
    else Write recB to FILEC;
        Go to step FM1.5".

FM2". [get record from B]

Read recB from FILEB;
If not EOF, then Go to step FM3".
Write recA to FILEC.

FM2.5". [get next from A]   Read recA from FILEA;
                                 If EOF, then Halt.
                                  else Write recA to FILEC;
                                   Go to step FM2.5".

   The net effect is that we handle the situation with one of the files being empty, as a special case. In the case where both files originally had some records and we have reached the end of one of them, the last few steps of the algorithm then need only be concerned with copying the rest of the list. This makes the main loop (steps FM3' and FM4') also easier to write, using structured C constructs.

   Using two "flags" results in a rather structured algorithm that can be converted into C code easily. When C performs a file read, using fgets(), it will return a NULL if the EOF is encountered, and a non-NULL if the read is successful (actually the value of the pointer to the string). We can store this return value into a flag for each file. The resultant algorithm is:

Algorithm FM (File Merge). Given two files, *FILEA* and *FILEB*, merge them into a single resultant file, *FILEC*. It is assumed that each file ends with an EOF, which is detected upon a read attempt, and that initially all files are positioned at their beginning. It uses two EOF flags, one for each source file, to control execution.

FM1. [get record from A]   Read recA from FILEA;
                                If EOF, then eofa = FALSE.
                                 else eofa = TRUE.

FM2. [get record from B]   Read recB from FILEB;
                                If EOF, then eofb = FALSE.
                                 else eofb = TRUE.

FM3. [loop]   While eofa and eofb are both TRUE, Perform
                                 step FM4.

FM4. [compare and write]   If recA < recB,
                                  then Write recA to FILEC;
                                   Read recA from FILEA;
                                   If EOF, then eofa = FALSE.
                                    else eofa = TRUE.
                                  else Write recB to FILEC;
                                   Read recB from FILEB;
                                   If EOF, then eofb = FALSE.
                                    else eofb = TRUE.

FM5. [copy rest from A]   While eofa is TRUE, then Perform step FM6.

FM6. [write/read]   Write recA to FILEC.
                                 Read recA from FILEA;
                                 If EOF, then eofa = FALSE.
                                  else eofa = TRUE.

FM7. [copy rest from B]	While eofb is TRUE, then Perform step FM8.
FM8. [write/read]	Write recB to FILEC.
	Read recB from FILEB;
	If EOF, then eofb = FALSE.
	else eofb = TRUE.

Because the fgets() function returns a result that matches our desired values for the flags, the steps in the algorithm with reads become, for example, FM1:

```
eofa = fgets(.....);
```

Tracing through the algorithm, you should be able to assure yourself that a write operation and a read operation are attempted only when the corresponding flag is TRUE.

11.6 C IMPLEMENTATION OF FILES

The simplest way that C deals with files is perhaps I/O redirection. Normally, scanf(), gets(), printf(), and the other simple read/write functions use the standard input (stdin)—the keyboard, and the standard output (stdout)—the screen. The screen, of course, serves two functions: 1.) To echo the keyboard, and 2.) To write the output from the program. Typically, C programs are written to take advantage of these two functions so that on the screen the entered values and the output are seen in the proper juxtaposition.

It is possible to redirect the input from a file and the output to a file by specifying the files on the command line when the program is executed. If the name of the program is CPROG, then

```
cprog >outfile
```

will cause all the ordinary output to be written to the file with the name *outfile* instead of the screen. This includes the prompt messages as well as the final results.

```
cprog <infile
```

will cause the program to attempt to satisfy all of its keyboard input by reading lines from the file with the name *infile*. It is important that all the data that the program requests is present in the proper order in the file.

These two may be combined so that the program gets all of its input from a file and writes all of its output to a file by:

```
cprog <infile >outfile
```

A C program can also open, read, write, and close external files. There are several ways to do this. Perhaps the most common is to use a set of library functions. These are declared in the "include" file:

```
<stdio.h>
```

The scheme is based on a special structure that has been defined to be of "type" FILE. File accesses are through a pointer to this structure. This pointer is returned by the open function and is used in the subsequent file I/O functions.

Example usage: `FILE *fp;`

Using this "type" specification, there are several library functions:

`FILE *fopen(filename, mode)`

filename is a string containing the name of the file

mode is one of:

> "r"   Opens for reading, if file does not exist, then the call will fail.

> "w"   Opens a file for writing, if file exists, its contents are destroyed; if the file does not exist, then it will be created.

> "a"   Opens file for writing at end of file, creates the file if it does not exist.

> "r+"   Opens for both reading and writing, the file must exist.

Returns a pointer to the open file if successful, NULL if not.

Example usage: `fp = fopen("infile","r");`

`int fclose(fp)`

Returns 0 if successful, EOF if not (EOF is defined in <stdio.h>).

Files should be closed when the write or read operations are concluded so that the operating system can correctly update the directory and sector usage tables.

Example usage: `fclose(fp);`

`char *fgets(string, n, fp)`

Reads the string from the file, with *n* as the maximum number of characters to be read, and the reading stops when *n*-1 characters are read or the first new-line character is found; the characters are stored in string and a NULL appended (note: the new-line character is retained and not replaced as with the gets() function); normally, a pointer to the string is returned, but if an EOF is encountered, then a 0 is returned.

Example usage: `fgets(buff,80,fp);`

int fscanf(fp,"format",list of addresses)

Returns number of fields successfully converted, EOF indicates an attempt to read end-of-file.

Example usage: `fscanf(fp,"%d %f",&n,&x);`

int fputs(string, fp)

Writes the string to the file pointed to by *fp*.

Example usage: `fputs(buff, fp);`

int fprintf(fp, "format", argument list)

Formats the values exactly like printf() but writes to the file pointed to by *fp*.

Example usage: `fprintf(fp,"%d %f\n",n,x);`

int rewind(FILE *fp)

Repositions the file pointer to the beginning of the file.

Example usage: `rewind(fp);`

The rewind function may also be performed by closing the file then reopening it.

To use a file, we must perform the following:

1. Define a file pointer of the FILE type.

2. Open the file.

3. Perform file input and/or output.

4. Close the file.

It is probably best to close a file as soon as it is no longer needed. This will cause the operating system to update the directory and other tables. If there is a problem, such as a power failure or an infinite loop or other program error, the information that has been previously written to the file is saved, without a problem.

When we implement an external sort on files, we discover that we need to create several temporary files. When the process is completed, these may be removed; indeed, it is probably best to delete these from the system.

The function `fclose(FILE *fp)` detaches the file from access by the program but the file itself still exists.

To delete a file takes the standard library function:

```
int remove(char *file_name)
```

This function returns 0 if the file is successfully deleted, otherwise it returns a -1. Note that this function uses the file name, not the special file pointer.

11.7   *RADIX SORT*

The Radix Sort is one type of distribution sort. Perhaps the original motivation for its development came from the need to perform a sort on a set of punched cards, using a mechanical card sorter. Such a device reads a set of cards and places each in one of a set of bins, depending upon the exact punch in a particular column. By a procedure of separation or distributing, recombining the separate piles in order, and repeating the process on a different column, the cards could be arranged in order, according to several columns. Fortunately, we no longer need to sort cards mechanically; however, the process is easy to visualize.

For a file, the Radix Sort proceeds by reading the items in the file and writing them to a series of auxiliary files. The particular auxiliary file that the item is stored in corresponds to the value in a particular byte. These files are then copied, in order, to the original file so that it is sorted on that particular byte. The not-so obvious aspect, is that the sort should proceed from the least-most significant byte to the most-significant byte.

11.7.1 Example sort

As an example, consider a series of items consisting of three-digit numbers.
Performing the distribution procedure on the right-most digit:

					—— Auxiliary Files ——						
File	0	1	2	3	4	5	6	7	8	9	File	
417	390	731	622	263	304	625	896	417	148	749	390	0
625			502		644			267	978		731	1
304								877			622⌐ 502⌐	2
749											263	3
390											304⌐ 644⌐	4
267											625	5
148											896	6
622											417⌐	
896											267⌐	7
978											877⌐	
731											148⌐	8
644											978⌐	
502											749	9
877												
263												

We proceed down through the file on the left, one element at a time, and copy each to the appropriate auxiliary file. That is, the first item, the 417, gets copied to the "7" file; the 625, to the "5" file; and so forth.

Finally, after copying all of the records in the original file to the auxiliary files, the auxiliary files are "rewound", and we copy from each of these files in turn and in order the elements to a new file on the right (which physically can be the original file). That is, we first copy from the "0" file the items found there, in order, from the first to last, then from the "1" file, then the "2" file, and so forth. The recombined file contains all of the records that were in the original file.

Note, that the final file is sorted according to the right-most digit—the one we performed the distribution and recombination procedures on. That is, all the records with a "0" in the right-most position are found before those with a "1", etc.

Using our rearranged list and repeating the distribution and copying back procedures, but now using the middle digit results in:

```
                 ┌──────────────── Auxiliary Files ────────────────┐
File     0     1     2     3     4     5     6     7     8     9    File
390     502   417   622   731   644         263   877         390   502┐
731     304         625               267   978         896   304┘  0
622                       749                                       417   1
502                                                                 622┐
263                                                                 625┘  2
304                                                                 731   3
644                                                                 644┐
625                                                                 148│  4
896                                                                 749┘
417                                                                 263┐
267                                                                 267┘  6
877                                                                 877┐
148                                                                 978┘  7
978                                                                 390┐
749                                                                 896┘  9
  ^                                                                 **
```

Now the resultant file is in order according to the last two digits. The file is no longer in order according to the right-most digit. However, the "02" occurs before the "04" because both of these were copied to the auxiliary file "0" and the "2" occurred before the "4" after the first pass. On the other hand, although the "22" did occur before the "04" after the first pass, it was copied to the "2" file and hence gets written to the final file after "02" and "04".

Note, that it is not necessary that each auxiliary file have items written to it. In this example, there were no items with middle digits of "5" or "8".

Finally, using this resultant file and performing the procedure on the left-most digit gives:

```
              ┌────────── Auxiliary Files ──────────┐
 File   0    1     2     3     4     5     6     7     8     9    File
 502        148   263   304   417   502   622   731   877   978   148   1
 304              267   390               625   749   896         263┐
 417                                      644                     267┘  2
 622                                                              304┐
 625                                                              390┘  3
 731                                                              417   4
 644                                                              502   5
 148                                                              622┐
 749                                                              625│  6
 263                                                              644┘
 267                                                              731┐  7
 877                                                              749┘
 978                                                              877┐  8
 390                                                              896┘
 896                                                              978   9
 ^                                                                ***
```

We see that the final file on the right is completely sorted, in ascending order!

After observing the sort operate, it does make sense to proceed right-to-left because the left-most digit does specify most strongly where, in the final file, the datum is to go. As an example, a 903 must go near the end of the file as compared to 178, even though the 78 is larger than the 03. It is the 9 that most strongly specifies the final order, hence, that digit position should be sorted on last. The right-most digits are scattered throughout the list and do not appear in order.

11.7.2 Analysis

It is difficult to compare this procedure with our other sorting techniques because, typically, we count the number of comparisons. The Radix Sort makes no comparisons of the data! However, we note that with each pass, each item in the list is examined and moved twice (once to one of the auxiliary files, and once back to the full file). Evidently the total time to execute this procedure is proportional to $2 \cdot n \cdot d$, where n is the number of items in the list and d is the number of digits. In terms of the size of the file, this procedure is O(n). However, the price that one pays for this is the necessity of managing a number of auxiliary files.

With tapes, or even disk storage, the amount of temporary space required is not as much a constraint as it might be using main memory.

11.7.3 Algorithm

An algorithm that implements the Radix Sort on a file is:

Algorithm RF (Radix Sort on a File). Given a file, FILE, rearrange the items consisting of d digits in the file so that they are in increasing order. Uses ten temporary files, FILE(i), i=0,1,...,9.

RF1. [initialize]   divisor=1.

RF2. [loop on digits]   Perform steps RF3 through RF8 for k=0,1,...,d−1.

RF3. [reset]   Set all files to beginning.

RF4. [read record]   Read rec from FILE;
                             If not EOF, then dgt = rec/divisor mod 10;
                                          Write rec to FILE(dgt);
                                          Go to step RF4.

RF5. [reset files]   Reset all files to beginning.

RF6. [read back over j]   Perform step RF7 for j=0,1,...,9.

RF7. [read & write record]   Read rec from FILE(j)
                             If not EOF, then Write rec to FILE;
                                          Go to step RF7.

RF8. [change divisor]   divisor=10 • divisor.

The algorithm and example above illustrate the Radix Sort using numeric data. This was convenient because the number of intermediate files is only 10—a somewhat reasonable number. However, this procedure may be used for alphabetic data. There are two problems that make this more difficult. The first is the large number of intermediate files that are required—at least 26, but probably 52, and possibly more if special characters are used. The second is that alphabetic data generally are longer than numeric data. For example, people's names may take up to 24 or more characters and consist of upper- and lower-case letters, spaces, commas (if last name first), periods (for initials), and other possible characters.

The primary limitation for file sorting is that 26 devices may not be available for the auxiliary files. If tapes are used, then one needs a total of 27 drives. If disk files are used, then it is possible to use a single drive with many files, but the head movement becomes excessive.

One way around this is to consider the binary representation of the data. At each bit position there is a 0 or a 1, regardless of the meaning of the data. Therefore, a file could be sorted with just two auxiliary files. Of course, this means that there will need to be many more passes through the data—one for each bit position in the sorting field.

If more devices are available, say five, then we can reduce the number of passes by considering combinations of bits—in this case two bits, dividing the information according to 00, 01, 10, or 11. By doubling the number of auxiliary files, the number of passes is cut in half and hence the time for sorting is reduced.

11.8   TWO-WAY MERGE SORT

Another, more fruitful, approach is to use a merge scheme; it is reasonably effective, operates on any type of data with equal ease, and also involves making copies of the data and intermediate files. The advantage is that it does not require as many intermediate files (only four at one time) and the number of passes is not as large as sorting with a Radix Sort, using only two bits at a time.

We have observed that a merge operation produces an ordered list if the original lists are ordered. Indeed, if there are n sorted elements in each of the two lists, then the resultant list will have $2n$ sorted elements. Hence, a merging operation might increase the size of sorted lists. It is also a sequential operation suited for files.

11.8.1   Example

Consider this example:

```
        23      18              18
        36      21   merging    21
        43      42              23
        51      48              36
                                42
                                43
                                48
                                51
```

The above suggestion has two practical difficulties that need sorting out! Since a merge operation doubles the number of sorted items, we must start somewhere, and the process may take a number of repeated operations. The first situation is easy. A file of one element is sorted. Hence, two files of one element each may be merged to become a sorted file of two elements. This may be repeated to produce a file of four sorted elements, etc. However, the merge operation takes two files and combines them into one; hence, for the next pass we have only one file, not two.

The most obvious way to proceed is to write n files of one element. We then merge these to create $n/2$ files of two elements (with the possibility that one file has only one element), then $n/4$ files each with four elements, and continuing on until only one file remains, which is sorted. However, it is not practical to have many hundreds of files, even for a temporary situation, especially if they involve tape drives where the typical number of available drives is just a few. One could, of course, mount and dismount tapes, but this would be cumbersome and slow the procedure down drastically.

We can resolve this problem and produce an effective sorting scheme by merging pieces from two files into two resultant files alternatively. Therefore, at each phase there are two files, each containing many independent pieces that are individually sorted. As the sort proceeds, the size of the sorted pieces increase until the entire file is sorted. Therefore, we will need only four files—two for input and two for output.

To perform this sort by the merging process, we need two files, but the original file is just one. Therefore, we will separate the original file by writing records alternatively to two files. If the original number of records is even, they will both contain the same number; if the original number is odd, then the first of the two files will contain one more record than the second.

Actually, this separation process is not magical. If the number of records were known in advance, then $n/2$ (n even) or $n/2+1$ (n odd) could be written consecutively to the first file and the remaining $n/2$ (both n even and odd) could be written to the second. The alternative writing scheme is convenient when we do not know the number of records.

Once the original file is separated into two files, the merging operations can take place. The first pass will take subfiles of one element from the two source files and merge them into lists of two to be written alternatively to the two destination files. We can think of these two input files as consisting of $n/2$ or $n/2\pm1$ sorted pieces of size one. When the pass is completed, the two destination files will contain half the number of sorted pieces, but the size of the pieces will be two. The next pass will process these two files of pieces with two sorted items and produce files with pieces with a size of four—this process will repeat until the entire file is contained in one sorted piece.

Consider an example with $n=19$ elements.

file	--0-> a	b	--1-> c	d	--2-> a'	b'	--3-> c'	d'	--4-> a"	b"	--5-> c"
13	13	42	⌐13	⌐17	⌐13	⌐18	⌐13	⌐12	⌐12	⌐28	⌐12
42	17	21	∟42	∟21	17	25	17	14	13	30	13
17	45	33	⌐33	⌐18	21	33	18	19	14	∟34	14
21	18	25	∟45	∟25	∟42	∟45	21	23	17		17
45	31	12	⌐12	⌐14	⌐12	⌐19	25	29	18		18
33	14	41	∟31	∟41	14	23	33	31	19		19
18	29	19	⌐19	⌐23	31	29	42	41	21		21
25	23	47	∟29	∟47	∟41	∟47	∟45	∟47	23		23
31	34	28	⌐28	30	⌐28		⌐28		25		25
12	30		∟34		30		30		29		28
14					∟34		∟34		31		29
41									33		30
29									41		31
19									42		33
23									45		34
47									∟47		41
34											42
28											45
30											∟47

In this example, we first note that files a and b do contain all of the original items taken from the original file alternatively.

Focusing our attention on files a,b and c,d; we note that the 13 and 42 from a and b get merged to 13,42 on c:

```
              --1->
    a   b         c   d
   13  42        ┌13
                 └42
```

The next two records from *a* and *b*, 17 and 21, get merged to 17,21 on *d*. This process is continued until all of the items are transferred to *c* and *d*.

```
    a   b      c   d
   13  42     13  ┌17
   17  21     42  └21
```

The next pass takes these files of two elements from *c* and merges them two-by-two into files of four on *a'* and *b'*. In particular, it takes the 13,42 from *c* and the 17,21 from *d*, produced during the previous pass, and merges them into 13,17,21,42 on *a'*.

```
    c   d     a'  b'
   13  17    ┌13
   42  21    │17
            │21
            └42
```

The next two two-element subfiles on *c* and *d*—33,45 and 18,25—get merged to *b'* as 18,25,33,45.

```
    c   d     a'  b'
   13  17    13  ┌18
   42  21    17  │25
   33  18    21  │33
   45  25    42  └45
```

The following pass will take those two subfiles of size four from *a'* and *b'* to produce 13,17,18,21,25,33,42,45 on *c'*.

```
    a'  b'     c'  d'
   13  18    ┌13
   17  25    │17
   21  33    │18
   42  45    │21
            │25
            │33
            │42
            └45
```

At each pass, the number of elements in the first file of the pair is greater than or equal to the number in the second. Eventually, all the records are contained in the first file of the destination pair and the second file is empty. The first file then contains all of the items and is totally sorted.

The process is thus:

pass 0:   Copy alternatively

pass 1:   Merge by one's into alternative destination files
pass 2:   Merge by two's into alternative destination files
pass 3:   Merge by four's into alternative destination files
pass 4:   Merge by eight's into alternative destination files
pass 5:   Merge by sixteen's into alternative destination files

If the number of elements is larger than the example, then additional passes of 32, 64, 128, ... (powers of 2) are performed until $b^{(n)}$ or $d^{(n)}$ is empty. At that time, the file is sorted (and stored in $a^{(n)}$ or $c^{(n)}$, respectively).

11.8.2 Analysis

Because of the doubling nature, this is an easy algorithm to analyze. The number of passes depends upon the logarithm of the number of elements. Specifically:

$$p = \texttt{ceil(lg n)+1}$$

For the example used, $n = 19$; hence, lg n = 4.248. Therefore, $p = 6$. Since each pass processes each element once, the number of operations is proportional to:

$$\texttt{n·p = n[ceil(lg n)+1]} \approx \texttt{n·lg n.}$$

And this is an O(n • lg n) procedure.

With some more programming we can eliminate pass 0, the separation pass. For pass 1' we read two elements from the original file, compare them in memory, and write them in order to c and d, alternately. This will not increase our memory requirements since the merge operation requires two records to be in memory at once.

```
                    1'
       file            c    d
       13┐ c         ┌13  ┌17
       42┘           └42  └21
       17┐ d         ┌33  ┌18
       21┘           └45  └25
       45┐ c         ┌12  ┌14
       33┘           └31  └41
       18┐ d         ┌19  ┌23
       25┘           └29  └47
       31┐ c         ┌28   30
       12┘           └34
       14┐ d
       41┘
       29┐ c
       19┘
       23┐ d
       47┘
       34┐ c
       28┘
       30  d
```

Therefore, the number of operations is proportional to:

$$n \cdot \mathtt{ceil(lg\ n)} \approx n \cdot \mathtt{lg\ n}.$$

We could eliminate another pass by reading in four records, sorting them and writing them out in order to the output files, but the programming begins to get complicated and additional memory is required. Sorting two elements involves just one comparison, sorting four takes three to six comparisons (using an insertion sort scheme).

Indeed, there is no reason why we cannot eliminate other passes. We could read in eight records, sort them, and write them alternatively to the two output files and eliminate passes 0, 1, and 2. Since a significant amount of time is taken by accessing and reading and writing external files, it might be time-effective to read a large number of records into memory (as many as possible), sort them internally, then write these sorted chunks alternatively to the output files. (It is only necessary for the number of records read and sorted internally to be the same so that the sorted pieces on the two output tapes are the same size.) Finally, finish the process with the Two-Way Merge Sort procedure.

Indeed, if the file is small, all of the records might fit into memory at once and all of the sorting could be done internally. This could save a large amount of file reading and writing and—therefore—time!

The change to the Two-Way Merge Sort Algorithms in the next section would involve substituting this procedure for Algorithm SF and modifying the initial value of NR in Algorithm T (step T2) to the actual number of records processed in these initial chunks.

However, while such a scheme might speed up the sorting process, it would not change the "big O" behavior.

With tapes, the Two-Way Merge Sort can be implemented with four drives. The first pass requires three drives—one to read the file and two to write the intermediate tapes; the other passes require four. However, only four physical tapes need to be used. Once the information is read from *a* and *b* and merged onto *c* and *d*, then *a* and *b* may be used to receive the data from the next pass, which reads from *c* and *d*. It is easy to see how a procedure might be developed that reads lists of size *n* (*n* is a power of 2) from drives 1 and 2 and writes lists of size 2*n* to drives 3 and 4. The tapes could be then swapped.

However, with a little more programming, the drives could be logically alternated and the entire process completely automated. The original tape is mounted on drive 1 and temporary scratch tapes are mounted on drives 2, 3, and 4. When the sort procedures are finished, then the sorted tape is found on one of the two drives, 1 or 3. The program could tell which one. Or if drive 3 did end up with the sorted file, then it would be easy with one more pass through the data to copy it back to the original tape, although a simple physical substitution is really all that is necessary. Thus, the net result is to rewrite the original unsorted tape with the sorted data.

While the Two-Way Merge Sort may be used in the very restricted circumstance of tapes, today it is more likely to be used for disk files.

11.8.3 Algorithms

Although a Two-Way Merge Sort is easy to explain, understand, and perform by hand, its proper implementation requires considerable thought. There are a number of special situations and complications that must be worked out so that the computer can handle all of the possible difficulties. Rather than develop a single algorithm, we will break the task up into a series of algorithms.

A key to efficient implementation is knowing that the central task is to merge subfiles from two files to one file. This one routine is called alternatively with different arguments to produce the two output files. The calling routine, is in turn, invoked by a procedure that alternately calls it with one pair of files as input, and the other as output—then calls it with the two sets reversed.

In order to implement the Two-Way Merge Sort, we must first modify the general File Merge Algorithm (Algorithm FM; which proceeds until an End-of-File mark is found), to merge only up to a certain specified number of records from each file; that is, we will stop reading records from a given file whenever the limit is reached or an EOF is found. It is also important that the algorithm communicate back to the calling procedure exactly why it finished.

Algorithm ML (File Merge with Limit). Given two files, *FILEA* and *FILEB*, merge up to *NR* records from each into a single resultant file, *FILEC*. It is assumed that each file ends with an EOF which is detected upon a read attempt. Returns a value which indicates if it found an EOF on *FILEA*, *FILEB*, both (1), or neither (0).

ML1. [initialize]   ia=0; ib=0;

ML2. [get record]   Read recA from FILEA;
                      If EOF, then eofa = FALSE.
                          else eofa = TRUE.

ML3. [get record]   Read recB from FILEB;
                      If EOF, then eofb = FALSE.
                          else eofb = TRUE.

ML4. [loop]   While eofa and eofb are both TRUE, Perform step ML5.

ML5. [compare & write]   If recA < recB,
                    then Write recA to FILEC;
                        ia = ia+1;
                        If ia=NR, then Go to step ML6.
                        Read recA from FILEA;
                        If EOF, then eofa = FALSE.
                              else eofa = TRUE.
                  else Write recB to FILEC;
                        ib = ib+1;
                        If ib=NR, then Go to step ML6.

Read recB from FILEB;
If EOF, then eofb = FALSE.
else eofb = TRUE.

ML6. [finish FILEA]   While eofa is TRUE and ia < NR, then Perform
step ML7.

ML7. [write and read]   Write recA to FILEC;
ia = ia + 1;
If ia=NR, then Go to step ML8.
Read recA from FILEA;
If EOF, then eofa = FALSE.
else eofa = TRUE.

ML8. [finish FILEB]   While eofb is TRUE and ib < NR, then Perform
step ML9.

ML9. [write and read]   Write recB to FILEC;
ib = ib + 1;
If ib=NR, then Go to step ML10.
Read recB from FILEB;
If EOF, then eofb = FALSE.
else eofb = TRUE.

ML10. [return status]   If eofa and eofb are both TRUE, then return 0.
else return 1.

As with Algorithm FM, the **Read record** instructions properly set the value of the *eofa* and *eofb* variables. In addition, since the Go To instructions simply branch to the statement following the loop, they may be implemented as C break statements.

This algorithm performs the crucial central procedure for the Two-Way Merge Sort. It merges two pieces of two files and writes the result to one file. It must be repeatedly invoked to merge all of the pieces of the two input files to two alternate output files. Therefore, we use this in the following algorithm:

Algorithm MA (Merge to Alternate Files). Given two files, *FILEX* and *FILEY*, merges up to *NR* records from each to two output files, *FILEM* and *FILEN* alternately. The EOF_flag is the value returned from Algorithm ML. Algorithm MA returns a value which indicates if the second output file is written to (1) or not (0).

MA1. [initialize]   second=0; Set all files to beginning.

MA2. [merge to first]   Invoke Algorithm ML with NR; FILEX and FILEY to
FILEM.

MA3. [check if done]   If EOF_flag ≠ 0, then Return (second).

MA4. [merge to second]   Invoke Algorithm ML with NR; FILEX and FILEY to
                                                         FILEN.

MA5. [set flag]   second = 1.

MA6. [check if done]   IF EOF_flag ≠ 0, then Return (second).
                                                         else Go to step MA2.

      This algorithm will also be invoked repeatedly. It reads the entire two input
files, invokes Algorithm ML, many times, to write the two output files.
      The final sub-process that needs to be defined (before we put everything
together) is one that separates the initial file into two. We will use the simple scheme
to copy records alternatively to the two destination files.

Algorithm SF (Separate File). Given a file, *FILE*, write alternative records to two
output files, *FILEA* and *FILEB*.

SF1. [get record]   Read rec from FILE; If EOF, then Return.

SF2. [write record]   Write rec to FILEA.

SF3. [get record]   Read rec from FILE; If EOF, then Return.

SF4. [write record]   Write rec to FILEB.

SF5. [loop]   Go to step SF1.

      Finally, we are able to combine everything into an algorithm for performing
the Two-Way Merge Sort.

Algorithm T (Two-Way Merge Sort). Given a file, *FILE*, sorts the contents into
ascending order. Uses four temporary files, *FILE1*, *FILE2*, *FILE3*, and *FILE4*. The
value flag is the result returned from Algorithm MA. The resultant sorted file is
contained in *FILE1* or *FILE3*.

T1. [separate]   Invoke Algorithm SF with FILE to FILE1 and FILE2.

T2. [set merge size]   NR = 1.

T3. [merge]   Invoke Algorithm MA with NR; FILE1 and FILE2 to
                                                 FILE3 and FILE4.

T4. [are we done?]   If flag = 0, then Copy FILE3 to FILE; Halt.

T5. [change size]   NR = 2 · NR.

T6. [merge]   Invoke Algorithm MA with NR; FILE3 and FILE4 to
                                                 FILE1 and FILE2.

T7. [are we done?]   If flag = 0, then Copy FILE1 to FILE; Halt.

T8. [change size] $NR = 2 \cdot NR$.

T9. [loop]   Go to step T3.

∎

   Depending upon where this algorithm finishes, the sorted file will be contained in *FILE1* or *FILE3*. This file may be copied back to *FILE* using Algorithm FC; then we can delete the temporary intermediate files before halting. Note, that Algorithm T repeatedly uses the four temporary files over and over—merging from one set to the other and back.

   Implementing these algorithms in C requires some care. First, it is very important to pass the file information via the parameter list of the individual functions. This way, a single function can perform its action independent of the actual files involved. That is, in step T3 we might have:

```
flag = merge_alt(nr, f1,f2, f3,f4);
```

and step T6 becomes:

```
flag = merge_alt(nr, f3,f4, f1,f2);
```

The function itself simply performs its action on two input files and two output files. By changing the arguments for the two invocations, we change which set we are using for input and output, respectively. The simplest way to pass the file information is via the file pointers for the open files.

   Going hand in hand with the parameter passing is writing each function, paying careful attention to what is required for each. As an example, the Merge to Alternate Files, Algorithm MA, is "Given two files, FILEX and FILEY, merges up to NR records from each to two output files, FILEM and FILEN alternately. Algorithm MA returns a value which indicates if the second output file is written to (1) or not (0)." Therefore, an appropriate function definition would be:

```
int merge_alt(int nr, FILE *fx, FILE *fy, FILE *fm, FILE *fn)
```

   The second concern is to open (via fopen()) the temporary output files just before performing the Merge Alternative Algorithm, closing (via fclose()) the input files immediately after. This will reposition the output files at their starting point and insure that subsequent write operations will indeed overwrite the contents.

   The most difficult function to implement in a structured manner is the File Merge with Limit, Algorithm ML. Perhaps the best way is to structure it according to the hints given for the File Merge (Algorithm FM) and write some redundant code. That is, follow step ML2 (FILEA empty) with the equivalent of ML7 and ML6 to copy the records from FILEB. Likewise, follow ML3 with the equivalent of ML8 and ML9. Within the loop, steps ML4 and ML5 set a variable which determines whether ML6 or ML8 is the appropriate process to finish up the algorithm. Then the "go to step MLx" can be replaced by "break".

Finally, while we can be consistent and pass the file information to each function via file pointers, it is convenient to pass the name of the file to the sort function which is invoked from the main program. This function implements Algorithm T. Within this function, the original file is opened for reading; the temporary files are opened; the file is separated; the original file is closed; the iterative two-way merge sort is performed; the original file is opened for writing and the appropriate temporary file is copied; the original file is closed; and, finally, the temporary files are removed. Note, that opening and removing files require having the names of the files. Therefore, all opening, closing, removing of files takes place in this one function.

11.8.4 Three-Way Merging

If Two-Way merging is an effective procedure, then why not use six files and implement a Three-Way Merge Sort. This will reduce the number of passes from ceil($\log_2$ n) to ceil($\log_3$ n). However, this changes the number of operations only by a constant—0.631, but the programming would be considerably more complicated. Merging on two files requires one comparison to know which to output. Merging with three files requires two comparisons to find the minimum each time, but since there are three possibilities, there need to be three coded comparisons.

Assume that we have three records: *reca*, *recb*, and *recc* that we have read from the three files, respectively. Merging these files requires that we compare the records and write the smallest one to the output file. The procedure to perform this might appear as:

```
if (reca < recb)
    if (reca < recc)
        write(reca)                          reca < recb and recc
        read another record from a
    else
        write(recc)                          recc < reca < recb
        read another record from c
else
    if (recb < recc)                         recb < reca and recc
        write(recb)
        read another record from b
    else
        write(recc)                          recc < recb < reca
        read another record from c
```

For two of these cases we do not know the exact order of all three, only that the smallest is found. For each case, there are only two comparisons that are executed; whereas, determining the complete order requires three.

11.9   *EXTERNAL SORTS APPLIED TO LISTS*

External sorts may also be applied to internal lists. The two presented above are reasonably efficient, comparing favorably with the Shell's Sort and the Quick Sort in terms of the number of operations required. The primary disadvantage is that the external sorts require extra storage.

A formal algorithm to implement the Radix Sort for items that are composed of a set of digits in an internal list is:

Algorithm RL (Radix Sort on a list). Given a list, LIST, of n elements of d digits, rearrange these items so that they are in increasing order. Uses auxiliary queues, QUEUE[10][SIZE], and queue indices, QI[10].

RL1. [initialize]   divisor=1.

RL2. [loop on digits]   Perform steps RL3 through RL13 for $k=0,1,...,d-1$.

RL3. [initial queues]   Perform step RL4 for $j=0,...,9$.

RL4. [set initial indices]   QI[j]=-1.

RL5. [loop over items]   Perform steps RL6 through RL8 for $i=0,1,...,n-1$.

RL6. [get digit]   dgt=(LIST[i]/divisor) mod 10.

RL7. [increment index]   QI[dgt]=QI[dgt]+1.

RL8. [store item]   QUEUE[dgt][QI[dgt]]=LIST[i].

RL9. [initialize list index]   i=0.

RL10. [loop over queues]   Perform step RL11 for $j=0,1,...,9$.

RL11. [move from queues]   Perform step RL12 for $m=0,1,...,$QI[j].

RL12. [store item]   LIST[i]=QUEUE[j][m]; i=i+1.

RL13. [change divisor]   divisor = 10•divisor.

We have called the auxiliary lists queue's because all of the insertions (during the distribution operation) are made at one end, and the deletions (during the recombination operation) are made at the other end. However, since the insertions take place and are finished before the deletions are made, and the deletions are all performed at one time, the full qpush and qpop algorithms need not be used. (And we need not worry about making the queues circular in nature.) It is sufficient to keep track of the total number of items appended into each.

We simply copy items to the end of the list (append) during the distribution phase, then begin at the beginning and copy items from the list until the end is reached during the combination phase.

A disadvantage of the Radix Sort on an internal list is that the size of each of the queues might need to be as large as the original list. It is possible that the keys at one of the digit positions contains the same digit. Thus, the total storage required for these auxiliary queues is $10n$ locations. However, only n of these will be used during any one pass. With some clever programming to manage memory, it might be possible to use only what storage is actually needed. A linked structure could perform this trick; however, that is looking ahead a bit.

The Two-Way Merge Sort holds more promise, but, on the surface, it would appear that it would require a possible $4n$ temporary storage locations to sort a list of n items. For files, this is not a problem. If we simply modified the algorithm to use lists rather than files, we would need to reserve the space even though it will not all be needed.

However, note that at any one time there are only two copies of the data in existence. Therefore, it should be possible to implement the Two-Way Merge Sort with only n additional storage location. This can be done with internal lists, whereby one has more freedom in accessing the lists. At each pass in the procedure, a list will contain pieces that are already sorted. We will merge from two distinct pieces of one list. For example:

```
        ab          cd
 i─  12      k ┌ 11
     15        │ 12
     22        │ 14
     24        │ 15
 j─  11        │ 18
     14        │ 19
     18        │ 22
     19        └ 24
```

Here we have merged two four-item pieces from *ab* to *cd* (as a single ordered eight-item piece). This requires two indices into *ab*, which move sequentially, which is not typically possible with files. The next two sets of four-item pieces from *ab* are merged onto *cd*, and so forth. The next pass will take two eight-item pieces from *cd* and merge them onto *ab*, etc. The original list can serve as one set of storage locations, hence, all we need is one other. Essentially by allowing two indices into a single list, we can combine the two input lists into one and the two output lists into one. When the procedure is complete, the sorted list will either be back in the original list or in the temporary one from which it can be copied back to the original.

Consider the example above:

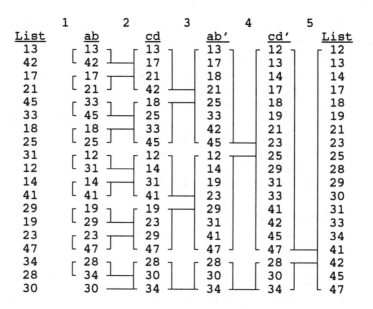

The heart of such a procedure is, again, a merge algorithm that merges from two positions in an input list to an output list, until a limit is reached or the end of the list is encountered.

At the pass where m items are to be merged, the initial indices in the input list start at locations 0 and m. Each will process m items to produce a list of $2m$ on the output list (where they go in locations 0 through $2m$-1). The next step is to start the indices at $2m$ and $3m$, respectively, in order to merge $2m$ items to the output list (where they will go in locations $2m$ through $4m$-1).

The same comment that applied to the Radix Sort is appropriate for the Two-Way Merge Sort. With the proper memory management—that is, using a different data structure—it is possible to implement a Two-Way Merge Sort on internal data without any extra storage.

11.10 SUMMARY

There have been a number of different types of external media for storing machine-readable data. A characteristic of many of these is a sequential access by the computer. Presently, magnetic disks are the primary type of media for secondary storage!

Storage and organization of data on the external medium becomes important with large amounts of data. These are typically organized into files consisting of many records, each record consisting of fields which contain the desired data.

Because of the nature of external files, the algorithms for accessing and manipulating the data are different from those appropriate for internal random access memory.

The standard C library contains a number of functions for accessing, reading from, and writing to files.

An external sort accesses data sequentially; hence, it can be used on a large data set stored in a file—a data set too large to fit into random access memory. In general, these sorts temporarily produce extra copies of the data.

The Radix Sort is a distribution type sort. It distributes the data according to the value in a given position, then catenates these pieces, and repeats with the next position to the left until all positions have been processed. It make no comparisons of the data, but it reads the data set twice for each position. Therefore, it is O(n).

The Two-Way Merge Sort stores sorted pieces on alternative files. Each merge operation doubles the size of the sorted pieces until the entire file is sorted. It is O(n • lg n). A very efficient file sort can combine an internal sort and the Two-Way Merge Sort by reading into memory as many records as possible, sorting these internally, and writing subsequent pieces to alternative starting files for the Two-Way Merge Sort which completes the sorting process.

The external sorts may be applied to internal lists; however, they need considerable extra storage compared to the "in place" internal sorts, and generally do not offer better "big O" behavior.

REFERENCES

Kernighan, Brian W., and Ritchie, Dennis M., *The C Programming Language*, 2nd ed., Prentice-Hall, Englewood Cliffs, New Jersey, 1988.

Knuth, Donald E., *The Art of Computer Programming*; Fundamental Algorithms, vol. 1., 2nd ed., Addison-Wesley Publishing Co., Reading, Massachusetts, 1973.

Knuth, Donald E., *The Art of Computer Programming*; Sorting and Searching, vol. 3., Addison-Wesley Publishing Co., Reading, Massachusetts, 1973.

Sedgewick, Robert, *Algorithms in C*, Addison-Wesley Publishing Co., Reading, Massachusetts, 1990.

QUESTIONS

Q11.1   Which of the following items that, typically consist of digits and appear to be numeric, are actually alphanumeric?

> phone number
> zip code
> birthday
> social security number
> house number as part of a street address

Q11.2   How would change the sense of the File Merge Algorithm to process files in descending order?

Q11.3   What are the differences in processing a file from:

      a.   Accessing an internal random access list of length n?

      b.   Accessing a string?

Q11.4   How does the fgets() differ from the gets() function?

Q11.5   Why does a computer system have a variety of different types of storage?

Q11.6   What is the smallest "chunk" of information called that may be accessed in one operation for the following?

      a.   RAM   c.   tape
      b.   disk

Q11.7   What is wrong with the following C code for opening a file?

```
FILE fp;

fp = fopen("datafile.in",'r');
```

Q11.8   What are the advantages of opening a data file internally in a program, rather than using I/O redirection? What are the disadvantages? When might you wish to choose one over the other?

Q11.9   A diskette rotates at 360 rpm. If each track contains 9 sectors of 512 bytes, how long does it take to read a given sector once the head is positioned at the beginning of the sector? How many Kbytes/sec is this? On the average, how long would one have to wait for the desired sector to rotate into the correct position, assuming the head is positioned on the relevant track?

Q11.10   A C programmer wrote a program that had, as part of its code:

```
printf("enter value:   ");
scanf("%d",&x[i]);
```

This was in a loop that would read in a series of values. When executed in the normal manner, it appeared on the screen as:

```
enter value:   12
enter value:   8
   ⋮
```

The final answer is 34.5 and -3.4

She grew tired of entering the same series of numbers while testing the program. Therefore, she put the values in a file and executed:

```
name <file
```

What would appear on the screen? Why?
If she executed:

```
name <file >prn
```

what would appear on the screen? On the printer?

Q11.11 We wrote the process of obtaining a record from a file as (example taken from Algorithm FM):

FM1. [get record from A]   Read recA from FILEA;
                            If EOF, then go to step FM6.

How might the C implementation of this step look? Note, that this appears within a loop and step FM6 follows the loop.

Q11.12 If you wished to check to see if a file exists before using it as a temporary file (one that information will be written to in the course of the execution of the program, but is not needed when the program is ended), what C code would tell you if the file does indeed exist?

Q11.13 How many comparisons does the Radix Sort perform (on the average) for a file or list of n elements?

Q11.14 The Radix Sort can be implemented with only two auxiliary files if one distributes the file by bit (0 and 1). If it is necessary to sort a file of names with 20 characters reserved for each name, how many passes would be required?

Q11.15 What is the "big O" behavior of the radix sort?

Q11.16 In a Two-Way Merge Sort, explain why the first of the file pairs always contains the same number of records as or more records than the second.

Q11.17 It was stated that to change from a Two-Way Merge Sort to a Three-Way would only change the number of operations by a factor of 0.631. What does this number represent, and why?

Q11.18 How would you modify the Radix Sort Algorithm, Algorithm RL to have it sort in descending order?

Q11.19   We developed the Two-Way Merge Sort Algorithm, Algorithm T, using three "subalgorithms." If it were to be written as one large procedure, how many copies of the basic merge algorithm, Algorithm ML, would need to be explicitly written?

Q11.20   It was suggested that it might be more efficient to read a large number of records from a file into memory, sort these internally, and write them alternatively to two output files; then when this process is finished, continue with a Two-Way Merge Sort. Does it matter how many elements the pieces we internally sort are, as long as they all contain the same number (except for the last)? That is, the Two-Way Merge Sort Algorithm, as expressed above, uses pieces that are powers of 2. Is it necessary that our internal pieces be powers of two in length?

Q11.21   The Two-Way Merge Sort is a rather efficient sort $O(n \cdot \lg n)$, and is comparable to the Quick Sort. Why is the Quick Sort a preferred sort for an internal list?

Q11.22   How could we use any of the sorts we have discussed to produce a sorted version of a list, yet leave the original list intact? How much storage would the Two-Way Merge Sort take in this case?

Q11.23   What is the best case number of comparisons for the Two-Way Merge Sort on a file of n items? The worst case? The average case?

Q11.24   How would you modify the Two-way Merge Sort Algorithm to have it sort in descending order?

Q11.25   Does the number of operations for a Radix Sort depend upon the initial order of the data? Why, or why not?

Q11.26   Does the number of operations for a Two-Way Merge Sort depend upon the initial order of the data? Why, or why not?

Q11.27   What is the essential difference between an internal sort and an external sort?

Q11.28   Can an external type sort be used on an internal list? Can an internal type sort be used on an external list? Explain.

Q11.29   Comment on the truth of the following statement; that is, explain if it is true or explain why it is not true:

"One cannot perform a sort with a better behavior than $O(n \cdot \lg n)$."

Q11.30 In implementing the Radix Sort, one might be tempted to read the items from the temporary files or lists and place them directly into the appropriate file or list based upon the next character position without first copying them back into a complete file or list and thereby saving some time. What problem would this cause?

Q11.31 In the file close function, fclose(), how is the argument first initialized?

Q11.32 What is the difference in closing a file, using fclose(), and deleting it, using remove()?

Q11.33 In the text, it was stated that to sort a tape of alphabetic data by the Radix Sort would require 27 tape drives—why 27?

Q11.34 The text suggested that a tape containing the original file be mounted on drive 1, and scratch tapes be mounted on drives 2, 3, and 4. When the Two-Way Merge Sort procedure is finished, then the sorted tape is found on one of the two drives, 1 or 3. Which drives are used as alternative pairs? Which two would the original be copied to first?

Q11.35 During the file separation algorithm for the Two-Way Merge Sort it was stated that we want the same number of records or one more record written to the first of the pair of files as to the second. Show that these number can be expressed as:

first: $(n+1)/2$ second: $n/2$

Hint, consider two cases: n even and n odd.

Q11.36 It was suggested that for the Two-Way Merge Sort, a number of records be read into memory, sorted internally, then written alternatively to the two initial files for the two-way merge procedure. If we could read 50 records into memory at one time, then what would be the sequence of the size of the pieces in the two-way merge process?

EXERCISES

E11.1 Write out a formal algorithm to insert a record after the k-th record in a file. That is, the new file consists of records $1,2,...,k,new,k+1,k+2,...$.

E11.2 Write out a formal algorithm to delete the k-th record from a file. That is, the new file consists of records $1,2,...,k-1,k+1,k+2,...$.

E11.3   Write a C function that behaves as gets() but reads from a file; that is, it replaces any new-line characters with a NULL rather that appending the NULL after the new-line as does fgets(). It should return the same value as does fgets():

```
char *file_gets(string, fp);
```

Use the #define to specify a SIZE of the string array.

E11.4   Perform the File Merge algorithm, Algorithm FM, on the following files, by hand:

a.	FILEA	FILEB	d.	FILEA	FILEB
	EOF	12		12	17
		31		14	21
		EOF		20	24
				27	26
b.	FILEA	FILEB		34	42
	17	EOF		36	EOF
	24			39	
	33			EOF	
	EOF				
c.	FILEA	FILEB			
	EOF	EOF			

E11.5   Rewrite Algorithm FM', using the suggested "redundant" steps.

E11.6   Programs that read data files can be written to include the name of the file on the command line. Write out the appropriate beginnings of a C program that behaves as:

```
process
Enter input file name:

process infile.dat

process ?
Program to process data file, ver 1.56, 1990

    process [filename]
```

E11.7   By hand, perform the Radix Sort on the following data which consist of octal (base 8, with digits 0,1,...,7) numbers:

1234
1101
7201
6443
4362
1275
0576
2475
2112
5020
3647
7472
4533

Show all of the intermediate lists, as well as the final sorted one.

E11.8   What would happen if you began with the most significant digit and worked to the least, using the Radix Sort Algorithm? Illustrate with the following data consisting of octal (base 8, with digits 0,1,...,7) numbers:

1234
1101
7201
6443
4362
1275
0576
2475
2112
5020
3647
7472
4533

Show all of the intermediate lists, as well as the final sorted one.

E11.9   A distribution sort may be developed for an internal list that sorts in place. It proceeds by bit, from the most significant bit, moving all of the items with a zero bit to the top of the list and those with a one bit to the bottom; thereby dividing the list into two parts. Each of these parts is individually and recursively processed, using the next bit to the right, until the last (right-most) bit is processed.

The key to this is a distribution algorithm that is similar to the partitioning algorithm of the Quick Sort. We keep two indices that grow from the left and right such that all items to the left of the left one contain a zero and items to the right of the right one contain a one. Check the unprocessed item next to the left index. If the bit is zero, increment the left index. If the bit is a one, swap with the item next to the right index, and decrement the right index. When the indices meet, the list is divided.

Write a formal algorithm to perform this in-place Radix Sort.

E11.10   The text suggested a scheme that eliminates one pass from the Two-Way Merge Sort by combining the original separation and the one-by-one pass. Read two records from the input file, compare them, and write them in order to the two output files.

        a. Write a formal algorithm that replaces Algorithm SF and eliminates the first pass from the Two-Way Merge Sort.

        b. What changes to the other algorithms involved in the Two-Way Merge Sort are required if this is used in place of Algorithm SF?

E11.11   By hand, perform the Two-Way Merge Sort on the following data:

```
1234
1101
7201
6893
4362
8285
0576
2975
2112
5020
3697
7472
4533
9183
3827
5026
7641
```

Show all of the intermediate lists, as well as the final sorted one.

E11.12   Modify Algorithm T to use the File Copy process, Algorithm FC, to copy the resultant file back to the original, if necessary.

E11.13   Write out a procedure similar to that in the text for merging four files. Hint: the most efficient scheme involves three comparisons at each step, but is rather messy to write out as nested comparisons.

E11.14   Rewrite the Two-way Merge Sort Algorithms to perform an internal sort on a list of items. Assume that there is sufficient storage for $4n$ items.

E11.15   Rewrite the Two-way Merge Sort Algorithms to perform an internal sort on a list of items, using only one additional block of storage of n elements.

E11.16   Write a Three-Way List Merge Algorithm. That is, read three internal lists and generate a fourth merged list.

E11.17   Write a Three-Way File Merge Algorithm. That is, read three external files and generate a fourth merged file.

PROBLEMS

P11.1   Implement, in memory, using three lists, the File Merge Algorithm. Fill the initial two lists with positive values, in ascending order, and terminate them with a -1 as an EOF mark. The final list should also be terminated with an EOF mark.

　　　　　The File Copy Algorithm (FC) may be modified to print the contents of a simulated file—print the record instead of writing it to the second file. Implement the print routine to print the contents of the original files and the final file.

P11.2   Implement the File Merge Algorithm to read two files consisting of strings of characters, names of animals in ascending order; and write a third merged file.

　　　　　To test your program, build two data files with 10 to 20 animal names in each.

P11.3   Write a C program that copies the contents of one file onto the end of another. This is file catenation. That is, the first file is read and the second file is written so that it contains its original contents followed by the contents of the first.

P11.4   Write a program to maintain an external file of records that looks like:

```
last_name[20]
first_name[20]
birthday
sex
```

Assume that the records are to be stored in ascending order, by last_name.

Hint: define a structure to contain each record. For insertions and deletions you will need to rewrite the file to a temporary, then copy it back.

Implement the following routines:

insert	insert a record
delete	delete a record
print	read and print the file
search	search for desired last name and print contents of record
exit	

Try it with:

1.	insert:	Bond	James	2/14/30	M
2.	insert:	Fatale	Natasha	5/ 1/36	F
3.	insert:	Badenov	Boris	7/21/32	M
4.	insert:	Rose	Tokyo	12/ 7/16	F
5.	insert:	Leader	Fearless	10/12/22	M
6.	insert:	Big	Mr.	5/29/13	M
7.	print				
8.	search:	Bond			
9.	delete:	Fatale			
10.	print				

P11.5   Write a C program to read a text file, identify words, and count the number of words. The file name is to be supplied on the command line, or if not supplied, have the program request it. If the file does not exist, then the program should exit gracefully with an appropriate message.

A word is a slippery thing to identify. It consists of letters and a possible apostrophe or hyphen. It must start immediately after the beginning of a line, a space, double quotes, or single quotes. It is ended by a non-letter, or the end of the line. An apostrophe may be detected because it is a single quote immediately preceded by a letter and immediately followed by a letter. Thus, "can't" is a single word. A hyphen at the end of a line probably suggests a word that is split; therefore, delete it and combine the two pieces. A hyphen in the middle of line suggests a hyphenated word. thus, "co-processor" is a single word. This scheme might miss some hyphenated words that happened to be split by the end of a line.

Test your program on a text file at least five pages in length.

P11.6   Write a C program that merges three internal lists containing numeric values. It should produce a fourth list that is the result of the merge operation.

P11.7   Write a C function to implement the Radix Sort Algorithm (Algorithm RL) on an internal list of items consisting of digits, (e.g. zip codes).

```
void radsort(long list[], int n, int d)
```

Write a main program that inputs a list of zip codes, prints the original list, sorts them via the Radix Sort routine, and prints the resultant list.

Generate a file of 50 to 100 zip codes. You can read them into your program by I/O redirection; that is

```
program <file
```

will cause all normal read operations that would come from the keyboard to access the contents of the file.

You should not need to enter the number of zip codes in the file, but read until an end-of-file is encountered, with the program counting the number of values.

Note: Because zip codes may range from 00000 to 99999, they might not be able to be stored in an int or even an unsigned int depending upon the computer.

Note: The C printf() format specification permits the printing of leading zeros—use it!

Change the number of zip codes by editing your data file and execute the program again.

P11.8   Write a C function to implement the Radix Sort Algorithm (Algorithm RF) on an external file of items consisting of digits, e.g. zip codes.

```
void exradsort(char *fname)
```

The function should read the file, create the auxiliary ones, write them, and read them back into the original file. Use the function in a program that requests the name of the original file and invokes the sort. When the sorting process is completed, delete the temporary auxiliary files.

Generate a file of 50 to 100 zip codes. Dump the contents of the file to the printer. Sort the file. Dump the sorted contents to the printer.

Hint: In testing the program, make a copy of the original file of zip codes to test the sort.

P11.9   Write a C program to implement a Two-Way Merge Sort on an internal list of random numbers. The original list should contain the final sorted version.

Include, in your program, the usual tests to check on the sorting process.

P11.10 Write a C program to implement a Two-Way Merge Sort on a file of strings. The program should request the file, sort it using four temporary files, copy the sorted file back to the original file, and delete the temporary ones. (Alternatively, delete the original, rename the last temporary file, and delete the other three temporary files—in any case, the net result should take an unsorted file with a given name and return a file by the same name that is sorted.

Build a file at least 70 book titles in length, and sort them. Each title should be less than 60 characters long; therefore, you can list them on the screen and print them conveniently.

When testing your sort program, make certain that you sort on a copy of the original data file so that you can repeatedly test your program without having to rebuild the data file each time.

P11.11 Modify the C program written for the above problem that implements a Two-Way Merge Sort to read a large number of records, say enough to fill a 40,000 byte buffer, sort the records internally, write them by pieces to the two output files, then finish up with a Two-Merge Sort. You may choose any of the $O(n \cdot \lg n)$ sorts (including a Shell's Sort) for the internal portion.

You will need to decide how many records to be read in to be internally sorted, since it is important that subsequent blocks contain the same number of records.

Test your sort routine by reducing the size of the internal buffer to 5000 and generating a file of at least 300 records.

P11.12 Write a C program that merges three files containing strings. It should produce a fourth file that is the result of the merge operation.

Chapter 12

Linked Lists

The Cat only grinned when it saw Alice. It looked good-natured, she thought: still it had <u>very</u> long claws and a great many teeth, so she felt that it ought to be treated with respect.

"Cheshire Puss," she began, rather timidly, as she did not at all know whether it would like the name: however, it only grinned a little wider. "Come, it's pleased so far," thought Alice, and she went on. "Would you tell me, please, which way I ought to go from here?"

"That depends a good deal on where you want to get to," said the Cat.

"I don't much care where—" said Alice.

"Then it doesn't matter which way you go," said the Cat.

"—so long as I get <u>somewhere</u>," Alice added as an explanation.

"Oh, you're sure to do that," said the Cat, "if you only walk long enough."

12.1 OBJECTIVES

The objectives for this chapter are to:

- Introduce the concept of a linked-list data structure.

- Discuss the advantages and disadvantages of such structures.

- Present algorithms for the access, searching, insertion, and deletion.

- Describe methods of sorting and merging linked lists.

- Generalize for doubly and multi-linked lists
- Give suggestions on the C implementation of linked-lists and manipulation algorithms.

12.2   INTRODUCTION

The simple lists in main memory that we have studied are easy to implement and understand. Searching and modification are relatively inexpensive processes. Searching takes approximately **lg n** operations (if the data are ordered), and replacement of an item takes only a few more constant operations once the item is located. However, insertion and deletion are more time consuming, taking roughly $n/2$ operations on the average. If each item is really a large record consisting of many bytes of data, then these data movement operations are slow.

However, if insertion and deletion are relatively rare, then the simple list is satisfactory. For the many situations for which insertions and deletions are frequent, then a more suitable data structure is desired. We will consider such a structure, called a **linked list**. Unfortunately, as we shall see, the linked list is efficient for insertions and deletions, but the searching process is slowed from a O(lg n) operation to an O(n) operation. Later, we can generalize the linked-list concept to speed up the searching process as well.

Essentially, a linked list is a structure where each record contains information to tell where the next record is located. We will study linked lists in the context of an internal implementation. However, they are also very useful for the disk storage of files—a very similar situation with each sector being a fundamental chunk of storage.

12.3   LINKED LISTS

The basic idea of a linked list is that each datum will be stored in memory and will also contain a link to the next item in the list. The order of the list is determined by following the links from one item to the next logical one. The actual items may be stored anywhere in memory—they do not have to be contiguous or arranged in physical order.

12.3.1   Views

We can picture each record as:

```
address
        ┌──────────┐
        │ data     │
        │     ┌────┤
        │     │link│
        └─────┴────┘
```

The link is contained in a link field that is simply one of the other fields in the record. The link gives the address (or index) of the next item in the list. A semi-physical (or physiological) view of a linked list might appear as:

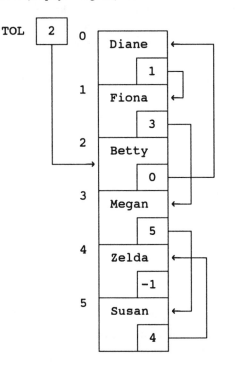

We have added extra lines to show how the links point to the next record in the list.

A more logical view of this list might be:

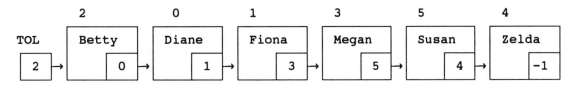

And a high-level logical view of the list is simply:

```
Betty
Diane
Fiona
Megan
Susan
Zelda
```

We have numbered the records in the list with the non-negative integers; that is, we have really used an index. However, we could also have used actual physical addresses in the computer. As we have seen, there typically is a simple linear polynomial that produces an address from an index. In reality, we do not have to perform any of this calculation but, rather, can let the computer do it for us. That is, we can implement a linked list using indices or pointers.

A physical view of the data as it might be actually stored in memory could be:

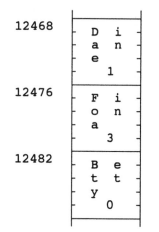

In addition to the link provided in each record, which points to the next logical record, we need a value which points to the first logical element of the list. This is indicated above by the top-of-list, *TOL*, variable.

12.3.2 Traversal

The process of traversing the list is to follow the sequence of links. Before we write an algorithm, we must establish a consistent notation. For the moment we will use the index to access the records. An index (or address) will be associated with each record. The index essentially tells where the record is stored. There are two quantities stored in each record: the data, which we will designate as *DATA[j]*— where *j* is the index—and the link to the next record, *LINK[j]*.

Each list has an end. Therefore, we need to be able to determine when we have reached the last element. We also need to select an appropriate value for a link that points to nothing. Actually, the solution to both is simple. Define an END mark and place it in the link field of the last logical record. If we are using indices which are all non-negative, then -1 is an appropriate choice. This is what we used in the example above. If we use actual addresses, or pointers, then a value of zero is appropriate.

If the list is empty, we can store the value END in the top-of-list variable.

An example using the links is provided by a simple algorithm to traverse and print the contents of the list.

Algorithm LP (Print Linked List). Follow the sequence of links and print the data stored in each record as it is encountered.

LP1. [initialize index]   j=TOL.

LP2. [test if done]   If j=END, then Terminate.

LP3. [print contents]   Output DATA[j].

LP4. [move to next]   j=LINK[j]; Go to step LP2.

∎

Tracing through the algorithm, through the example above, gives us:

      LP1   j = TOL = 2

      LP2   j is not equal to -1, therefore continue

      LP3   output DATA[2] which is: "Betty"

      LP4   j = LINK[2] = 0

      LP2   j is not equal to -1, therefore continue

      LP3   output DATA[0] which is: "Diane"

      LP4   j = LINK[0] = 1

      LP2   j is not equal to -1, therefore continue

      LP3   output DATA[1] which is: "Fiona"

      LP4   j = LINK[1] = 3

      LP2   j is not equal to -1, therefore continue

      LP3   output DATA[3] which is: "Megan"

      LP4   j = LINK[3] = 5

      LP2   j is not equal to -1, therefore continue

      LP3   output DATA[5] which is: "Susan"

      LP4   j = LINK[5] = 4

      LP2   j is not equal to -1, therefore continue

      LP3   output DATA[4] which is: "Zelda"

      LP4   j = LINK[4] = -1

      LP2   j is equal to -1, therefore we halt

Generally, a linked list is maintained in some sort of order. The searching procedure is thus similar to searching an ordered simple list. Because of the nature of the linked list, it is not possible to use a binary search procedure. We cannot compute the location of the mid-point of the list. We cannot jump into the middle of the list, but can get to a particular record only by following the links in sequence from the beginning until the record is found (or it is determined the record is not present).

Therefore, the algorithm for searching the linked list is essentially a serial search on an ordered list; it is given by:

Algorithm LS (Search Linked List). Follow the sequence of links in an ordered linked list for the occurrence of the item *KEY*.

LS1. [initialize index]   j=TOL.

LS2. [test if done]   If j=END, then Terminate.   (not found)

LS3. [is this it?]   If DATA[j]=KEY, then Terminate.   (found)

LS4. [past it?]   If DATA[j]>KEY, then Terminate.   (not found)

LS5. [move to next]   j=LINK[j]; Go to step LS2.

12.3.3   Deletion

The primary advantage of a linked list is that the operations of deletion and insertion may be done without moving data. These are accomplished by reassigning the links. As an example, deleting the record "Megan" from the above list would look something like:

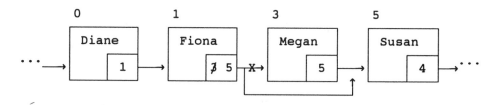

We have "cut" the link from record 1 to record 3 by changing its value. All we have to do is change the link of "Fiona" from 3 (which points to "Megan") to 5 (which points to "Susan"); that is, we change the link field of the record that points to the record we wish to delete—to the value of the link field of the record being deleted.

This gives us:

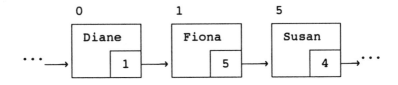

Since we are not moving any data, all of the records actually remain in their prior locations. Our physiological view would still be:

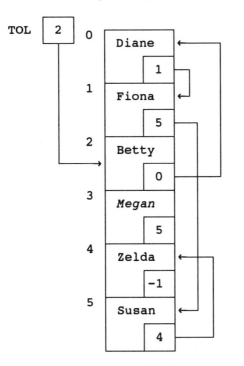

Shortly, we will deal with what to do about the physical storage associated with the record that we have just deleted. Note that it is really unnecessary to change either the contents of the data part of the deleted record or the link field; even though it points to record 5, it cannot be reached by following the links, hence it is not part of the list.

12.3.4 Insertion

Insertion may also be performed without moving data—only changing the links. For example, let us consider inserting the record "Emily" (stored in location 3) into the list, in order. Clearly, "Emily" needs to be logically inserted between "Diane" and "Fiona." To perform this, we copy the link from "Diane" (the 1) to "Emily" and change the link of "Diane" to point to 3 (the location of "Emily").

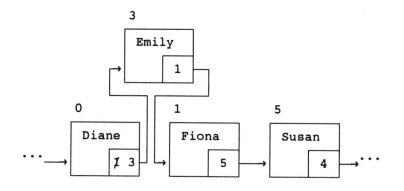

Thus, the list becomes:

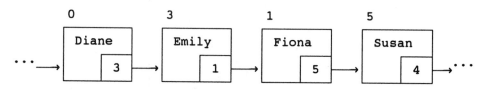

The physiological view of the list after the insertion is:

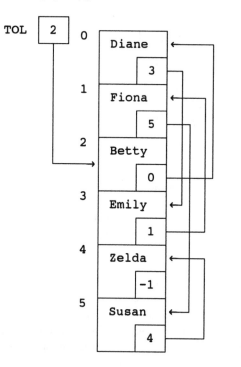

The general process is:

1. Copy the link of the record just before the place where the new record is to be inserted to the link field of the new record.
2. Change the link field of the previous record to the location of the new record.

Of course, we still need to determine the physical location of the new record.

12.3.5 Empty Records

Before we present specific algorithms for performing insertion and deletion, we need to decide how to handle empty records—records that have not been assigned a value and incorporated into the list and records that have been deleted from the list.

It is important that a record that is in use is not accidently reused; it is also important that the physical storage of records that have been deleted is not "lost." In general, we will place the deleted record into a pool of storage locations that may be used and reused, as needed.

There are two major ways to do this. The simplest one to visualize uses indices or pointers and entails linking the entire memory that will be allocated to the list into a list of empty locations. Access to the list will be through a variable that indicates the top-of-the-empties, *TOE*.

Since the actual list is empty, we will place our END marker (a −1) in the *TOL* variable.

Therefore, the empty list and its initial indices would appear as:

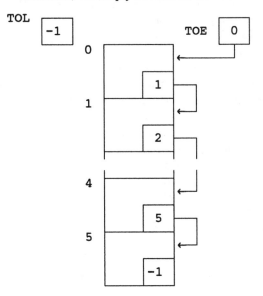

We have used the same link field for the empty link and the list link; however, since a record is never in the two lists at the same time, we could use any convenient field.

This scheme of linking available memory explicitly, is what we will use for the present. The other method (and a preferred one with C) is to implement pointers to the records as the link information and use the system memory allocation functions malloc() and free() to maintain the empty memory for us. Using these also makes the size of the linked list dynamic: growing and shrinking, as needed.

The formal algorithm to initialize memory is, thus:

Algorithm LM (Initialize Memory). Link all of the selected memory into a linked list of empty records. The variables *TOL*, top of list, and *TOE*, top of empties, are used to provide access to the list structure.

LM1. [set top pointers]   TOL=END; TOE=0.

LM2. [loop thru memory]   Perform step LM3 for j=0,1,...,N−2.

LM3. [set empty links]   LINK'[j]=j+1.

LM4. [set last link]   LINK'[N−1]=END.

The empty links may be any convenient field in the record—a good choice is the forward link field for the list. It is not necessary, and indeed is a waste of space, to design a record structure that has both the empty link fields and the regular link fields present at all times. The empty links are indicated as LINK'[] to remind us that they are a part of the empty records and not the ordinary link field of those records that are part of the list. They may be stored physically in the same bytes as the ordinary links, but may occupy any convenient part of the record.

Keep in mind that at any one time, a record is in one of two lists, but never both. In essence, we have two independent lists that are stored in a section of shared memory. A chunk of physical storage moves from one list to the other, and back, as insertions and deletions are made. What indicates whether a specific chunk is in one list or the other are the links. It is in the empty list if you can trace the chain of links starting with *TOE* and encounter it. It is part of the data list if you can do the same, starting with *TOL*. It can never be reached from both.

The list of empties will be maintained as a stack. The next insertion will be placed in the record pointed to by *TOE*. When we delete from the list, we will link it into the top of the empty list.

12.3.6 Insertion and Deletion Algorithms

To insert, we first find an empty record, remove it from the empty stack, and store the data in it.

Algorithm LU (Setup for Insertion into a Linked List). Store the item, *KEY*, in an empty record and set up for insertion into the linked list. Returns location, *loc*, where item is stored.

LU1. [set up]   loc=TOE.

LU2. [check if full]   If loc=END, then Terminate.   (no memory)

LU3. [update TOE]   TOE=LINK'[loc].

LU4. [store record]   DATA[loc]=KEY.

■

After invoking this algorithm, a datum will be stored and the empty stack will be updated, but the original list will not have been changed. We now have three logical entities sharing memory: the list (initially, it contains no records), the empty stack, and the record (where we have stored our new datum).

The physiological view of things will appear as:

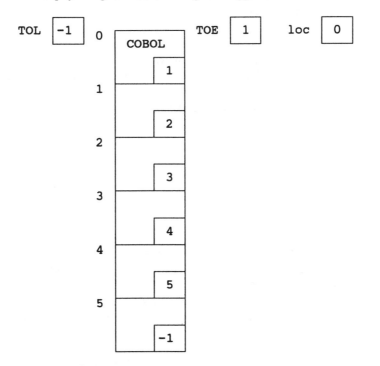

We are now ready to actually insert the record into the list in the appropriate logical position. First, there are two complications that must be taken care of.

On the surface, the procedure should involve searching the list until the proper logical position is found, and then inserting the new record. Perhaps we could use

Algorithm LS. To find the proper position, we search until we find the record that is just past the new one; that is, we insert it before the first one that is greater in value than it is. In order to insert, we must modify the link field of the record that logically precedes the new one. The problem is that the records are linked in the forward direction only. There is no way to "back up" in the list, and Algorithm LS "forgets" where it has been when it moves to the next record. Therefore, we need to modify this process so that it remembers the one previous record as we search the list.

The second problem is that there are two distinct situations where we can insert, and each involves something a little different. We could insert a record at the beginning of the list, which means we modify the value of *TOL*, or we could insert into the middle of the list so we modify the link field of an ordinary record. We need to take care of both of these situations.

There is actually a third situation as well—insertion at the end of the list (append)—but this will be taken care of automatically the same way insertion in the middle is, since it involves modifying the link field of an ordinary record.

The following algorithm implements solutions to both problems. It finds the appropriate position in the list and modifies the required link fields and variables to put the record into the list.

Algorithm LG (Graft a Record into a Linked List). Follow the sequence of links in an ordered linked list to find the appropriate location to insert an item stored in location, *loc*. The linked list is linked only in the forward direction.

LG1. [set up indices]   prior=END; j=TOL.

LG2. [test & move]   If j≠END and DATA[j] < DATA[loc], then prior=j;
                                              j=LINK[j]; Go to step LG2.

LG3. [update links]   If prior=END, then LINK[loc]=TOL; TOL=loc.
                                    else LINK[loc]=LINK[prior];
                                         LINK[prior]=loc.

The "grafting" terminology is borrowed from binary trees (discussed in the next chapter), where it is also convenient to separate the functions of setup and actual placement into the structure.

The algorithm uses a variable *prior* to remember the location of the prior record in the list. Essentially, it points back one record. Initially it is set to END, i.e., equivalent to *TOL*. Therefore, step LG2, in reality, performs a serial search on the ordered list.

The step LG3 checks to see if we need to update the *TOL* (insertion before the first record of the existing list) or update an ordinary record's link field (anywhere else). We use the special value of END, which is initially stored in the variable *prior*, to differentiate between these two cases. Once the search goes past the first logical record, *prior* will contain a valid index (or address) of an actual record in the list.

After invoking this algorithm, the physiological view of the memory becomes:

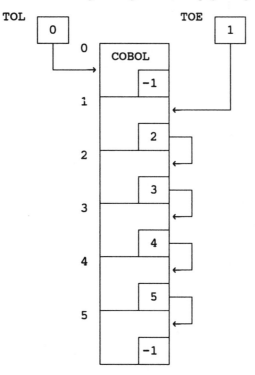

The logical list is simply: COBOL

In this case, the *TOL* is updated because the list was initially empty.

The complete insertion algorithm then combines the setup and grafting procedures as:

Algorithm LI (Insert a Record into a Linked List). Follow the sequence of links in an ordered linked list for the appropriate location to insert an item *KEY*. The linked list is linked only in the forward direction.

LI1. [find storage]   Invoke Algorithm LU, gives location loc.

LI2. [graft into list]   Invoke Algorithm LG with loc.

■

The two separate algorithms, LU and LG, could be combined, of course, into a single algorithm. However, by separating them we can use the grafting algorithm, Algorithm LG, for sorting, as we will see shortly.

After inserting LISP, Pascal, FORTH, and Ada in turn, the list becomes:

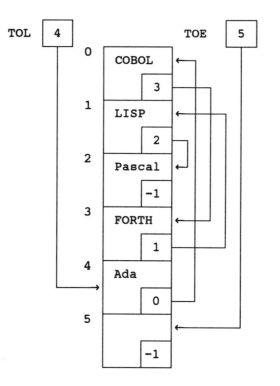

The logical list is: Ada, COBOL, FORTH, LISP, Pascal.

Now let us consider the process of deletion in detail. It involves searching for the record, finding it, removing it from the list, and placing the space on the empty list. As with insertion, we must remember the previous logical record and we must distinguish between deletions at the beginning of the list (update the TOL) and those in the middle (update an ordinary link field).

An algorithm to accomplish this is:

Algorithm LD (Deletes a Record from a Linked List). Follow the sequence of links in an ordered linked list to find an item, *KEY*, and delete it. The linked list is linked only in the forward direction.

LD1. [set up]   prior=END; j=TOL.

LD2. [check if at end]   If j=END or DATA[j]>KEY, then Terminate.(not found)

LD3. [test & move]   If DATA[j]≠KEY, then prior=j; j=LINK[j];
                                      Go to step LD2.

LD4. [update links]   If prior=END, then TOL=LINK[j].
                                      else LINK[prior]=LINK[j];

LD5. [put on empty]   LINK'[j]=TOE; TOE=j.

■

Again, similar to the grafting algorithm, steps LD2 and LD3 perform the search. Step LD4 differentiates where the link update will take place and, finally, step LD5 performs the opposite of the setup algorithm. We have included both the manipulation of the list and the stack of empties in a single algorithm since there is no need to separate them.

As an example of how the deletion algorithm works, let us now delete LISP from our list. It is found in location 1 with *last*=3. Therefore, LINK[3] is set to LINK[1]=2. This effectively removes it from the list. The location is then placed on the stack of empties.

The physiological view of the situation after deletion is:

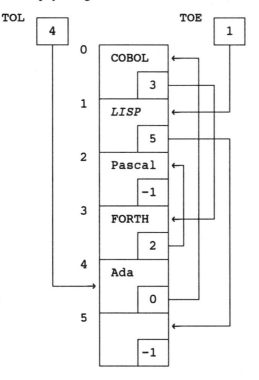

The logical list is: Ada, COBOL, FORTH, Pascal.

Notice that the data for LISP is still present, but it is effectively lost. It is no longer part of the data list; that is, it cannot be reached from TOL. It is part of the empty list and, hence, may be reused; that is, new data may be stored there.

Finally, to complete the example, let us insert SNOBOL into this list. Because the last location that was deleted is available and is placed on the top of the empties, it is the location that will be used for the next insertion. Thus, SNOBOL will stored in location 1.

The physiological view of things after inserting the new record becomes:

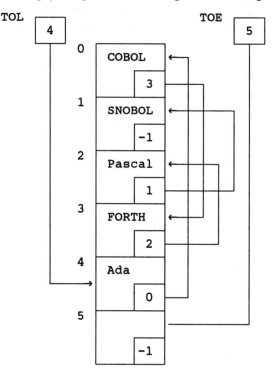

The logical list is: Ada, COBOL, FORTH, Pascal, SNOBOL.

Because of the sequential nature and the typical ordering of a linked list, searching will take:

Best	Average	Worst
1	n/2	n

Insertions and deletions will also take roughly the same number of operations. However, because data does not have to be moved, these are considerably faster than the simple procedures we studied for a simple list. For the example we have considered, this may not be a significant savings, but if each record contained several hundred bytes, moving a few hundred or thousand of them for each insertion or deletion might take a significant amount of time.

12.4   *C IMPLEMENTATION*

There are several ways one can implement a linked list in C. We have used a notation that suggests using arrays and indices. That is, we have used a data structure that could be defined as:

```
int data[SIZE],link[SIZE],tol,toe;
```

We would access the *j*-th record with:

```
data[j] and link[j]
```

where *j* is defined to be int.

However, this does not make use of the best possibilities of C, which allow us to define a record structure. Maintaining an index to access records, we could use:

```
struct record {int data;
               int link;
              };

struct record list[SIZE];
int tol,toe;
```

where *list[]* is defined to be a vector of records. To access the *j*-th record we would use:

```
list[j].data and list[j].link
```

The definition of *list[]* could be combined alternatively with the structure declaration as:

```
struct record {int data;
               int link;
              } list[SIZE];
int tol,toe;
```

Even using a C structure in this way does not fully exploit the features of the C language—to do so, would be to use pointers. First, we define the record as:

```
struct record {int data;
               struct record *link;
              };

struct record list[SIZE],*tol,*toe;
struct record *ptr;
```

To access a record we must initialize the pointer to the structure:

```
ptr = &list[j];
```

Then we can use:

```
ptr->data and ptr->link
```

Actually, we would not explicitly use the index notation except, perhaps, to initialize the *tol*, *toe*, and link fields.

Since we are using pointers, the END mark is normally a zero (or NULL) rather than -1, since a zero is an invalid address or pointer value.

In reality, things would appear little different. There would be actual addresses stored in the link fields rather than a simple index. As an example, our previous list might appear as:

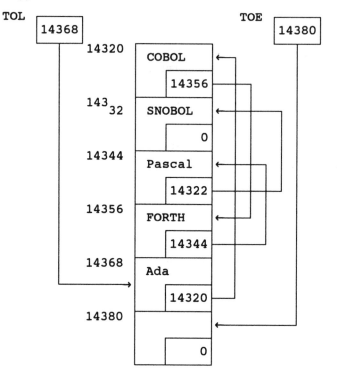

The preferred scheme in C is to use the memory allocation library functions:

malloc(size)   Returns a pointer to usable memory of size bytes.

free(pointer)   Frees memory so that is can be reused.

With these is a very useful C operator:

sizeof (data type)   Returns size in bytes of *data type*.

Using these means, the C system handles the "empty" memory. We need only allocate a chunk of memory to store our record—malloc() gives us a pointer to that memory. When we delete the record, free() permits that storage to be reused.

For the previous examples we have used a very simple record structure. The data field has been an integer; however, in a realistic situation the data might be more complicated. For example:

```
struct record {char name[24];
               char street[20];city[16], state[3];
               long int zip;
               char phone[13];
               char sex;
               int age;
               struct record *link;
               };
```

Such a record could be suitable for storing a name, address, phone number, sex, and age. Remember, structures may also contain structures as members.

12.5 I/O RESTRICTED LISTS

We have already seen how a linked list can be utilized as a stack. Indeed, because we always have access to the top of the list, this is a natural use.

A linked list can also be easily established as a queue. However, now we will find it convenient to maintain an "end of the list" pointer which contains the location of the record with a link of END. Because knowing which record this is does not tell us which record points to it, it is difficult to delete from this end. We will insert at this end; we have already seen how we can delete from the other end.

The operations of insertion and deletion then follow rather directly. We do not have to be concerned about a full queue and an empty queue, as we did with the simple list formulation. The ordinary insertion and deletion algorithms for the linked list will take care of these cases.

12.6 SORTING

Typically, a linked list is maintained in order. The algorithms that we have examined, above, do this. However, it is important to be able to perform a sort operation on a list that is in random order. Even if the list is built and maintained in order for one field in the record, it might be desirable to reorder it according to another field.

Because the linked lists that we have studied are linked only in the forward direction, this eliminates, at first consideration, those algorithms that need to pass both ways through the list or need to jump around in the list—algorithms such as Bubble Sort, Insertion Sort, Shell's Sort, Quick Sort, etc. This leaves us with a pretty limited selection of sorts, none of which are very good.

12.6.1 Insertion Sort

We included the Insertion Sort in our list of unusable sorts because it involves an index that moves backwards. The reason for this, with a simple list structure, was the necessity to move data forward, one at a time, to make room for the new item that was being inserted into the already sorted list. We needed to do this because we were sorting in place.

However, linked lists do not involve the movement of data! We can insert anywhere in the list without having "to make room" for the new item. Therefore, we can perform the insertion by scanning from the beginning of the list and inserting the new item in the proper position in the already sorted list.

To do this, we first create an empty list, then logically remove a record from the beginning of the old list and insert into the proper position in the new linked list, using the graft algorithm. This process is repeated until the old list is empty. The new list is sorted! Since we are not actually moving data, but merely rearranging the values of link fields, this can be accomplished easily, without data duplication. Removal from the beginning of a list is easy, and we already have an algorithm for grafting a record into the appropriate position.

In reality, we are implementing the fundamental essence of the Insertion Sort. We are not trying to force a particular algorithm based upon a certain data structure, on another. We are stepping back to examine the concept rather than simply looking at the specific scheme.

An algorithm to perform this Insertion Sort on a linked list is given by:

Algorithm LN (Performs a Linked List Insertion Sort). Removes records one at a time from an old list and grafts them into a new linked list, in order. The linked list is linked only in the forward direction.

LN1. [set indices]   told=TOL; TOL=END;

LN2. [get next record]   loc=told.

LN3. [are we done?]   If loc=END, then Terminate.

LN4. [remove from old]   told=LINK[loc].

LN5. [insert in new]   Perform Algorithm LG with loc.

LN6. [loop]   Go to step LN2.

Because this is an insertion type sort, the average number of operations is $O(n^2/4)$. This is not an extremely efficient sort for large numbers of records, and it is difficult to modify into a Shell's Sort procedure since that involves jumping around in the list and implicit separation and combining, which are easiest when the list is maintained physically as a contiguous simple list.

12.6.2 Quick Sort

A more fruitful approach is the Quick Sort procedure. On the surface, with the swapping and right index moving backwards, it would not seem possible. But the essence of the Quick Sort scheme is to form two lists and a single item. All the records in one list are smaller than the single item, and all the records in the other list are larger. These two are sorted recursively, and finally all three can be combined into a single sorted list.

Separating the original list into two lists plus a single element is relatively easy with linked lists. We can remove one records from the beginning of the original list and insert it at the beginning of one of the two sublists. The record can be inserted at the beginning of the "small" sublist or the beginning of the "big" sublist, since we do not care about the internal order of these.

When the original list is separated into the three pieces, we simply need to sort each piece recursively and recombine the pieces. To do this efficiently, we need to know the location of the last item in the "small" and "big" sublists. There is some additional complication because the "small" or "large" sublist might be empty at the end of the process.

The algorithm that we will use will take the first item in the list as the pivot element. It will return the new beginning and the location of the last element of the list so that we can easily hook the pieces together. It is given by:

Algorithm LQ (Linked List Quick Sort). Sorts a forward-linked linked list using a Quick Sort procedure. Returns the location of the first and last element of the list and the appropriate links. It is invoked with the location, *loc*, of the top of the list to be sorted (initially *TOL*). The ends of the two pieces are given in *ends* and *endb*, for the small and big list, respectively.

LQ1. [empty?]   If loc = END, then Return (END).

LQ2. [initialize]   pvt=loc; tols=END; tolb=END.

LQ3. [get partition]   part=data[pvt]; j=link[pvt].

LQ4. [at end?]   If j = END, then Go to step LQ8.

LQ5. [get next]   nxt=link[j].

LQ6. [test]   If part > data[j], then link[j]=tols; tols=j.
                                          else link[j]=tolb; tolb=j.

LQ7. [loop]   j=nxt; Go to step LQ4.

LQ8. [recurse]   Invoke Algorithm LQ with tols; Set ends to returned value.
                       Invoke Algorithm LQ with tolb; Set endb to returned value.

LQ9. [hook on big]   link[pvt]=tolb.

LQ10. [small empty?]   If ends ≠ END, then link[ends]=pvt; loc = tols.

LQ11. [return end]   If endb = END, then Return (pvt).
                                    else Return (endb).

If the "small" list is empty, then our location of the top of the list, which already indicates the pivot item, does not change. Otherwise, we set the top of the list to the top of the "small" list and connect the pivot to its end.

If the "big" list is empty, then we return the location of the pivot as the last element of the recombined list. Otherwise, we return the location of the end of the "big" list.

When we implement this in C, since a C function can return only one value, we will pass a pointer to the function that contains the address of the top of the list and allow the function to return the location of the end of the list. For the index version, the function could be defined as:

```
int lqsort(int *loc)
```

The function is invoked as:

```
lqsort(&tol);
```

Part of step LQ8 might then appear as:

```
ends = lqsort(&tols);       /* recurse, sort small */
```

For the pointer version, things are more interesting. Assuming we have a list defined in terms of a struct record, our sort function would be defined as:

```
struct record *lqsort(struct record **loc)
```

It would be invoked the same way. Here, however, *tol* contains an address to a structure. We pass the address of this variable. Thus, inside the function *loc* is an address of a variable containing an address; that is, a pointer to a pointer to a record (perhaps we should name it *loc_add*). The variables, such as *j*, *pvt*, *ends*, and *tols*, etc. are also defined to be pointers.

In both cases, *loc* must be referenced internally as *loc* since we want to modify the value of the variable. The variable *pvt* is used because we may need to modify *loc* inside the function (step LQ10), but we may need to return its original value (step LQ11).

Essentially, we partition the list into the usual three pieces. If the "small" list is empty, then the location of the pivot becomes the first value in the list. If the "big" list is empty, then the end of the list is the location of the pivot. We use the values in the "end" variables to determine these details.

12.6.3 External Type Sorts

Other possibilities for sorting a linked list come from the external sorts. After all, a linked list is a sequential structure, and the two external sorts we discussed access the data in a sequential manner.

A disadvantage of the external sorts, for simple lists, is that they require considerable extra storage. There is at least n extra storage locations for a list that is n elements in length. However, a real advantage of linked lists is that the records can be arranged in a variety of ways without moving data—simply by rearranging the links; therefore, it should be possible to implement such sorts without any extra storage.

The Radix Sort required m auxiliary lists. With a linked list we can simply establish m "top of list" pointers or indices, then sequentially access the records of the linked list, and append each record to the appropriate auxiliary linked list. This is fast if we also keep m "end of list" pointers (or indices) which point to the last record in the auxiliary lists. When the records are all distributed into the auxiliary linked lists, then we simply copy the pointer of the top of the $m+1$ list to the link of the bottom record of the m list, and the list is reassembled. This procedure may then be repeated on the next bit, character, or digit.

Since the only extra storage involves approximately $2m$ pointers, it is practical to make m as large as conveniently possible. Therefore, to sort strings of letters, we could use 26 auxiliary lists (or even 52 or 255). The number of operations required to sort a list of n elements is therefore n times the number of letters.

The following algorithm is used for sorting a linked list where the data consists of digits.

Algorithm LR (Radix Sort on a Linked List). Given a linked list, *LIST*, of elements of d digits with the top of the list *TOP*, rearrange these items so that they are in increasing order. This uses auxiliary linked lists with *TOL[10]* and *EOL[10]*.

LR1. [initialize]	divisor=1.
LR2. [loop on digits] $k=0,1,...,d-1$.	Perform steps LR3 through LR17 for
LR3. [initial queues]	Perform step LR4 for $j=0,...,9$.
LR4. [set initial indices]	TOL[j] = END; EOL[j] = END.
LR5. [start into list]	loc = TOP.
LR6. [are we done]	If loc = END, then Go to step LR12.
LR7. [get digit]	dgt = (DATA[loc]/divisor) mod 10.
LR8. [put in auxiliary]	If TOL[dgt] = END, then TOL=loc. else LINK[EOL[dgt]]=loc.

LR9. [update link of record]	nxt=LINK[loc]; LINK[loc]=END.
LR10. [update bottom]	EOL[dgt]=loc.
LR11. [go get next record]	loc=nxt; Go to step LR6.
LR12. [set up index]	j=0.
LR13. [find non-empty]	If TOL[j] = END, then j=j+1; Go to step LR13.
LR14. [restore top]	TOP=TOL[j];
LR15. [loop over list]	Perform step LR16 for i=j+1,...,9.
LR16. [relink list]	If TOL[i] ≠ END, then LINK[EOL[j]]=TOL[i]; j=i.
LR17. [change divisor]	divisor = 10 • divisor.

The Two-Way Merge Sort can also be implemented for linked lists without using any additional storage. The original list is accessed and linked together into two linked lists, *a* and *b*, the same as it is for files. These two are sequentially accessed and alternately merged 1 by 1 into pieces of two long onto two other lists, *c* and *d*. These, in turn, are merged 2 by 2 into pieces that are four long, onto alternative lists. The important thing to keep in mind is that these temporary lists are created by manipulating links. There does not need to be any movement or duplication of data.

12.7 MERGING

Two linked lists may also be merged. Since linked lists are typically maintained as ordered lists, the resultant list will also be ordered.

We typically merged simple lists or files into a third list such that we retained the original two lists. We need not do this with the linked lists. Indeed, we can accomplish this task without moving data; that is, we combine two logical lists into one, using the same physical storage.

Initially, we have two mutually exclusive lists sharing memory. Access to these lists will be via two "top of the list" variables: *tola* and *tolb*, giving us access to lists A and B, respectively. For convenience, we will use *tola* to be the top of the list variable for the resultant list. That is, we will merge list B into list A.

We will perform this efficiently, taking one record at a time from list B and moving through list A to find the proper place to link it in. Since we will assume that list A is ordered, this is done by continuing from the last record we examined; that is, if the record in list A is less than the top record in list B, then we will move to the next record in A. If not, then we will remove the record from list B and graft it into list A.

It is important to keep in mind that we are dealing with two logical linked lists; however, these two occupy one physically defined list of memory. Therefore, the data and the link fields are the same. There is no need to use *DATAA* and *DATAB* or *LINKA* and *LINKB* in the algorithm. In reality, we have a group of records linked together into two logical lists. The algorithm re-links them into one logical list without moving them—just adjusting the link fields.

The following algorithm will perform this.

Algorithm MG (Merge Two Linked Lists). Given a linked list, *LIST* with top of list variable *tola* and a second list, *LIST* with top of list variable *tolb*, merge these. When done *tola* provides access to the top of the resultant linked list, *LIST*.

MG1. [initialize]   Set prior=END; k=tola.

MG2. [end of B?]   If tolb = END, then Halt.

MG3. [get next B]   Set j=tolb; tolb=LINK[j].

MG4. [end of A?]   If k = END, then Go to step MG8.

MG5. [compare]   If DATA[k] < DATA[j], then prior=k; k=LINK[k];
                                      Go to step MG4.

MG6. [merge]   If prior = END, then LINK[j]=k; tola=j.
                              else LINK[j]=LINK[prior]; LINK[prior]=j.

MG7. [loop]   Set prior=j; Go to step MG2.

MG8. [tack on B]   If prior = END, then tola = j.
                              else LINK[prior]=j.

In order to clean up the two list access variables, it is important to set *tolb* to END after executing this algorithm since, presumably, the second list is now empty—all of the records that were in it have been merged into the first list.

In C, using our scheme for defining a single physical list to store the lists, we would have:

```
struct record {int data;
               int link;
               } list[SIZE];
int tola,tolb,toe;
```

The references in Algorithm MG (appearances of DATA[k]) would become:

```
list[k].data    list[j].data
```
and
```
list[j].link    list[k].link    list[prior].link
```

That is, they are references to a single physical set of records. It is the links that keep these organized into two logical lists.

12.8 DOUBLY LINKED LISTS

We have described a linked list with forward links only, but it is also possible to define both forward and backward links. This helps alleviate some of the problems we encountered earlier when searching for the proper position for a record to be inserted or deleted, but it increases the complexity of the algorithms that modify the links, because we now have two links to be updated. We also need to keep two link fields in each record as well as a variable that points to the end of the list, *EOL*.

Such a list might look like:

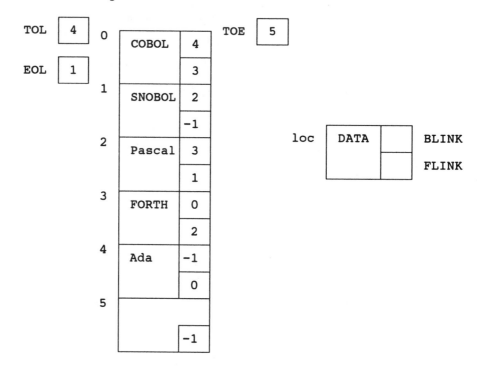

Tracing the backward links from EOL produces: SNOBOL, Pascal, FORTH, COBOL, Ada.

Linking a list both forwards and backwards does serve to provide some redundancy; therefore, if a link gets corrupted, the list might be able to be reconstructed.

12.9 MULTI-LINKED LISTS

Not only might we wish to link a list both forwards and backwards, but we might wish to link a list into several logical lists, each with the same data but linked in different order. This would be more appropriate if the data in each record contained several items of data. We can link the same data in several different ways, if we wish.

This is particularly useful if we want to access the data regularly in different order. This is a common situation with a database containing complicated records.

As a simple example, consider the following list of records containing a NAME and an AGE field. We supply two link fields (forward links) one for each of the ordering that we desire: *LINKN[]* for the names and *LINKA[]* for the ages. Access to the lists are through the top-of-the-list variables: *TOLN* for the NAME order and *TOLA* for the AGE order.

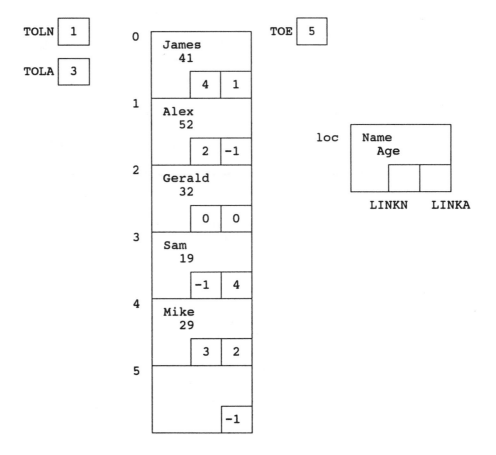

Tracing the LINKN links, starting with *TOLN*, produces:

Alex	52
Gerald	32
James	41
Mike	29
Sam	19

Tracing the LINKA links, starting with *TOLA*, produces:

Sam	19
Mike	29
Gerald	32
James	41
Alex	52

Insertion involves invoking Algorithm LU, Setup, to find an empty storage location and storing the new data, then invoking Algorithm LG, Graft, twice—once for each logical list.

Deletion involves invoking Algorithm LD, Deletion, steps LD1-LD4, for one logical list and the entire algorithm for the second one.

12.10 VARIABLE SIZE RECORDS

If all of the records in the list are the same size, then the above discussion should be sufficient to implement a linked list. However, all too often the records differ in size. One way to handle the situation is to reserve sufficient storage for each record to contain the largest anticipated amount of data. However, this is wasteful of space; therefore, it is desirable to handle variable sized records. On the other hand, the general situation with all possible record sizes is rather messy. Deleting and inserting records of different sizes may result in small pieces of memory that become unusable.

A compromise is to allocate memory in fixed chunks; this will be the basic size of all records and is selected to handle the majority of the cases we need. For those records that are too large to fit into this storage, we will allocate a second (or third, or fourth,...) chunk and link it to the first as a continuation record. When such an extended record is deleted, all of the storage is released back to the empty pool. Because all of the chunks are the same size, memory management is easy.

We can designate a field in the original record structure as a continuation field to point to any necessary continuation records. Originally, these have the END value but, as needed, will point down a chain of strange chunks that make up the entire record. Thus, our record will appear as:

Consider the example where we insert the records: Pascal, COBOL, and Ada. These are the keys, and each record contains other data (Perhaps, a list of versions!) Let us imagine that all the data for Pascal and Ada will fit into one of the record chunks, but the COBOL record takes two chunks. The "almost physical" view of the linked list structure will appear as:

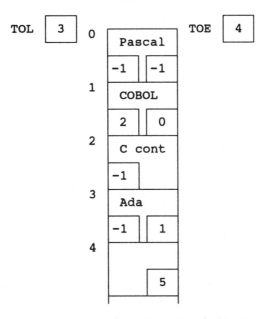

A more logical view of the list which illustrates the continuation record would appear as in the diagram at the top of the next page.

Because we were inserting records into an empty list without deletions, the continuation record for FORTRAN appeared in the next physical record. In general, this would not be the case. The continuation record would be taken from the next available chunk of memory from the empty list and might be located anywhere in memory.

If more than one continuation record were necessary, then the *CONT* could point to another in the "side branch."

In general, the data stored in the continuation record is different than the data stored in the main record. As an example, different link fields are used. The effective implementation of continuation records using the same physical memory as the primary records requires the use of the C union construct. This allows the same piece of memory to contain different data of different types.

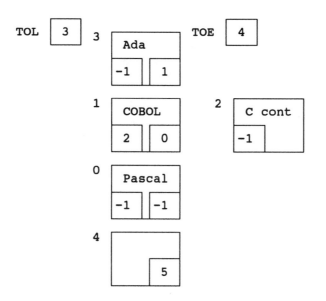

12.11 ELIMINATION OF TOP-OF-LIST

We needed to make a distinction in the grafting and deletion algorithms about whether the operation modified the *TOL* or the link field of an ordinary record. The algorithms may be simplified if the first physical record of the list contains a data value that is less than any allowed value in the list and is, hence, used to contain the *TOL* information. The printing algorithm simply skips over this record. Actually, we do not have to store any data in this record if all of the algorithms that search or print simply start with the second in the list.

This scheme wastes space in the list, but might actually provide an overall savings by simplifying and decreasing the size of the code required for the algorithms.

The "physiological" view of the list we used previously appears as in the diagram at the top of following page.

Because the *TOL* information is contained in the link field of a record, the appropriate steps in grafting and deletion can be simplified. When these two algorithms are executed, the variable, *prior*, is first set to 0, the location of this "top" record, rather than END.

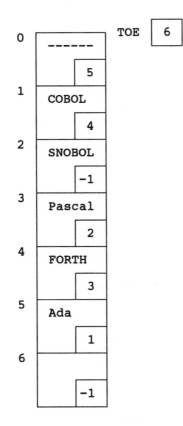

12.12 SUMMARY

A linked list is a powerful data structure. It permits insertion and deletion without the movement of data. To implement such a structure requires a link field in each record that tells where the next logical record is located. By following the trail of links, you can process the entire list.

The disadvantage of the linked list is that it is a serial structure; therefore, we cannot perform an efficient search, such as the binary search.

Because of the linked nature of these lists, we can implement sorting, merging, and other manipulation algorithms without moving data or without providing extra storage for the records. However, we must rethink the essence of the algorithms and adapt them for this linked structure.

REFERENCES

Knuth, Donald E., *The Art of Computer Programming*; Fundamental Algorithms, vol. 1., 2nd ed., Addison-Wesley Publishing Co., Reading, Massachusetts, 1973.

Knuth, Donald E., *The Art of Computer Programming*; Sorting and Searching, vol. 3., Addison-Wesley Publishing Co., Reading, Massachusetts, 1973.

Sedgewick, Robert, *Algorithms in C*, Addison-Wesley Publishing Co., Reading, Massachusetts, 1990.

QUESTIONS

Q12.1   What fraction of extra memory would be taken for the link field of a linked list if each record consisted of:

name	20	characters
number	1	integer
price	1	float

Q12.2   Declare a C record structure for a linked list that would be appropriate for:

last name	15 characters
first name	15 characters
team	10 characters
uniform number	1 integer
at bats	1 integer
hits	1 integer

The list is to be maintained using only a forward link ordered according to last name.

Q12.3   Explain why insertion and deletion in a linked list take roughly the same number of operations as searching (best, average, worst cases). If we used a simple list, how many operations would be required for insertion and deletion once we were given the key of the record to be deleted or inserted?

Q12.4   What are the advantage(s) and disadvantage(s) of using a doubly linked list (with both forward and backward links) compared to a singly linked list (with only forward links)?

Q12.5   Could a linked list be implemented on a magnetic tape medium? Explain.

Q12.6   How could a linked structure be used to handle files stored on a disk?

Q12.7   How could one maintain several independent linked lists in memory? Assume that the record size of all of these are is the same. Do you need to have more than one empty?

Q12.8   If a linked list is maintained in a computer's main memory with both forward and backward links, could you use a binary search to find a given record? Why or why not?

Q12.9   A simple random access list, a string, and a sequential file structure all had differences in their access algorithms because of their structure. For example, the length of a string and a file were not generally known whereas the number of records of a simple list was known. A file's record had to be read once and then the internal buffer needed to be accessed; whereas, for the simple list and string there could be repeated access. Compare these with a linked list. How are they the same? Different?

Q12.10   A beginning programmer decided to implement a linked list using a structure that looked like:

```
struct record {int data;
               int link;
               int empty_link;
               } list[NUMB];
```

Comment on the inclusion of the empty_link variable which was to link the unused records together. Is it necessary? Is it a good idea? Why, or why not?

Q12.11   Using a Two-way Merge Sort on a linked list requires how much extra storage? How many operations would it take?

Q12.12   We discussed using a Straight Insertion Sort on a linked list. Why (or why not) could you use a Shell's Sort and gain tremendous efficiency?

Q12.13   Of the various internal and external sorts that we have discussed, which could be applied to a linked list structure? Why or why not?

Q12.14   If it were desired to maintain a linked list as an unordered list, then where would it be best to implement an insertion? At the beginning or the end? Why?

Q12.15   Does it matter where in the record the linked field is located? Why or why not?

Q12.16   Is a linked list a random-access or a sequential access structure? Does this depend upon whether you are considering the logical view or the physical view, or something in between?

Q12.17   What are the advantages of implementing a linked list using pointers rather than indices as links?

Q12.18   Write a suitable C structure which could be used for a main record, that stores a person's first and last names, birthdate, sex, and number of children, and permits a single forward link as well as a continuation link, to a record that contains the same information for each of their children. Do not worry about the children of the children!

Q12.19   Why is the list of empties a stack?

Q12.20   If we wanted to maintain a linked list as a queue, what additional information would be useful to make this process efficient?

Q12.21   How many link fields (not counting the empty links) need to be changed in order to

       a. Delete a record?

       b. Insert a record?

Q12.22   Why is it not necessary to "blank" or modify the data areas of a record that has been deleted?

Q12.23   What would you need to do to "undelete" the last record that was deleted, before making any subsequent insertions?

Q12.24   In the Quick Sort Algorithm for a linked list, Algorithm LQ, we used:

       LQ9. [hook on big]   link[pvt]=tolb.

to connect the "big" list to the pivot. There are two possible situations: 1.) The "big" list is empty, 2.) The "big" list is not empty. Show that this one step correctly handles both cases.

Q12.25   In the linked-list merge procedure, Algorithm MG, we could halt immediately when we came to the end of one of the lists, without having to process the remaining records of the other as we did for the simple list merge. Why?

Q12.26   The Quick Sort for a simple list exhibited tail recursion, which we eliminated. Does the Quick Sort for the linked list, Algorithm LQ also exhibit tail recursion? Explain.

Q12.27   We defined the C function for the Quick Sort for a linked list as:

```
int lqsort(int *loc)
```

or

```
struct record *lqsort(struct record **loc)
```

In both cases, it is invoked as:

```
lqsort(&tol);
```

What is the significance of the *'s in the function definitions? In particular, why, in the pointer version, do we use **? Could we have used:

```
struct record *lqsort(struct record *loc[])
```

What would be the problem with this?

EXERCISES

E12.1   Diagram the "almost-physical" or "physiological" view of a linked list. Originally, the list is initialized to a list of empties that has 8 records. Include all necessary link fields and any variables necessary to access the list. Draw the configuration; that is, a DUMP for each of the following consecutively applied actions:

        a. Empty list

        b. List after insertion of 'P'

        c. List after insertion of 'S'

        d. List after insertion of 'G'

        e. List after insertion of 'M'

        f. List after **deletion** of 'P'

        g. List after insertion of 'B'

E12.2   Modify the Linked List Search Algorithm, Algorithm LS, to return not only the location of the desired record (or END if not found) but also the location of the logically previous record that points to it.

        This modified search algorithm then may be used to simplify the graft and deletion algorithms.

E12.3   Modify the linked list insertion and deletion algorithms (LG and LD) to handle the situation with both forward and backward links. Note that using both links both simplifies and complicates the algorithms.

E12.4   Consider the following "physiological" view of a linked list. What are the values of the *TOL* and *TOE* variables, as well as the values of the other link fields within each record? Assume that the list is ordered alphabetically.

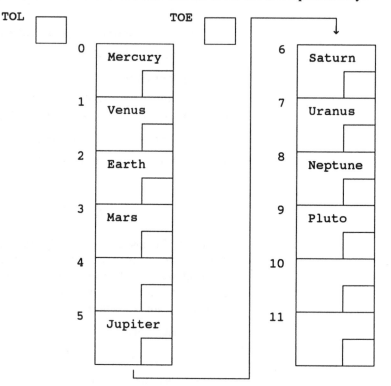

Note: The link fields are unique for the records containing valid data; the values of link fields are not unique for the empty list.

E12.5   Modify the linked-list algorithms to use the first element of the list to maintain the top-of-list information and not contain any useful data.

E12.6   Catenation of two lists is an operation that may be easily implemented using linked lists. Write a formal algorithm for catenating a linked list onto the end of a linked list. There should be no movement of data.

E12.7   A common situation is having to maintain the order in a single list according to more than one key. As an example, a list of baseball players might be maintained in order by team (the primary key) by last name (the secondary key). Modify the appropriate algorithm(s) (for inserting into the list) that finds the proper location using both the primary and secondary keys. Note, this is not the same as maintaining the list with two independent orderings. In reality, these two "keys" form an ordered pair that is the actual sort key.

E12.8   In order to speed up a linked-list search, it is possible to maintain several top-of-list pointers that allow entrance into the list at several places. For example, if the task was to maintain a list of names in alphabetical order, then one could establish a list of 26 indices or pointers that would tell where the first name starting with an 'A' was located, where the first starting with 'B' was found, etc. Therefore, to find a "Turner" one would begin searching at some place in the list where the first 'T' appeared—and effectively skipping all the names starting with 'A' through 'S'. Assuming the entire list is maintained in alphabetical order, with both forward and backward links, modify the list-manipulation algorithms to also maintain this list of indices or pointers. Note, that the list is to be maintained as one list; therefore, it would be possible to find "Turner" by starting with 'A'—it would just not be as quick.

E12.9   With a simple random access list, an easy "insertion" operation was appending a new item onto the end of the list. For a linked list, the straightforward analogous operation is to insert at the beginning of the list, or prepend. Write a formal algorithm to prepend a new item at the logical beginning of a linked list. Note, that the list will, generally, no longer be in order.

E12.10   Another possible sorting procedure for a linked list is the Two-way Merge Sort. A disadvantage of this sort, for simple lists or files, is that it takes additional storage; however, this is not a problem with linked lists. The four temporary lists used in the procedure turn into four temporary linked lists; however, there does not need to be a duplication or movement of data, only a rearrangement of the links.

Rewrite the Two-way Merge Sort Algorithms to sort a linked list.

E12.11   A queue is to be maintained as a linked list. Insertions are to be made at the top and deletions made at the other end. Write out formal algorithms for performing the two queue operations. Define a BOL variable to keep track of the bottom of the list and maintain a doubly linked list structure.

E12.12   Modify the linked-list maintenance algorithms to permit the use of continuation records. Use *CONT[j]* as the designation of the continuation link field.

E12.13   Show that the Insertion Sort on a linked list is $O(n^2/4)$ by counting the number of comparisons to insert the k-th item in a list of already sorted k items. To insert the $k=3$ item into a sorted list of two, as an example, assume that half the time only one comparison is needed, and half the time two comparisons are required (see Exercise 5.8).

PROBLEMS

P12.1   Write C functions to implement the linked list maintenance algorithms:

```
void initial()
void print()
int insert(item)  returns:    0 if successful
                             -1 if not successful
int delete(item)  returns:    0 if successful
                             -1 if not successful
void dump()
```

These will act upon a global linked-list structure containing 12 elements. The data will be integer values in the range 100-999. Let the initial() routine fill the data fields with 0.

The dump() routine should print out the location, the data, and the link values as well as the contents of *tol* and *toe* variables.

```
struct record {int data;
               int link;
              } list[12];
int tol,toe;
```

Write a main program that requests a command and value, if needed.

Perform the following in order:

1.	INITIAL		14.	PRINT
2.	DUMP		15.	DUMP
3.	INSERT	275	16.	DELETE 275
4.	INSERT	851	17.	PRINT
5.	INSERT	576	18.	DUMP
6.	INSERT	105	19.	INSERT 931
7.	INSERT	634	20.	PRINT
8.	PRINT		21.	DUMP
9.	DUMP		22.	INSERT 444
10.	DELETE	576	23.	PRINT
11.	PRINT		24.	DUMP
12.	DUMP		25.	DELETE 493
13.	INSERT	734		

P12.2   Write a C program that implements the linked-list algorithms using a pointer as a link:

```
struct record {int data;
                   struct record *link;
              } list[12],*tol,*toe;
```

Test it with the data for the previous problem.

P12.3   Implement a linked-list Insertion Sort function. Enter items into the list by inserting only at the beginning—this does not involve any searching down through the list, and consists of:

```
list[loc].link = tol;
tol = loc;
```

or

```
loc->link = tol;
tol = loc;
```

where *loc* is the location where the datum is stored.
    Print the list in order; sort it; then print it again.

P12.4   Implement a linked-list Quick Sort function. Enter items into the list by inserting only at the beginning—this does not involve any searching down through the list, and consists of:

```
list[loc].link = tol;
tol = loc;
```

or

```
loc->link = tol;
tol = loc;
```

where *loc* is the location where the datum is stored.
    Print the list in order; sort it; then print it again.

P12.5   Implement a Radix Sort on an internal linked list using a linked-list structure for the auxiliary queues. This eliminates the necessity for needing $10 \cdot n$ storage locations for the ten lists (assuming we are sorting digits). How much storage is now required?
    Use your program to sort a list of social security numbers which look like:

xxx-xx-xxxx

Hint: Treat the nine digits as a single nine-digit integer and break them apart for I/O. Use a list of 100 such values.

P12.6   Implement a C program to maintain a linked list linked in the forward direction by two independent links, as illustrated by the name and age example in the text.

Use either pointers:

```
struct person {char name[30];
               int age;
               struct person *nlink,*alink;
               } list[50],*toln,*tola;
```

or indices:

```
struct person {char name[30];
               int age;
               int nlink,alink;
               } list[50];
int toln,tola;
```

P12.7   An astronomy data base for stars might include:

name	24 characters
designation	12 characters
constellation	3 characters
right ascension	2 unsigned integers
declination	1 signed integer
	1 unsigned integer
visual magnitude	1 signed float

The right ascension (R.A.) is essentially a longitude type coordinate measured in hours and minutes (0:00 through 23:59) around the equator; the declination is a latitude type coordinate measured in degrees and minutes (-90:00 through +90:00) north and south of the equator; and the visual magnitude is a measure of the apparent brightness of the star (brightest star is the one with smallest or most negative visual magnitude).

It is desired that the data be stored in a linked list and logically ordered into three lists according to name, right ascension, and visual magnitude.

Write a C program to implement the linked list. It should permit:

    insert
    delete
    search by name
    list
            name
            right ascension
            visual magnitude
    dump
    exit

The program should handle all abnormal situations such as deletion from an empty list and insertion into a full list.

The data to be used are those of the brightest stars:

	name	des	cons	R.A.	dec	mag
1.	Archernar	alpha	Eri	01:37	−57:20	0.51
2.	Polaris	alpha	UMi	02:13	+89:11	1.99
3.	Mirfak	alpha	Per	03:23	+49:47	1.80
4.	Aldebaran	alpha	Tau	04:35	+16:28	0.86
5.	Rigel	beta	Ori	05:14	−08:13	0.14
6.	Capella	alpha	Aur	05:15	+45:59	0.05
7.	Bellatrix	gamma	Ori	05:24	+06:20	1.64
8.	Elnath	beta	Tau	05:25	+28:36	1.65
9.	Alnilam	eta	Ori	05:35	−01:13	1.70
10.	Alnitak	zeta	Ori	05:40	−01:57	1.79
11.	Betelgeuse	alpha	Ori	05:54	+07:24	0.41
12.	Canopus	alpha	Car	06:24	−52:41	−0.72
13.	Sirius	alpha	CMa	06:44	−16:42	−1.47
14.	Adhara	eta	CMa	06:58	−28:57	1.48
15.	Castor	alpha	Gem	07:33	+31:56	0.97
16.	Procyon	alpha	CMi	07:38	+05:17	0.37
17.	Pollux	beta	Gem	07:44	+28:05	1.16
18.	Regulus	alpha	Leo	10:07	+12:04	1.36
19.	Acrux	alpha	Cru	12:25	−62:59	1.30
20.	Spica	alpha	Vir	13:24	−11:03	0.91
21.	Hadar	beta	Cen	14:02	−60:16	0.63
22.	Arcturus	alpha	Boo	14:15	+19:17	−0.06
23.	Rigel Kentaurus	alpha	Cen	14:38	−60:46	0.00
24.	Antares	alpha	Sco	16:28	−26:23	0.92
25.	Vega	alpha	Lyr	18:36	+38:46	0.04
26.	Altair	alpha	Aql	19:50	+08:49	0.77
27.	Deneb	alpha	Cyg	20:41	+45:12	1.26
28.	Fomalhaut	alpha	PsA	22:57	−29:44	1.15

where "des" is the designation within the constellation (a letter of the Greek alphabet, generally in order of decreasing brightness) and the constellation is abbreviated in the "cons" column.

Perform in order:

a. Enter all the odd numbered data.

b. List by name

c. List by right ascension

d. List by visual magnitude

e. Delete all stars with a visual magnitude greater than or equal to 1.70. Note, there are only a few of these, identify them manually, and delete them one-by-one by name.

f. List by name

g. Enter all the even numbered data.

h. List by name

i. List by right ascension

j. List by visual magnitude

k. Dump

l. Search for 'Spica'

m. Search for 'Alkaid'

l. end

Your print routine should generate one line for each record, similar to the format above.

P12.8   Write a C function that merges two linked lists.

```
int llmerge(int tola, int tolb)
```

or

```
struct record *llmerge(tola, tolb)
 struct record *tola,*tolb;
```

where it returns the location of the top of the combined list.

Build two ordered lists (you need only one initial stack of empties); dump the memory; print each list; merge them; print the result; and dump the memory.

Chapter 13

Binary Trees

This time Alice waited patiently until it chose to speak again. In a minute or two the Caterpillar took the hookah out of its mouth, and yawned once or twice, and shook itself. Then it got down off the mushroom, and crawled away into the grass, merely remarking, as it went, "One side will make you grow taller, and the other side will make you grow shorter."

"One side of <u>what</u>? The other side of <u>what</u>?" thought Alice to herself.

"Of the mushroom, " said the Caterpillar, just as if she had asked it aloud; and in another moment it was out of sight.

Alice remained looking thoughtfully at the mushroom for a minute, trying to make out which were the two sides of it; and, as it was perfectly round, she found this a very difficult question. However, at last she stretched her arms round it as far as they would go, and broke off a bit of the edge with each hand.

"And now which is which?" she said to herself, and nibbled a little of the right-hand bit to try the effect.

13.1 OBJECTIVES

The objectives of this chapter are to:

- Introduce the concept of a binary tree data structure.

- Give basic tree terminology.

417

- Illustrate the order properties of a binary tree.

- Discuss the advantages of a tree structure.

- Provide tree manipulation algorithms such as insertion, deletion, searching, and traversal.

- Analyze the tree algorithms.

- Discuss balancing a tree.

- Provide an overview of other tree structures.

13.2   INTRODUCTION

A simple linear list is easy to visualize and the algorithms for manipulating it are straightforward. If it is maintained as an ordered list, then searching is quick—a binary search is O(lg n). Insertion and deletion are relatively slow, O(n/2), and involve moving data.

A linked list overcomes the slow insertion and deletion inherent in the simple linear list, but searching is no longer as effective as it was. Since insertion and deletion often involve searching, then we have not significantly changed the functional way that these grow—we have only eliminated data movement.

Is it possible to gain the best of all worlds? Can a data structure be devised that implements searching O(lg n) and insertion and deletion without moving data? Fortunately, the answer is an emphatic "yes!"

13.3   BINARY TREES

We will expand our concept of a linked list to include two forward links for each record. These will allow us to move down one of two directions. In so doing, the collection of data will no longer be "physiologically" a single sequential list but will be a tree structure—a binary tree.

13.3.1   Views

Our record will appear as:

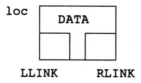

LLINK   RLINK

The link fields allow us to construct a "two-dimensional" structure that might appear as an upside-down tree. Because each element of the structure links forward to a maximum of two subsequent elements, this is termed a **binary tree**.

Displaying just the data of the list, a tree might appear as:

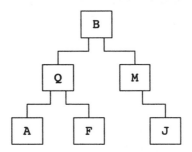

13.3.2 Terminology

As might be expected, tree structures have their own particular terminology. The records that hold the data are called **nodes**. Connecting the nodes are **arcs** or **branches**.

Each node in a binary tree, except one, has exactly one branch that comes into it from above. The one exception is called the **root**—the node containing 'B' in the example above. This forces the tree structure to be hierarchical in nature.

Each node in a binary tree has zero, one, or two branches leaving it to connect to nodes below. In the example, above, the nodes with 'A', 'F', and 'J' have zero branches leaving them; the node with 'M' has one; and the nodes containing 'B' and 'Q' have two branches. The nodes with zero branches are sometimes called **leaves**. It is customary to draw trees as growing downward, with the root at the top.

We can also describe the situation by saying that each node has exactly two branches; however, some of those branches may connect to null or empty nodes. Each node does have exactly two link fields to other nodes.

The **level** of a node is defined by the number of branches that it takes to get to that node from the root. The level of the root is zero. In the example above, nodes with 'Q' and 'M' are level 1, and nodes holding 'A', 'F', and 'J' are at level 2. The maximum level of a tree is sometimes called the **depth** of the tree.

Other traditional terminology refers to the node that branches to a given node from above as the **parent** of that node. In the example above, the node with 'Q' is the parent of the nodes containing 'A' and 'F'. The one or two nodes that branch downward from a given node are that node's **children** (or child). They are referred to as the "left child" and "right child."

```
                parent
           ┌──────┴──────┐
      left child     right child
```

13.3.3   Order

Just as an ordinary list may be unordered, so the items in the tree may be placed at random (see the example above); however, a binary tree is usually ordered. Indeed, this is what makes a binary tree so useful. A typical ordered binary tree is:

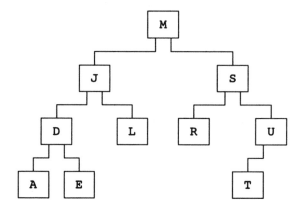

At first glance this may not appear to be ordered; however, note that each left child is smaller than the parent and each right child is greater than its parent. This is true for all of the nodes in the tree.

left child < parent < right child

or, more precisely, using our notation for linked structures:

```
DATA[LLINK[j]] < DATA[j] < DATA[RLINK[j]].
```

Not only is this relationship valid for nodes connected by a single branch, but all the nodes that are linked directly or indirectly through the left link of a node are smaller than the value of the node, and all nodes that are linked directly or indirectly through the right link of a node are greater. The following is NOT a properly ordered tree:

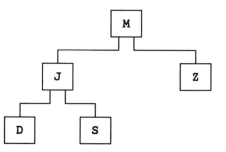

We observe that 'J' < 'M' < 'Z' and 'D' < 'J' < 'S'; however, the 'S' is not less than 'M', yet it appears as a descendent of 'M' on its left side.

Actually, there are other ways of ordering a binary tree, but we will consider this particular ordering. It is sometimes referred to as **LNR** order (for Left Node Right or L < N < R) or *inorder*.

Consider a simple list of names. The very high-level logical view of the data is just the ordered list:

Annie	Jolie
Cathy	Lynn
Ellen	Rose

If we are interested only in the data that is in alphabetical order, then the implementation is unimportant. However, if we are considering the implementation, then it is easier to visualize the tree structure. Without links or location information, the list may be diagrammed as lower-level logical view or "physiological" view:

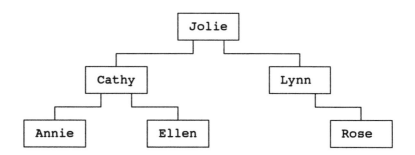

The tree may be diagrammed with more details, but we still have a fairly high-level view:

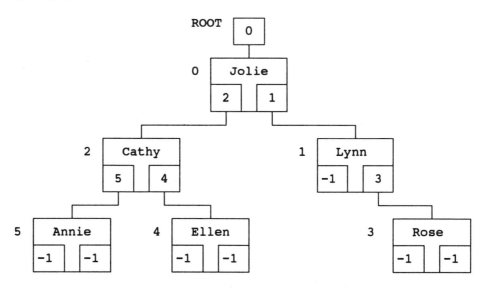

To get closer to the physical view (the actual storage details in memory), we can simply place the records in sequential order according to location. Now, the data no longer looks like a tree—it is no longer a logical view; although since it does not display the actual storage details; it is not quite a purely physical view, either:

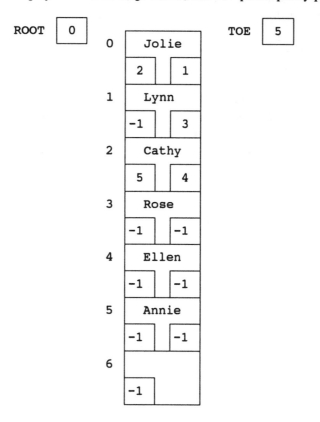

We will display the tree structure in the view most relevant for a given purpose.

It is important to realize that a binary tree is not unique. For a given list of data, there are many different binary trees that properly store the data. A linked-list may be stored in different order, but the links make the list into a single unique list. A binary tree may also store its records scattered throughout memory; however, the logical structure of the tree may be quite different and still store the data in the proper order. The tree illustrated on the top of the next page is a properly constructed tree that represents the same data as the example above.

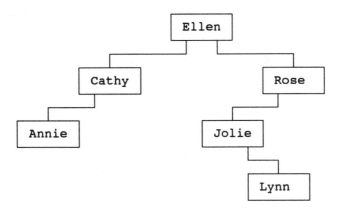

This representation uses a maximum of 4 levels (the node containing "Lynn" is at level 3). Therefore, its depth is 3. For searching, it is not as efficient as the first arrangement because it will take more "looks."

Another representation is:

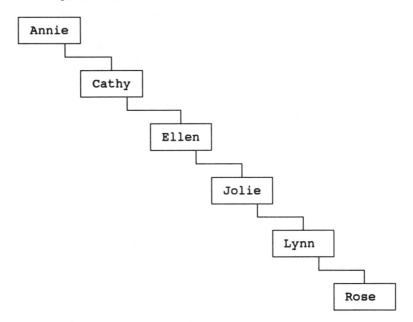

This last tree is an example of the worst possible case (another would be having "Rose" and "Lynn" reversed so that the last link is to the left; however, the maximum level of the tree would still be the same.) This tree is effectively a linked-list since all of the left-child links are END, there is a single sequential path through the data, and there is no branching. It takes the largest number of branches to get from the root to the last item—five. No efficiency is gained when one searches this tree, compared to a sequential structure.

The number of possible logical tree structures grows rapidly, but not nearly as rapidly as the number of possible permutations of a list of **n** elements.

n	Number Possible Trees	Number Permutations
1	1	1
2	2	2
3	5	6
4	14	24
5	42	120
6	132	720
7	429	5,040
8	1,430	40,320
9	4,862	362,880
10	16,796	3,628,800

The best representation is a tree that is balanced. This is a tree with the nodes as close to the root as possible—a tree that has nodes on the least number of levels as possible. This is achieved if, at each level, the number of descendants (children, grandchildren, etc.) on the left is close to the number on the right.

If the number of nodes is one less than a power of 2 (3, 7, 15, ...), then the tree can be perfectly balanced:

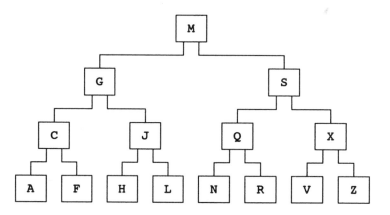

If the number of nodes is not one of these magic numbers, the tree can also be balanced. However, it will not be perfectly symmetric. Consider adding one more record to the tree, above, that has 15 records. This record could be attached to the tree in any one of 16 possible positions—there are 8 leaves each with 2 possible sites for a child. With the new record in any one of these, the worst-case number of looks to find it is the same and is a minimum (5). The total number of looks to find each of the records once is the same, and is a minimum (54). Therefore, we will consider all these trees of 16 nodes to be balanced.

If we add a second new record (for a total of 17) there are 15 possible places to attach the second one after we have attached the first. Therefore, there are $16 \cdot 15/2 = 120$ possible "balanced" trees of 17 elements. The worst-case number of looks for any one element is 5, and the total number of looks to search for all of them is a minimum at 59. If we keep going, then we discover that the number of possible balanced trees grows, then starts to diminish until we reach 1 tree at the next magic value of a power of 2 less one, where we "fill up the bottom level."

n	Number Balanced Trees	n	Number Balanced Trees
1	1	10	56
2	2	11	70
3	1	12	56
4	4	13	28
5	6	14	8
6	4	15	1
7	1	16	16
8	8	17	120
9	28	18	560

13.3.4 Searching

With a perfectly balanced tree, a search process can eliminate half (plus one) of the tree at each step, exactly like the binary search procedure on a simple list of the same number of items. The reason is that if a search key is less than the value of a node, then that node and <u>all</u> of the nodes on the right can be eliminated since they are all larger than the node.

As an example, if we search this tree for an 'H', then the first comparison with the root, 'M', will send us down the left-child branch, eliminating not only 'M', but 'S', 'Q', 'X', 'N', 'R', 'V', and 'Z'. The next comparison with 'G', sends us down its right branch, eliminating 'G' and its three left descendants 'A', 'C', and 'F'. The third comparison with 'J' sends us down its left branch, eliminating 'J' and 'L'. The fourth comparison finds the value. The number of comparisons is equal to the number of levels.

The average number of comparisons to find a given item for the balanced tree of 15 items is 3.27. The best case is 1, and the worst case is 4. This is precisely the situation that we found for a binary search on a list of 15.

Of course, if the tree is not balanced, then the search is not as efficient. In the worst case, if this data were located in a tree that stretched out to 15 levels, then the average would be 8. The best case would still be 1, but the worst case would be 15.

Thus, the analysis becomes even more difficult as compared to a binary search on an ordered simple list. To come up with an average search for an arbitrary number of items stored in an arbitrary tree, we have to consider all of the possible logical tree structures that correctly contain the given set of data Therefore, we will be content to consider the best, average, and worst cases for the best possible tree structure—balanced, and the worst possible tree structure—stretched out. In general, the average tree structure will be somewhere in between.

A formal algorithm for performing a search on an ordered binary tree is:

Algorithm TS (Search Binary Tree). Follow the sequence of links recursively in a binary tree (LNR ordering) for the occurrence of the item, *KEY.* This is originally invoked with an argument of *ROOT.*

TS1. [test if done]   If arg = END, then Terminate.   (not found)

TS2. [is this it?]   If DATA[arg] = KEY, then Terminate.   (found)

TS3. [go to child]   If DATA[arg] > KEY,
                                     then Invoke Algorithm TS with LLINK[arg].
                                     else Invoke Algorithm TS with RLINK[arg].

The C implementation can return the location of the desired record or an END indicating that it was not found.

Because Algorithm TS involves simple tail recursion, it may be rewritten to avoid the extra memory requirements:

Algorithm TS' (Search Binary Tree). Follow the sequence of links in a binary tree (LNR ordering) for the occurrence of the item *KEY.*

TS1'. [initialize index]   j=ROOT.

TS2'. [test if done]   If j = END, then Terminate.   (not found)

TS3'. [is this it?]   If DATA[j] = KEY, then Terminate.   (found)

TS4'. [go to child]   If DATA[j] > KEY, then j=LLINK[j].
                                         else j=RLINK[j].

TS5'. [move to next]   Go to step TS2'.

This is very similar to the search scheme for a linked list (Algorithm LS), except that step TS4 (as compared to step LS4) does not terminate but tests to see which child-branch to pursue. Even though the tree is ordered, the search does not terminate if the item is not present until we have encountered an END mark—no node.

13.4 INSERTION AND DELETION

Given a tree that is structured according to the scheme outlined above, this algorithm will produce the location of a desired item or will report that it is not found. We now need to devise algorithms for building and maintaining a tree structure.

13.4.1 Memory Management

A binary tree is essentially a linked structure. Therefore, much of the same memory and link management schemes that we used for a linked list will work (with the appropriate modifications) for a binary tree.

We could use the library memory allocation functions to manage memory but, for the present, let us handle the memory ourselves and treat the links as indices. We can link into a stack of empty locations, the entire memory that we will be using for the tree. We also have a variable, *ROOT*, that gives access to the tree by pointing to the root node.

The algorithm to initialize things and set up an empty tree is almost exactly the same as the one for the linked-list situation (Algorithm LM) and is:

Algorithm TM (Initialize Memory). Link all of the selected memory into a linked list of empty records. The variables *ROOT*, root of the tree, and *TOE*, top of empties, are used to provide access to the tree structure.

TM1. [set top indices]   ROOT=END; TOE=0.

TM2. [loop thru memory]   Perform step TM3 for j=0,1,...,N−2.

TM3. [set empty links]   LINK'[j]=j+1.

TM4. [set last link]   LINK'[N−1]=END.

The empty links may be any convenient field in the record—a good choice is the left-child link field for the tree.

After initialization, our memory would appear as a linked list of empties:

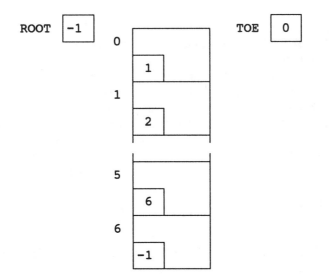

13.4.2   Insertion

Insertion into the tree is somewhat easier than insertion into a linked list. This is because all new records will be inserted as leaves. Thus, insertion into a binary tree will be more in the spirit of appending onto a list—the big difference is that a tree has many "ends" (i.e., each record with an END link; that is, no children or only one child). We will use a scheme similar to the one we used for insertion into a linked-list and will divide the insertion process into two phases. The first is to find storage, store the data, and set the children links.

Algorithm TU (Setup for Insertion into a Binary Tree). Store the item, *KEY*, into an empty record and set up for insertion into the binary tree. Returns location, *loc*.

TU1. [get empty record]   loc=TOE.

TU2. [check if full]   If loc=END, then Terminate.   (no memory)

TU3. [update TOE]   TOE=LINK'[loc].

TU4. [store item]   DATA[loc]=KEY.

TU5. [set links]   LLINK[loc]=END; RLINK[loc]=END.   ∎

At the end of this procedure, the record appears as:

```
loc  ┌─────────────┐
     │   xxxxx      │
     ├──────┬──────┤
     │ -1   │ -1   │
     └──────┴──────┘
```

Next, we graft the record into the tree. There will need to be no subsequent changes in the link fields of this record as we graft it, since it will be a leaf when it finally is placed in the tree.

To graft, we search until the proper place is found and change a link field to point to this location. Just like with the linked list, we need to remember the location of the parent, but now we also need to remember if we are grafting the new record as a right or a left child. If the tree is initially empty, then the new record will become the root of the tree. Note that this is the only case where the *ROOT* variable will be modified.

An algorithm to graft the record into a binary tree is:

Algorithm TG (Graft a Record into a Binary Tree). Find the appropriate location for insertion of a record, with location, *loc*, into the binary tree.

TG1. [check if empty]   If ROOT = END, then ROOT=loc; Terminate.

TG2. [initialize]   j=ROOT.

TG3. [compare]   If DATA[j] < DATA[loc], then nxt=RLINK[j]; dir='r'.
                                                   else nxt=LLINK[j]; dir='l'.

TG4. [found leaf]   If nxt ≠ END, then j=nxt; Go to step TG3.

TG5. [now graft it]   If dir = 'r', then RLINK[j]=loc.
                                          else LLINK[j]=loc.

                                                                            ■

      Note that the graft algorithm does not modify any of the fields of the new record. This is because each new record is a leaf.

      We have written Algorithm TG in its non-recursive form; however, this, as with most of the binary tree manipulation algorithms, may be written in a recursive form.

      The two algorithms, Algorithms TU and TG, then may be combined to form the tree insertion algorithm.

Algorithm TI (Insert an Item from a Binary Tree). Given an item, *KEY*, insert into a tree.

TI1. [find storage]   Invoke Algorithm TU, gives location loc.

TI2. [graft into tree]   Invoke Algorithm TG with loc.

                                                                           ■

      As an example, let us insert the record COBOL into an empty tree. The binary tree becomes:

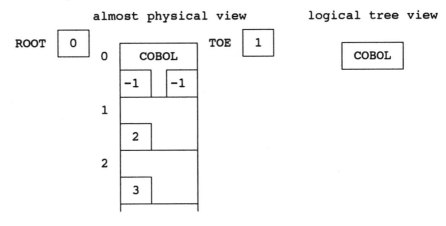

Next let us insert LISP:

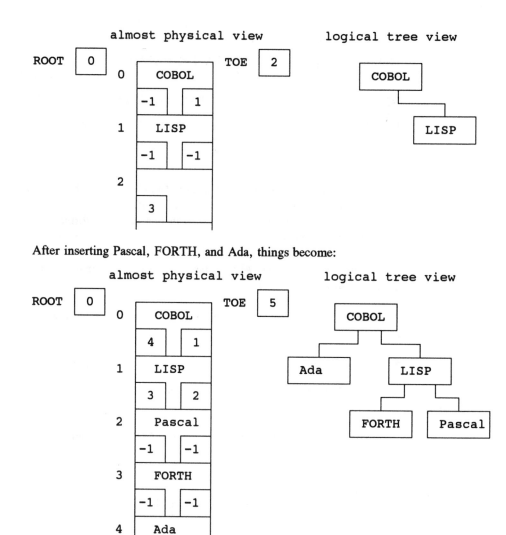

After inserting Pascal, FORTH, and Ada, things become:

13.4.3 Deletion

Deletion from a binary tree is not quite so simple. The record we wish to delete may be a leaf, it may be in the middle of the tree, or it may be the root record. In general, except for leaves, there will be one or two child subtrees to be taken care of. One child subtree is relatively easy to take care of; it may be handled in much the same way as a linked list. The possibility of a second child subtree is more interesting.

Our scheme will follow these general steps:

1. Find the record to be deleted.

2. Get the link of the parent that points to it, to END.

3. Put deleted storage space onto the empty stack.

4. Graft the right-child subtree, if it exists.

5. Graft the left-child subtree, if it exists.

Step 2 of this scheme will restore the remaining structure (except for the two orphan child subtrees) to a correct binary tree. Into this tree we can graft the orphan child subtrees—remember that grafting does not modify any of the fields of the record that it grafts. This means that the record will continue to link to whatever children it pointed to originally.

Therefore, the deletion process will use the graft routine that we used for insertion!

A formal algorithm to implement deletion of a record from a binary tree is given by:

Algorithm TD (Delete a Record from a Binary Tree). Follow the sequence of links in a binary tree to find an item, *KEY,* and delete it.

TD1.	[initialize]	parnt=END; j=ROOT.
TD2.	[check if there]	If j = END, then Terminate. (not found)
TD3.	[test]	If DATA[j] = KEY, then Go to step TD7.
TD4.	[parent index]	parnt=j.
TD5.	[move to child]	If DATA[j] > KEY, then j=LLINK[j]. else j=RLINK[j].
TD6.	[loop]	Go to step TD2.
TD7.	[set children]	rght=RLINK[j]; left=LLINK[j].
TD8.	[set indices, root]	If parnt = END, then ROOT=END; Go to step TD10.

TD9. [not root]   If DATA[parnt] > KEY, then LLINK[parnt]=END.
                                             else RLINK[parnt]=END.

TD10. [put on empty]   LINK'[j]=TOE; TOE=j.

TD11. [insert children] If rght ≠ END, then Invoke Algorithm TG with rght.
                                If left ≠ END, then Invoke Algorithm TG with left.

Deleting the record, LISP, results in the following views at the end of step TD10, where we have the two orphan child subtrees:

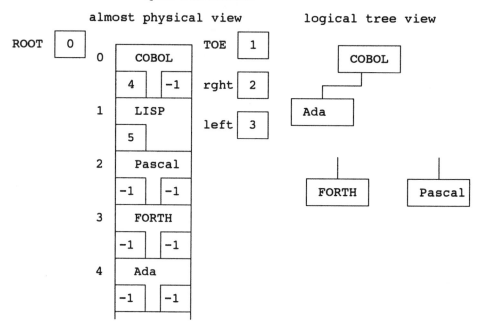

After grafting in the right-child subtree (step TD11) we get:

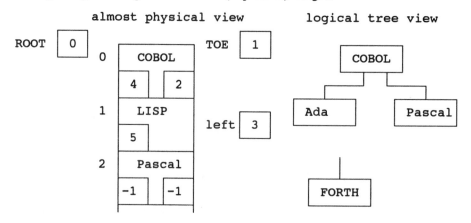

continuing:

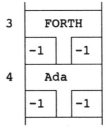

Finally, after grafting in the left-child subtree, we obtain the final binary tree:

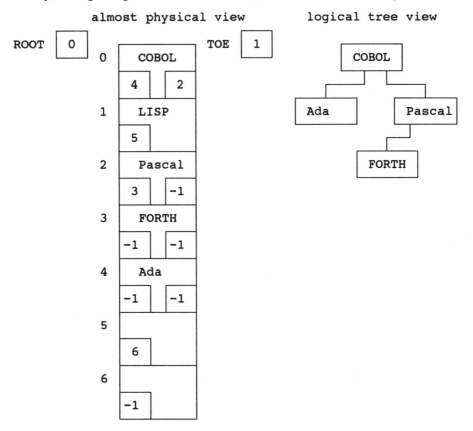

It does not really matter whether we graft the left-child subtree first or the right one. The final tree will have a different structure, but it will still be a correctly built binary tree. As an example, if we had inserted the left orphan first, and then the right one, we would obtain the equivalent logical tree:

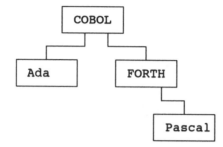

In the example above, the orphan subtrees consist of only one record. In general, there may be many records that might be linked from each of the two immediate orphan child subtrees. Grafting the orphan records will simply and properly graft in the entire subtree.

In general, the first orphan subtree to be grafted back into the tree will go in the same logical place as the record that was deleted. Therefore, it would save a searching step by changing the parent link (the parent of the deleted record) to point to one of the child subtrees then graft in the other. There are four possibilities where j is the location of the deleted record:

1. No children,   LLINK[j] = END and RLINK[j] = END

2. Left child only,   LLINK[j] $\neq$ END and RLINK[j] = END

3. Right child only,   LLINK[j] = END and RLINK[j] $\neq$ END

4. Both children exist, LLINK[j] $\neq$ END and RLINK[j] $\neq$ END

In each of these respective cases, we need to perform the following:

1. Simply set the appropriate link of the parent of j to END

2. Set the appropriate link of the parent of j to LLINK[j]

3. Set the appropriate link of the parent of j to RLINK[j]

4. Set the appropriate link of the parent of j to RLINK[j] and graft the record with location LLINK[j]

All of these cases complicate the algorithm for deletion, but do save some time.

We could save some further time by noting that the second orphan subtree will be connected somewhere into the first orphan subtree, rather than elsewhere in the tree. Therefore, we could begin the grafting search with the "root" element of the first orphan subtree after we have reconnected it.

Because the binary tree is a linked structure, insertion and deletion do not involve any movement of data. Because of the "two-dimensional" structure that "splits" the data at each level, searching is reasonably efficient. The number of comparisons for searching, if the tree is balanced, is O(lg n) hence the number of operations for insertion and deletion is also O(lg n). A binary tree is a good structure for inserting data and searching for it.

13.5   *TREE TRAVERSAL*

Because of the nature of the tree, it is not as convenient as it is for a simple linked list to traverse the tree and print the contents in order. We need a scheme that will allow us to visit every node in an orderly fashion and print the contents as we go. Because there are no links from a child to its parent in the structure we have described, we cannot proceed directly "up" a tree.

13.5.1   Traversal Order

We have constructed our tree as an LNR ordered binary tree where the L (left child) is less than the N (node or parent) is less than the R (right child). There are other ways of ordering a tree, and even if the tree is not ordered we can traverse it in a particular order.

Consider the following binary tree which is ordered in the usual LNR ordering:

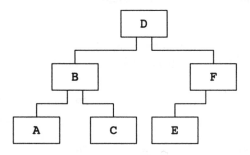

If we traverse the tree in the LNR order, it means that we print the left child, then the node, then the right child. Applying this to the root, we must print the 'B', except it is a parent, so we print the 'A', then the 'B', then the 'C'. This takes care of the left branch from the root, so we can print 'D', then process its right-child branch. The 'F' is a parent, so we print its left child, 'E', and then finally the 'F'. Such a procedure is clearly recursive in nature. Indeed the simplest way to describe and implement a tree traversal routine is a recursive one.

However, let us consider several different traversal orders:

LNR A B C D E F   Inorder

LRN A C B E F D   Postorder

NLR D B A C F E   Preorder

NRL D F E B C A

RNL F E D C B A

RLN E F C A B D

The typical ones are LNR (inorder), NLR (preorder), LRN (postorder), and RNL (backwards inorder).

13.5.2 Algorithm

An algorithm to traverse a tree in the LNR order is:

Algorithm TP (Traverse and Print Binary Tree). Follow the sequence of links and print the data stored in each record in a LNR ordering. The algorithm is invoked recursively, utilizing the parameter, *loc*. It is initially called with *ROOT*.

TP1. [done?]	If loc = END, then Return.
TP2. [do left child]	Invoke Algorithm TP with LLINK[loc].
TP3. [print contents]	Output DATA[loc].
TP4. [do right child]	Invoke Algorithm TP with RLINK[loc].

■

Invoking Algorithm TP on the Ada, COBOL, FORTH, LISP, and Pascal tree, above, we begin with *loc* = 0 (since *ROOT* contains 0). It executes as:

```
TP (0)                                                                1
        TP (4)                         TP2  left child of COBOL       2
                TP (-1)                TP2  left child of Ada          3
                                            return TP1
                output (4)      Ada    TP3                             2
                TP (-1)                TP4  right child of Ada         3
                                            return TP1
                                            end of function level 2
        output (0)              COBOL  TP3                             1
        TP (1)                         TP4  right child of COBOL       2
                TP (3)                 TP2  left child of LISP         3
                        TP (-1)        TP2  left child of FORTH        4
                                            return TP1
                        output (3)  FORTH  TP3                         3
                        TP (-1)        TP4  right child of FORTH       4
                                            return TP1
                                            end of function level 3
                output (1)      LISP   TP3                             2
                TP (2)                 TP4  right child of LISP        3
                        TP (-1)        TP2  left child of Pascal       4
```

			return TP1	
output (2)	Pascal		TP3	3
TP (-1)			TP4 right child of Pascal	4
			return TP1	
			end of function level 3	
			end of function level 2	

13.5.3   **C Implementation**

The C code is particularly simple. First, we assume the tree is defined as:

```
struct record {char data[SIZE];
               int llink,rlink;
               } tree[NUMB];
```

The function then becomes:

```
/*********************************************************
 *
 *      function to traverse binary tree in LNR order
 *
 *          param:  loc     location to begin
 *
 *********************************************************/
void traverse(int loc)
{

    if (loc == END)
        return;

    traverse(tree[loc].llink);        /* process L */

    printf("%s\n",tree[loc].data);    /* process N */

    traverse(tree[loc].rlink);        /* process R */

}
```

In reality, all we need to do is rearrange these statements in order to traverse the tree
in different orders.

It is important to realize that the order in which you traverse a tree is
independent of the actual ordering of the tree—if the tree is even ordered.

Consider the tree diagramed at the top of the following page. Traversing this
tree in the LNR order results in C O M P U T E R. However, this tree is not
ordered alphabetically.

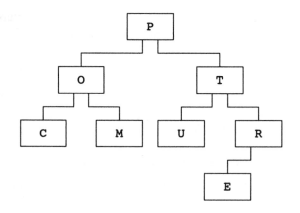

13.5.4 Non-Recursive Algorithm

As might be expected, it is possible to avoid a recursive algorithm by using a stack. The general scheme is to place, on a stack, the location of a record whenever a left child is encountered. If no left child exists, then print the data contained in the record, and move to any right child. If there is no right child, then pop a location from the stack, print it, and check for a right child.

A formal algorithm is:

Algorithm TA (Traverse and Print Binary Tree). Follow the sequence of links and print the data stored in each record in an LNR ordering. The algorithm uses a stack to keep track of parent location.

TA1. [initialize]	Set stack to empty; j=ROOT.	
TA2. [done?]	If j = END, then Terminate.	(empty tree)
TA3. [do left child]	If LLINK[j] ≠ END, then Push j; j=LLINK[j]; Go to step TA3.	
TA4. [print contents]	Output DATA[j].	
TA5. [do right child]	If RLINK[j] ≠ END, then j=RLINK[j]; Go to step TA3.	
TA6. [find next node]	If stack is empty, then Halt. else Pop j; Go to step TA4.	(all done)

It is more difficult to see how to modify this algorithm to achieve a different traversal order than is the simple recursive one.

13.5.5 Analysis

Our first impression is that the behavior of the tree traversal algorithms in O(n), since we are basically visiting each node and printing the contents. This, is indeed the case. However, we note that each node with a left child is visited twice—once on the way down the left branch to process its left child and once when we are ready to process its contents. A node with no left child is visited exactly once.

Consider a tree that has no right children:

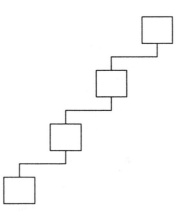

We move down the tree to the leaf, which involves visiting each node once; that is, n operations. We then print the leaf and move back up the tree taking $n-1$ operations for a total of $2n-1$ operations.

On the other hand, a tree consisting of only right children would take only n operations since we print each node as we visit it and move down to the right until we get to the leaf.

Clearly, the number of operations to process any possible trees with n nodes must lie between these extremes. Indeed, it is not difficult to show that full balanced trees (trees with 3, 7, 15, or $n = 2^m - 1$ nodes) take $(3n-1)/2$ operations.

The bottom line, of course, is that tree traversal is O(n), regardless of the shape and physiological structure of the tree.

13.6 BALANCED TREES

The effectiveness of using a binary tree will vary depending on the logical structure of the tree. If the tree is well balanced, so that all the nodes are as close to the root as possible, then the worst case for search is approximately lg n operations, and the average case is $\approx$ (lg n) -1. However, in the worst possible structure, with the tree stretched in a linear structure, the worst case is n operations and the average is $\approx n/2$.

The structure of the tree will depend upon the order in which we insert new items into the tree. The worst case will occur when the items are already sorted. In general, with random data a binary tree will behave only about 38% worse than a properly balanced tree.

13.6.1 Algorithm

It is possible to balance a tree. A simple scheme is to create a linear list of the locations of the records of the tree. If the records are large, they may not fit into a random-access list, but the list of locations may. Set the root to END; that is, an empty tree. Perform a "binary search" type access in this simple list of locations, generating a middle index. Graft the record that is associated with that location into a new tree. Recursively generate a middle index for each of the two sublists, and insert those records. Continue with the four sublists, then eight, and so forth until all the records in the original tree have been inserted into the new tree. Because of the linked nature of the records in the tree, no actual data need to be moved.

A formal algorithm becomes:

Algorithm TB (Balance a Binary Tree). Given a binary tree, balance it using an auxiliary list of locations.

TB1. [get keys]	Invoke Algorithm TP, except store the locations in a list.
TB2. [initialize tree]	ROOT=END.
TB3. [rebuild tree]	Invoke Algorithm TR.

Once the entire tree is represented as a list of locations, the original root may be initialized to "empty" without losing the data stored in the tree.

Algorithm TB invokes an algorithm to rebuild the tree. This process will be recursive, hence it needs to be a separate procedure.

Algorithm TR (Rebuild a Binary Tree). Given a linear list, *LIST*, of the ordered locations from a binary tree delimited by *LOWER* and *UPPER* indices, select the appropriate one to graft into the tree in the proper order to produce a balanced tree.

TR1. [are we done?]	If UPPER < LOWER, then Terminate.
TR2. [get midpoint]	$i=(LOWER+UPPER)/2$; loc=LIST[i];
TR3. [graft record]	LLINK[loc]=END; RLINK[loc]=END; Invoke Algorithm TG with loc.
TR4. [do left branch]	Invoke Algorithm TR with LOWER, $i-1$.
TR5. [do right branch]	Invoke Algorithm TR with $i+1$, UPPER.

It does not matter whether we recursively rebuild the left branch or the right branch first—since these are independent, we will end up with the same tree.

Consider the following example:

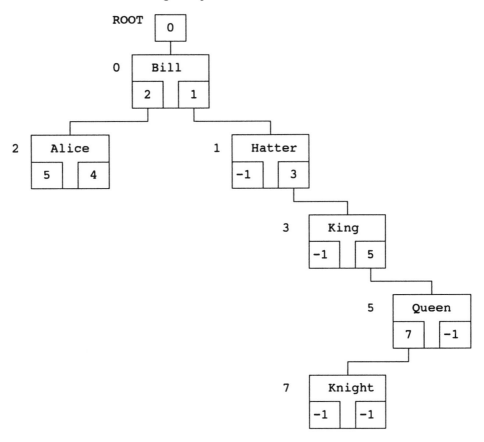

This tree certainly is not balanced. After traversing the tree in an LNR order we obtain the following list of locations:

0	1	2	3	4	5
2	0	1	3	7	5

And an empty tree:

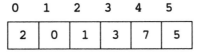

Applying Algorithm TR, with *lower*=0 and *upper*=5, gives *i*=2 for the first record located at 1 that will be inserted into the tree:

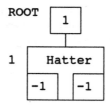

The algorithm is then invoked recursively with *lower*=0 and *upper*=$i-1$=1. This produces i=0, and the record located at 2 is next grafted into the tree:

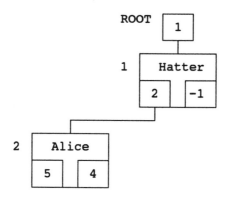

Continuing this process, we will graft the records into the tree, in order:

1   2   0   7   3   5

The resultant tree is:

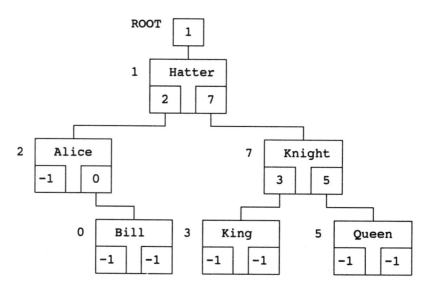

Our scheme to rebalance the tree can also provide a mechanism for reordering the tree. The general idea is to traverse the tree and get the list of pointers to the records. These will be in the order of the original ordering of the tree. Sort this list, using a sort that manipulates pointers, according to the new field. This involves comparing data from the actual records, but only the movement of pointers. Then, rebuild the tree according to Algorithm TR; the tree will not only be reordered, but also balanced.

13.6.2 An In-place Balancing Scheme

While the operation of rebalancing a binary tree is somewhat analogous to sorting a list, we could consider the possibility of actually reorganizing the tree, perhaps in an order according to a different field in each record.

The first thought might be to traverse the tree in an LRN or RLN order, removing leaves and grafting them into a new tree. In this case, we will be deleting leaves only, and the deletion algorithm may be simplified. This process allows us to rebuild the tree in place without any extra storage. Note that the actual records need not be moved. However, this process is O(n • lg n).

A scheme was published in 1986 that permits balancing a binary tree "in-place;" that not only requires less storage, but is more efficient than the scheme outlined above.

The key to this is a concept known as a rotation. This involves adjusting the structure of the tree to move some nodes from one side of the tree to the other. Consider the following tree:

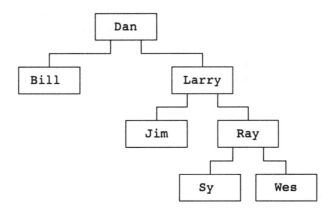

A balanced tree would have "Larry" as the root node. A rotation makes this possible. We will not simply turn the picture, but the action will appear as if we have rotated the entire structure counterclockwise.

A rotation essentially interchanges a node with its parent. We have no difficulty in removing a branch and making a new tree so that "Larry" is indeed the root node, as:

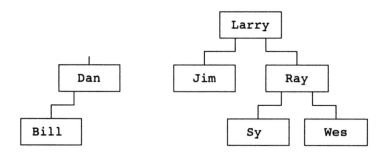

We note that the parent of a node and all of its left children are less than the value of the node. Hence, it would be appropriate to connect to the left child of the node; however, to do so, we need to disconnect the present left child of the node to make room. Thus:

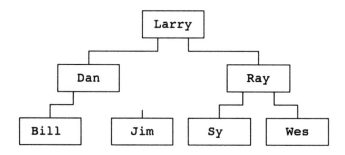

However, because the node (Larry) was previously connected to the right child of the prior parent (Dan), there is now a place to reconnect the previous left child of the node (Jim). Note that this child and all of its possible children, are greater than the value of the parent; therefore not only can it connect physically, but the order of the tree is maintained.

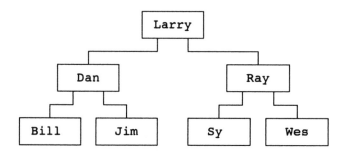

We have illustrated the rotation as taking place at the root; however, it can take place with any node that is on the right side of the tree. Actually, we could describe a clockwise rotation that could take place on the left side of the tree. However, we need only the counterclockwise rotation illustrated above for our present purposes.

Our tree-balancing procedure takes place in two stages. The first seems to make the situation worse, but it simplifies the structure of the tree so that we can easily balance it.

Consider the following unbalanced tree with fifteen items. It is quite unbalanced. Indeed, it contains nodes on six levels. A perfectly balanced tree would need only four levels. A balanced tree of fifteen nodes will be a full tree.

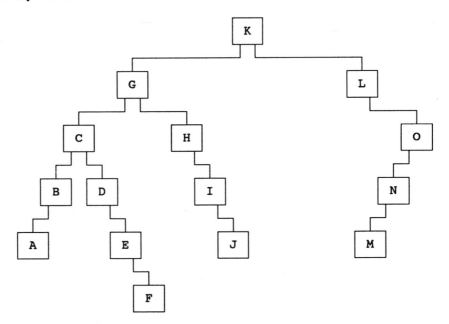

First, we restructure the tree so that it is completely "stretched out," with no left children.

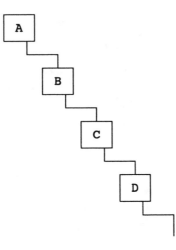

continuing:

The procedure for performing this is based on the tree traversal scheme we used to print the tree or to determine the ordered list of locations in the previous balancing procedure. There is one additional thing we need to determine with this process; the total number of nodes in the tree.

A formal algorithm to perform this is:

Algorithm TL (Change a Binary Tree into a Right-Hand List). Given a binary tree, proceed recursively to restructure it as a stretched out tree with no left children. Invoke originally with ROOT. This uses a variable, *last*, to keep track of the last node in the tree. *NN* is a count of the number of nodes.

TL1. [done?]	If loc = END, then Return.
TL2. [do left child]	Invoke Algorithm TL with LLINK[loc].
TL3. [move node]	If last = END, then ROOT = loc. else RLINK[last] = loc. LLINK[loc]=END; last=loc; NN=NN+1.
TL4. [do right child]	Invoke Algorithm TL with RLINK[loc].

The algorithm is initially invoked with *last* set to END and *NN* set to 0.

Next we perform several steps, each consisting of a series of counterclockwise rotations on every other node starting with the child of the root node (the node with a B). Since our original tree had fifteen nodes, we will perform seven rotations.

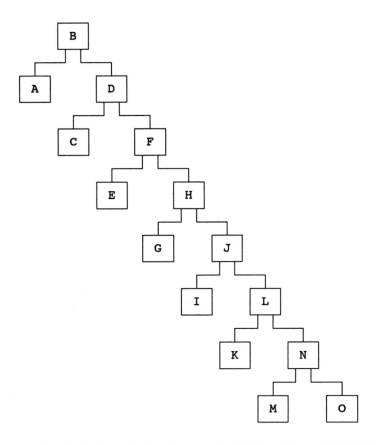

Since, for example, in the "stretched out" tree node B did not have a left child, the A node will not have a right child.

We have shortened the tree from fifteen levels to eight.

The rotation process is next repeated three times, using every other node, again starting with the child of the root node (the node with a D). The resultant tree is illustrated on the top of the next page. It now contains only five levels.

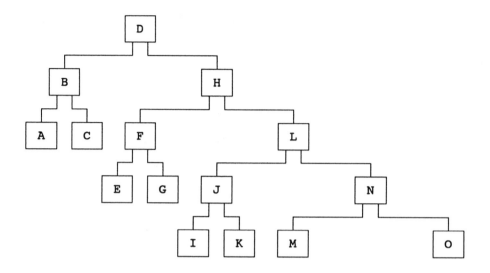

We repeat the rotation process one more time. This last step will consist of only one rotation on this tree, again with the node that is the child of the root node (the node with H).

The tree is now balanced.

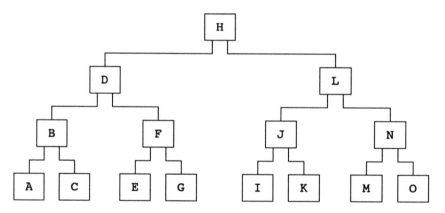

Now that we have an overview of the process, let us consider the procedure in more detail and then present a formal algorithm.

First, each rotation operation requires the adjustment of three link fields, one in the node (left link), one in its parent (right link), and one in its grandparent (right link). These need to be performed in a specific order. The following tree segment illustrates these.

The "before" picture is:

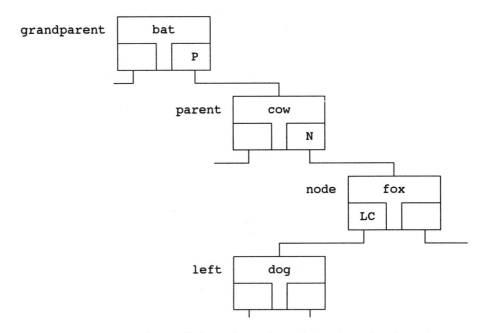

First, we change the *RLINK[grandparent]* to point to the node. Second, we move the *RLINK[node]* to *RLINK[parent]*. Finally, we set the *LLINK[node]* to point to the parent.

The resultant picture is:

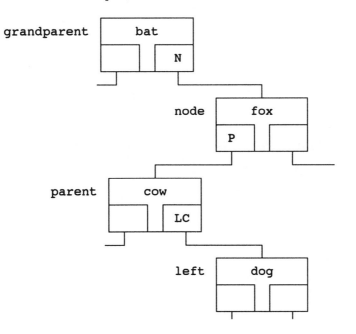

For clarity, we have retained the original designations for the nodes even though the "grandparent" is now the parent, the "parent" is now a left child, and the original left child is now a "left-right grandchild."

Second, we noticed in the tree balancing example above, that we performed a series of seven rotations as we moved down the original fifteen nodes. The second series of rotations were three in number, and the last was only one. This is characteristic of this procedure. In general, if there are $n = 2^m - 1$ nodes (making a full tree when balanced), then we perform the following sequence of rotations:

$$2^{m-1} - 1, \quad 2^{m-2} - 1, \quad 2^{m-3} - 1, \ldots, 7, 3, 1$$

If the tree does not contain $2^m - 1$ nodes, as is usually the case, then for $2^{m+1} - 1 < n < 2^m - 1$ we perform only enough rotations in the first step to produce a tree with $2^m - 1$ nodes down the right side. We then follow with the sequence above.

As an example, consider a tree with eight nodes. After processing it with Algorithm TL, we obtain:

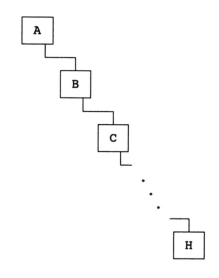

The first rotation step will want to remove one node from the right-hand side to leave seven. Thus, we rotate once at node B to obtain:

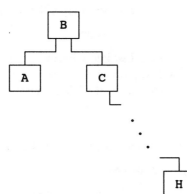

The next step performs three rotations, since we have seven nodes, (at nodes C, E, and G).

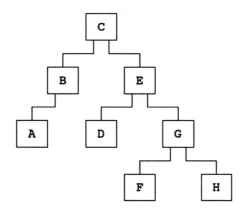

The last step performs one rotation at node E, to leave:

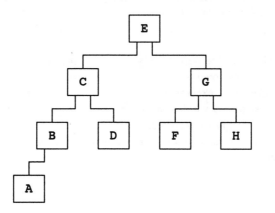

With these ideas in mind, we can write a formal algorithm for performing the series of rotation operations.

Algorithm TC (Change a Right-hand List into a Balanced Tree). Given a binary tree that is structured as a right-hand list, proceed with a series of rotation steps to restructure it as balanced tree. *NN* is a count of the number of nodes.

TC1. [initialize]   p=1.

TC2. [get power]   If p ≤ NN, then p=2p+1; Go to step TC2.

TC3. [number rotations]   p=p/2; nr=NN−p.

TC4. [adjust]   If nr = 0, then p=p/2; nr=p.

TC5. [set next]   nxt=p/2.

TC6. [rotation step]   Perform steps TC7 through TC13 as long as nr > 0.

TC7. [setup]   grndprnt=END; prnt=ROOT; node=RLINK[prnt].

TC8. [do rotations]   Perform steps TC9 through TC12 for i=1,2,...,nr.

TC9. [grandparent]   If grndprnt = END, then ROOT=node.
                                       else RLINK[grndprnt]=node.

TC10. [parent]   RLINK[prnt]=llink[node].

TC11. [node]   LLINK[node]=prnt.

TC12. [get next node]   grndprnt=node; prnt=RLINK[node];
                          node=RLINK[prnt].

TC13. [ready for next]   nr=nxt; nxt=nxt/2.

Note that p (and *nxt*) is an integer and is always equal to 2^m-1 for some m, even though we obtain the next value in the sequence by a simple division. For example, if it were originally 15, then 15/2 is 7, 7/2 is 3, 3/2 is 1, and, finally, 1/2 is 0.

The first five steps simply determine the number of rotations for the first and the second pass down the right side of the tree. It is necessary to do this because the first number is an exception to the normal sequence of one less than a power of 2.

In step TC9 we determine whether the "grandparent" is a node or the root variable, and adjust the correct one.

Putting these two algorithms together gives us the tree-balancing algorithm we are after:

Algorithm TT (Balance a Binary Tree). Given a binary tree, balance it in-place.

TT1.	[initialize]	last=END; NN=0.
TT2.	[make list]	Invoke Algorithm TL with ROOT, last, and NN.
TT3.	[balance]	If NN > 2, then Invoke Algorithm TC with NN.

There is no need to invoke Algorithm TC if the size of the tree is less than three, since a tree of one or two nodes is already balanced.

13.6.3 Analysis

We have seen that the tree traversal algorithm is $O(n)$. Therefore, Algorithm TL, to make a right-hand list, is also $O(n)$.

The number of rotations to reorganize the tree into a balanced one proceeds, as for $n=2^m-1$:

$$2^{m-1}-1, \quad 2^{m-2}-1, \quad 2^{m-3}-1, \quad \ldots , \quad 7, \quad 3, \quad 1$$

The sum of these quantities may be written as:

$$2^{m-1} + 2^{m-2} + 2^{m-3} + \ldots + 8 + 4 + 2 - (m+1)$$

where we have collected all of the 1's. The sum of the powers of 2 is easily evaluated as:

$$2^{m-1} + 2^{m-2} + 2^{m-3} + \ldots + 8 + 4 + 2 + 1 = 2^m-1 = n$$

Therefore, the number of operations is $n-m$. Since m is related to lg n, we see that the "big O" behavior is $O(n)$.

Therefore, the behavior of the entire process, Algorithm TT, is just $O(n)$.

13.7 EXTENSIONS

There were several extensions to the basic linked list, that we described in the previous chapter, that can be applied to a binary tree.

13.7.1 Parent Link

The tree that we have discussed implements links from a parent to its children. It is sometimes useful, also, to maintain a link back to its parent. This allows easy movement up and down a tree. The records would appear as:

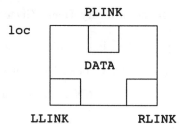

where the *PLINK* field contains the location of parent. In the case of the root records, the *PLINK* would contain the END value.

Exactly like the case with the linked list, we could maintain several logical binary trees using the same data set. We would need a set of link fields for each logical tree, and we could then traverse the data set in different ways.

13.7.2 Continuation Record

We could also implement a "continuation record" if we were implementing records that varied in size. The implementation would be exactly the same as for a linked list; indeed, each chain of continuation records would be a little linked list hanging off the main tree record somewhat like the elongated blossoms of some biological trees.

13.8   OTHER TREE STRUCTURES

The binary tree structure that we developed in this chapter is not the only possible tree structure that is useful as a data structure. It is perhaps the simplest, and hence is appropriate for the first exposure. Regardless of the details of the tree structure, the primary concern is to increase efficiency in the manipulation algorithms.

One concern is that a tree structure behave as efficiently as possible. For binary trees, this means that they should be balanced, or close to balanced. We could balance the tree after several insertions, using Algorithm TB. This would be analogous to appending to a simple list then sorting it at intervals. While it would work, it would seem to be better to attempt to maintain the list as a sorted list or to maintain the tree as a balanced structure at each step.

13.8.1 AVL Trees

In 1962, a scheme that produces a type of binary tree, termed an AVL tree (from the initials of the two Russian mathematicians, G. M. Adel'son-Vel'skii and E. M. Landis), was published. This uses two extra bits per node that indicate how well the subtree is balanced. For this purpose, a binary tree will be considered to be balanced if the height of the two subtrees of every node differs by no more than one.

When an insertion produces an "off-balance" condition, then the root is adjusted (a rotation) to restore balance.

This condition of balance is somewhat less restrictive than the one discussed above. This procedure may produce leaves on more than two levels.

For example, to illustrate how this might work, consider:

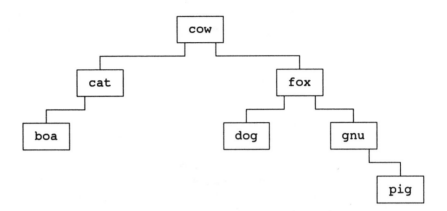

This tree is not exactly balanced in the traditional sense; however, it is reasonably balanced.

If we now insert "rat", the tree becomes "too unbalanced." The subtrees of the root, "cow", have heights of two and four, which differ by more than one.

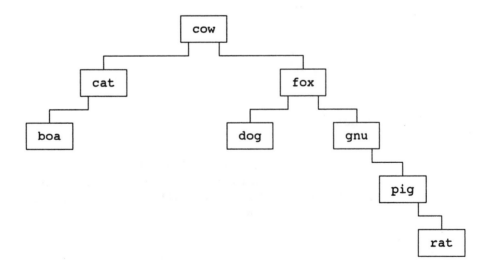

What we would like to do is change the root from "cow" to "fox" so that "cow" becomes a child of "fox". Unfortunately, performing this in a naive manner would give "fox" three children. No problem; "cow" would only have one, and "dog" would fit there!

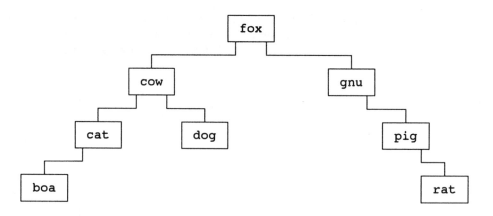

This process is termed a rotation.

This tree is still not balanced even in the restrictive sense we use for AVL trees. The node "gnu" has subtrees with heights of zero and two. We need a further rotation to move "pig" up in the tree.

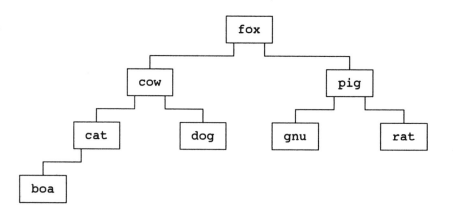

Each node contains an extra field that takes on three values, $+1$, 0, or -1; that tells how well the subtree using that node as the root is balanced. The AVL algorithms give details on how this field is maintained by insertion and rotation, and give the directions for rotation.

13.8.2   B-Trees

Another approach to creating and maintaining a balanced structure is to use a tree that allows more than two children. One such approach is called a B-tree. Basically, each node contains several keys and links. The keys and links are arranged in order as:

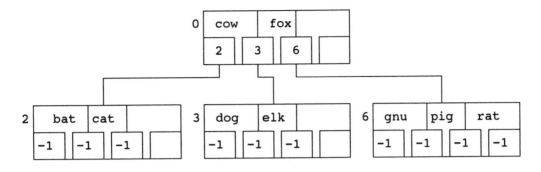

We see that, from the root node, the left-most link points to a node that contains keys less than the smallest one in the root. The middle link points to a node that contains keys that lie between the two keys in the root. The right-most link points to a node that contains keys larger than the largest one in the root.

We can specify the "order" of the B-tree as the maximum number of links that may be contained in a node. In the example above, we have used four. Each node then may contain three keys and four links to children nodes.

All insertions of new records occur at the leaves. To insert "boa" is quite simple. We change the node at 2 to:

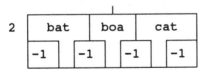

That is, to insert a record in a node that is not filled, we simply add it to the node. Since this node is a leaf, with no children, we do not need to be especially concerned with any of its link fields.

To insert "hog" is more of a problem. There is no room in the node at location 6 since it can contain only three keys. The solution is to split it into two nodes which contain all previous keys (plus the new one) except for the middle one:

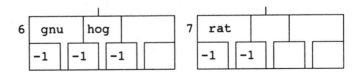

That is, node 6 is left with "gnu", node 7 is created with "rat", the new record "hog" is inserted in node 6, and the previous median record, "pig", is pulled out to be inserted in the parent of 6 and 7.

We must now move back toward the root and insert the middle key there:

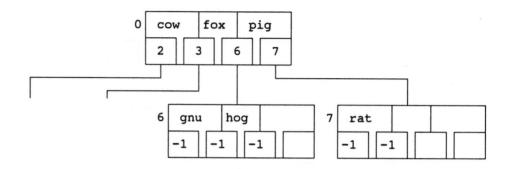

If the root already contains a maximum number of keys, then it is split and a new root is created that contains one key. It is in this that way the B-tree grows by one level.

Deletion is more complicated than insertion.

Because of the way the B-tree grows, it is a balanced structure. Therefore, searching is optimized.

Note that each B-tree of order *m*, has the following characteristics:

a. Every node has no more than m children.

b. Every node, except for the root, has at least m/2 children.

c. All leaves occur on the same level.

13.8.3 A Trie

So far we have built a structure so that each record contains the entire key. All comparisons were performed using the entire key. However, it is possible to use individual characters in the key to drive a search. An example is the thumb index found in many dictionaries. This uses the first letter of the key (the word to be searched for) to direct us to the appropriate part of the dictionary. Imagine one level of thumb indices for each letter in the word, and you have a physical model of a structure termed a trie. (This, presumably, comes from re*trie*val and was suggested in 1960.)

Essentially, a trie is a tree composed of nodes with many children. Each node corresponds to a character or digit, and the list of links point to the next character in the key.

Consider, for example, storing the telephone area codes for the United States, Canada, and the U.S. possessions in the Caribbean in an efficient search structure. These are three digits in length; however, there are restrictions so that not all 1,000 combinations are used.

The first digit must form the set {2,3,4...,9}. The second digit is either a 0 or 1. The third digit may be selected from the set {1,2,...,9}, with the exception that if the second digit is a 1, then the third digit cannot be.

We might form a trie that looks like:

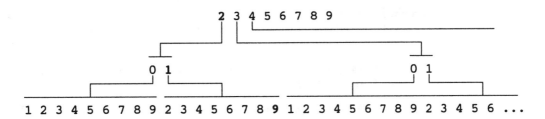

where we have indicated only part of the trie. Presumably, the last level would contain a link to where information about the particular area code is stored.

To search for a particular area code, we break it into its individual digits. We look in the root node to see which node to examine next. For example, 219 (Northern Indiana) would first give us a 2; looking in the root node would tell us which node to examine next. The next digit is a 1. The appropriate second-level node would direct us to the third and final level. The last digit, a 9, would direct us to where the data is stored. If no information were stored—that is, if the particular area code was not assigned, then an END link could indicate that this particular key was not present.

The example above uses a fixed length (three digits) key; however, it is not difficult to incorporate variable length keys as well.

The trie structure offers very efficient searching once the trie is built. It would be suitable, for example, for a dictionary which contains thousands of words. Typically, the trie would be generated once and used many times to search for words.

13.9 SUMMARY

The linked list of the previous chapter had a number of advantages compared to a simple list; however, searching was relatively slow. A tree structure overcomes this drawback yet retains the advantages of a linked structure.

A binary tree contains a maximum of two children for each node.

Whereas an ordered linked list has only one logical structure, the same data may be stored in many different binary tree configurations. The most efficient tree is one that is balanced.

Searching a binary tree, and indeed most operations are O(lg n).

A binary tree may be balanced in-place in an operation that is O(n).

There are other tree structures that maintain their balance as data is inserted and deleted.

REFERENCES

Aho, Alfred V., Hopcroft, John, E., and Ullman, Jeffrey D., *Data Structures and Algorithms*, Addison-Wesley Publishing Co., Reading, Massachusetts, 1983.

Knuth, Donald E., *The Art of Computer Programming*; Fundamental Algorithms, vol. 1., 2nd ed., Addison-Wesley Publishing Co., Reading, Massachusetts, 1973.

Lee, E. Stewart, *Algorithms and Data Structures in Computer Engineering*, Jones and Bartlett Publishers, 1992.

Sedgewick, Robert, *Algorithms in C*, Addison-Wesley Publishing Co., Reading, Massachusetts, 1990.

QUESTIONS

Q13.1   Declare a C record structure for a binary tree that would be appropriate for:

last name	15 characters
first name	15 characters
team	10 characters
uniform number	1 integer
at bats	1 integer
hits	1 integer

The list is to be maintained using only children links ordered according to last name.

Q13.2   Draw all of the possible ordered binary trees containing the three elements: ABC. Note that there are 3!=6 different permutations of the three items. The trees may be constructed by inserting these elements one at a time in order. Not all of the permutations will generate unique trees. Repeat for four elements: ABCD.

Q13.3   The presentation, above, used distinct keys. Where, in the following tree, would another key with the value ALICE be placed? Use the algorithms given.

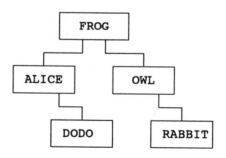

Q13.4 In what ways are a linked list and a binary tree the same? In what ways do they differ?

Q13.5 Consider the following binary tree:

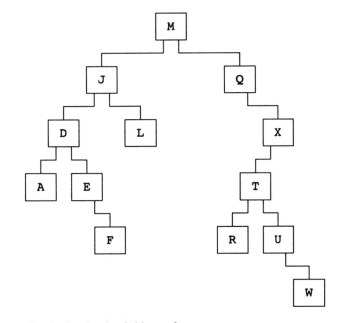

a. What is the depth of this tree?

b. What would be the depth if the tree were balanced?

c. Redraw the tree as a balanced binary tree.

d. Is the answer to part c. unique?

Q13.6 A beginning programmer decided to implement a binary tree using a structure that looked like:

```
struct record {int data;
               int left_link;
               int right_link;
               int empty_link;
              } tree[NUMB];
```

Comment on the inclusion of the empty_link variable which was to link the unused records together. Is it necessary? Is it a good idea? Why, or why not?

Q13.7 Could a binary tree be implemented on a magnetic tape medium? Explain.

Q13.8   As was mentioned in the text, the following is also a maximum-depth binary tree.

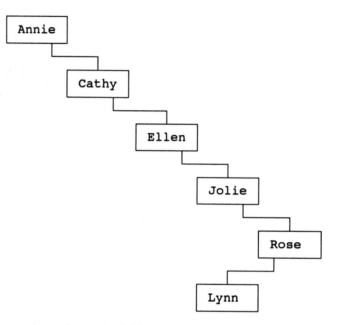

How many such maximum-depth binary trees are there for these six items?

Q13.9   What does the following tree give when traversed in the designated orders?

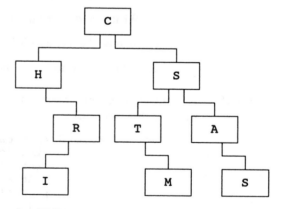

a. Inorder (LNR)

b. Preorder (NLR)

c. Postorder (LRN)

Q13.10 In the tree balancing algorithm, Algorithm TB, step TB1 reads as:

> TB1. [get keys]   Invoke Algorithm TP, except store the locations in a list.

How would Algorithm TP need to be modified in order to store the locations rather than print the data?

Q13.11 What is the order of the tree balancing algorithm; that is, using the "big O" notation, how does the behavior of this process depend upon n, the number of items in the tree?

Q13.12 It was stated that if a binary tree is traversed in LRN or RLN order, deleting records as they are visited, then only leaves will be deleted. Explain why.

Q13.13 What is the "big O" behavior of the tree reorganization if it is performed in place, without rebalancing, by deleting leaves and grafting them into a new tree structure?

Q13.14 What are the advantage(s) and disadvantage(s) of maintaining not only children pointers but also a parent pointer with each record?

Q13.15 Discuss, with diagrams, how continuation records could be implemented with a binary tree structure.

Q13.16 For the linked list case, the algorithms were simplified if the first node was designated as the top of the list rather than using a special *tol* index or pointer. Would there be a similar gain for using such a record for the root node in a binary tree?

Q13.17 In balancing the tree, we first obtained a list of the locations, then we set the *ROOT* to END, effectively creating an empty tree but in the process we lost access to our original tree. Why do we not have to be concerned about losing records?

Q13.18 If a node in an AVL tree requires a field that contains three possible values, how many bits are required to contain it?

Q13.19 If telephone area codes are constructed as indicated in the text, then how many possible three-digit codes are there?

Q13.20 If a B-tree node contains two keys, how many links does it contain?

Q13.21 A B-tree node, of order 5, already contains four keys. If another key is to be inserted into it, then it will be split. How many keys will the original and the new node each contain?

Q13.22 A binary tree contains *n* nodes. How many different places are available to insert the next record?

Q13.23 Does the Tree Rebuilding algorithm, TR, display tail recursion?

Q13.24 What is the average number of looks needed to find a record in the unbalanced tree consisting of the six records: Alice, Bill, Hatter, etc.? After balancing the tree, what is the average number of looks?

Q13.25 When a node is deleted, one of the children will be grafted back to the same location as the deleted node. Show that the other child will be grafted into the first child subtree, rather than somewhere else in the tree.

Q13.26 As we traversed a tree and restructured it into a right-hand only tree, we simply appended the node onto the new list without changing its parent link to END. Why was this unnecessary?

Q13.27 As we traversed a tree and restructured it into a right-hand only tree, we set the left child links of each to END; however, we did not adjust the right child link of any of them, including the last node in the list. Why not?

Q13.28 In the in-place tree-balancing procedure using rotations, after the first pass down the right-hand list, which nodes became leaves in the final balanced tree? (Consider full trees with $n=2^m-1$ nodes.)

Q13.29 Why does a rotation operation leave a tree properly ordered?

Q13.30 We have used a counterclockwise rotation operation. What would a clockwise rotation operation look like? What would be the sequence of link changes to perform this?

Q13.31 On a tree of 50 nodes, what is the sequence of rotation operations required to balance it once it is stretched into a right-side only tree?

Q13.32 How does a rotation operation change the number of levels in a tree?

Q13.33 The number of operations to stretch a tree into a right-side only tree is approximately $3n/2$. The number of rotation operations is roughly $n+\lg n$. What is the "big O" behavior of the combined operations? Why?

EXERCISES

E13.1 Draw, by hand, the "almost physical" view of a binary tree at each of the following operations (assume alphabetic ordering, not month within the year):

a. empty tree

b. insert 'MAY'

c. insert 'FEB'

d. insert 'OCT'

e. insert 'AUG'

f. insert 'APR'

g. insert 'JUN'

h. insert 'SEP'

i. **delete** 'Feb'

E13.2 Modify the Tree Traversal Algorithm, Algorithm TP, to perform its traversal in NRL order.

E13.3 Modify the stack version of the Tree Traversal Algorithm, Algorithm TA, to perform its traversal in NLR order.

E13.4 Show that when a node in a binary tree is deleted, then either one of the orphan branches will be attached where the node was originally located.

E13.5 Modify the Tree Insertion Algorithm, Algorithm TI, to attach one of the orphan branches directly and graft the other if necessary.

E13.6 If each node contains a link to its parent, it is possible to derive a procedure for traversing a tree in preorder (LNR) without utilizing a stack. This allows us to move through the tree at will.

To begin the analysis, note that we can arrive at a node from only five different ways:

1. Straight down (from ROOT).
2. Down to the left; that is, from a LLINK.
3. Down to the right; that is, from a RLINK.
4. Up from the left; that is, from a left child.
5. Up from the right; that is, from a right child.

When we arrive at a node, we will find four possibilities:

1. No children
2. Left child only
3. Right child only
4. Both child present

Form a table with the arrival ways as rows and the findings as columns. Fill in each entry as to whether the contents are printed and where one goes afterwards:

print contents of node

move to left child
move to right child
move to parent

quit

	No Children	Left Only	Right Only	Both Children
1. straight down				
2. down to left				
3. down to right				
4. up from left	------		------	
5. up from right	------	------		

There are four entries in the table that are "impossible". For each of the others we can decide if we wish to print the contents and what action to take. In reality, several rows are identical, which simplifies the algorithm. However, by including all possible situations explicitly, we are ensured not to overlook something.

Note, that "quitting" requires checking if a parent exists; that is, are we at the root arriving from a particular direction?

After simplifying the table, write a formal algorithm for traversing a binary tree in LNR order if parent links are available.

E13.7   Another algorithm for deleting from a binary tree recognizes that of the four possible configurations of children, there is only one that presents any problems. If the node to be deleted has:

1. No children—then delete it by setting a link to it from its parent to END.

2. Only a left child—then connect the left child to the parent by setting the link to the deleted node to its left child link.

3. Only a right child—then connect the right child to the parent by setting the link to the deleted node to its right child link.

4. Both a left and a right child—then we find the next node in the LNR sequence; that is, we move down the right child branch and find the first node with no left child. We delete that node from the tree and write its contents into the location of the one we really wish to delete.

As an example:

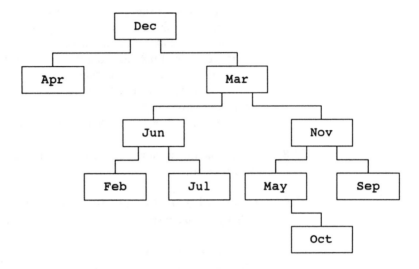

If we wish to delete the node containing "Mar", we find that it has links to two children. The next datum in the LNR sequence is "May". Moving down the right branch of "Mar", then following the LNR order, "May" is the first one we come to with only one child; that is, after "Nov" is it the first left descendent that does not have a left child. We delete "May" (by connecting its only child to "Nov", its parent) and copy the contents to the node with "Mar". The tree becomes:

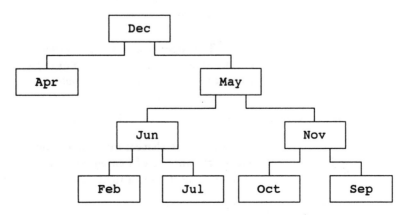

In all cases the resultant tree will be properly ordered. Show this by considering:

  a. The relationship of the "next" node with the left children of the deleted node.
  b. The relationship of the "next" node with the right children of the deleted node.

The process suggested above involves copying the contents of the "next" record to the location of the deleted record; however, this is not necessary if the links of the deleted node are copied to the link fields of the "next" record, and the link from the parent of the deleted record is adjusted to point to the location of the "next" one.

The deletion of the "next" record is easy, since it has either no children or only a right child.

Write a formal algorithm to perform this deletion process.

E13.8   Modify the tree-manipulation algorithms to include the use of a parent link in each record.

E13.9   An interesting problem is to determine the number of possible distinct trees with a given number of nodes. For the first few it is easy to count them.

```
n = 1:   A                                    1 tree
n = 2:   A       B                            2 trees
          B     A
n = 3:   A       A       B       C       C    5 trees
          B       C     A C     A         B
               C     B           B     A
n = 4:   A               B                    14 trees
          B      ...    A C     ...
           C               D
            D
n = 5:                                        42 trees
```

The larger trees may be determined by considering how they are composed of smaller trees. As an example, for n = 5, we get (using a number to indicate the size of a subtree):

```
a.  1      b.  1        c.  1        d.  1      e.  1
     4         3   1         2   2        1   3          4
```

That is, the five element tree may be composed of a root (of one element) and a left child tree of four elements (case a) or a root of one, a left child of three elements, and a right child of one element (case b), etc.

We can determine the number of possible trees for each of these if we know the numbers of the simpler trees. In this case we get:

   a.   14   b.   5·1   c.   2·2   d.   1·5   e.   14

for a total of 42.

Each term (except for the first and last) will consist of a product of two factors, each containing the number of possible subtrees corresponding to the two children.

If we define P(0) = 1, then each term may be written as a product of two factors:

```
P(5) =
    P(4)·P(0)+P(3)·P(1)+P(2)·P(2)+P(1)·P(3)+P(0)·P(4)
    = 14·1 + 5·1 + 2·2 + 1·5 + 1·14 = 42
```

Note:

```
P(4) = P(3)·P(0)+P(2)·P(1)+P(1)·P(2)+P(0)·P(3)
     = 5·1 + 2·1 + 1·2 + 1·5 = 14
```

and

```
P(3) = P(2)·P(0)+P(1)·P(1)+P(0)·P(2)
     = 2·1 + 1·1 + 1·2 = 5
```

This expression is in the form of a recurrence relation. Write it out as:

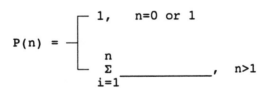

Evaluate this and calculate a table P(n) for n=1 through 10.

E13.10   It can be derived that a closed form solution to the number of possible binary trees can be expressed as:

$$P(n) = \frac{1}{n+1} C(2n,n)$$

where C(n,r) is the combination of *n* things taken *r* at a time, and is given by:

$$C(n,r) = \frac{n!}{(n-r)!\, r!}.$$

Evaluate this for $n=1$ through 10, and compare with the values given in the previous exercise.

E13.11   Rewrite the Tree Grafting Algorithm, Algorithm TR, to be a recursive algorithm.

E13.12   Rewrite the Tree Rebuilding Algorithm, Algorithm TR, to eliminate tail recursion.

E13.13   In a rotation, it was stated that the root node becomes a child node of the new root, taking the place of a child node of the new root, which can be connected to the old root node. Show that this will be the proper place for that branch to connect, to maintain the LNR order of the tree.

E13.14   Using the example B-tree after we inserted "rat" as a starting point, insert the key "ant" and draw the resultant structure. Assume that locations 9 and 10 are the next available ones.

E13.15   Write out the algorithm for searching a B-tree.

E13.16   Write out the algorithm for insertion into a B-tree.

E13.17   The number of possible balanced trees can be computed by considering that a tree with $n = 2^m - 1$ is perfectly balanced and there are $p = 2^m$ possible places to insert new records. Therefore, show that the number of possible balanced trees is given by:

$$B(n) = C(p, n-p+1) \qquad p \le n < 2p$$

Using this expression, compute a table for $n=1$ through 31 giving the number of possible balanced trees.

E13.18   By considering full balanced trees with $n = 2^m - 1$, $m=1,2,3,...$ nodes show that the total number of node visits is given by:

m	n	Visits
1	1	1
2	3	4
3	7	10
4	15	22
5	31	46

Since dealing with a tree with m involves two subtrees of $m-1$ plus visiting the root node twice, we get a recurrence relation:

$$V(m) = \begin{cases} 1, & m = 1 \\ 2V(m-1)+2, & m > 1 \end{cases}$$

Show that the closed-form expression for the table and the recurrence relation is given by:

$$V(m) = 3 \cdot 2^{m-1} - 2$$

Hence, derive the closed form for $V(n)$.

E13.19 The tree restructuring algorithm, Algorithm TL, traversed the tree in a LNR order and appended nodes to a list. For this process, it was convenient to maintain a variable which gave the location of the last node. However, we could eliminate this need by traversing the tree in the RNL order and always inserting new nodes at the root end of the right-hand tree. Rewrite Algorithm TL to do this.

E13.20 We have used a right-hand list and counterclockwise rotations to balance a binary tree. It would be possible to build, initially, a left-hand-only tree and use clockwise rotations. Rewrite Algorithms TL and TC to rebalance a tree from the left.

PROBLEMS

P13.1 Write C functions to implement the binary tree maintenance algorithms:

void initial()

void print()   LNR order

int search(item)   returns: location if found
                                        -1 if not found

int insert(item)   returns: 0 if successful
                                        -1 if not successful

int intsetup(item)   returns: loc if successful

void graft(loc) -1 if not successful

int delete(item)   returns: 0 if successful
                                        -1 if not successful

void dump()

These will act upon a global binary-tree structure containing 12 elements. The data will be integer values in the range 100-999. Let the initial() routine fill the data fields with 0.

```
struct record {int data;
               int llink,rlink;
              } tree[12];
```

The dump() routine should print out the location, the data, and the link values as well as the contents of root and top of empty variables.

Write a main program that requests a command and value if needed. Perform the following commands in order:

1.	INITIAL	19.	PRINT
2.	DUMP	20.	DUMP
3.	PRINT	21.	DELETE 500
4.	INSERT 444	22.	DELETE 444
5.	INSERT 222	23.	PRINT
6.	INSERT 333	24.	DUMP
7.	INSERT 111	25.	INSERT 600
8.	INSERT 777	26.	PRINT
9.	INSERT 555	27.	DUMP
10.	INSERT 666	28.	INSERT 100
11.	INSERT 999	29.	PRINT
12.	INSERT 888	30.	DUMP
13.	PRINT	31.	SEARCH 222
14.	DUMP	32.	SEARCH 300
15.	DELETE 222	33.	SEARCH 999
16.	PRINT	34.	SEARCH 111
17.	DUMP	35.	SEARCH 600
18.	DELETE 888		

P13.2   Modify the tree to store alphabetic names of up to ten characters. Test it on names that are inserted, deleted, printed, dumped, and searched, as above.

P13.3   In C the appropriate scheme to implement a binary tree would be to use pointers for the links:

```
struct record {int data;
               struct record *llink,*rlink;
              } tree[12],*root,*toe;
```

Implement the binary tree maintenance routines that use pointers and this structure. Test it using the data provided above.

P13.4   Using one of the programs you developed for maintaining a binary tree with an integer data field implement the binary tree balancing routines. Use a tree that contains 24 records.

Perform the following operations in order:

1.	INITIAL	17.	DUMP
2.	DUMP	18.	INSERT 800
3.	PRINT	19.	INSERT 810
4.	INSERT 444	20.	INSERT 820
5.	INSERT 222	21.	INSERT 830
6.	INSERT 333	22.	INSERT 840
7.	INSERT 111	23.	INSERT 850
8.	INSERT 777	24.	INSERT 860
9.	INSERT 555	25.	INSERT 870
10.	INSERT 666	26.	INSERT 880
11.	INSERT 999	27.	INSERT 890
12.	INSERT 888	28.	PRINT
13.	PRINT	29.	DUMP
14.	DUMP	30.	BALANCE
15.	BALANCE	31.	PRINT
16.	PRINT	32.	DUMP

P13.5   Rewrite the Tree Rebuilding Algorithm, Algorithm TB, and implement the appropriate C function to balance a tree using a stack rather than recursion. Test it with the operations for the previous problem.

P13.6   Another traversal order for a binary tree is called "level order." This essentially visits and processes the root, then its two children, then its four grandchildren, etc. As an example, consider the following tree:

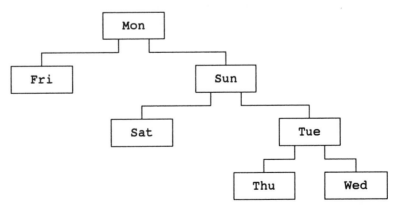

The level order traversal of the tree would be:

Mon, Fri, Sun, Sat, Tue, Thu, Wed

Write a C function that would perform a level order traversal of a binary tree and print the data for each node. Hint, a queue data structure is a useful structure for this problem. Each time you visit a node, place its two child links (including any with END) onto a queue. You "visit" a node by taking it from the queue. The queue is initialized by first placing the root into the empty queue.

P13.7   Write a C function that prints out a binary tree in logical form; that is, it prints, on each line, all of the nodes on that level. Space over to the middle of the paper or screen for the root. The two possible nodes at level 1 should go one quarter and three quarters across, etc.

```
void display()
```

Illustrate its use with the data for problem P13.4, displaying the logical structure whenever it calls for a DUMP command (perform both DUMP and DISPLAY).

The first output should look like:

```
                    444

        222                         777

    111         333         555             999

                                666     888
```

Hint, this is similar to the "level order" visits of the previous problem. A queue data structure is particularly useful.

P13.8   Rewrite the Tree Rebuilding Algorithm, Algorithm TB, and implement the appropriate C function to balance a tree using a stack rather than recursion.
Test it with the operations for problem P13.4.

Chapter 14

Heaps

"Here!" cried Alice, quite forgetting in the flurry of the moment how large she had grown in the last few minutes, and she jumped up in such a hurry that she tipped over the jury box with the edge of her skirt, upsetting all the jurymen on to the heads of the crowd below, and there they lay sprawling about, reminding her very much of a globe of goldfish she had accidentally upset the week before.

"Oh, I <u>beg</u> your pardon!" she exclaimed in a tone of great dismay, and began picking them up again as quickly as she could, for the accident of the goldfish kept running in her head, and she had a vague sort of idea that they must be collected at once and put back into the jury-box, or they would die.

"The trial cannot proceed," said the King, in a grave voice, "until all the jurymen are back in their proper places—<u>all</u>," he repeated with great emphasis, looking hard at Alice as he said so.

Alice looked at the jury box, and saw that, in her haste, she had put the Lizard in head downwards, and the poor little thing was waving its tail about in a melancholy way, being quite unable to move. She soon got it out again, and put it right; "not that it signifies much," she said to herself; "I should think it would be <u>quite</u> as much use in the trial one way up or the other."

14.1 OBJECTIVES

The objectives for this chapter are to:

- Describe a heap and its properties.

- Present algorithms for insertion and deletion.

- Illustrate the uses of heaps.

- Derive a sort algorithm based upon a heap.

- Analyze the algorithms.

14.2 INTRODUCTION

Often one does not want to sort a list completely, but to find the largest element in the list easily. An example might be a list of priorities, with the highest priority being the one that you want to find quickly. Thus, a data structure that provides this is useful. Certainly a sorted list does this, but insertion into and deletion from a sorted list may be time consuming. The largest element in a binary tree is not in a fixed convenient location—one must search for it.

A suitable structure for maintaining a list, where the largest element is readily available, is an interesting data structure called a **heap**. Insertion into and deletion from the heap is O(lg n) because a heap is, in reality, a binary tree. However, the order of the elements is different from the typical tree, and the structure may be implemented in a list with no extra memory taken up with links.

Because insertion is at one end of a list (that internally has certain tree properties) and deletion is at the other end, a heap behaves generally as a queue. However, a newly inserted element is moved up through the heap to find its appropriate position in the structure.

As an example, a computer system may have a number of jobs to execute. It selects the next one to work—one based upon its priority, which depends on a number of factors such as the resources needed and the time it has been waiting. Thus, its priority may dynamically change after being set initially. If the job name's are stored in a heap along with its priority, and the heap is maintained according to the priority, it is easy for the scheduler to select the next one and delete it from the heap. As jobs are added to the system, they are inserted into the heap.

We have also considered a number of different sorts for arranging a list of values, in place. As it turns out, a heap data structure is a wonderful starting point for an interesting sort algorithm that—while, in general, is not as good as a Quick Sort—does not have a very bad worst case.

14.3   A HEAP

A heap is a data structure for representing a collection of data. Superficially, it can be thought of as a binary tree. An example of a heap is:

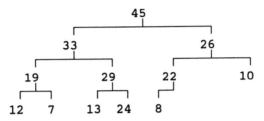

14.3.1   Properties

However, there is more to a heap than its being a simple binary tree. There are two properties that make this tree, or a collection, a heap:

1. order: The value of any node is greater than or equal to the values of its two children.

2. shape: The terminal nodes (leaves) are on, at most, two levels, with those on the bottom level as far "left" as possible; that is, no "holes" in the tree.

In order to sharpen our understanding, the following collection of the same values is not a heap because it violates the order property. The value of the root (29) is not greater than or equal to its left child (45).

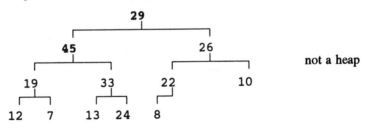

not a heap

Similarly, the following arrangement illustrated on the top of the next page is not a heap because it violates the shape property. Even though the terminal nodes are only on two levels, there is a "missing" child (of 29) and hence, a "hole" exists. The nodes on the bottom level are not as far to the left as possible.

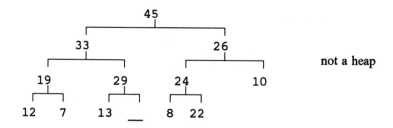

not a heap

Because of the shape property, the heap is as balanced as possible; that is, each node is as close to the root as possible.

Note that a given heap is not unique for a specified set of data. The following arrangement of the same set is also a heap:

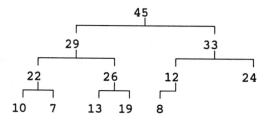

We observe that the root value is the same in both arrangements, but the other values may be found in different locations in this tree structure.

Finally, the typical order found in a binary tree is not found in a heap. The left child may be less than, greater than, or equal to the right child. The only ordering is that **both** children are less than or equal to the parent.

14.3.2   Representation

Because of the shape property, we can represent a heap as an implicit binary tree without the formal links; that is, we can store the heap in a simple list and calculate the locations of the children and parent. We will number the nodes as:

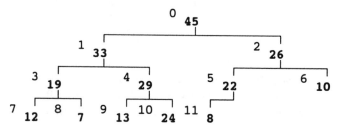

Thus, this structure may be stored in a list as:

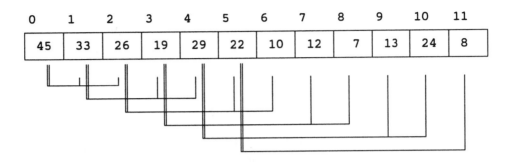

0	1	2	3	4	5	6	7	8	9	10	11
45	33	26	19	29	22	10	12	7	13	24	8

The lines connect a parent with its two children. The "list" is a heap even if it is difficult to see that it has the heap properties.

Because of the shape property we can compute, rather than check, a link field for the location of a parent or a child. For a given node, i, we can compute the location of the children and parent by:

left child	$2i+1$
right child	$2i+2$
parent	$(i-1)/2$

with the root given by 0, all values of i must then satisfy

$$0 \leq i < n.$$

where n is the number of items stored in the heap. We need not specify the floor function (greatest integer less than or equal to) since we are assuming integer arithmetic on positive quantities.

14.3.3 Insertion

The useful operations that we need to consider are insertion and deletion. We demand that the structure be a heap before and after each of these operations. This will mean that we will have to rearrange some of the elements as we perform each operation.

We can implement insertion into a heap by entering an element in the list at the end of the heap, then moving it up the tree structure toward the root until the heap property is regained.

Consider the heap of ten elements stored in locations 0 through 9 of a simple list:

0	1	2	3	4	5	6	7	8	9	10	11
45	29	33	22	26	12	24	10	7	13		

Or a more logical view that displays the heap structure:

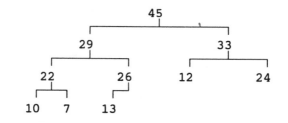

If we now put item 42 in location 10, then the structure of eleven elements (including the new one) is no longer a heap.

0	1	2	3	4	5	6	7	8	9	10	11
45	29	33	22	26	12	24	10	7	13	42	

not a heap

The process to regain the heap structure is to move it up the path denoted by its successive direct ancestors; that is, 26, 29, and 45, until the order property of the heap is restored. Clearly the resultant heap of eleven elements is:

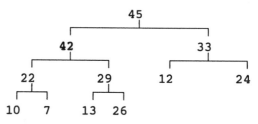

where we have moved the 26 and the 29 down and inserted 42. In list form:

0	1	2	3	4	5	6	7	8	9	10	11
45	42	33	22	29	12	24	10	7	13	26	

Such a process can be called **Move Up**. It adds an element to an already existent heap. It is basically an insertion-type process, but the increments change as we move from a node to its parent, etc., to the root. For the example above, we needed to move items along locations 10, 4, 1, and 0 until a proper place for the new item could be found. That is, the increments are 6, 3, and 1. However, rather than focusing on the increments, it is easier simply to compute the parent location for a given node until either a place is found to insert the item, or the root is reached.

A formal algorithm to perform this heap insertion is:

Algorithm MU (Move Up). Insert item onto the end of a heap and move it up toward the root of the heap until the heap property of the structure is regained. Initially, we have a heap stored in *LIST* with H elements (stored in $0,1,...,H-1$) and the new item is in *LIST[H]*; when finished, the heap contains $H+1$ elements.

MU1. [initialize]   j=H; k=LIST[j].

MU2. [compute parent]   i=(j−1)/2.

MU3. [at root?]   If j = 0, then Go to step MU6.

MU4. [compare]   If LIST[i] > k, then Go to step MU6.

MU5. [move to parent]   LIST[j]=LIST[i]; j=i; Go to step MU2.

MU6. [store key]   LIST[j]=k.

With this algorithm it is easy to convert any random list into a heap by inserting each subsequent item into the heap. We can begin the process by noting that a list of one element satisfies both heap properties and is, hence, a heap. Therefore, we really start by inserting element number two into the initial heap of size one.

Algorithm MH (Make heap). Take a list of n values stored in *LIST* and insert them one at a time to make a heap structure of *n* items.

MH1. [loop over new items]   Perform step MH2 for H=1,2,...,n−1.

MH2. [move up]   Invoke Algorithm MU with length H.

14.3.4 Analysis

As time progresses, the random list shrinks and the heap grows. What makes this relatively efficient is that the heap is a balanced structure, hence there are no more than lg H operations to insert a new item into a heap of H elements, and an average that is close to (lg H)/2. Because we start with a heap of one element and add to it $n-1$ elements, then the total number of operations is approximately dependent upon the changing size, as:

$$(lg\ 1)/2 + (lg\ 2)/2 + (lg\ 3)/2 + ... + (lg\ n)/2$$
$$= [lg\ 1 + lg\ 2 + lg\ 3 + ... + lg\ n]/2$$
$$= lg(1·2·3·\ ...\ ·n)/2 = (lg\ n!)/2.$$

We can evaluate the logarithm of the factorial by using Stirling's approximation (see Appendix A). The net result is that the heap-making process is $O(n \cdot \lg n)$.

The primary advantage of a heap is that the largest item in the heap is located at the root—at location 0, and the heap is relatively cheap to build. To form a heap from a list of n items takes $O(n \cdot \lg n)$ operations, but to add (or delete, as we shall see) a single item from a heap takes, at most, $O(\lg n)$ operations. Thus, it is an appropriate data structure where the largest item is needed but the rest of the items are not needed. Of course, if the list is built first, the elements are removed at a later time; then sorting the list might be preferred. But if items are being added dynamically and the largest is always needed, then the heap is a good structure. An example of such a situation is a list of tasks to be performed, each with a designated priority. The next task to be performed is the one with the highest priority. As tasks are completed they are removed from the structure, and new tasks are being added constantly as others are being processed.

Another application is a relatively efficient sort, as we shall explore shortly.

14.3.5 Deletion

Before we consider sorting, we need to determine what we mean by deletion and how to effect it. Because the largest element is located at the root node, it is easy to access, and is typically the one that is desired and, hence, deleted from the heap. However, removing it creates two problems: what do we put in its place, and how do we maintain a heap structure?

We will define heap deletion as removing the root item. This reduces the number of items in the heap; therefore, we will simply move the last item, stored in location H-1 to location 0, and reduce the size of the heap by one. This restores the heap shape property but not its order. We need a scheme to move this element **down** an appropriate branch, thereby moving larger elements up until the heap property is restored. This process is called **Move Down**. Move Up was straightforward because there was only one path to the root, but Move Down involves a decision about which of two possible child branches to move down. The answer is easy—we will always attempt to move the **largest** child up towards the root. This will ensure that the heap order property is maintained.

As an example, consider our previous heap of size $H=11$. If we now remove the contents of location 0 (the 45) and move the contents of location $10=H-1$ (the 26) to location 0, the size of the structure, which is not a heap, becomes $H=10$:

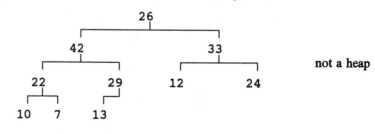

In list form this would appear as:

26

0	1	2	3	4	5	6	7	8	9	10	11
26	42	33	22	29	12	24	10	7	13		

We wish to use to move the root element (26) down the tree until the heap order property is restored using an insertion-type procedure.

There are two possible children that we might consider moving up as we move the given item down. The choice is not difficult. We will always attempt to move the **larger** of the two children. This will insure that we do not move a smaller child up to become the parent of a larger one. In this case, we will choose the 42 located at 1 because it is the largest child.

26

0	1	2	3	4	5	6	7	8	9	10	11
42	42	33	22	29	12	24	10	7	13		

The children of location 1 are located at 3 and 4. Again, choose the largest, which is 29. Since it is larger than 26, we move it up.

26

0	1	2	3	4	5	6	7	8	9	10	11
42	29	33	22	29	12	24	10	7	13		

Continuing, we discover that location 4 has only one child, which is located at 9 (the other would be at location 10, which is not part of the heap). Since the element there, 13, is smaller than the 26, we simply insert the 26 at location 4. The heap properties are now restored.

0	1	2	3	4	5	6	7	8	9	10	11
42	29	33	22	26	12	24	10	7	13		

or in logical form:

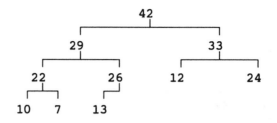

An algorithm for implementing this insertion type Move Down process is given below.

Algorithm MD (Move Down). Move item originally in LIST[0] down in the structure to regain the heap property. The heap has H elements and is stored in *LIST* $(0,1,2...,H-1)$.

MD1. [initialize]	k=LIST[0]; j=0.
MD2. [compute child]	i=2·j+1.
MD3. [too big?]	If i >= H, then Go to step MD8.
MD4. [at end?]	If i = H−1, then Go to step MD6.
MD5. [find largest child]	If LIST[i+1] > LIST[i], then i=i+1.
MD6. [compare]	If LIST[i] < k, then Go to step MD8.
MD7. [move to child]	LIST[j]=LIST[i]; j=i; Go to step MD2.
MD8. [store key]	LIST[j]=k.

Incorporating this algorithm, we can define an algorithm to delete the root from a heap, store it, and reheap the resulting structure.

Algorithm DH (Heap deletion). Removes the item located at location 0 in a heap of length H stored in a list, *LIST*, replaces it with the last item, and reheaps the result with length H-1.

DH1. [remove root]	ITEM=LIST[0].
DH2. [move last]	LIST[0]=LIST[H−1].
DH3. [change length]	H=H−1.
DH4. [reheap]	Invoke Algorithm MD with length H.

Because of the tree nature of a heap, the Move Down process takes a maximum of lg n operations and may take closer to (lg n)/2 operations on the average.

14.4   HEAP SORT

We can incorporate the Move Up and Move Down Algorithms to perform a sort. The general scheme is to form the random list into a heap using Algorithm MH. Then we swap the item at location 0 with the one in location n-1. Since the item that was at location 0 is the largest item in the heap, it will be moved to its final location in the sorted list. We then reheap the remaining n-1 elements (located in 0 through n-2) into a heap using the Move Down Algorithm. This largest element in this list will then be located at location 0. We swap this with the element in location n-2, and reheap the remaining n-3 elements. This process is continued until the heap is only one element long. This will be the smallest item in the list and will remain in location 0.

Consider our heap example. After taking a random list and adding one element at a time to the heap that starts with one element, we obtain a heap that incorporates all of the items of the list.

0	1	2	3	4	5	6	7	8	9	10
45	42	33	22	29	12	24	10	7	13	26

Or in more logical form:

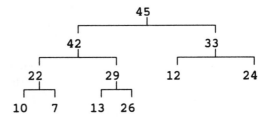

Now we swap the root element with the last one:

0	1	2	3	4	5	6	7	8	9	10
26	42	33	22	29	12	24	10	7	13	45

Now reheap the elements, except for the last; that is, the heap of ten (locations 0 through 9).

0	1	2	3	4	5	6	7	8	9	10
42	29	33	22	26	12	24	10	7	13	*45*

In a logical display, this becomes:

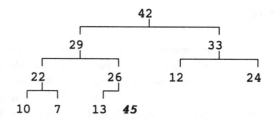

where we have indicated the heap as well as the elements in the list that are "beyond the end" of the heap.

Repeating this process, we obtain:

0	1	2	3	4	5	6	7	8	9	10
33	29	24	22	26	12	13	10	7	*42*	*45*

In a logical display, this becomes:

The general procedure is to transform the random list into a heap that grows from location 0 until the entire list is a heap. This uses the Move Up Algorithm repeatedly. Then, using the Move Down Algorithm, we transform the heap into a sorted list that grows from the last location downward as the heap shrinks.

A formal algorithm to implement the Heap Sort is:

Algorithm H (Heap Sort). Given a list, *LIST*, of *n* elements, rearrange these items in place so that they are in increasing order by first heaping them, then repeatedly extracting the largest, which is located at the root, swapping it with the last element and reheaping the result.

H1. [make heap]   Perform step H2 for H=1,2...,n−1.

H2. [move up]   Invoke Algorithm MU on LIST with H.

H3. [make sorted list]   Perform steps H4 through H5 for H=n−2,n−3,...,1,0.

H4. [swap]   Swap LIST[0] and LIST[H+1].

H5. [remake heap]   Invoke Algorithm MD on LIST with H.

Note that the first step of Algorithm MD is to store the value of *LIST[0]* in a variable. This may be incorporated with the storing of *LIST[0]* in a temporary variable for the swap in step H4 to save two assignments. That is, if one writes the Move Down process as part of the function that performs Algorithm H, rather than invoking it as a separate function, then a small efficiency is gained in addition to the elimination of a function call:

```
t = list[0];        /* swap */
list[0] = list[h+1];
list[h+1] = t;

k = list[0];        /* step MD1 */
j = 0;
```

may simply be replaced by:

```
k = list[h+1];      /* combine swap & step MD1 */
list[h+1] = list[0];
j = 0;
```

Diagrammatically, the Heap Sort may be portrayed as:

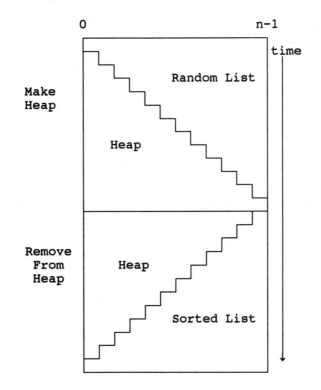

Because the Make Heap process is O(n • lg n), as a worst case, and the Unheap process to the final sorted list follows a similar analysis and is also O(n • lg n), the Heap Sort does not have a very bad worst-case. On the average, it will sort slightly more slowly than the Quick Sort or the Shell's Sort, but, whereas the Quick Sort has a very bad worst-case, the Heap Sort does not.

14.5   INTERNAL SORTING SUMMARY

Let us time the heap sort, just as we did for the other internal sorts. The following tables were constructed using a series of C function implementations of the listed sorting algorithms. They were run on an 80286 processor with a clock speed of 6 MHz. The items were 16-bit integers to be sorted into ascending order. The timings were determined by using the internal clock and are precise to better than 5% and, typically, better than 1%.

TIMINGS FOR VARIOUS SORT ROUTINES

Times in Seconds for 1,000 Items

Sort	Random	Ascending	Descending	Constant
Simple swap	11.40	8.91	13.95	8.91
Improved bubble	10.67	0.02	13.84	0.02
Insertion	4.65	0.04	9.26	0.04
Shell's	0.37	0.17	0.29	0.17
Heap	0.35	0.46	0.32	0.35
Quick	0.33	0.26	0.33	11.79
Quick + Insert	0.30	0.20	0.27	11.81

Times in Seconds for 3,000 Items

Sort	Random	Ascending	Descending	Constant
Simple swap	102.1	80.1	125.6	80.1
Improved bubble	96.4	0.05	124.6	0.04
Insertion	41.7	0.11	83.2	0.11
Shell's	1.38	0.62	1.00	0.62
Heap	1.22	1.64	1.14	1.21
Quick	1.15	0.89	1.15	105.4
Quick + Insert	1.06	0.69	0.99	105.5

<u>Times in Seconds for 10,000 Items</u>

Sort	Random	Ascending	Descending	Constant
Simple swap	1118	890	1395	890
Improved bubble	1071	0.15	1384	0.15
Insertion	461	0.35	924	0.35
Shell's	5.92	2.66	3.74	2.66
Heap	4.67	6.40	4.45	4.64
Quick	4.47	3.35	4.42	1169
Quick + Insert	4.15	2.78	3.95	1169

The four columns are labeled according to the initial ordering of the items. The column labeled "random" is the average for several randomly generated lists. The same lists were used for all of the sort algorithm executions.

The Quick Sorts used a median-of-three to select the pivot element, and the Quick + Insertion used a minimum sublist size of 14.

We quickly note the drastic differences between the $O(n^2)$ sorts, the first four, and the others on random and descending data. However, for ascending or constant data, the simplest sorts were the best.

Generally speaking, the Quick + Insertion is overall the fastest sort, except for its very bad worst case. The Heap Sort and Shell's Sort are slightly slower, but have no extremely bad worst case.

14.6 SUMMARY

A heap structure is an extension of the concept of a binary tree. Because of its shape property, it may be implemented as a list without explicit links. You can always calculate where the children are located and where the parent is. Because of its order property, the largest element is always conveniently located at the root (location 0) of the heap.

Insertion is at the end of the heap, and the item is moved upward to regain the heap order property. Deletion is at the "root" end, the last item is moved to the root and moved downward until the heap order property is regained. Both of these operations are $O(\lg n)$.

A heap is a suitable structure for maintaining a priority queue, where items are inserted at one end and deleted at the other; however, inserted items are moved up through the structure according to its "priority." The highest priority item is the one that is deleted.

The heap structure is the basis for a sort algorithm that has no really bad worst case. The scheme is to build the unordered list into a heap, then swap the largest item in the heap with the last item; that is, to its final position, and Move Down to regain the heap order property. The resulting algorithm is, on the average, slightly slower than the Quick Sort.

REFERENCES

Bentley, Jon L., *"Thanks Heaps"*, *Communications of the ACM*, vol. 28, no. 3, March 1985, Association for Computing Machinery, New York, p 245.

Knuth, Donald E., *The Art of Computer Programming*; Fundamental Algorithms, Vol. 1.,2nd ed., Addison-Wesley Publishing Co., Reading, Massachusetts, 1973.

Knuth, Donald E., *The Art of Computer Programming*; Sorting and Searching, vol. 3., Addison-Wesley Publishing Co., Reading, Massachusetts, 1973.

Sedgewick, Robert, *Algorithms in C*, Addison-Wesley Publishing Co., Reading, Massachusetts, 1990.

QUESTIONS

Q14.1   In what ways is a heap analogous to a queue?

Q14.2   Is a list that is sorted into descending order a heap? Why, or why not?

Q14.3   A heap is a binary tree structure, so why do we not need links?

Q14.4   A heap is not necessarily unique. There is only one heap of one element; there is only one heap of two distinct elements; for three elements, there are two distinct heaps. As an example,

For four distinct elements, how many different heaps are there? For five? For six?

Q14.5   If the root of the heap is located in location 1 rather than 0, (that is, the array contains values from 1 through *n*, rather than 0 through *n*-1) how do the formulas change for computing the locations of the children given the parent and the location of the parent of a given child?

Q14.6   In a conventional heap, the largest element is always located at the root. Where might the second largest element be located? The third largest element? The smallest element?

Q14.7   What are the relative advantages of a Heap Sort over a Quick Sort? The relative disadvantages?

Q14.8   An ordered binary tree was characterized by a recursive definition; that is, it consists of an element and each of the children are ordered binary trees. Does this concept hold for a heap? That is, is the structure consisting of each of the two descendants of the root, a heap?

Q14.9   In the table comparing various C functions that sort 10,000 items, the fastest time for the Heap Sort that was for the descending case—the opposite order of the desired one. Why?

Q14.10   What modifications would be needed to implement a Heap Sort that would sort the list into descending order?

Q14.11   The heap that we developed is an implicit binary tree structure—the links were not needed because of the shape. Could a heap be constructed explicitly? How?

Q14.12   What broad classification of a sort is a Heap Sort; that is, is it a selection, an enumeration, an insertion, or an exchange sort?

Q14.13   What would happen to the heap structure if we did not choose the larger of the two children in the Move Down process? That is, what would happen if we always chose the right child?

Q14.14   In the Move Down process, how many comparisons are there between elements of the heap for each iteration of the algorithm?

Q14.15   The Slow Sort, described in an exercise in Chapter 5 based upon a selection scheme that selects the smallest element not already found and moves it to a new list, is $O(n^3)$. If it takes 5.7 seconds to sort a list of 100 random elements (this was determined in the same way that the tables above were calculated), then how long would it take to sort a list of 1,000 elements? Of 3,000 elements? Of 10,000 elements?

Q14.16   What is the advantage(s) of the Quick Sort over the other types of internal sorts we have studied? Its disadvantage(s)?

Q14.17   What is the advantage(s) of the Heap Sort over the other types of internal sorts we have studied? Its disadvantage(s)?

Q14.18   Our heap examples have displayed distinct values. What happens if two or more values in the original list to be heaped are the same?

Q14.19   Show that a process that is $O(\ln n!)$, is $O(n \cdot \ln n)$. Use Stirling's Approximation.

Q14.20   Is the following a heap? Why or why not?

42 18 25 21 9 15 6 12 8 4

Q14.21   If you are inserting the n-th item into a heap of $n-1$ elements, then what is the exact expression that gives:

      a. The maximum number of comparisons?

      b. The average number of comparisons?

Hint: make a table, count the number, write out an expression in terms of n.

Q14.22   The Shell's Sort may have a bad worst case. For the general situation, it is not easy to find. How does this differ for the Heap Sort?

Q14.23   The heap examples that we illustrated, all items have been unique. What happens if there are repeated values? In particular, form the following into a heap:

4, 8, 15, 21, 21, 33, 42, 42

EXERCISES

E14.1   Write a formal algorithm to examine a list of n elements (indices 0 through $n-1$) and determine if the list is a heap.

E14.2   Rewrite the Move Up and Move Down Algorithms to implement a heap structure where the value of the parent is less than or equal to each of its children. The root value will then be the smallest item in the heap. As an example:

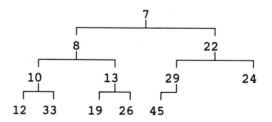

E14.3   We generally implemented the heap structure using indices. What would you need to do to use pointers? How would it modify the calculations of the parent and child locations?

E14.4   If you add a constant to all items of a heap, will it remain a heap? Explain why, or why not.

E14.5   If one takes two heaps:

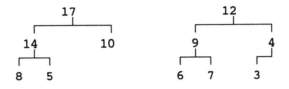

Treat them as simple lists:

    17   14   10   8   5   and   12   9   4   6   7   3

and merge them using a "descending order" merge and, thereby, obtain:

    17   14   12   10   9   8   5   4   6   7   3

which we discover is also a heap, as can be seen by putting it into a two-dimensional tree structure:

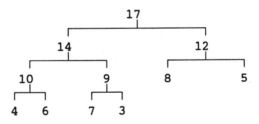

    Therefore, in this example, merging two heaps by the List Merge Algorithm (Algorithm M with the "order" reversed) results in a heap. Is this generally true? If not, can you find a counter example? Hint, try various heaps with three elements each.

E14.6   Which is the best sort to use on a set of internal data? Explain your answer.

E14.7   The heap manipulation algorithms, Move Up and Move Down, may be expressed using a swap process rather than an insertion process; that is, we compare two elements, and if they are out of order, swap them, then move up or down the heap. Write out the formal algorithms using a swap process.

E14.8   If you multiply all items of a heap by a constant, will it remain a heap? Explain why, or why not.

E14.9   In reality, each of the internal sort routines we have studied require additional storage for indices and for copies of an item. As an example, the simple Swap Sort, Algorithm W, requires one copy of the item for swapping, and two indices. In addition the code requires storage, but let us concentrate on the data storage. The enumeration sort required $n+2$ locations capable of storing indices, hence we have an example of a procedure that requires considerable extra storage.

Complete the following table. Count the required occurrences of variables that hold indices or pointers separately from those that hold a copy of a record. It is suggested that instead of the recursive version of the Quick Sort, you analyze the stack version. It is easier to account for storage. In that case, the amount of storage will depend upon the list—use the worst case.

For the two external sorts, consider their internal version.

Sort	Algo-rithm	Number index Variables	Number Record Variables
Simple Swap	W	2	1
Selection	L		1
Enumeration	C	n+2	
Insertion	I		
Bubble Up	BU		
Improved Bubble	BI		
Shell's	S		
Quick	QA		
Radix	RL		
Two-Way Merge	T,etc		
Heap	H		

E14.10 Given your knowledge of the behavior of the various sorts and the information given in the chapter on the times for sorting 1000, 3000, and 10,000 elements, compute the approximate times and complete the table:

Times in Seconds for 30,000 Items

Sort	Random	Ascending	Descending	Constant
Simple swap				
Improved bubble				
Insertion				
Shell's				
Heap				
Quick				
Quick + Insert				

E14.11 Sort by hand, using a Heap Sort and showing all of the intermediate conditions of the following list:

    Tiger-lily
    Rose
    Daisy
    Violet
    Larkspur

E14.12 In the text it was stated that the approximate number of operations in building a heap was given by:

$$(lg\ 1)/2\ +\ (lg\ 2)/2\ +\ (lg\ 3)/2\ +\ \ldots\ +\ (lg\ n)/2$$

This was sufficient to lead us to the "big O" behavior of $O(n \cdot lg\ n)$.

However, let us now consider carefully the problem of inserting items into a heap. We will insert, using Move Up, the *n*-th item into a previous heap of *n* elements. Make a table and count the average number of comparisons:

n	average comparisons	cumulative average
1	0	0
2	1.0	1.0
3	1.0	2.0
4	1.5	3.5
5		
6		
7		
8	2.0	

Hint: draw the heap in its logical structure. To insert item 2, takes one comparison (with the root). To insert item 3 takes one comparison (again with the root). To insert item 4 takes an average of 1.5 comparisons. That is, half the time there is one comparison (with its parent) and half the time there are two (once with its parent and once with the root). Therefore,

$$1.5\ =\ (1/2) \cdot 1\ +\ (1/2) \cdot 2$$

For item 8, one third of the time there is one comparison, one third of the time there are two, and one third of the time there are 3:

$$2.0\ =\ (1/3) \cdot 1\ +\ (1/3) \cdot 2\ +\ (1/3) \cdot 3$$

Continue this table, especially for 15 and 31 items.

Next compute the cumulative averages. Concentrating on those values of *n* that are 1, 3, 7, 15, and 31; that is for:

$$n = 2^m - 1$$

write out an expression for the cumulative average in terms of *m*.

Hint 1: it may be easier to work with twice the cumulative average values to get integers—you can always throw in a factor of 1/2 later.

Hint 2: this is almost exactly like the analysis for the binary search (Algorithm B).

Obtain:

$$\texttt{cumulative average} = \frac{(m-1) \cdot 2^m}{2}$$

Write this in terms of *n* and take the situation where *n* is large to obtain the "big O" behavior. Note that, strictly speaking, this expression is valid only for these special values of *n*; however, the actual expression will not differ very much for values of *n* in between.

PROBLEMS

P14.1   A heap is an ideal structure for maintaining a list of prioritized jobs to be performed. A difficulty, which it shares with a stack, is that a given job might never get executed. In the case of a stack, unless the stack gets emptied regularly, the first job submitted may wait for very long time. In the situation of a priority queue, if new jobs are submitted that have a higher priority than a given job, it might never be run. A way around this is to increase periodically the priority of every job that is waiting in the priority queue.

Implement, using a heap a simulation for a priority queue. There should be two types of commands:

ADD   Insert a job with given priority.

EXECUTE   Delete the highest priority job.

END   End program.

When a job is executed, then all of the other jobs in the heap get one added to their priority.

Maintain a structure that contains the name of the job and its priority. The collection is to be maintained as a heap according to the priority.

When a job is executed, print its name and its current priority. If an attempt is made to EXECUTE and the heap is empty, simply give an appropriate message.

Perform in order:

1.	EXECUTE		13.	ADD	job8 4
2.	ADD	job1 5	14.	EXECUTE	
3.	EXECUTE		15.	EXECUTE	
4.	ADD	job2 3	16.	ADD	job9 7
5.	ADD	job3 7	17.	EXECUTE	
6.	ADD	job4 8	18.	ADD	job10 5
7.	EXECUTE		19.	EXECUTE	
8.	ADD	job5 6	20.	EXECUTE	
9.	EXECUTE		21.	ADD	job11 8
10.	ADD	job6 9	22.	EXECUTE	
11.	ADD	job7 4	23.	EXECUTE	
12.	EXECUTE		24.	EXECUTE	

P14.2   Write a C function to implement the Heap Sort Algorithm.

```
void heapsort(int list[], int n)
```

Write a main program to invoke and execute the sort function. Have it perform, in order:

a. Fill the list with 100 random integers in the range 0-1,000.

b. Print the list in five columns as:

1	2	3	4	5
6	7	8	9	10
.	.	.	.	.
.	.	.	.	.
.	.	.	.	.
96	97	98	99	100

c. Sort the list into ascending order using the Heap Sort.
d. Print the list in five columns

P14.3   Implement C functions for the Straight Insertion Sort, the Shell's Sort, the Quick Sort, the Quick plus Insertion Sort, and the Heap Sort that count the number of comparisons. Construct a table similar to the timings table but displaying the number of comparison operations.

P14.4   Write a Heap Sort function that takes a list of pointers to the items to be sorted and sorts the items by rearranging the list of pointers. Write a main program that builds the list of pointers, invokes the Heap Sort routine, and prints the list in sorted order.

P14.5   One of the advantages of a linked list or a binary tree is that the items may be rearranged without moving data. On the other hand, the heap structure that we developed does not need link fields, but data is moved. Develop the algorithms for implementing an explicit heap structure. Write a C program that will request a string, insert it into a record, then place it in a heap (Move Up) without moving the datum. The program should also permit deletion that rebuilds the heap without moving data (Move Down).

Test your program and print out the contents of the heap, the actual locations of the items, and the appropriate link fields as you insert and delete a variety of strings.

Chapter 15

Hashing

> *"We <u>must</u> have a bit of a fight, but I don't care about going on long," said Tweedledum, "What's the time now?"*
>
> *Tweedledee looked at his watch, and said "Half-past four."*
>
> *"Let's fight till six, and then have dinner," said Tweedledum.*
>
> *"Very well," the other said, rather sadly: "And <u>she</u> can watch us—only you'd better not come <u>very</u> close," he added: "I generally hit everything I can see—when I get really excited."*
>
> *"And <u>I</u> hit everything within reach," cried Tweedledum, "whether I can see it or not!"*
>
> *Alice laughed. "You must hit the <u>trees</u> pretty often, I should think," she said.*
>
> *Tweedledum looked round him with a satisfied smile. "I don't suppose," he said, "there'll be a tree left standing, for ever so far round, by the time we've finished!"*

15.1 OBJECTIVES

The objectives for this chapter are to:

- Review the "big O" behavior of maintaining the various data structures we have studied.

- Introduce the concept of hashing.

- Consider direct addressing schemes.

- Discuss collisions and collision resolution using open addressing.

- Present the analysis of a hash based procedure.

- Describe how non-numeric keys may be used; that is, converted to numeric values.

15.2   INTRODUCTION

We have considered several schemes for storing and retrieving information, each with its advantages and disadvantages:

Unordered Simple List

Insertion	constant
Searching	$O(n/2)$
Deletion	$O(n/2)$

If order does not matter, then we can simply append to the list. To delete, we find the information, then move the last element to its location.

Ordered Simple List

Insertion	$O(\lg n) + O(n/2) = O(n)$
Searching	$O(\lg n)$
Deletion	$O(\lg n) + O(n/2) = O(n)$

To insert or delete takes, on the average, lg n operations to find the proper place (searching via a binary search) and n/2 operations to move the data. Since the $O(n/2)$ term grows so much more rapidly than the $O(\lg n)$ term, insertion and deletion are dominated by the $O(n/2)$ term. Indeed, if the records are large, then the movement of data can be quite expensive.

Ordered Linked List

Insertion	$O(n/2)$
Searching	$O(n/2)$
Deletion	$O(n/2)$

The primary advantage of a linked list over simple lists is that the data may remain ordered with insertions and deletions, and no data movement takes place. The $O(n/2)$ operations for each of these come from the searching for the record or searching for the proper location to store a new one. Even though the operations of insertion and deletion are the same order as the ordered simple list, the $O(n/2)$ searching operations may take much less time than the $O(n/2)$ operations of data movement required by the simple list. However, some extra memory is required to store the links.

Binary Tree

Insertion	O(lg n)
Searching	O(lg n)
Deletion	O(lg n) + O(lg n) = O(lg n)

The binary tree combines the best of the ordered simple list and the linked list in that searching is fast and no data need be moved. For deletion we must first search to find the correct record to delete, graft back one of its children, then search to find the appropriate place to graft the other child. A randomly constructed tree will not normally be balanced, so the depth is somewhat greater than lg n, and, of course, in the worst case it is *n*, but on the average it will not be too much larger than lg n. Some additional memory is required to store the links.

To refresh our memory, these various functions grow as:

n	n/2	lg n
10	5	3
30	15	5
100	50	7
300	150	8
1000	500	10
3000	1500	12
10,000	5000	13
30,000	15,000	15
100,000	50,000	17
300,000	100,000	18
1,000,000	500,000	20
3,000,000	1,500,000	22
10,000,000	5,000,000	23

It is clear that for large lists we want to avoid anything that grows O(n/2), if possible. The binary scheme of "divide and conquer" that can be fully implemented in a binary tree gives us a great efficiency. We can manipulate a list of one million elements with no more than approximately twenty operations for each use. Even if those operations are lengthy and complex, twenty is minuscule compared to half a million.

We might be tempted to think that we could not do better, and we might not wish to do better. However, there is a scheme that does take fewer operations than even a binary tree. This is a **hashing** method.

Essentially, a hashing method is a scheme that computes an address directly from a key. Ideally, this avoids any searching. In practice, a limited amount of searching is still required.

15.3   DIRECT ADDRESSING

Consider a simple situation. Assume we have a computer programming language that allows the use of single-letter (upper-case) variable names. There are exactly 26 such variables: A, B, ..., Z. We wish to establish an appropriate data structure to store the values that might be associated with these variables. A simple list is suitable.

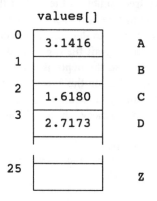

If we define the list to be 26 elements, then we can readily compute the address (actually the index) by a simple C expression:

```
index = v_name - 'A';
```

A given program written in this language might involve only a few variables. Thus, we would be "wasting" the unused locations. However, in the worst case we would only have 26 unused elements, which is probably far less than the code that would be needed to implement more sophisticated data structure algorithms.

Because there is a one-to-one relationship between the variable name and the index, there is no need to store the actual name. Only the value associated with a given name needs to be stored.

Unfortunately, real situations tend to be more complicated. Even the simplest languages usually allow more variety in variable names. The original BASIC permitted variable names that looked like:

Single letter: A, B, C, ... ,Z
Letter and Digit: A0, A1, ... , A9, B0, ... , Z9

The total number of possible variable names is 26 + 26 • 10 = 286.

An appropriate index calculation expression, assuming the variable name is stored in a two element character array, could be:

Single Letter:
```
index = v_name[0] - 'A';
```

Letter and Digit:

```
index = v_name[0]-'A' + (v_name[1]-'0'+1)*26;
```

This would establish the variable names and indices in the order:

```
Variable:  A, B,  ... , Z, A0, B0, ... ,Z0, A1, ... , Z9
Index:     0, 1,       ,25, 26, 27,     ,51, 52,      ,285
```

A given program might only use a few of these, so reserving a list of 286 elements might be marginal. The situation gets worse as the language allows for a greater variety of variable names. Applesoft BASIC uses the first two characters; the first must be a letter, the second could either be a letter or a digit. Therefore, there are $26 + 26 \cdot 36 = 962$ possible variables. (Actually, Applesoft BASIC permits longer names, but only uses the first two characters!) In this situation, reserving 962 locations—of which only a handful may be used—is too wasteful of memory.

FORTRAN allows at least six character variable names (some versions permit more), with the same syntax rules as the Applesoft BASIC. However, the possible number of variable names is now:

```
letter                           26       =               26
letter, character                26·36    =              936
letter, character, character     26·36·36 =           33,696
letter, 3 characters             26·36³   =        1,213,056
letter, 4 characters             26·36⁴   =       43,670,016
letter, 5 characters             26·36⁵   =    1,572,120,576
    total:                                       1,617,038,306
```

Clearly, it is not possible to use the simple direct addressing scheme we have suggested and reserve storage for over 1.6 billion items, especially when only one hundred or less might actually be used.

However, if we could allocate the storage and use a direct addressing scheme, we note that to insert, delete, or access the list requires no lengthy searching. We compute the index, or address, directly from the key. The best case, the average case, and the worst case number of "looks" to access the list is one—regardless of the number of elements. Unfortunately, such an ideal is not practical.

We could, of course, simply select a binary tree for our data structure, accept the $O(\lg n)$ operations, and be done with it. However, even when direct addressing is not possible, the idea of generating an address from a key by a simple procedure is appealing.

15.4 HASHING

The difficulty, in general, for direct addressing is that the number of possible keys is often quite large, compared to the number of items we wish to use or the amount memory we have available. Indeed, the situation is usually:

$$K > M \geq n$$

where K is the number of possible keys, M is the memory locations available, and n is the number of items we wish to store. We would hope that the number of locations would equal or exceed the number of items!

With direct addressing, each key leads to a unique address. If we wish to find a much smaller number of addresses from a given large set of possible keys, then it is quite likely that two different keys might lead to the same address. In the terminology of hashing, this situation is termed a collision. At first, it might seem to be an insurmountable problem, but in reality, this can be taken care of rather easily. Collisions will increase the average number of "looks" when one searches above the one for direct addressing, but, hopefully, less than would be required even for a binary tree.

Thus, the general scheme for a hashing procedure is to generate an address, or index, from the key. If there is nothing stored at that address, then the key and associated information is stored there. If there is a collision; that is, some other key is already at that address, then an additional address or sequence of addresses are generated until a place is found for the item. Generally, most items can be stored at their initial or hash address, a few items at the second address, fewer at a third, and so forth. The item is retrieved by the same process, looking first at the hash address; if it does not match, then looking at the second address in the sequence, and so on until it is found. Because there are, hopefully, few items stored and found at an address other than their initial hash address, the average number of looks will not be too much larger than one.

In order to understand and implement such a hashing scheme, there are a number of details that need our attention.

First, for simplicity, we will consider unsigned numeric keys. This is not a great restriction since it is easy, in practice, to convert alphanumeric keys to unsigned numeric values.

15.4.1   Insertion and Searching

Our first task is decide how we can convert the numeric key into an address or index—the hash function. For an example, consider the following list of telephone area codes:

	Code	Area
1.	907	Alaska
2.	616	Western Michigan
3.	801	Utah
4.	503	Oregon
5.	602	Arizona
6.	913	Northern Kansas
7.	615	Eastern Tennessee
8.	619	South Eastern Calif

Our data structure will use the area codes as keys. An appropriate C structure for storing these is:

```
struct record {int area_code;
                char area[24];
               } phone_list[M];
```

If we set M to 1000, then we could use direct addressing, since the area codes are only three digits in length, but this is quite wasteful for storing only $n=8$ records. Clearly, M must be at least eight. If M is large, then there will be few collisions. If M is eight or only slightly larger, then one would anticipate more collisions as we try to convert the possible 1000 keys into only a few possible addresses.

In C, the valid indices for a list of M elements is 0, 1, ... , $M-1$. An arithmetic function that naturally produces these values is a modulo or remainder function. We will adopt this for our basic hash function. Therefore, the index into our list of structures may be computed as:

```
index = area_code%M;
```

In order to apply this, we need to choose M. The larger M is, the fewer collisions; hence, the average number of "looks" is less, but more space is required. We can conserve memory at the expense of access time. For several values of M, we can compute the hash indices for this set of keys:

	Key		M 30	20	15	10	8
1.	907	Alaska	7	7	7	7	3*
2.	616	Western Michigan	16	16	1	6	0
3.	801	Utah	21	1	6	1	1*
4.	503	Oregon	23	3	8	3*	7*
5.	602	Arizona	2	2	2	2	2
6.	913	Northern Kansas	13	13	13	3*	1*
7.	615	Eastern Tennessee	15	15	0	5	7*
8.	619	South Eastern Calif	19	19	4	9	3*
		collisions =	0	0	0	1	3

One collision is formed when a second key maps to the same address or index where a previous key is stored. It appears that $M=10$ is a reasonably good selection. There does exist one collision, but the storage list is almost full—very few unused locations.

For short lists, there can be large random fluctuations. The above data have been selected to illustrate a point; however, a large list selected at random will illustrate a similar behavior. For a given number of keys, a smaller list will generally have more collisions.

We are almost ready to insert these items in our list. Before we do that, we need to decide upon a scheme to handle collisions, and we will need to specify an "empty" value and initialize our list.

Because there may be more than one key that produces the same address or index, we must store the key with the record along with the other information. Therefore, when we take a key and generate an index, we can examine that location to see if indeed the key is stored there. In general, there are three possibilities:

1. The key is stored there.

2. Some other key is already stored at that location.

3. The location is "empty."

To indicate an "empty" location it is necessary and sufficient to find a value that is not a possible key. For the telephone area codes, a zero is perfectly adequate to indicate an empty location.

To initialize the list we simply store this "empty" value in every key field. Therefore, our empty list will look like:

phone_list[]	Key	Area
0	0	
1	0	
2	0	
3	0	
4	0	
5	0	
6	0	
7	0	
8	0	
9	0	

We are now ready to begin inserting items into the list. The general scheme is:

Generate address from key.

Check if that address is empty.

If it is empty, then store record.
If not, then resolve collision and store the record.

Inserting the first item—we will take them in the order presented above—we get a hash location of 7. That location is empty since the key field is 0, therefore, we can store the item. This results in:

phone_list[]		Key	Area
0		0	
1		0	
2		0	
3		0	
4		0	
5		0	
6		0	
7		907	Alaska
8		0	
9		0	

If we attempt to find this record and follow the same procedure as storing it, then we have no difficulties. The key 907 will generate the address (actually, index) 7. Examining the contents of that record in the list gives the record associated with the key.

Repeating this process for the next four items in our list is easy, since all the keys map to a location that is presently empty. The table appears as in the diagram at the top of the next page.

So far, everything is quite simple. Each record is stored at its hash address. Retrieval is straightforward also. We simply use the same hash function to compute a location, then go to that location to find our record.

The next item in our original list to be inserted is:

913 Northern Kansas

This key generates a hash address of 3. Unfortunately, a record is already stored there. We have a collision! One solution is to ignore the record, but that is not really satisfactory. We need an orderly way of handling such a situation.

The scheme that we will adopt is to generate a sequence of indices beginning with the initial hash index—a **probe sequence**. The simplest is to use consecutive locations. For this situation we have:

3, 4, 5, 6, 7, 8, 9, 0, 1, 2

phone_list[]	Key	Area
0	0	
1	801	Utah
2	602	Arizona
3	503	Oregon
4	0	
5	0	
6	616	Western Michigan
7	907	Alaska
8	0	
9	0	

When we reach the end of the list, we move to the beginning, much like a circular buffer. We will examine each of these locations, in turn, until an empty one is found, and store our record there. This **probe sequence**, since it gives the order in which we will probe the table to try to find an empty location to store our record.

In this situation, location 3 is the original hash index. Location 4 is empty, so we need not look any further. Thus, the list becomes:

phone_list[]	Key	Area
0	0	
1	801	Utah
2	602	Arizona
3	503	Oregon
4	913	Northern Kansas
5	0	
6	616	Western Michigan
7	907	Alaska
8	0	
9	0	

Perhaps the most obvious question is how we might ever retrieve this record. After all, it is not stored in the expected location. The answer is that we follow the same procedure in looking for a record as we used in storing it!

To find key 913, we first generate its hash index, which is 3. We check to see if indeed it is stored at that location. Since it is not, and the location is not empty, then we follow the same probe sequence that was generated originally to store it; that is, we next look in location 4, and find it!

Now consider what would happen if we attempted to search our list for key 603 (New Hampshire). It hashes to location 3; location 3 contains 503. We next check location 4; this contains 913. Therefore, we keep going and check location 5, which is empty. Because we have found an empty location before finding the key we are looking for, it is not present in the list. If we had been storing this particular key, then we would have followed the probe sequence until we found an empty location, and then stored it at that location. Since we found an empty location before finding the key, it evidently is not in the list.

The procedures that we have explored by this example are basically all there is to hashing! A specific algorithm that implements insertion is:

Algorithm HI' (Insert into a Hash List). Insert an item with a key, *KEY*, into a hash list, *HLIST*, that contains *M* elements. Use linear probing to resolve collisions.

HI1'. [get initial location] $loc = h(KEY)$.

HI2'. [check if found]   If HLIST[loc] = EMPTY, then HLIST[loc] = KEY;
                         Store record; Halt.

HI3'. [move to next] $loc = loc + 1$; If $loc = M$, then $loc = 0$.

HI4'. [loop]   Go to step HI2.

This algorithm will need to be revised slightly to obtain our final version of the Hash List insertion routine. It handles the insertion correctly except in the case where we might wish to delete an item. This is why we indicate it with an apostrophe!

The searching algorithm is given by:

Algorithm HS (Search a Hash List). Search for an item with a key, *KEY*, in a hash list, *HLIST*, that contains *M* elements. Use linear probing to resolve collisions.

HS1. [get initial location] $loc = h(KEY)$.

HS2. [check if found]   If HLIST[loc] = KEY, then Halt.   (found)

HS3. [found empty]   If HLIST[loc] = EMPTY, then Halt.   (not found)

HS4. [move to next] $loc = loc + 1$; If $loc = M$, then $loc = 0$.

HS5. [loop]   Go to step HS2.

In both of these algorithms, we indicate the original hash function as h(KEY), which in practice is (*KEY* mod *M*). Steps HI3' and HS4, after incrementing the index, in effect apply the modulo function so that when the index reaches the end of the list, location *M*-1, then the next location is item 0.

It is important to note that the Insert and Search algorithms are essentially the same.

We will need to modify the Insert Algorithm slightly after we consider deletion, but it will not change the basic scheme.

Algorithm HI, the Hash List Insertion procedure, does not check if the list is full. Indeed, if the list is full it will loop endlessly. We could prevent this by counting the number of items inserted in the list, we could count the number of times step HI3 is executed, or we could store the value of the original hash location and if *loc* ever reaches it as it is changed throughout the probe sequence, then halt.

However, proper use of a Hash List suggests that the list never becomes full. If the size of the list is large compared to the number of items to be inserted, then there will be few collisions, but a large amount of extra space is required. If the size of the list is comparable to the number of items, then little extra space is needed, but more collisions and, hence, more time is required. A rule of thumb is to choose *M* so that the list will be about 80% filled; that is:

$$M = n/0.8$$

Moreover, for some of the collision resolution schemes (to be discussed later), it is best that *M* be a prime number. Therefore, we choose *M* to be the first prime number greater than *n*/0.8.

15.4.2   Deletion

Deletion introduces a new wrinkle. In the example above, if we deleted record 503 Oregon in location 3 and set the space to empty, then we could not find 913 Northern Kansas. It hashes to location 3 which is empty, hence the record is not found. The chain down the probe sequence would be broken. Therefore, it is important when a record is deleted that it be marked as "once used," so that any possible chain is not broken. We will adopt a value called USED that, like EMPTY, is not a valid key in the actual list of records. It is this value that will be placed in the key field when a record is deleted.

With this concept in mind, the algorithm for deletion becomes:

Algorithm HD (Delete from a Hash List). Delete an item with a key, *KEY*, from a hash list, *HLIST*, that contains *M* elements. Use linear probing to resolve collisions.

HD1. [get initial address]   loc=h(KEY).

HD2. [check if found]	If HLIST[loc] = KEY, then HLIST[loc]=USED; Halt.
	(found)
HD3. [found empty]	If HLIST[loc] = EMPTY, then Halt. (not found)
HD4. [move to next]	loc=loc+1; If loc = M, then loc=0.
HD5. [loop]	Go to step HD2.

■

There is no reason why we cannot reuse a USED location, from which a record has been deleted, for further insertions. The important thing is that we do not break the chain along the probe sequence. Therefore, we can insert a new record if the location is empty or previously used.

Thus, our modified version of Algorithm HI' to insert into a Hash List becomes the final complete:

Algorithm HI (Insert into a Hash List). Insert an item with a key, *KEY*, into a hash list, *HLIST*, that contains *M* elements. Use linear probing to resolve collisions.

HI1. [get initial location]	loc=h(KEY).
HI2. [check if found]	If HLIST[loc] = EMPTY or HLIST[loc] = USED,
	then HLIST[loc]=KEY; Store record; Halt.
HI3. [move to next]	loc=loc+1; If loc = M, then loc=0.
HI4. [loop]	Go to step HI2.

■

With Algorithms HI, HS, and HD we have all the basic tools to maintain a simple hash list.

15.4.3 Analysis

The analysis of a hashing scheme is more complex than the situation presented by a simple list, a linked-list, or a binary tree. Intuitively, we would expect the average number of "looks" in the hash list to be close to one if the list is not very full. Indeed, for random data most of the keys will be found in their hash location, a few will be found at the second value in their probe sequence, and fewer, still, will be found further down the probe sequence.

It turns out that the important parameter that determines the average behavior of a hashing scheme is:

$$\alpha = N/M.$$

where N is the number of items stored in the table, n, plus the number of "used" locations.

This "load factor" of the table varies from 0 (for an empty list) to 1 (for a full one). As it turns out, the average number of "looks" depends on α only, and not on N. The "used" records do contribute to the number of "looks" because they are generally part of a probe sequence and hence need to be examined. Therefore, deletion does not reduce the effective loading of the table. On the other hand, if the insertion of a new item takes place in a previously used location, then the load factor is not increased.

For the scheme that we have used to resolve collisions (linear probing with $p = 1$), the average number of "looks" if the item is present is approximately:

$$L = 1/2 [1 + \frac{1}{1-\alpha}].$$

Or evaluating this formula:

AVERAGE NUMBER OF LOOKS FOR P=CONSTANT

α	Average Looks
0.00	1.00
0.20	1.13
0.40	1.33
0.60	1.75
0.70	2.17
0.80	3.00
0.90	5.50
0.95	10.50

It is important to realize that this result depends only upon α and not upon n. Therefore, for a list of 1,000,000 items stored in 1,250,003 (the first prime larger than 1,000,000/0.8) locations, the average number of looks to find an item is 3, as compared to 19 for a binary tree (assuming that the tree is balanced), and 500,000 as compared to searching a simple list.

15.5 COLLISION RESOLUTION

The scheme that we have presented for resolving collisions is a simple one, but has some problems. Essentially we wish to generate a probe sequence that has M unique values beginning with the hash address (or index); that is, it is a permutation of the integers 0 through $M-1$ with the initial value of h(k). We will move along this sequence until the record is found or an empty or used location is discovered. Note that it is important as we move along the probe sequence that we "visit" each location before finally repeating one—typically the original hash location.

One fairly general scheme is to generate the probe sequence by:

```
[h(k) + i·p] mod M,      i = 0, 1, 2, ..., M-1.
```

where k is the value of the *KEY* and p and M are chosen so that there are M unique values; that is, the sequence will generate M distinct values before repeating. Clearly, p cannot be zero.

When $i=0$, then the original hash location is used. The use of the modulo function insures that all values generated lie in the range of 0 through $M-1$.

15.5.1   Linear Probing

The scheme that we have discussed is termed **linear probing**. Essentially:

```
p = 1.
```

Thus, we generate the probe sequence:

```
h,  h+1,  h+2,  ...,  M-1,  0,  1,  ...  ,  h-1
```

With linear probing, there is only one probe sequence used for all values. Different values of *h(k)* simply begin the sequence at different points.

This type of probing, using one sequence for all keys, results in the clustering of data in the hash list. A **cluster** is a group of contiguous data. Clusters tend to grow in size as items are added to one end (any key that hashes to a location in the cluster or the EMPTY at either end) and two smaller clusters coalesce. If all the members of the cluster are located in their original hash location, then there is not a problem. However, this would be unusual. A cluster increases the number of locations along the probe sequence that must be used, on the average, and hence increases the time it takes to access a key. Such clustering is termed **primary clustering**.

One might be tempted to try some constant other than p=1. However, this will not really make a difference. The clusters will no longer be physically contiguous, but will cluster on sequential values of the probe sequence. We still have one probe sequence to be used for all values and hence still get primary clustering.

15.5.2   Secondary Clustering

Clustering may be reduced if we use a different probe sequence for different hash locations. We can do this by determining p as a function of h:

```
p = p(h).
```

One possible function is:

$$p = \begin{cases} [h(k)+4] \text{ mod } M, \text{ if not zero} \\ 1 \end{cases}$$

Note that this means we use the upper expression unless its value is zero, then we use the lower one; that is, $p = 1$. This way we avoid $p = 0$.

As example, if $M=13$:

For h(k) = 7 (perhaps for $k = 813$), we get $p = 11$; therefore the probe sequence becomes:

$$7, \ 5, \ 3, \ 1, \ 12, \ 10, \ 8, \ 6, \ 4, \ 2, \ 0, \ 11, \ 9$$

Note that $7+11 = 18$ which becomes 5 (modulo 13); that is, the remainder of 18 when divided by 13 is 5. Continuing, $5+11 = 16$, which becomes 3.

For h(k) = 4 (perhaps for $k = 420$), we get $p = 8$; therefore the probe sequence becomes:

$$4, \ 12, \ 7, \ 2, \ 10, \ 5, \ 0, \ 8, \ 3, \ 11, \ 6, \ 1, \ 9$$

For h(k) = 9 (perhaps for $k = 165$), we get $p = 9+4 = 13$, which becomes 0. In this case, we use $p = 1$.

In essence, this scheme generates $M-1$ different sequences, each for a different value of $h(k)$. If $h(k) = M-4$, then we use $p=1$ which is the same for $h(k)=1$. This avoids $p=0$. Therefore, p is selected from: $\{1,1,2,...,M-1\}$.

However, we get the same sequence for two keys that generate the same hash location.

Such a scheme does reduce clustering, but still may increase unduly the number of values in the probe sequence needed for values that hash to the same address—this is termed **secondary clustering**. However, this scheme reduces the average number of looks if the key is present as compared to linear probing:

AVERAGE NUMBER OF LOOKS FOR P=P(H)

α	Average Looks
0.00	1.00
0.20	1.12
0.40	1.31
0.60	1.62
0.70	1.85
0.80	2.21
0.90	2.85
0.95	3.52

15.5.3 Double Hashing

We can improve on this method by using a more general formula that computes a value for p that depends upon the key, not just h:

```
p = p(k).
```

A typical specific function is:

$$p = \left\{ \begin{array}{l} \text{(k/M) mod M, if not zero} \\ 1 \end{array} \right.$$

As an example, if $M=13$:

For $k = 657$ we get h(k) = 7 and (k/M) = 50, hence $p = 11$ (the remainder of 50 when divided by 13 is 11); therefore the probe sequence becomes:

7, 5, 3, 1, 12, 10, 8, 6, 4, 2, 0, 11, 9

For $k = 137$ we get h(k) = 7, and (k/M) = 10, hence $p = 10$; therefore the probe sequence becomes:

7, 4, 1, 11, 8, 5, 2, 12, 9, 6, 3, 0, 10

This scheme is termed **double hashing**, and also generates $M-1$ different sequences, but two keys that generate the same *h(k)* may not necessarily generate the same probe sequence. This tends to spread them out and reduce clustering even more.

For both of the last two schemes, it is important that the probe sequence encompasses M values before repeating. This may be ensured if M is selected to be prime. Consider the non-prime situation where $M=12$. The second scheme for *h(k)*=2, will use *p*=6. Therefore, the probe sequence will be:

2, 8, (2)

which oscillates between only two values and does not include all M possible values.

For this double hashing scheme, the average number of looks if the key is present is approximately:

AVERAGE NUMBER OF LOOKS FOR P=P(K)

α	Average Looks
0.00	1.00
0.20	1.12
0.40	1.28
0.60	1.53
0.70	1.72
0.80	2.01
0.90	2.56
0.95	3.15

We can easily incorporate any one of these schemes into our Hash List maintenance algorithms—Algorithm HI, HS, and HD—by adding the appropriate computation of p in steps HI1, HS1, and HD1 and by replacing steps HI3, HS4, and HD4 by:

loc=loc+p; If loc $\geq$ M, then loc=loc−M.

15.6   ALPHABETIC KEYS AND OTHER HASHING SCHEMES

For the numeric keys that we have considered so far, it is easy to generate an appropriate location from this by the remainder operation. However, there are other possible schemes. The important criteria in selecting a hashing function is to choose one that is fast to calculate and spreads the keys over the addresses as uniformly as possible.

15.6.1   Parts of Numeric Keys

Some methods use just portions of the key, such as:

1. low order digits
2. middle digits
3. high order digits
4. selected digits

In general, these may not uniformly spread the keys over the possible locations, especially if care is not taken to select the appropriate digits.

15.6.2   Alphabetic Keys

Alphabetic keys can be converted to integers by a variety of methods. Of course, the computer representation of character data is in terms of bits which may be directly interpreted as an integer. If a long int is 32 bits, then the first four characters of an alphabetic key may be treated directly as a long int.

Alternately, the letters may be treated as digits of a base 26 number where $A=0$, $B=1$, ..., $Z=25$. Therefore, KERMIT would become:

$$K \cdot 26^5 + E \cdot 26^4 + R \cdot 26^3 + M \cdot 26^2 + I \cdot 26 + T$$
$$= 10 \cdot 26^5 + 4 \cdot 26^4 + 17 \cdot 26^3 + 12 \cdot 26^2 + 8 \cdot 26 + 19$$
$$= 120,948,795.$$

and for $M = 673$, $h = 600$ (since the remainder of 120,948,795 when divided by 673 is 600).

There are two concepts that permit this to be evaluated more easily. The expression above is essentially a polynomial in the value 26. We can use Horner's method to evaluate this. We observe that this, and any polynomial, may be written as:

$$((((10 \cdot 26 + 4) \cdot 26 + 17) \cdot 26 + 12) \cdot 26 + 8) \cdot 26 + 19$$

Starting with the inner-most parenthesis, that is, with the left-most coefficient, we obtain successively:

```
10·26 + 4           =              264
264·26 + 17         =            6,881
6,881·26 + 12       =          178,918
178,918·26 + 8      =        4,651,876
4,651,876·26 + 19   =      120,948,795
```

Evaluating the expression this way avoids raising a quantity to a power.

The second concept is that for these calculations we wish the result to be modulo M. Therefore, we can take the modulo after any arithmetic operation. Since the multiplication operation is the one that can increase the size of the number rapidly, let us use the remainder function to keep these as small as possible.

```
(10·26  +  4) mod 673  =  264
(264·26 + 17) mod 673  =  151
(151·26 + 12) mod 673  =  573
(573·26 +  8) mod 673  =  100
(100·26 + 19) mod 673  =  600
```

The appropriate application of modulo arithmetic may keep the size of the intermediate numbers within reason even for keys that are quite long.

Other characters may be included in the key by assigning them a value and increasing the base.

15.7 SUMMARY

The advantages of a hash list are that insertion and searching are quite fast, especially for large lists. However, there are certain disadvantages. A hash list uses more memory than other data structures—typically, 20% more than a simple list. It must be remembered, however, that a binary tree also uses extra memory.

The most serious disadvantage is that there is no convenient way to print the contents of a hash list in order. We can print the contents of the list in order of location, but because a hash function should scatter the keys all over the list, these will not be in order.

Therefore, the situation where a hash list might be used is where there will be a large number of insertions and searches. In particular, a hash list is quite appropriate for the symbol table for a compiler. Each variable, as it is encountered, must be placed on the symbol table. We must quickly determine if it is already present, and if not, insert it. The hash list does this with a minimum of overhead.

If the situation is to search and insert items all at one time, and after the list is built, to process the items in order, then a hash list may also be used. The procedure is to build the hash list, and then compress the list by moving items up to fill any empty holes. (This step destroys the hash list.) Finally, sort the resultant simple list. This will result in a final list that is in the desired order. This might be useful when processing symbols within a computer program as part of the translation process and in the final generation of an alphabetical cross-reference table or the processing of a text: identifying words, counting the number of times each word occurs, and producing a alphabetical list of word usage or a concordance.

REFERENCES

Knuth, Donald E., *The Art of Computer Programming*; Fundamental Algorithms, vol. 1., 2nd ed., Addison-Wesley Publishing Co., Reading, Massachusetts, 1973.

Knuth, Donald E., *The Art of Computer Programming*; Sorting and Searching, vol. 3., Addison-Wesley Publishing Co., Reading, Massachusetts, 1973.

Sedgewick, Robert, *Algorithms in C*, Addison-Wesley Publishing Co., Reading, Massachusetts, 1990.

QUESTIONS

Q15.1   What is a collision?

Q15.2   How many elements would you use for a hash table to store 50 items?

Q15.3   A researcher wishes to build a hash table capable of holding 10,000,000 records. She makes it large enough to be only 80% full and uses the double hashing scheme where $p = p(k)$. What is the average number of looks to access a value?

Q15.4   Assuming an 80%-full hash table and double hashing, how big a list of items would make the hash scheme faster than a binary tree? Explain your reasoning.

Q15.5   For a list of M locations, how many different possible probe sequences are there? That is, how many different possible arrangements are there of the M values, 0 through $M-1$?

Q15.6   Why must deleted items be counted in the numerator when computing the loading factor α?

Q15.7   Why is it important that a probe sequence take on M unique values before repeating?

Q15.8   A student wished to store 80 zip codes of nearby communities. He decided to use a list of 100 locations and compute the hash address by using the two most significant digits. Is this a good idea? Why, or why not?

Q15.9   What are the possible values of p in the probe sequence generation expression?

```
[h(k) + i·p] mod M,      i = 0, 1, 2, ..., M-1.
```

Hint, while p may in principle be chosen from all possible integers, some of these may not produce a practical difference.

Q15.10 A hash table has certain advantages over a binary tree. What are the advantages of a binary tree structure? When might you wish to use a binary tree rather than a hash table? When might you wish to use a hash table?

Q15.11 A well constructed hashing scheme would take the keys and distribute these uniformly over the address space. If the keys are uniformly distributed, then it is not difficult to generate a good hashing scheme—the one above, which uses modulo arithmetic for numeric keys is one. In practice, would you expect keys to occur uniformly? Why, or why not? Illustrate with examples.

Q15.12 Assuming a 16-bit unsigned integer and ASCII representation, what is the decimal value of the bit pattern for the two characters 'pi'?

Q15.13 For the schemes that are illustrated in the chapter, what would happen if the list really did become full?

Q15.14 Why is it important to establish a hash list that contains a prime number of locations? Is this necessary if linear probing is used?

Q15.15 What is the "big O" behavior for a hash list search?

Q15.16 What is the largest intermediate value in the example of hashing "KERMIT" using base 26 and $M = 673$ when we evaluated it using Horner's method and performed a modulo operation after each step? What would be the largest possible intermediate result?

Q15.17 In changing an alphabetic key to a number, we considered upper-case letters and gave them the values:

```
A=0, B=1, ..., Z=25
```

Write a C statement that would produce the correct numeric value for an alphabetic character (either upper- or lower-case).

Q15.18   If four characters stored together are to be treated as a 32-bit integer, what is the largest value of the integer, assuming the four characters are alphabetic letters (either case)?

Q15.19   Rather than using a modulo process to compute the initial hash address, sometimes a series of digits from the original key is used. As an example, for zip codes we might catenate the third, first, and fifth digits together:

                  49103   becomes 143

Why might this be used? Why might the modulo procedure be preferred?

Q15.20   With direct addressing it is not necessary to store the value of the key in the record. Why is it necessary to store it in a hash table? What about a binary tree?

Q15.21   As you search a hash table for a given item, will all of the values you encounter along the probe sequence be items that originally hashed to the same address? Why, or why not?

Q15.22   If we have an alphabetic key or k characters that we wish to convert to a numeric address, then how many arithmetic operations (such as addition, subtraction, multiplication, division, and modulo) will it take using the "best" scheme described in the text?

Q15.23   If you had a situation where there were going to be a large number of insertions, many searches, and, finally, you were to produce a sorted list, then which type of data structure might you implement?

Q15.24   To incorporate a more sophisticated collision resolution scheme it was suggested that we replace:

        loc=loc+1; If loc = M, then loc=0.

with

        loc=loc+p; If loc $\geq$ M, then loc=loc-M.

Why not use:

        loc=(loc+p) mod M.

EXERCISES

E15.1 A C variable name may consist of up to 31 characters. The first character may be selected from an underscore (_), an upper-case letter, or a lower-case letter. Succeeding characters may also include a digit.

    a. How many possible C variable names are there? Hint, the total number of possible names is closely approximated by the number of 31-character names, since the number of 30-character names, 29-character names, etc. are all considerably smaller—see the FORTRAN variable name example.

    b. If you adhere to the traditional C practice and do not use upper-case letters, how many possible C variable names are there?

E15.2 Write out a C expression to compute the index for the 962 Applesoft type variable names that consist of two characters; the first is an upper-case letter, and the second, if present, is an upper-case letter or digit. Assume that the name is stored in the two-character array v_name[2].

```
A,  B,  ...,  Z,  A0,  B0,  ...,  Z0,  A1,  ...,  Z9,  AA,  ....,  ZZ
0,  1,       ,25,  26,  27,       , 51,  52,       ,285,286,        ,961
```

E15.3 With our general scheme of generating a probe sequence:

$$[h(k) + i \cdot p] \bmod M, \qquad i = 0, 1, 2, \ldots, M-1.$$

and for $M = 13$, write out all of the different probe sequences if p is computed from:

$$p = \begin{cases} [h(k)+4] \bmod M, & \text{if not zero} \\ 1 \end{cases}$$

Hint, consider all the possible values of h.

E15.4 With our general scheme for generating a probe sequence:

$$[h(k) + i \cdot p] \bmod M, \qquad i = 0, 1, 2, \ldots, M-1.$$

and for $M = 13$, write out all the different probe sequences if p is computed from:

$$p = \begin{cases} (k/M) \bmod M, & \text{if not zero} \\ 1 \end{cases}$$

Hint, consider all of the possible values of (k/M); that is, all the different values of p and begin the "circular" set of sequences with 0.

E15.5   Using the same scheme that was illustrated for KERMIT, what would be
the hash location for $M = 157$ for:

      a. PIGGY   c. BIGBIRD

      b. OSCAR   d. MARIA

E15.6   Write out a procedure that would take a hash list that is stored in M
locations and store it in N locations. This would be a procedure that would
be required if the number of items in the original hash list increased beyond
the anticipated 80% of M so that N would be larger than M. For
simplicity, assume that both tables can exist in memory at once.

E15.7   Another collision resolution scheme is to use a probe sequence generated
by:

```
[h(k) + i²] mod M, [h(k) - i²] mod M
                  for i = 0,1,...,(M-1)/2
```

Except for $i=0$, the above definition will produce two subsequent terms in
the sequence for each value of i:

```
h(k), h(k)+1, h(k)-1, h(k)+4, h(k)-4, ....
```

This scheme is termed **quadratic residue**, and is valid for:

    $M = $ prime and $M = 4j+3$; that is, $(M \bmod 4) = 3$

to generate M distinct indices.

      a. For value of $j = 0,1,...,100$ which corresponding values of M
are prime?

      b. Write out the probe sequence for $M=19$.

      c. Is this scheme analogous to p=1, p=p(h), or p=p(k) above?
That is, quadratic residue behaves in a similar fashion to which
of these?

E15.8   A scheme to handle collisions is to construct a linked list of items that
originally hash to the same address. Develop and write out the insertion
and searching algorithms for this scheme. That is, we do not follow a
probe sequence, but rather link these items together in a list that is accessed
at their common hash address.

E15.9   Build, by hand, a hash table of length 7; use linear probing, and perform the following:

a.	insert	23	e.	insert	16
b.	insert	39	f.	**delete**	17
c.	insert	17	g.	insert	44
d.	insert	41			

E15.10   A common operation with a hash list is to combine searching and insertion. That is, the list is first searched to see if a key is present, and if not, then it is inserted. If the key is not present, then the searching stops when an EMPTY location is found—at the proper place for insertion. Therefore, insertion takes little extra time beyond searching. However, it is best to insert into a USED location if one is encountered along the search sequence. This is easy to do by remembering where the first USED location along the sequence occurred, if one actually was there, and storing the new record in that location.

Write a formal algorithm that searches and inserts if not present.

E15.11   Telephone area codes within the United States and Canada are selected so that they are three-digit codes. The left and right digits are non-zero and the middle digit is a zero or 1.

a. How many possible area codes are there?

b. A programmer wished to store these in a 200-long array using direct addressing. Devise a scheme that would take the three digits and generate an address in the range 0 — 199 directly; that is, do not use modulo arithmetic.

c. Write out the C code segment that would perform this.

E15.12   In the text it was pointed out that any of the open addressing collision resolution schemes of p=c, p=p(h), or p = p(k) could easily be incorporated into any one of our Hash List maintenance algorithms (HI, HS, and HD) by adding the appropriate computation of p in steps HI1, HS1, and HD1 and by replacing steps HI3, HS4, and HD4 by:

loc=loc+p; If loc $\geq$ M, then loc=loc−M.

However, this will involve computing a value of p even in those situations where there is no collision and the value of p will not be required. If we have set things up properly, the majority of the searches into the table will fall into the category of no collisions. Modify the three algorithms so that p will be computed only if there is a collision. Note, this will increase the complexity and/or size of the algorithms.

PROBLEMS

P15.1   For probing schemes other than linear probing it is important that the length of the hash list, and hence the value used for computing the index via modulo arithmetic, be prime. A prime number is one that is evenly divisible only by itself and 1. By agreement, 1 is not considered prime. Thus the prime values are: 2, 3, 5, 7, 11, 13, 17, 19, 23, ...

Except for 2, all prime numbers are odd. Furthermore, except for 5, they all end in 1, 3, 7, or 9; that is, numbers ending in 5 are divisible by 5. Because a prime number cannot be divisible by 2 or 3, all prime numbers greater than 3 must have remainders of 5 or 1 when divided by 6.

A simple scheme to determine whether a number is prime is to first check whether 2 is a factor. If not, then try all odd numbers from 3 onward until the trial factor squared is larger than the number. That is, in looking for a factor one needs only to check all possible values up to the square root of the number. Any factor larger than the square root must be matched up with a factor that is smaller.

This procedure is reasonably efficient. Even to determine whether a number around 1,000,000 is prime requires checking odd values up to 1,000; this is only 500 possible trials.

Write a C program to determine whether an entered number is PRIME or NON-PRIME.

Test your program on 1, 2, 3, 4, 5, 23, and 666. What is the largest prime less than 1,000,000? What is the smallest prime larger than 10,000?

P15.2   Write C functions to implement the hash list maintenance algorithms:

```
void initial()

int search(key)     returns:    item index
                             -1, not found

int insert(item)    returns:    0 if successful
                             -1 if not successful

int delete(key)     returns:    0 if successful
                             -1 if not successful

void dump()
```

The keys will be 4-digit telephone extension numbers and the information associated with each key will be a 20-character name. Therefore, a C structure such as:

```
struct record {int phone;
               char name[21];
              };
```

would be appropriate with the item above defined by:

```
struct record item;
```

but the key above need only be a phone number; i.e. an int.

A key of 0 will indicate an empty record and a key of -1 will indicate a previously used record.

These routines will act upon a global hash-list structure containing 23 (a prime number) elements. Let the initial() routine fill the information fields with " ", and the keys with 0.

Use modulo 23 arithmetic to compute the initial hash address and resolve collisions with linear probing.

The dump() routine should print out the location, the key, and the information.

Write a main program that requests a command and values, if needed, and prints appropriate messages.

Perform the following in order:

```
 1. INITIAL                          19. DUMP
 2. DUMP                             20. SEARCH   3516
 3. INSERT   1701  Kirk, James T.    21. SEARCH   3275
 4. INSERT   0007  Bond, James       22. SEARCH   6879
 5. INSERT   3413  Fearless Leader   23. SEARCH   3161
 6. INSERT   3516  Squirrel, R. J.   24. SEARCH   6100
 7. INSERT   3425  Badenov, Boris    25. DELETE   3413
 8. INSERT   6879  Prefect, Ford     26. DELETE   6859
 9. INSERT   3214  Sherman           27. DUMP
10. INSERT   3426  Moose, Bullwinkle 28. SEARCH   6859
11. INSERT   3251  Fatale, Natasha   29. SEARCH   3275
12. INSERT   3422  UNIX Lab          30. INSERT   5986  Mr. T
13. INSERT   3446  Fort L            31. DUMP
14. INSERT   3390  Barracks          32. SEARCH   3390
15. INSERT   3631  The Tower         33. SEARCH   6003
16. INSERT   3275  Bookkeeper
17. INSERT   3161  Feedbag
18. INSERT   6859  Mr. Peabody
```

P15.3   Modify the program in the problem above (P15.2) to use double hashing to resolve collisions. Execute with the same data and operations.

P15.4   Write a C function that takes an alphabetic key and hashes it to an index:

```
int hash(char *key, int m)
```

where it returns a value of 0 through $m-1$. Use the 7-bit ASCII equivalent to represent the value of each character and perform:

```
val = key[0] mod m
val = (val*128 + key[i]) mod m,    for i=1,...
```

This scheme keeps the intermediate values small.

Try it for:

	Key	m
a.	"Wizard of Oz"	149
b.	"Dorothy"	251
c.	"Glenda"	877
d.	"Scarecrow"	53

P15.5 Write a C program to read a text file, identify words, and count the number of words. Use a hash table that stores the word and the number of occurrences. If the program encounters a word that is in the table, then it increments the count. If it encounters a word that is not in the table, then it inserts it with a count of one.

For convenience use:

```
struct word_count {char word[16];
                          int count;
                   } hash_table[M];
```

where *M* is a large prime number, selected to make the table as large as memory limitations will conveniently allow. Note that this limits words to 15 characters—longer words will be truncated to this length. Different words that have the same first 15 characters will be treated the same, but that should be rare.

Convert all letters to lower-case so that "The" and "the" will count as two occurrences of the same word.

For a hash function, see the previous problem.

A word is a slippery thing to identify. It consists of letters and a possible apostrophe or hyphen. It must start immediately after the beginning of a line, a space, a double quote, or a single quote. It is ended by a non-letter or the end of the line. An apostrophe may be detected because it is a single quote immediately preceded by a letter and immediately followed by a letter. Thus, "can't" is a single word. A hyphen at the end of a line probably suggests a word that is split; therefore, delete it and combine the two pieces. A hyphen in the middle of a line suggests a hyphenated word; thus, "co-processor" is a single word. This scheme might miss some hyphenated words that happened to be split by the end of a line.

Once the hash table is built (note, there will be no deletions) and the entire source document is processed, then there is no need to preserve the actual hash location, so move items to fill in the "holes" in the table, sort the resultant simple list according to the decreasing number of occurrences, and in the case of several words with the same occurrence, in ascending alphabetical order; print the list of words and occurrences.

There is sufficient information to compute the number of different words in the document, the number of total words, and their ratio. This ratio is an interesting measure of the style of the author.

Test your program on the following paragraphs (note, enter the paragraphs line-by-line, each line exactly as given):

This is a paragraph to test the word identification program. According to Turner, "A word is a slippery thing to identify." It isn't difficult to identify ordinary words, but hyphenated words are higher-order problems. And if we have a '"quote" inside a "quote"' or a "'quote' inside a 'quote'", things are more interesting. A hyphen-ated word at the end of line should challenge your program. We must also handle in a graceful manner, numbers such as: 2 and 12:30 pm.

Some paragraphs begin with a tab. "Smile, aren't you having fun yet?" If you had more RAM you could handle a larger text file; however, a math co-processor probably wouldn't help much!

Execute your program on the above two paragraphs as well as on a text file at least 5 pages in length. Supply a copy of the original text as well as the output.

Chapter 16

Dynamic Memory Allocation

There seemed to be no use in waiting by the little door, so she went back to the table, half hoping she might find another key on it, or at any rate a book of rules for shutting people up like telescopes: this time she found a little bottle on it ("which certainly was not here before," said Alice), and tied round the neck of the bottle was a paper label with the words "DRINK ME" beautifully printed on it in large letters.

...This bottle was <u>not</u> marked "poison", so Alice ventured to taste it, and, finding it very nice, she very soon finished it off.

"What a curious feeling!" said Alice. "I must be shutting up like a telescope!"

And so it was indeed: she was now only ten inches high, and her face brightened up at the thought that she was now the right size for going through the little door into that lovely garden....

After a while, she decided on going into the garden at once; but, alas, for poor Alice! when she got to the door, she found she had forgotten the little golden key, and when she went back to the table for it: she found she could not possibly reach it ....

Soon her eye fell on a little glass box that was lying under the table: she opened it, and found in it a very small cake, on which the words "EAT ME" were beautifully marked in currents. "Well, I'll eat it," said Alice, "and if it makes me grow larger, I can reach the key;

and if it makes me grow smaller, I can creep under the door: so either way I'll get into the garden, and I don't care which happens!
    "Curiouser and curiouser!" cried Alice. "Now I'm opening out like the largest telescope that ever was!"

16.1   OBJECTIVES

The objectives for this chapter are to:

- Discuss dynamic memory allocation.

- Describe the C library functions that allocate memory and how they may be used.

- Show how these functions may be used with linked structures.

- Introduce unions.

- Present pointers to functions.

- Describe how to write generic C data structure functions.

16.2   INTRODUCTION

Perhaps no discussion of data structures using C would be complete without including the preferred C scheme for handling memory. Up to this point, we have explicitly managed the memory by using static arrays and linking the linked structures together in an empty list. This is appropriate from the standpoint of learning how this might be accomplished at a fundamental level. However, in a practical situation it is more convenient to let the C system handle some of these details.

Another particular advantage of dynamic memory allocation is that the storage requirements for a particular problem can be adjusted at execution time and hence, depend upon the size of the problem rather than the choice of the programmer when he or she writes the program. If it is useful, the memory requirements can grow and shrink just like our heroine.

Some languages allow an array to be adjusted in shape and size within the program as needed. Many others implement only static arrays. C takes an intermediate approach, implementing only static arrays, yet standard library functions allow you to grab as much memory as is needed (within the constraints of the computer resources) and use this as desired, implementing arrays using the addressing schemes and pointers discussed earlier.

16.3   *MEMORY ALLOCATION FUNCTIONS*

The standard C library includes two functions that allow us to allocate memory dynamically:

`void *malloc(size)`	returns a pointer to usable memory of size bytes
`void free(pointer)`	frees memory so that is can be reused

Using these functions does mean that the "empty" memory is handled by the C system rather than the programmer maintaining it explicitly, as we have done previously.

There is one more "function" that is necessary in order to allow C to handle memory for us—actually it is not a function, but an operator. This is:

`sizeof (data item)`	returns size in bytes of data item, which can be an identifier or a data type

Even though it looks similar to the standard library functions, it is actually one of the fundamental constructs of C and, indeed, "sizeof" is one of the reserved words in the C syntax.

In use, it returns an integer constant; however, this value may not fit in the int that is implemented, and standard C specifies a special data type. The most portable use is to employ it as:

```
(int) sizeof (data item)
```

where the result is cast to an int, or whatever the desired data type.

The "data item" may be an identifier or fundamental type, or an array or a structure. As an example, to determine the total storage taken up by an array, we could use:

```
char list[20][30];
int num_bytes;

num_bytes = (int) sizeof (list)
```

which should give 600.

16.3.1   Malloc

The standard library function malloc() is used to allocate memory for use within a program. It is typically declared in:

```
<stdlib.h>
```

The function is called with an argument that specifies how many bytes of storage is needed. (This is where the sizeof operator comes in.) The function first determines if that amount of contiguous memory is available; if so, then it allocates the memory and keeps track so that it cannot be allocated a second time (unless it is first released), and, finally, the function returns a pointer to that chunk of memory.

The pointer that is returned is a generic pointer. Since malloc() has no way of knowing what data type is going to be stored in the chunk of memory, it simply returns a pointer. If that pointer is to be used in a situation where pointer arithmetic is planned, then it is important to cast the pointer to the correct pointer type. It is probably best to cast it explicitly to the correct pointer type, in any case, for program readability.

For example, to allocate a piece of memory to store a double precision quantity, one might use:

```
double *xptr;

xptr = (double *) malloc(sizeof (double));
```

or to allocate storage for a structure:

```
struct person {...
               } me, you, *finger;

finger = (struct person *) malloc(sizeof (me));
```

It is important to realize that the size returned by the sizeof operator on a structure may be greater than the sum of the bytes for each of the members of the structure. The reason is that certain data types require being aligned with respect to word boundaries. As an example, on a byte machine with 16-bit words that begin with an even address, int cannot be positioned starting with an odd word.

If there is insufficient memory available to satisfy the request, then malloc() returns a NULL.

The block of memory that has been reserved by using malloc() can be returned to the pool of unused memory (so that it may be used again) by a call to free() as:

```
free(pointer);
```

where *pointer* points to the beginning of the block that was previously allocated.

16.4 DYNAMIC ARRAYS

Using the malloc() function to allocate storage for a simple variable is hardly worth the effort. However, it is not really any more difficult to allocate storage for an array. For example, to allocate storage for a list of 50 integers is simply:

```
int *list;

list = (int *) malloc(50*sizeof (int))
```

We have used the sizeof operator to give us the actual storage required for an int, which may vary from computer to computer.

Note that the variable list (a pointer variable) contains the address of the beginning of the contiguous block of available storage. We could access various elements of the list as:

```
list[i]  or *list
```

It probably is best to treat *list* as a pointer constant even though it is a pointer variable. If you ever wish to free up the memory before the end of the program for reuse later in the program, then the original value of list is required. This is performed as:

```
free(list);
```

Multi-dimensional arrays may be allocated in a similar manner, except that we have no way to provide the shape information—only the total storage requirements. Therefore, it is important to access the various elements of the array using the formulas for the address polynomials developed in an earlier chapter. For example:

```
#define R 10
#define C 20

int *table;

table = (int *) malloc(R*C*sizeof (int));
```

The i,j element of this table, assuming standard zero-origin C indexing, is then given by:

```
table + C*i + j
```

or if we prefer to provide an index function:

```
table[index(i,j)]
```

where index() is a function that returns:

```
C*i + j
```

To free up this memory for reuse, we simply use:

```
free(table);
```

A very good example of the value of such dynamic arrays could be found in the implementation of the Radix Sort on a List. The temporary queues could be dynamically allocated, used, then released.

16.5   LINKED STRUCTURES

We previously implemented linked lists and binary trees using a C structure both with index addressing and the use of pointers. However, because we defined the storage requirements statically, we did not fully exploit the features of the C language.

To do so first requires us to use pointers as links. As we have done previously, we declare a record appropriate for a linked list as:

```
struct record {int data;
               struct record *link;
               };
```

Of course, in reality the "data" portion might be much more complex. We will need a pointer variable to point to the top of the list:

```
struct record *tol;
```

However, note that we do not need to define a list of records nor do we need a pointer to the empty stack. Indeed, we are allowing the C system to handle all of the empty memory for us. It turns out that for most programmers, the use of the memory allocation functions simplifies the implementation of linked structures considerably.

The initialization of the top-of-list pointer to create an empty list is the same as used previously:

```
tol = NULL;
```

Remember, we use NULL since it is not a valid pointer value.

Our Setup Algorithm, which finds a storage place for the new data, becomes as a C implementation:

```
struct record *loc;

loc = (struct record *) malloc(sizeof (record));
```

The C system now has allocated sufficient storage for us to store the data. This storage will not be overwritten unless we release it explicitly.

Continuing, we next store the required data.

```
loc->data = new_item;
```

The Graft Algorithm inserts this into the proper location in the linked list structure. For this case, since the list was initially empty, we get:

```
loc->link = tol;
tol = loc;
```

This result follows from Algorithm LG as adapted for use with pointers.

Note that we do not have to know the values of links as long as we are careful to follow the algorithms for maintaining them.

The deletion process is also simpler. After modify the appropriate links to remove a record form the list, we release the space:

```
free(loc);
```

Using the record structure we have defined above, a C function to perform a print of the list would look like:

```
/**********************************************************
 *
 *      linked list print
 *
 *           params:  tol    pointer to top of list
 *
 **********************************************************/
void llprint(struct record *tol)
{

    struct record *j;

    j = tol;

    while (j != NULL) {
        printf("%d\n",j->data);
        j = j->link;
    }


}
```

We could have written the while () with its condition simply as:

```
while (j)
```

This, however, would have been less readable!

In a real situation, the printing of the data in each record might be more complicated. Note that the only information provided to the function is an address where the first record is to be found.

The linked list insertion function is similar. We have to provide the function with the top-of-the-list pointer, *tol*, and whatever new data is to be stored. However, the *tol* variable might need to be modified. Therefore, we will access it indirectly within the function. This requires that we pass its address as an argument—essentially a pointer to a pointer!

```
/**********************************************************
 *
 *      linked list insertion
 *
 *           params:  tolptr    pointer to tol variable
 *                    item      item to be inserted
 *
 *           returns: 1, successful; 0, failed
```

```
          *
          *******************************************************/
          int llinsert(struct record **tolptr, int item)
          {

              struct record *loc,*last,*j;
/*        setup     */
              loc = (struct record *) malloc(sizeof (record));

              if (loc == NULL)    /* check if memory available */
                  return (0);

              loc->data = item;
/*          graft    */
              last = NULL;
              j = *tolptr;

              while (j != NULL && j->data < loc->data) {
                  last = j;
                  j = j->link;
              }

              if (last == NULL) {
                  loc->link = *tolptr;
                  *tolptr = loc;
              } else {
                  loc->link = last->link;
                  last->link = loc;
              }

              return (1);

          }
```

We have implemented both the Setup Algorithm and the Graft Algorithm in one C function, since the Setup is now so simple.

We have declared *tolptr* as a pointer to a pointer to a structure, and accessed it indirectly. This allows us to modify the value of the *tol* pointer and pass the value back. The function would be invoked as:

```
          err = llinsert(&tol, new_item);
```

If we needed to pass the address of *tol* to another function from within the llinsert() function, we would invoke the secondary function as:

```
          sec_fun(tolptr);
```

since *tolptr* already contains the address of *tol*. Within this function, we could access (and change) the value of *tol* by:

```
void sec_fun(struct record **tolptr)
{

    struct record *loc;

    loc = *tolptr;

    *tolptr = loc;

}
```

This is precisely how we used it in the llinsert() function. It could also be called directly from the main() program.

The binary tree functions are similar to those for the linked list. The Setup Algorithm must also include:

```
loc->llink = NULL;
loc->rlink = NULL;
```

since each new item inserted in a binary tree is inserted as a leaf.

16.6 UNIONS

A union allows two different data types to share the same memory. One possible use would be in a situation where we have continuation records and would like to have the data stored in the continuation record be different from that stored in the main record. It is convenient to be able to allocate memory with the same size chunks for all different records, and yet place different types of information in the record.

A union declaration and definition of a union variable appears like that for a structure except with the specifier "union":

```
union same {double x;
            int k;
           } val;
```

In this case *x* and *k* occupy the same memory locations. They are accessed as:

```
val.x     and   val.k
```

where the first is treated as a double and the second is treated as an int.

Because the bit patterns for a given value differ whether the value is stored in a floating point representation or an integer representation, it is up to the programmer to make certain that the program references the value according to the way the value was last stored.

The size of the construct is that of the largest member.

A union should be used with care. It is easy to produce very difficult to find bugs when using unions.

16.7 POINTERS TO FUNCTIONS

In calling a function, we have considerable versatility in specifying arrays, values, addresses, etc. This allows us to generate functions that are more general than, if for example, all of the variables were global. Parameter passing is a major strength of a language like C. One possibility, allowing us to develop even more general functions, is the ability to pass the name of a function as an argument to a function. This permits us to select, from the outside, which of several functions we want to have available for a given routine to use.

The way that C implements this versatility is, as you might expect, through the use of a pointer to a function!

We declare functions as:

```
int fun();
```

and we declare pointers to a value as:

```
int *ptr;
```

In a similar manner, we can declare:

```
int *funny();
```

However, this declares a function that returns a pointer to an int. We want a pointer to a function. This is easy:

```
int (*funprt)();
```

The reason the parentheses are necessary is the relative precedence of the indirect operator, *, and the function attribute operator, (), which binds first.

As one might expect, using our simple function as an example, the use of:

```
.... fun() ....;
```

invokes the function. On the other hand, the use of:

```
fun
```

is a pointer constant. Therefore, we could initialize our pointer variable as:

```
funprt = fun;
```

A function that is looking for a function pointer as a parameter could then be invoked as:

```
myfun(list, n, fun);  or  myfun(list, n, funprt);
```

where *list* and *n* are other arguments.

Now that we can pass a pointer to a function as an argument to another function, we need to examine how this is treated inside the function. For this example, we might define:

```
myfun(int list[], int n, int (*fn)())
```

where *fn* is a pointer variable to a function. This would be used within the function as:

```
.... (*fn)(a,b) ....;
```

where *a* and *b* are arguments to the function pointed to by *fn*; that is, the function fun().

The value in this use of a pointer is that there could be several functions that we wished myfun() to use as it is called from different places in the program:

```
int fun1(), int fun2(), int fun3();

myfun(list ,n, fun2);
    ⋮
myfun(vect, m, fun1);
    ⋮
myfun(arry, k, fun3);
```

If myfun() were a complicated function and the series of functions fun1(), fun2(), and fun3() were simple or very specific ones, then we would not have to modify or replicate the complicated myfun(). Indeed, it might be placed in a library and not have to be recompiled each time it was to be used in a different way.

16.8   GENERIC FUNCTIONS

We have discussed (and hopefully written) various functions to implement the algorithms for manipulating data structures. These were specific for the type of data that we wished to store in the structure. It would be convenient if we could develop a "generic" routine for some procedure.

As an example, the basic statements of the linked list print function presented above could be used on any linked list, provided we could set the appropriate data type for the variables and supply an appropriate "print a record" function. We know how to pass a print function name to the overall linked list print processing function. We still need to consider how to specify a "variable data type."

The answer to this last piece of the puzzle is a pointer! In this case, a generic pointer. Notice that in the linked list print function, we are not using any pointer arithmetic. The only pointer operations are assignment and referencing a member of a structure.

A generic pointer is one that is defined to point to a void. It is often used in the declaration of a function parameter when pointers of more than one function are acceptable.

Let us rewrite the linked list print function to make it as general as possible:

```
/********************************************************
 *
 *     general linked list print
 *
 *     params:  loc    top of list pointer to list
 *              prnt   pointer to print record function
 *
 ********************************************************/
void llprint(void *loc, void (*prnt)())
{

    while (loc) {
       (*prnt)(loc);
       loc = loc->link;
    }

}
```

Here we have made use of the fact that the parameter references a copy of the value of the argument; therefore, we can modify this local copy of *loc*.

In the calling program, this would be invoked as:

```
struct record { ....;
                  struct record *link;
                };

struct record *tol;
void prnt_rec();

llprint(tol,prnt_rec);
```

Of course, the "print a record" function would be defined as:

```
void prnt_rec(struct record *ptr)
{
    .
    .
    .
}
```

We could use this basic llprint() function on any linked list using a structure as a record, as long as a member of the structure is called *link* and it points to that type of structure! We would need to customize the actual structure and the *prnt_rec*.

Another useful example is a generic simple list sort function. It really does not matter which of the various sort algorithms we are interested in. They all have about the same requirements. We need to pass to the routine the data—actually a pointer to the data structure—and an int indicating the number of items.

Within the body of the routine, we probably will need a temporary variable of the same type. The other variables we might typically need are integers or pointers. There are various common operations. One of these is pointer arithmetic, so we will need to know how big each item in the list is. Other operations include assignment and comparison. Occasionally, a swap is used rather than an assignment. If we could specify to the sort routine the names of functions that were of the required type to perform these operations, then the sort function itself could be written in a generic manner.

Let us modify the Straight Insertion Sort that we implemented earlier so that it becomes a generic function. You will recall that Chapter 5 presented a version for integer data and Chapter 9 presented the same routine for strings.

```
/**********************************************************
 *
 *        function to implement a straight insertion sort
 *
 *           params:   list     list of integers
 *                     n        number, indexed 0 - n-1
 *
 **********************************************************/
void insert_sort(list, n, item, size, assign, compare)
 void *list, *item;
 int n, size;
 void (*assign)();
 int (*compare)();
{

    int i,j;

    for (i=last+size; i<last+n*size; i+=size) {
        j = i-size;
        (*assign)(item,i);
        while (j >= list && (*compare)(j,item) > 0) {
            (*assign)(j,j+size);
            j -= size;
        }
        (*assign)(j+size,item);
    }

}
```

We have used pointers rather than indices, throughout, to reference the elements of the list. This is because we have control over the values used without having to cast the list so that the indexing would work properly.

The use of this sort function would require us to define two other, specific functions:

```
int comp(void *, void *);     /* comparison function */
void assign(void *, void *);  /* assignment function */
```

We have declared, and will define, our comparison function to have two arguments. It will compare the values and return:

> if first < second, then return negative
> if first = second, then return zero
> if first > second, then return positive

This is similar to the string comparison function.

The assignment function also has two parameters. The value of the second is stored in the first. Therefore, we need to give it the address of the first.

Finally, to use this function as an example on an integer list, we would invoke it as:

```
int list[N],item;
void assgni(int *, int *);
int compi(int *, int *);
int n;

insert_sort(list, n, &item, sizeof (list[0]), assgni,
                                                 compi);
```

We would need to write the two specific functions.

On a list of strings, this use would look like:

```
char strngs[N][M],item[M];
void assgns(char *, char *);
int comps(char *, char *);
int n;

insert_sort(strngs, n, item, sizeof (strng[0]), assgns,
                                                 comps);
```

We would also need to write the two specific functions.

16.9   SUMMARY

C provides functions which allow us to allocate memory dynamically. This means that we can select, at execution, the appropriate size arrays depending upon the problem. More importantly, C can manage the unused memory for us when we use linked structures. This actually simplifies the algorithms. To do so, we must implement our structures using pointers for the link information.

The standard C library function of malloc() and free(), along with the C operator of sizeof () provide the basic tools.

A C union allows different data types to share the same memory. This also gives us more freedom in setting up a data structure.

We can establish a pointer to a function which can be passed as an argument to a function. This permits us to write generic functions. As an example, a sort function typically needs a comparison and an assignment function appropriate for the data type of the list to be sorted. If we supply such functions and a few extra storage locations, the sort function can be written to handle any list, regardless of the data stored in it.

REFERENCES

Kernighan, Brian W., and Ritchie, Dennis M., *The C Programming Language*, 2nd ed., Prentice-Hall, Englewood Cliffs, New Jersey, 1988.

Koenig, Andrew, *C Traps and Pitfalls*, Addison-Wesley Publishing Co., Reading, Massachusetts, 1989.

QUESTIONS

Q16.1   What is the difference between sizeof and functions found in C, such as printf(), gets(), and sqrt()?

Q16.2   Why is it important to study how to handle the memory in static arrays for our linked structures, as we have done up to now, rather than using the C library functions from the beginning?

Q16.3   What is the significance of the return type for malloc()? That is:

```
void *malloc();
```

Q16.4   How would you write a cast expression so that malloc() produces a pointer to a struct record?

Q16.5   Write a C statement that would dynamically allocate storage for a list of 100 integers.

Q16.6   When we have a statement such as:

```
malloc(30*sizeof (int))
```

At which point are each of the operations performed—at compilation or execution?

   a. sizeof (int)   b. multiply

   c. malloc()

Q16.7   In the linked structure algorithms for Setup (Algorithms LU and TU), how can you tell if the memory is full when you are dynamically allocating memory?

Q16.8   When we allocated memory for our list of 50 integers, why did we use:

```
malloc(50*sizeof (int))
```

rather than:

```
malloc(100)
```

Q16.9   Which algorithms for maintaining a linked list need to be modified for the use of pointers rather than indices? Which need to be modified for allocating memory dynamically rather that using a stack of empties?

Q16.10   Which algorithms for maintaining a binary tree need to be modified for the use of pointers rather than indices? Which need to be modified for allocating memory dynamically rather that using a stack of empties?

Q16.11   Since the linked list routine manipulates only one value, the *tol* pointer, write the insertion function header to return this value explicitly rather than modifying a parameter.

Q16.12   What happens if you try the following definitions:

```
#define NULL '\0'
#define END NULL
```

Does it matter in which order these appear?

Q16.13   In the llprint() function we used a pointer variable *j*. Could this function be written without any local automatic pointer variable? Explain.

Q16.14   What would you get if you tried:

```
union test {double x;
            int y;
            } var;

var.y = 5;

printf("%f",var.x);
```

Q16.15   Why do we want to write generic routines? After all, they are more complicated than specific ones. Might it not be easier to write several specific ones instead of one generic one?

Q16.16   For the following situations, write out examples of both the function invocation and the function header, and an example of use within the function:

    a. argument is an int

    b. argument is an address of an int (use &)

    c. argument is an int pointer

    d. argument is an address of an int pointer

Q16.17   What would the declaration of a pointer to a function returning a pointer to an int look like?

Q16.18   What does malloc() return if there is insufficient memory to allocate?

Q16.19   What would the assignment function (as described in the text for use in a generic sort routine) to perform an integer assignment look like?

Q16.20   The text suggested an explicit cast to the appropriate type for the pointer value returned by malloc():

```
double *xptr;

xptr = (double *) malloc(sizeof (double));
```

What would happen if you used the following?

```
xptr = malloc(sizeof (double));
```

Q16.21   We implemented *tolptr* as a pointer to a pointer and declared it as:

```
int **tolptr
```

We have also passed an array of pointers to a function and declared it as:

```
int *arrpts[]  or  int **arrpts
```

What is the difference in these declaration for *tolptr* and *arrpts*?

Q16.22   Assume we have:

```
int *fun();
```

We invoke this as:

```
.... fun(...) ...;
```

What is *fun*?

Q16.23   How would you declare a pointer variable that points to a function that returns a pointer to a char?

EXERCISES

E16.1   On the computer system you are using, determine the sizeof() for the following:

a. char   d. float
b. int   e. double
c. long   f. double *

E16.2   On the computer system you are using, determine the sizeof() for the following:

```
a.     struct record1 {char name[12];
                       int age;
                       struct record *link;
                       };
b.     struct record2 {char name[13];
                       int age;
                       struct record *link;
                       };
c.     struct record3 {char name[14];
                       int age;
                       struct record *link;
                       };
d.     struct record4 {char name[15];
                       int age;
                       struct record *link;
                       };
```

E16.3   Write the index() function for indexing into a two-dimensional table as a macro, as given in the text concerning the table example.

E16.4   Check the reference manual for the C implementation and computer that you are using to determine what the limits are on the amount of memory that is available to be allocated dynamically.

E16.5   Consider how the C system might go about allocating memory dynamically. Initially, there is a large pool of available memory. A call to malloc() supplies a requested size for the block. It returns a pointer. Later the value of this pointer used as an argument to free() releases the block. Consider what tables must be maintained. As a specific example, consider a vector of char, say memory[50000]. Develop two functions, and any necessary tables, that allocate and free this memory.

E16.6   Modify and rewrite the Linked List Setup Algorithm, Algorithm LU, and the deletion algorithm, Algorithm LD, to handle the memory dynamically.

E16.7   Modify and rewrite the Binary Tree Setup Algorithm, Algorithm LU, and the deletion algorithm, Algorithm LD, to handle the memory dynamically.

E16.8   Perhaps the cleanest way to pass several data items to be stored in a record to an insertion function for a linked list or binary tree is to pass a copy of the structure. Modify the linked list insertion function to use a parameter of the "type" struct record to pass the information to the function. How will this modify the rest of the function? What happens to the link field in the structure? That is, does it need to be initialized before passing? If so, to what?

E16.9   Write C functions that correspond to:

```
int comp(void *, void *);        /* comparison */
void assgn(void *, void *);      /* assignment */
```

Where the data types are int.

E16.10   In the text, we allocated space for a table "dimensioned" R by C using malloc() as:

```
table = (int *) malloc(R*C*sizeof (int));
```

The i,j element of this table, assuming standard zero-origin C indexing, is then given by:

```
table + C*i + j
```

If we prefer to provide an index function, then:

```
table[index(i,j)]
```

where index() is a function that returns:

```
C*i + j
```

Another possibility would be to use a macro that would permit the use of:

```
tabl(i,j)
```

to access the (i,j)-th element of table. Define such a macro.

E16.11   One of the problems with dynamic memory allocation is that the available memory can become fragmented. Consider a table that is used to control the allocated memory. Let each entry hold the beginning address and the size of the block; assume that it is ordered according to increasing beginning address. Write a formal algorithm that moves the blocks of used memory down to fill in the pieces that are unused and updates that table. In a realistic situation, it may be necessary that blocks that begin with an even or odd address be moved to a location that also begins with an even or odd address, respectively.

PROBLEMS

P16.1   Write a C function to implement the Radix Sort Algorithm (Algorithm RL) on an internal list of items consisting of digits, e.g. zip codes.

> void radsort(long list[], int n, int d)

Write a main program that inputs a list of zip codes, prints the original list, sorts them via the Radix Sort routine, and prints the resultant list.

The Radix Sort routine should dynamically allocate the memory for the temporary queues and release the storage before returning to the main program.

Generate a file of 50 to 100 zip codes. You can read them into your program by I/O redirection; that is:

```
program <file
```

will cause all normal read operations that would come from the keyboard to access the contents of the file.

You should not need to enter the number of zip codes in the file, but read until an end-of-file is encountered with the program counting the number of values.

Note: because zip codes may range from 00000 to 99999, they might not be able to be stored in an int or even in an unsigned int depending upon the computer.

Note: C printf() format specification permits the printing of leading zeros—use it!

P16.2   Write C functions to implement the linked-list maintenance algorithms:

```
void print()
int insert(item)      returns:  0 if successful
                               -1 if not successful
```

```
        int delete(item)        returns:  0 if successful
                                         -1 if not successful

        void dump()
```

These will act upon a linked-list structure that is to be allocated dynamically. The data will be integer values in the range 100-999.

The dump() routine is different from the one that we used for a statically defined list. It performs much like the print() function except that it should print out the location, the data, and the link values as well as the contents of the *tol* variable.

Each record should use a pointer to link it with the next record, and your functions should use the C library functions to allocate memory dynamically.

```
        struct record {int data;
                       struct record *link;
                       };

        struct record *tol:
```

Write a main program that requests a command and value, if needed.

Perform the following:

1.	INITIAL	14.	PRINT
2.	DUMP	15.	DUMP
3.	INSERT 275	16.	DELETE 275
4.	INSERT 851	17.	PRINT
5.	INSERT 576	18.	DUMP
6.	INSERT 105	19.	INSERT 931
7.	INSERT 634	20.	PRINT
8.	PRINT	21.	DUMP
9.	DUMP	22.	INSERT 444
10.	DELETE 576	23.	PRINT
11.	PRINT	24.	DUMP
12.	DUMP	25.	DELETE 493
13.	INSERT 734		

P16.3   Write C functions to implement the binary tree maintenance algorithms:

```
void print()        LNR order
struct record *search(item)
                    returns:  location if found
                             -1 if not found
int insert(item)    returns:  0 if successful
                             -1 if not successful
  struct record *intsetup(item)
```

```
struct record *intsetup(item)
                          returns:  loc if successful
    void graft(loc)                 -1 if not successful
int delete(item)     returns:  0 if successful
                                -1 if not successful

void dump()
```

These will act upon a binary tree structure that is to be allocated dynamically. The data will be integer values in the range of 100-999.

Each record should use a pointer to link it with the next record, and your functions should use the C library functions to allocate memory dynamically.

```
struct record {int data;
                  struct record *llink,*rlink;
                  };

struct record *root;
```

The dump() routine is different from the one that we used for a statically defined tree. It performs much like the print() function, except that it should print out the location, the data, and the link values as well as the contents of the root variable.

Write a main program that requests a command and value, if needed.

Perform the following commands in order:

1. INITIAL	19. PRINT
2. DUMP	20. DUMP
3. PRINT	21. DELETE 500
4. INSERT 444	22. DELETE 444
5. INSERT 222	23. PRINT
6. INSERT 333	24. DUMP
7. INSERT 111	25. INSERT 600
8. INSERT 777	26. PRINT
9. INSERT 555	27. DUMP
10. INSERT 666	28. INSERT 100
11. INSERT 999	29. PRINT
12. INSERT 888	30. DUMP
13. PRINT	31. SEARCH 222
14. DUMP	32. SEARCH 300
15. DELETE 222	33. SEARCH 999
16. PRINT	34. SEARCH 111
17. DUMP	35. SEARCH 600
18. DELETE 888	

P16.4   Using one of the programs that you developed for maintaining a binary tree with an integer data field, implement the binary tree balancing routines.

Perform the following operations in order:

1. INITIAL	19. INSERT 810
2. DUMP	20. INSERT 820
3. PRINT	21. INSERT 830
4. INSERT 444	22. INSERT 840
5. INSERT 222	23. INSERT 850
6. INSERT 333	24. INSERT 860
7. INSERT 111	25. INSERT 870
8. INSERT 777	26. INSERT 880
9. INSERT 555	27. INSERT 890
10. INSERT 666	28. PRINT
11. INSERT 999	29. DUMP
12. INSERT 888	30. BALANCE
13. PRINT	31. PRINT
14. DUMP	32. DUMP
15. BALANCE	
16. PRINT	
17. DUMP	
18. INSERT 800	

P16.5   Write a C program to read a text file, identify words, and count the number of words. Use a hash table that stores the word and the number of occurrences. If the program encounters a word that is in the table, then it increments the count. If it encounters a word that is not in the table, then it inserts it with a count of one.

For convenience use:

```
struct word_count {char word[14];
                       int count;
                   };
```

Allocate memory dynamically to a list of M such records, where M is a large prime number, that are selected to make the table as large as memory limitations will conveniently allow. Note, this limits words to 13 characters—longer words will be truncated to this length. Different words that have the same first 13 characters will be treated the same, but that should be rare.

Convert all letters to lower-case so that "The" and "the" will count as two occurrences of the same word.

A word is a slippery thing to identify. It consists of letters and a possible apostrophe or hyphen. It must start immediately after the beginning of a line, a space, a double quote, or a single quote. It is ended by a non-letter or the end of the line. An apostrophe may be detected because it is a single quote immediately preceded by a letter and immediately followed by a letter. Thus, "can't" is a single word. A hyphen at the end of a line probably suggests a word that is split; therefore, delete it and combine the two pieces. A hyphen in the middle of a line suggests a hyphenated word. Thus, "co-processor" is a single word. This scheme might miss some hyphenated words that happened to be split by the end of a line.

Once the hash table is built (note, there will be no deletions) and the entire source document is processed, then there is no need to preserve the actual hash location; therefore move items to fill in the "holes" in the table, sort the resultant simple list according to decreasing number of occurrences, and in the case of several words with the same occurrence, in ascending alphabetical order. Then print the list of words and occurrences.

There is sufficient information to compute the number of different words in the document, the number of total words, and their ratio. This ratio is an interesting measure of the style of the author.

Test your program on a text file at least 5 pages in length.

P16.6   Write a C function to implement the Shell's Sort as a generic list sort routine.

```
void ssort(list,n,k,size,assign,compare)
 void *list, *k;
 int n, size;
 void (*assign)();
 int (*compare();
```

Write necessary comparison, assignment, or swap functions as well as a read_list and print_list functions that are specific for the data type.

Write a main() program to read a list of at least 50 random floating point items, print it out, invoke the sort function, and print the final list.

Modify it for a list of strings that input to the main program. You will need to change the specific functions, but you should not have to modify the sort function.

P16.7   Write a C function to implement the Recursive Quick Sort, Algorithm Q.

```
void qksort(left, rght, size, swap, compare)
 void *left, *rght;
 int size;
 void (*swap)();
 int (*compare();
```

Test it. Modify it for a minimum recursion limit of 14, and implement Algorithm QS, using your previously tested Algorithm Q and the Straight Insertion Sort function developed previously.

Write necessary comparison, assignment, or swap functions as well as read_list and print_list functions that are specific for the data type.

Write a main() program to read a list of at least 50 random floating point items, print it out, invoke the sort function, and print the final list.

Modify it for a list of strings that input to the main program. You will need to change the specific functions, but you should not have to modify the sort functions.

Appendix A

Mathematical Relations

... said the Mock Turtle with a sigh. "I only took the regular course."

"What was that?" enquired Alice.

"Reeling and Writing, of course, to begin with," the Mock Turtle replied; "and then the different branches of Arithmetic--Ambition, Distraction, Uglification, and Derision."

SUMMATIONS OF INTEGERS

Summations of integers occur often in the analysis of algorithms, since many processes will take n operations to eliminate one item out of n, then $n-1$ operations out of the remaining $n-1$ items, and so forth.

sum of first n integers

$$1+2+3+\ldots+n \quad = \quad \frac{n(n+1)}{2} \quad = \quad \frac{n^2}{2} + \frac{n}{2}.$$

sum of squares of first n integers

$$1+2^2+3^2+\ldots+n^2 = \frac{n(2n+1)(n+1)}{6} \quad = \quad \frac{n^3}{3} + \frac{n^2}{2} + \frac{n}{6}.$$

sum of integers m through n inclusive

$$m+(m+1)+\ldots+(n-1)+n = \frac{n(n+1)}{2} - \frac{m(m-1)}{2}$$

POWERS OF TWO

Powers of 2 occur very frequently in the entire discussion of computers, data structures, data representation, and the analysis of algorithms.

POWERS OF 2

n	2^n	n	2^n
0	1	16	65,536
1	2	17	131,072
2	4	18	262,144
3	8	19	524,288
4	16	20	1,048,576
5	32	21	2,097,152
6	64	22	4,194,304
7	128	23	8,388,608
8	256	24	16,777,216
9	512	25	33,554,432
10	1,024	26	67,108,864
11	2,048	27	134,217,728
12	4,096	28	268,435,456
13	8,192	29	536,870,916
14	16,384	30	1,073,741,832
15	32,768	31	2,147,483,664

FACTORIAL

The factorial function is loosely defined to be the product of the first n integers:

$$n! = 1 \cdot 2 \cdot 3 \cdot \ldots \cdot n.$$

By definition $0! \equiv 1$.

The normal recursive definition in mathematical notation is:

$$n! = \begin{cases} 1, & n \leq 1 \\ n(n-1)!, & n > 1 \end{cases}$$

It is an extremely rapidly growing function as the table of the top of the next page illustrates.

Note that even 13! exceeds the size of a typical unsigned long int.

Fortunately, there is a way of getting at the size of large factorials by using logarithms--Stirling's approximation.

FACTORIAL

n	n!	n	n!
0	1	10	3,628,800
1	1	11	39,916,800
2	2	12	479,001,600
3	6	13	6,227,020,800
4	24	14	87,178,291,200
5	120	15	1,307,674,368,000
6	760	16	20,922,789,888,000
7	5040	17	355,687,428,096,000
8	40,320	18	6,402,373,705,728,000
9	362,880	19	121,645,100,408,832,000

LOGARITHMS

While natural logarithms (base e) have some useful mathematical properties and common logarithms (base 10) were once used extensively for numerical calculations, many algorithms tend to eliminate half of the items at a time. Therefore, logarithms to base 2 are relevant.

$$\lg x \equiv \log_2 x$$
$$\ln x \equiv \log_e x \qquad e = 2.171828$$
$$\log x \equiv \log_{10} x$$

Since calculators and computers tend to give natural logs, it is fortunate that it is easy to convert from one base to another.

$$\lg x = \frac{\ln x}{\ln 2} \approx 1.442695 \cdot \ln x$$

$$= \frac{\log x}{\log 2} \approx 3.321928 \cdot \log x$$

The table on the next page shows how slowly this function grows.

Properties of logarithms:

$$\lg ab = \lg a + \lg b \qquad\qquad \lg a/b = \lg a - \lg b$$
$$\lg a^n = n \cdot \lg a \qquad\qquad\qquad \lg 1/a = -\lg a$$
$$\lg 1 + \lg 2 + \lg 3 + \dots + \lg n = \lg(1 \cdot 2 \cdot 3 \cdot \dots \cdot n) = \lg n!$$
$$\ln n! \approx n(\ln n - 1) + \ln \sqrt{(2\pi n)} \qquad \text{Stirling's Approximation}$$

LOGARITHMS BASE 2

n	lg n	n	lg n
1	0.000	100,000	16.610
2	1.000	200,000	17.610
5	2.322	500,000	18.932
10	3.322	1,000,000	19.932
20	4.322	2,000,000	20.932
50	5.644	5,000,000	22.253
100	6.644	10,000,000	23.253
200	7.644	20,000,000	24.253
500	8.966	50,000,000	25.575
1,000	9.966	100,000,000	26.575
2,000	10.966	200,000,000	27.575
5,000	12.288	500,000,000	28.897
10,000	13.288	1,000,000,000	29.897
20,000	14.288	2,000,000,000	30.897
50,000	15.610	5,000,000,000	32.219

GEOMETRIC SERIES

Geometric series occur when each term is a constant times the previous one:

$$a + ar + ar^2 + \ldots + ar^n = a\frac{(1-r^{n+1})}{1-r}.$$

In particular in the representation in binary, we get

$$1+2+4+\ldots+2^n = 2^{n+1}-1 \quad \text{and} \quad 1/2+1/4+\ldots+1/2^n = 1 - 1/2^n.$$

FIBONACCI SERIES

This sequence was suggested in 1202 by Leonardo Pisano who was also called Leonardo Fibonacci. The sequence is a solution to the problem of determining the number of pairs of rabbits at the end of a year, starting with a single pair. Each month, each pair produces a new pair. The new pair becomes fertile when they are one month old, and rabbits never die.

At the end of one month, there is the original pair plus their offspring for a total of two pairs.

At the end of two months, there are these two plus another pair produced by the original pair, for a total of three pairs.

At the end of three months, there are three plus two pairs, one from the original pair and one from their first litter, for a total of five pairs.

At the end of four months, there will be five plus three for eight pairs.

The sequence is formally defined in a recurrence relation by:

$$F_n = \begin{cases} 1, & n = 1 \text{ and } 2 \\ F_{n-2} + F_{n-1}, & n > 2 \end{cases}$$

Note: it is customary to associate n with F_n so that $F_5 = 5$.

FIBONACCI NUMBERS

n	F_n	n	F_n
1	1	17	1,597
2	1	18	2,584
3	2	19	4,181
4	3	20	6,765
5	5	21	10,946
6	8	22	17,711
7	13	23	28,657
8	21	24	46,368
9	34	25	75,025
10	55	26	121,393
11	89	27	196,418
12	144	28	317,811
13	233	29	514,229
14	377	30	832,040
15	610	31	1,346,269
16	987	32	2,178,309

Fibonacci numbers are related to the Golden Ratio.

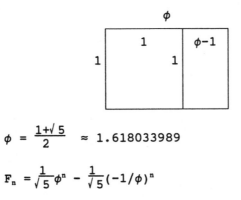

$$\phi = \frac{1+\sqrt{5}}{2} \approx 1.618033989$$

$$F_n = \frac{1}{\sqrt{5}}\phi^n - \frac{1}{\sqrt{5}}(-1/\phi)^n$$

as n gets large $(-1/\phi)^n$ goes to zero, hence $F_{n+1}/F_n \approx \phi$.

FUNCTIONAL GROWTH

In analyzing algorithms, we see that it is common for these to grow faster than linear. The following table illustrates several functions that typically appear in the behavior of

algorithms in this book. Such functional growth is characteristics of the sorting
algorithms.

n	n·lg n	$n^{1.3}$	$n^{1.5} = n\sqrt{n}$	n^2
1	0	1	1	1
2	2	2	3	4
5	12	8	11	25
10	33	20	32	100
20	86	49	89	400
50	282	162	354	2,500
100	664	398	1,000	10,000
200	1,529	980	2,828	40,000
500	4,483	3,226	11,180	250,000
1,000	9,966	7,943	31,623	1,000,000
2,000	21,932	19,559	89,443	4,000,000
5,000	61,439	64,367	353,553	25,000,000
10,000	132,877	158,489	1,000,000	100,000,000
20,000	285,754	390,246	2,828,427	400,000,000
50,000	780,482	1,284,284	11,180,340	2,500,000,000
100,000	1,660,964	3,162,278	31,622,777	10,000,000,000
200,000	3,521,928	7,786,441	89,442,719	40,000,000,000
500,000	9,465,784	25,624,831	353,553,391	250,000,000,000
1,000,000	19,931,569	63,095,734	1,000,000,000	1,000,000,000,000

At the other end, we find algorithms that grow much more slowly than linear.
Examples include the binary search and the tree searching algorithms.

n	lg n	$\sqrt{n}$	n/2
1	.000	1.00	0.5
2	1.000	1.41	1
5	2.322	2.24	2.5
10	3.322	3.16	5
20	4.322	4.47	10
50	5.644	7.07	25
100	6.644	10.00	50
200	7.644	14.14	100
500	8.966	22.36	250
1,000	9.966	31.62	500
2,000	10.966	44.72	1,000
5,000	12.288	70.71	2,500
10,000	13.288	100.00	5,000
20,000	14.288	141.42	10,000
50,000	15.610	223.61	25,000
100,000	16.610	316.23	50,000
200,000	17.610	447.21	100,000
500,000	18.932	707.11	250,000
1,000,000	19.932	1,000.00	500,000

MATHEMATICAL INDUCTION

Mathematical induction is a way of proving the correctness of closed-form expressions. Note that it generally does not derive an expression, but rather proves that a given one is correct. Unfortunately, it is often easier to find a recurrence relation than it is to find a closed-form expression. However, if the closed-form expression can be guessed, then it may be rigorously proved.

Mathematical Induction involves three steps:

1. Show that the expression is true for the first case.

2. Assume that it is true for the n-th case.

3. Show that it leads to the correct expression for the $(n+1)$-th case.

As an example, let us prove the closed-form expression for the sum of the first n integers:

$$1+2+3+\ldots+n \quad = \quad \frac{n(n+1)}{2} \quad = \quad \frac{n^2}{2} + \frac{n}{2}.$$

1. For $n=1$, the expression gives $1 \cdot (1+1)/2 = 1$, which indeed is correct.

2. Assume that it is true for the n-th case.

$$1+2+3+\ldots+n \quad = \quad \frac{n(n+1)}{2}$$

3. Show that it is true for $(n+1)$-th case.

   If it is indeed true, then

$$1+2+3+\ldots+(n+1) \quad = \quad \frac{(n+1)(n+1+1)}{2} \quad = \quad \frac{(n+1)(n+2)}{2}$$

   but

$$1+2+3+\ldots+(n+1) = 1+2+3+\ldots+n + (n+1)$$
$$= n(n+1)/2 + (n+1)$$

   where we have used the assumption for the n-th case. Now we only need to show that this is the same as $(n+1)(n+2)/2$.

$$n(n+1)/2 + (n+1) = [n(n+1) + 2(n+1)]/2$$
$$= (n+1)(n+2)/2$$

   which is the same. Therefore, if our expression is true for the n-th case, then it is true for the $(n+1)$-th case. Since it is true for the first case, it is true for the second. Since it is true for the second, it is true for the third. Since it is true for the third, etc.

LOGICAL RELATIONS

Typically, it is most obvious to express a logical expression as the opposite of that which is most useful for the program. For example, we might know the condition for terminating a loop, whereas C needs to use the condition for the loop to continue. Therefore, we need a way to negate a condition easily.

The easiest way is to use the ! operation; however, it might be preferable to rewrite the expression. First we have the unary operation of negation:

$$\text{not A} \equiv \text{!A} \qquad\qquad \text{not(!A)} \equiv \text{A}$$

where the $\equiv$ symbol indicates that the two sides are identically equal to each other.

In reality, the simple comparison operations divide the continuous number line into three pieces. Therefore:

$$
\begin{array}{llll}
\text{not(x == y)} & \equiv & \text{x != y} & \qquad \text{not(x != y)} \equiv \text{x == y} \\
\text{not(x < y)} & \equiv & \text{x >= y} & \qquad \text{not(x >= y)} \equiv \text{x < y} \\
\text{not(x > y)} & \equiv & \text{x <= y} & \qquad \text{not(x <= y)} \equiv \text{x > y}
\end{array}
$$

These simple comparisons are often combined with the logical operations of <u>and</u> and <u>or</u>. The negation of such a combined expression is obtained through the use of DeMorgan's Law.

$$\text{not(A or B)} \equiv \text{(not A) and (not B)}$$
$$\text{not(A and B)} \equiv \text{(not A) or (not B)}$$

PRIME NUMBERS

A prime number is defined to be a positive integer whose only factors are 1 and itself. By agreement among mathematicians, the value 1 is not prime. Therefore, the list of prime numbers begins:

2   3   5   7   11   13   17   19   23   29   31   37   41

There are an infinite number of primes, which is easily proved.

All primes, except the first few, must end with one of the digits: 1, 3, 7, or 9. The reason is that those ending with 0, 2, 4, 6, or 8 are even and are divisible by 2. Those ending with 5 (and 0) are divisible by 5.

Further, all primes, except the first few, are 1 greater or 1 less than a multiple of 6. That is,

$$\text{p mod 6 = 1 or 5}$$

The reason for this is that those integers that are congruent to 0, 2, or 4 modulo 6 are even, and those congruent to 3 modulo 6 are multiples of 3.

Every integer may be factored into a unique set of prime factors.

To test small numbers (in a range up to a billion) for primality, it is sufficient and reasonably quick to attempt to divide it by first 2, then odd values beginning with

3. We can stop when we reach a trial factor whose square is larger than the number we are testing for primality. If we have not reached a factor by the time we have reached the square root of the number, then we cannot find a larger factor. If such a larger factor existed, then it would need to be paired with a smaller one that we have already checked. Therefore, to check for primality for a number around 1 billion, would require trying only about 15,812 possible factors. We could reduce this to around 10,541 by using the sequence:

$$5 \quad 7 \quad 11 \quad 13 \quad 17 \quad 19 \quad 23 \quad 25 \quad 29 \quad 31 \quad 35 \quad 37 \quad 41 \quad 43$$

that is, we add 2 then 4, then 2, etc., rather than trying all the odd numbers. This sequence consists of those values that are one less or one more than a multiple of 6.

MODULO ARITHMETIC

Modulo arithmetic begins with the concept of a remainder. If a positive integer is divided by another positive integer, the result is an integer quotient and an integer remainder.

$$a/m = q + r/m,$$

where

$$0 \leq r < m.$$

Indeed,

$$a = qm + r.$$

The operation of finding a remainder, or modulo function, is often denoted as:

$$r = a \bmod m.$$

The important thing to keep in mind is that the modulo function takes any integer and changes it to a value in the range 0 through m-1, inclusive. We can envision this as subtracting or adding sufficient multiples of m until the result is within the correct range.

We can perform various arithmetic operations, such as addition, subtraction, and multiplication using modulo arithmetic. If the result is to be reduced to a remainder, then the intermediate results in a lengthy process can be reduced. In particular:

$$(a \pm b) \bmod m = [(a \bmod m) \pm (b \bmod m)] \bmod m$$

and

$$(ab) \bmod m = [(a \bmod m)(b \bmod m)] \bmod m$$

Note, that (a mod m) are both in the range 0 through $m-1$. Therefore, as an example, adding them may result in a quantity that is in the range 0 through $2m-2$. The [ ] mod m on the right-hand side reduces this to the proper range.

BIG O NOTATION

The precise definition of the "big O" behavior can be expressed as:

> *A function g(n) is said to O(f(n)) if there exist constants c_o and n_o such that g(n) is less than $c_o f(n)$ for all $n > n_o$.*

This essentially puts an upper-bound functional performance on g(n). Strictly speaking, as an example:

$$g(x) = 3x + 2 \quad is: \quad O(x) \quad and \quad O(x^2) \quad and \quad O(x^3), \quad etc.$$

since all of these satisfy the definition for some values of the constants.

Of course, the least upper bound is generally what is desired, namely O(x).

Appendix B

C Style

*She was standing before an arched doorway, over which were the
words "QUEEN ALICE" in large letters, and on each side of the arch
there was a bellhandle; one was marked "Visitors' Bell," and the other
"Servants' Bell."*

*"I'll wait till the song's over," thought Alice, "and then I'll ring
the—the—<u>which</u> bell must I ring?" she went on, very much puzzled by
the names. "I'm not a visitor, and I'm not a servant. There <u>ought</u> to be
one marked 'Queen,' you know—"*

It is easy to write C code that is readable. It is also easy to write C code that is
unreadable. The following suggestions are to help make your C programs more
readable and hence decrease the amount of time it takes to develop the program. It is
important that you write your program initially with style in mind and not simply wait
until after you get it working to "pretty it up." A well written C program that is
developed with attention to stylistic neatness will avoid many potential bugs!

<u>variables</u>

- Use mnemonic variable names that are appropriate in length.

    —Single letters such as i,j,k,m,n for loop variables and where
    there is algebraic meaning attached from formulae.

    —Variable names that are too long may be cumbersome.

—Use _ (underscore) where appropriate for readability.

- Use upper-case for #define identifiers, variable names should be lower-case.

- Avoid the use of global variables except where a good case may be made for using them.

- Use `#define  ID  value` for constant values in order to enhance the generality and readability.

- Avoid the use of the variable name l (el) since it is so easily confused with 1 (one).

functions

- Use appropriate mnemonic names for functions.

    —Avoid standard names that are typically found in the standard library.

- Explicitly define each function type.

    —Do not use the default of int for all functions.

    —Define as **void** in all cases where the function does not return an explicit result.

    —Declare functions as fully as possible—use function prototyping where possible.

- Definition should declare parameters as:

    ```
    int funny(double x, int na, int list[])
    ```

    rather than

    ```
    int funny(x,na,list)
     double x;
     int na, list[];
    ```

- If the function returns a pointer to a variable that is defined within the function, declare the variable static.

- If a function is not of void type, then return a value; do not simply exit off the end of the function.

- When writing a function, think carefully what data must be supplied, what does it communicate back to the calling module, and what data does it use internally on a temporary basis; define the function and variables appropriately.

<u>comments</u>

- Use comments to enhance the readability.

- If at end of a statement, then space as far to right as possible on the screen or printed page;

```
    statement;                        /*  comment  */
```

rather than

```
    statement;/*  comment  */
```

- Use comments appropriately.

    —Do not omit all comments.

    —Do not comment the obvious.

- Separate logical sections with comments and/or blank lines.

- Document all functions liberally.

    —Use a full line of * or some other characters to separate visually functions.

    ——Do not use the full line of asterisks for other comments.

    —Describe what the function is to perform.

    —Document all parameters.

    —Document what is returned, if the function is not void.

    —Describe any restrictions on parameters values and/or return values.

    —Document the main() program.

——Include your name, date written, course, assignment, etc.

■ Do not obscure the code with comments; that is, the code should be easy to see and read—it should stand out as the most important thing to read. As an example of a function that is difficult to read, consider:

```
/*****************************************************
*
*        function to perform simple swap sort
*
*            params:  list     list of integers
*                     n        number, indexed 0 - n-1
*
*****************************************************/
void swap_sort(int list[] ,int n)
{

/******************************************
*    variable definitions
******************************************/
    int i,      /*  outer index  */
        j,      /*  inner index  */
        temp;   /*  temporary variable for swapping  */
/******************************************
*    loop over first n-2 values
******************************************/
    for (i=0; i<n-1; i++ ) {
/******************************************
*    loop from i+1 to end
******************************************/
        for (j=i+1; j<n; j++) {
/******************************************
*    test if out of order
******************************************/
            if (list[i] > list[j]) {
/******************************************
*    out of order, swap using temp
******************************************/
                temp = list[i];/* store i-th item */
                list[i] = list[j];/* move j-th item */
                list[j] = temp;/* retrieve i-th item */
            } /*  end of if (), no else  */
        } /*  end of loop over j  */
    } /* end of loop over i   */

} /*  end of function swap_sort()  */
```

<u>indentation</u>

- Generally four spaces for each level of indentation is reasonable.

- Indent one "unit" further for each block within a block.

- There are several possible styles for braces and indentation:

```
for ( ;    ;   ) {           /* preferred */
    xxxxx;
    xxxxx;
}
```

or

```
for ( ;    ;   )
{
    xxxxx;
    xxxxx;
}
```

In both cases, the closing brace { is directly below the beginning of the statement that opens the block, and the statements in between are indented.

More difficult for readability, and hence to be avoided is:

```
for ( ;    ;   )
    {
    xxxxx;
    xxxxx;
    }
```

and never:

```
for ( ;    ;   ) {
    xxxxx;
    xxxxx;}
```

Choose a comfortable style and be consistent!

- Use braces for readability even if they are not necessary, e.g.

```
for (i=0; i<n-1; i++) {
    for (j=i+1; j<n; j++) {
        if (list[i] > list[j]) {
            temp = list[i];
            list[i] = list[j];
            list[j] = list[i];
        }
    }
}
```

The only set of braces that are required are those on the if () statement. The braces on the for loops are unnecessary because, logically, they each execute only one C statement; however, because each "statement" takes several lines, the explicit use of braces for the for loops enhances readability.

- Place a null statement on a separate line:

```
while (        )
     ;
```

not

```
while (        );
```

Following this consistently means that if the following constructs are spotted, then an error has occurred:

```
for (  ;  ;  );
```

```
while (        );
```

```
if (        );
```

Note: do/while structures should be written as:

```
do {
} while (    );
```

even if the braces are not necessary.

white space

- Use white space within a statement to enhance readability as desired:

```
     x = expression;
```

space between for and the (

```
     for ( ; ; )  /* since for is not a function */
     while (   )
     if (     )
```

but use

```
     printf(       )  /* printf is a function */
```

- Use white space, including indentation, consistently.

- Use blank line(s) to separate logical units of the source code.

initialization

- Take care with a combination of definition and initialization, such as:

    int n=0;

    Use only when initializing to a constant.

- Do not initialize and then not use the value—it is confusing, e.g.

```
     int i=0;

     for (i=n-1; i>=0; i--) {

     }
```

control structures

- Do not use labels and goto statements.

Appendix C

Glossary

"I don't know what you mean by 'glory,'" Alice said.

Humpty Dumpty smiled contemptuously. "Of course you don't—till I tell you. I meant 'there's a nice knock-down argument for you!'"

"But 'glory' doesn't mean 'a nice knock-down argument,'" Alice objected.

"When I use a word," Humpty Dumpty said, in rather a scornful tone, "it means just what I choose it to mean—neither more nor less."

"The question is," said Alice, "whether you <u>can</u> make words mean so many different things."

"The question is," said Humpty Dumpty, "which is to be master—that's all."

Alice was too much puzzled to say anything; so after a minute Humpty Dumpty began again. "They've a temper, some of them—particularly verbs: they're the proudest—adjectives you can do anything with, but not verbs—however, I can manage the whole lot of them! Impenetrability! That's what I say!"

"Would you tell me, please," said Alice, "what that means?"

"Now you look like a reasonable child," said Humpty Dumpty, looking very much pleased. "I meant by 'impenetrability' that we've had enough of that subject, and it would be just as well if you'd mention what you mean to do next, as I suppose you don't mean to stop here the rest of your life."

"That's a great deal to make one word mean," Alice said in a thoughtful tone.

"When I make a word do a lot of work like that," said Humpty Dumpty, "I always pay it extra."

ACCESS. To retrieve the value or store a value in a given location of a data structure.

ADDRESS. The physical location of the data entity in the computer memory or secondary storage.

ADDRESS POLYNOMIAL. A function that gives the actual address in terms of the indices for an item located in an array; for rectangular arrays the function is a linear polynomial in each of the indices.

ALGORITHM. A finite step-by-step procedure or recipe for solving a particular problem with the following characteristics: zero or more inputs, one or more outputs, unambiguous, finite time, and effective.

APPEND. To add a record to the end of a list.

ARGUMENT. A value that is supplied to a function by the calling module (see parameter).

ASCENDING ORDER. The items are arranged such $x_i \leq x_j$ for all $i<j$.

ASCII. American Standard Code for Information Interchange, a 7-bit code which relates a character with its internal representation.

AVL TREE. A binary tree structure that uses an extra field in each node to indicate how well balanced the tree is so that is can be maintained in an approximate balanced condition.

BALANCED TREE. A tree with its nodes as close to the root as possible so that the total number of "looks" to find each of the elements once is a minimum.

"BIG O" NOTATION. A mathematical expression that describes the gross behavior of a function as the relevant parameter gets large.

BINARY SEARCH. A search in an ordered list that successively divides the list by two by examining the middle element of each remaining list until the desired item is found or the entire list is eliminated.

BINARY TREE. A linked structure, so that each record may have two links that point to the two possible successors of that item.

BLOCK. A chunk of data that is written to or read from a tape with a single "write" or "read" operation.

BOX. A three-dimensional array.

B-TREE. A multi-way tree where each node contains up to m keys and m+1 links.

BUBBLE SORT. An exchange sort that operates by comparing adjacent elements and exchanging them if they are out of order.

BUFFER. A queue typically used as a temporary storage between two processes that either operate at different speeds or operate asynchronously.

BUS. A data or address path used for various parts of the computer to pass information back and forth.

CATENATE. Appending the contents of one list onto the end of another list.

CHILD. One of the two successor records in a tree structure.

CLUSTERING. The tendency for items inserted in a hash table to be located in contiguous locations along a probe sequence, which increases the number of looks it takes to find a record.

COCKTAIL SHAKER SORT. A bubble-type sort that alternates between bubbling out-of-place items up in the list and down in the list.

COLLISION. The situation where two distinct keys hash to the same location.

COLUMN. Strictly speaking, a vertical line—usually considered to be the right-most dimension of a table or a multi-dimensional array (see row).

COLUMN-MAJOR. An ordering or slicing of a multi-dimensional array so that the left-most index varies most rapidly; in a table the vertical dimension or column is stored contiguously (see row-major).

COMMAND LINE. All of the information on the line when a program is executed, available to a C program through parameters for main().

CONTINUATION RECORD. A chunk of memory that is linked to an ordinary record to hold additional data that will not fit into the regular record.

DATA. The internal value of some information; singular is *datum*.

DATA STRUCTURE. A scheme for storing data inside a computer that is concerned with the relationship between the data and efficient manipulation of them.

DELETE. To remove a data element from a structure and adjust the structure so that it is consistent.

DEQUE. Double-ended queue—a restricted I/O (Input/Output) list that allows insertions and deletions at both ends.

DESCENDING ORDER. The items are arranged such that $x_i \geq x_j$ for all $i < j$.

DISTRIBUTION SORT. A general classification of "sorting" schemes that operates by distributing the original items into discrete sets, then recombining them into an ordered list.

DOUBLE HASHING. A scheme that resolves collisions by adding a value, that is a function of the original key, to each subsequent address in the probe sequence.

DOUBLY LINKED. A linked list with both forward and backwards links.

EBCDIC. (Extended Binary Coded Decimal Interchange Code) An 8-bit code which relates a character to its internal representation.

ENUMERATION SORT. A sort procedure that uses a counting process to determine where in the final list an item is to go.

EOF. (End-of-File mark) A character or characters that designate the logical end of the data stored on a file.

EXCHANGE SORT. A sort procedure that swaps or exchanges the positions of out-of-order elements.

EXTERNAL SORT. A sort that uses sequential access only and thus is suitable for sorting lists that are too large to fit into random access memory.

FIBONACCI SEQUENCE. A sequence formed by adding the last two values to produce the next one in the sequence.

FIELD. A logical portion of a record, typically containing one datum.

FILE. A collection of records typically located in secondary storage on a serial access device.

FLOWCHART. A graphical form of an algorithm that emphasizes the flow of control.

GOLDEN RATIO. The ratio of the sides of a rectangle such that taking a square out leaves a smaller rectangle with the same proportions; the ratio is designated as $\phi = (1+\sqrt{5})/2 \approx 1.618$.

GRAFT. To connect a record into a linked structure.

GRANULARITY. The smallest difference between two possible consecutive values of stored data that relates to the number of significant digits of floating point quantities.

GREATEST COMMON DIVISOR. The largest integer that divides two other positive integers evenly.

HASH. To compute an address or an index directly from the value of a key.

HEAP. A binary tree structure that may be represented implicitly with each parent greater than or equal to both of the child values, and all items located as close to the root and towards the left side of the tree as possible.

HEAP SORT. A sort that operates by transforming the random list into a heap and then exchanging the root of the heap with the last element of the heap, hence removing it from the heap and reheaping the remaining elements of the heap until the heap is reduced to one element.

HYPERBOX. A four-dimensional array.

INDEX. A logical value that indicates the position in an array of data items, measured from the beginning of the dimension in the array and in terms of individual storage units—in C the indices begin with zero.

INDEX VECTOR. A vector of indices that provides the order in which a random list should be accessed so that it will be accessed in a sorted order.

INFORMATION. The meaning given to data when it is interpreted by a human being.

INORDER. A traversal of a tree in an LNR order where the left-child is processed first, followed by the parent, then the right-child; it is typically applied recursively.

INSERT. To place a new data item into a data structure.

INSERTION SORT. A sorting technique that operates by inserting an element into a previously sorted list.

INTERBLOCK GAP. A gap between blocks in the data recorded on a magnetic tape, used so that the tape can accelerate and decelerate.

INTERNAL SORT. A sort that may be implemented in internal random access memory; it involves random access and, in many cases, the swapping of out of order elements.

ITERATION. The repetition or looping, typically implemented in C via a for (; ;) or a while ( ) construct.

K. An abbreviation that stands for 1,024; it is derived from **k**, the metric prefix "kilo" which is a unit of 1,000.

KEY. The field that uniquely identifies a record.

LEVEL ORDER. A tree traversal order that visits the root, then its possible children, and then their possible children, etc.

LINEAR PROBING. A scheme to resolve collisions when hashing by adding a constant to each subsequent address when looking for an item.

LINK. A datum that is part of a record (a field) that indicates where the next logical record is stored; it may be a pointer (an actual address) or an index.

LINKED LIST. A data structure consisting of records that are not necessarily located contiguously, but are linked together in a linear structure by links that tell where that next logical item in the list is to be found.

LOCATION. The physical location of an item, expressed as an index or an address.

LOGICAL VIEW. The high-level view of how the data is perceived by the user without the details of the actual storage.

MERGE. To combine two lists by comparing elements in the list and moving the appropriate one to a resultant list by making one pass through each list—if the initial lists are ordered, then the resultant list will be ordered.

MODULO. Essentially, the remainder after integer division.

MOVE DOWN. To move an item at the root of a heap down in the heap structure until the heap property of order is restored.

MOVE UP. To insert an item at the end of a heap and move it toward the root until the heap property of order is restored.

MULTILINKED. A linked structure with several link fields where the same set of records may be logically linked into different structures.

NODE. A record in a tree structure.

NULL. A null character with a value 0, or '\0', used to signal the termination of a string.

PARAMETER. The variable in the function definition that references a value supplied by the calling module (see argument).

PARENT. The record in a tree structure that points to the given record.

PARITY. An extra redundant bit that is used for error detection; its value depends upon the scheme selected and the other bits.

PARTITION SCHEME. A method that divides a list into at least two independent pieces.

PHYSICAL VIEW. The way the data is stored in the computer.

PHYSIOLOGICAL VIEW. A coinage that describes a view of the data that is part way between—or a blend of—the physical details of the storage and the high-level logical view.

PIVOT. In a quick sort, it is the item that is used to partition the list so that there will be a sublist of items smaller than the pivot, or the pivot as a sublist of one item, and a sublist of those items greater than the pivot.

PLANE. Strictly speaking, a two-dimensional structure consisting of rows and columns; for multi-dimensional arrays, taken to be the third dimension from the right.

POINTER. An address.

POP. To delete an item from the top of a stack.

POSTORDER. A traversal of a tree in an LRN order where the left child is processed first, followed by the right child, then the parent, and is typically applied recursively.

PREORDER. A traversal of a tree in an NLR order where the parent is processed first, followed by the left child, then the right child, and is typically applied recursively.

PRIORITY QUEUE. A structure where items are added at one end and deleted at the other, but in the order of value; it is typically implemented as a heap.

PROBE SEQUENCE. The sequence of locations in a hash table, starting with the original hash location, that will be examined in turn until the desired key is found or an empty location is encountered.

PUSH. To insert an item onto the top of a stack.

QUEUE. A restricted I/O list that allows insertions only at one end and deletions at the other—also know as a FIFO structure.

QUICK SORT. A partition sort that separates the original list into three parts—one part with all elements less than the partitioning element, the partitioning element itself (which is in its final location in the sorted list), and a part with all elements larger than the partitioning element.

RADIX SORT. A distribution-type sort that examines the values in a right-to-left scheme according to the value in that part of the item, and distributing them into auxiliary lists and recombining.

RAM. Random access memory—the type of memory found in the main memory of a computer; each word of memory has its own address and can be directly accessed by the CPU.

RANDOM ACCESS. The capability to access any item directly via its address or index without having to process a series of items to find the desired one.

RECORD. The fundamental collection of items in a file that stores data concerning a unique entity.

RECTANGULAR ARRAY. An array that for each dimension contains the full range of values for every other dimension; as an example, a rectangular table contains the same number of rows for each column and the same number of columns for each row.

RECURRENCE RELATION. A mathematical description of a sequence that describes one term in terms of the previous ones.

RECURSION. A procedure that is defined in terms of itself; generally, a function that invokes itself with a more restricted value until a value is reached that can be evaluated directly.

REPLACE. Take an existing value in a data structure and change it to another value.

REVERSE POLISH NOTATION. A notation for writing an arithmetic expression that is parentheses free; the two operands are followed by the binary operator that combines them.

ROOT. The one node in a tree structure that has no parent node.

ROTATION. Moving the root of a tree to one of its children, thereby producing a more balanced tree.

ROW. Strictly speaking, a horizontal line, that is usually taken to the next to right-most dimension of a multi-dimensional array; for a two-dimensional structure—a table—it is the left-most dimension (see column).

ROW-MAJOR. An ordering or slicing of a multi-dimensional array so that the right-most index varies most rapidly; in a table the horizontal dimension or row is stored contiguously (see column-major).

SEARCH. To look for the occurrence of some desired item in a data structure.

SECTOR. A division of a disk track into a physical chunk of storage that is written or read with a single operation.

SELECTION SORT. A sorting procedure that examines the random list and selects a desired element—typically the largest or smallest—moves it, and repeats the process on the remaining list.

SEQUENTIAL. An access scheme that requires processing items in turn until the desired one is found.

SERIAL ACCESS. Access that requires processing (at least "reading") a sequence of data items in order to get to the desired one.

SHELL'S SORT. A diminishing increment insertion sort.

SIMPLE SWAP SORT. An exchange sort that compares a given element with all the rest in the list and swaps elements if they are out of order.

SORT. To arrange a list of items into ascending or descending order.

STACK. A restricted I/O list that allows insertions and deletions only at one end—also known as a LIFO structure.

STRING. A sequence of characters internally stored in C in a character vector and terminated with a NULL character.

STRUCTURE, C. A C language construct that permits the building of complicated records, designated by **"struct."**

STRUCTURED PROGRAM. A computer program that is written in an organized manner, typically avoiding the use of labels and GoTo statements.

SWAP. To exchange the values of two variables.

TABLE. A two-dimensional array, also referred to as a matrix.

TAIL RECURSION. A recursive call that is the last operation of a function.

TOKEN. A single syntactical entity in a statement; as an example, an arithmetic expression consists of the possible tokens of variables, constants, binary arithmetic operators, unary operators, and parentheses.

TRACK. A circular trail where data is stored on a disk; typically a disk will hold a number of concentric tracks.

TREE. A data structure that for each node may contain links to several other nodes in a hierarchal fashion.

TRIE. A tree structure with the characters of the keys stored in each node so that a key is found by accumulating characters as one moves down the tree.

TRUNCATION. A scheme to reduce the storage size of a datum by discarding least-most-significant bits.

TWO-WAY MERGE SORT. A distribution-type sorting scheme suitable for an external serial access medium that reads sorted pieces from two files, merges them into a sorted piece twice as long, and writes these alternatively to two files, proceeding until all the elements are contained on one file in a sorted order.

TYPE. A description of the datum giving its size and representation in the computer; examples are: int, char, float.

UNION. A C scheme that allows two different date types to share the same memory location.

VECTOR. A one-dimensional array, also referred to as a list or a singly-dimensioned array.

WORD. The smallest unit of computer storage that is assigned a unique single address.

Appendix D

Selected Answers

"Have you guessed the riddle yet?" the Hatter said, turning to Alice again.

"No, I give it up," Alice relied.

"What's the answer?"

"I haven't the slightest idea," said the Hatter.

"Nor I," said the March Hare.

Alice sighed wearily. "I think you might do something better with the time," she said, "than wasting it in asking riddles that have no answers."

chapter 1

Q1.1   "… data are …"

Q1.4

	X	O
0	2	1
1	0	1
2	0	0
3	1	1
4	0	1
5	1	0
6	1	0
7	1	0

Play is in lower right corner square which is common to line 5 and 7, makes these configured as 2 0

Q1.5   Each square may contain a blank, an X, or an O for 3 possible values. There are 9 squares, hence there is a maximum of $3^9 = 19,683$ possible board positions.

However, this overestimates the possible legal configurations. The constraint is that the number of X's and O's cannot differ by more than 1.

Q1.6   ileac

Q1.9   It is less ambiguous than "take three tablets, three times per day" Generally it is well understood that three times a day one takes one tablet, for a total of three spread over the day.

Q1.12   Generally, $\lg x = \ln x / \ln 2$

Q1.14 $O(n^2)$

If process A were to be executed n^2 times or process B n times, then we would have $O(n^3)$

Q1.15 $O(d)$

Q1.18   The assignments are performed right to left; therefore, m and n will both have the value of r.

Q1.19   For readability! Writing a program with style will help eliminate bugs and help you find those that exist more easily. It also is helpful if you try to have someone help you with the code.

Q1.20   Human time is more expensive than computer time.

E1.2   4!=24 permutations; anagrams are: stop, spot, tops, opts, pots, post

E1.5   assume m < n

E1   m/n is zero with a remainder r=m
E2 $r \neq 0$
E3   m=n, n=m   they are reversed

E1.11   For *n* cities, there are $(n-1)!$ possible paths. For n = 48, this evaluates to 2.586×10^{59}. At 1,000,000 per second, this gives 2.586×10^{53} seconds. There are 3.15×10^7 sec/yr. Therefore, it would take 8.2×10^{45} years.

P1.4   b.   7,22,11,34,17,52,26,13,40,20,10,5,16,8,4,2,1

P1.6   c.   2/315

chapter 2

Q2.1   Less general, you may wish, sometime, to perform some other action than printing.

Q2.4   a.   5, 9, 12, 15, 17, 27, 31, 32, 42, 45, 53, 67

Q2.5   `list[k] = list[--n];`

Q2.7   **Algorithm LR** (Replacement in a Simple List) Given a new item, *ITEM*, and a location *K*, replace existing item with new one in the list, *LIST*. Uses Algorithms IL and DL.

LR1. [delete old]   Invoke Algorithm DL with K.

LR2. [insert new]   Invoke Algorithm IL with K and ITEM.

                                                          ∎

Q2.9   Any value that is not a valid index; i.e., < 0 or $\geq n$.

Q2.10 $O(n)$

Q2.12   100x

Q2.15   The test at M2 or M3 will detect it, and the algorithm will copy all the records in the other list via steps M7 or M8.

Q2.17 $> =$ is more robust and does not take any extra time.

Q2.19 $120 + 330 = 450$
$330 + 450^2/2 = 101{,}580$

Q2.20   Change step M4 to read:
M4.[find, move largest]   If LISTA[i] > LISTB[j],
then LISTC[k]=LISTA[i]; i=i+1.
else LISTC[k]=LISTB[j]; j=j+1.

Q2.22 $i <= n$ || list[i] > k

E2.1 $1 + 2 + 3 + ... + n = n(n+1)/2 \approx n^2/2$

E2.4   For the line with 8 sublists, merging operations = 768

E2.8   **Algorithm FL** (Find Largest Value in List). Given a list, *LIST*, of *n* elements, find the location of the largest item.

FL1. [initialize]   loc=0; i=1.

FL2. [at end?]   If i >= n, then Halt.

FL3. [compare]   If LIST[i] > LIST[loc], then loc=i.

FL4. [loop]   i=i+1; Go to step FL2.

P2.3   When printing the entire list, then use something like:

```
for (i=0; i<n; i++) {
    if (i%5 == 0)
        putchar('\n')
    printf("2d 5d    ",i,list[i]);
}
```

This will print the list across the page rather than down—hence will save paper!

The final list is: 42,34,17,67,12,21,8,29,78

chapter 3

Q3.1   SO4. [gone past?]   If KEY > LIST[i], then Halt.

Q3.2   No, Yes, Algorithm SU.

Q3.3   It is an extreme value placed at one end of the list. The innermost loop of the algorithm is shortened by eliminating a test if an index is out of range. This speeds the operation of the algorithm, but does not change the "big O" behavior.

Q3.4 $26(26+1)/2 = 351$, average = 13.5
A—M, $13(13+1)/2 + 1 = 92$ and N—Z, 92; total = 184, average = 7.08

Q3.7   By adopting the convention that all searches return an index of -1, then we do not have to specialize our calling program regardless of the search function.

Q3.9   On the average Algorithm B takes lg n − 1 looks with two comparisons each time less one. That is, $2 \cdot \lg n - 3$ comparisons. With this modification, approximately half of the time only one comparison would be made and the rest both. Therefore, is would save $\approx (\lg n)/2$ comparisons. Of course, the minimum number of comparisons in the best case is now 2.

Q3.10   Total looks = 49, average = 3.267

Q3.11   Each key that is present will be searched for the same number of times; that is, they all occur with a uniform distribution. Therefore, the average depends upon the distribution of keys, whereas the best and worst cases are extreme and depend upon the one extreme value.

Q3.13   For n=10,000; best case = 1, worst case = 14, average case = 12.36

Q3.15   Binary Search

Q3.17   For overall speed, Algorithm BA.

Q3.18   List must be ordered and randomly accessible.

Q3.22   Since the list is normally greater than 10, this would slow down the searches by one extra comparison. It would also increase the total length of the code for the program. Even for short lists, the binary search is still very fast.

E3.1   **Algorithm SU'** (Serial Search on Unordered List). Given a list, *LIST*, of *n* elements, find the location of the key, *KEY*.

SU1'. [initialize]   i=0.

SU2'. [sentinel]   LIST[n]=KEY.

SU3'. [compare]   If KEY = LIST[i], then Go to step SU5.

SU4'. [loop]   i=i+1; Go to step SU2.

SU5'. [determine] If i = n, then Halt.   (not found)
                      else Halt.   (found)
                                                          ∎

E3.10   a.   lwr = 0
              upr = 8 --> i=4 (>) ==> lwr = 0
                                  upr = 4 --> i=2 (>=)
              ==> lwr = 2
                  ipr = 4 --> i=3 (>=) ==> lwr = 3
                                          upr = 4 found at 3

P3.1   500 is found at location 249 with 1 look

P3.4   a. $n = 10$, $max = 4$, $L = 29$,   average = 2.900

chapter 4

Q4.1   A circular definition has no stopping point. A recursive definition sooner or later reaches a point where it can stop and be evaluated without invoking itself again.

Q4.2   Values of the local variables, the parameters, and the return address.

Q4.5   No, even numbered disks always are next to an odd numbered disk.

Q4.6 $F_{46} = 1,836,311,916$, $F_{47} = 2,971,205,095$

Q4.8 $N(n)$ has the same growth function as F_n.

Q4.9   ABCD ABDC ACBD ACDB ADBC ADCB
              BACD BADC BCAD BCDA BDAC BDCA
              CBAD CBDA CABD CADB CDBA CDAB
              DBCA DBAC DCBA DCAB DABC DACB

Q4.10 $20! = 2,432,902,008,176,640,000$

Thus, we have 2.433×10^{15} seconds $= 7.715 \times 10^7$ years

Q4.12   Number of operations are the same. Execution time is probably increased somewhat. Memory requirements are increased.

Q4.20   After the recursive call there is a mathematical operation, namely addition.

Q4.22   This would not be an algorithm since there is no way of telling if it would ever end. Generating all the permutations systematically does result in algorithm, although both of these are terribly ineffective!

E4.4   31 moves, top disk goes first to B the final destination pile since there is an odd number of disks

E4.7   For $n=2$, $n! = 2$, $n^n = 4$.
              $n=10$, $n! = 3,628,800$, $n^n = 10,000,000,000$.

E4.10

n	G(n)
0	0
1	1
2	1
3	2
4	3
5	3

P4.8   i. 210

chapter 5

Q5.1   n!

Q5.3   Use: NEWLIST[n$-$1$-$INDEX[i]]=LIST[i], i=0,1,...,n$-$1

Q5.5   C2. [set index]   INDEX[i]=1.

Q5.7   Insertion Sort and Improved Bubble Sort

Q5.9   Depending upon the order, the number of **swap** operations is changed.

Q5.10   The fundamental operation is selection; that is, select a desired element.

Q5.14   Slightly faster and takes less space unless performed in many different places.

Q5.18   For 10,000; expect 1,140 seconds.

Q5.22   b.   address

E5.9   c. $O(n^3)$

P5.1   It is suggested that in order to save space and paper when printing the execution, that you print the list across the page rather than down; that is, use:

   13456 87394 83453   3455 78783 19262   621
   49153 73524

Rather than:

$$
\begin{array}{r}
13456 \\
87394 \\
83453 \\
3455 \\
78783 \\
19262 \\
621 \\
49153 \\
73524 \\
\end{array}
$$

or what is even more spaced out, to double space each line!
This may be accomplished by:

```
for (i=0; i<n; i++) {
    if (i%7 == 0)
        putchar('\n');
    printf("%7d",list[i]);
}
```

where the if () statement will generate a new line after every seventh number printed. Actually, you could use 10 rather than 7 since each number will take 7 characters. This totals 70 characters per line out of 80 possible on a typical printed line or screen.

P5.2   See previous answer.

P5.3   See answer for P5.1.

chapter 6

Q6.1   So the final sorting can get the elements into the correct order, a simple insertion sort is needed. If the last increment is not one, then the final list is not necessarily sorted.

Q6.5   Prime: 13, 1093, 797,161

Q6.6   1, 3, 7, 15, 31, 63, ...   not necessarily

Q6.7   1, 3, 7, 25, 121, 721, ...   yes

Q6.11   Q2. [setup]   i=LEFT; j=RIGHT; dir=1.

Q6.13   Because with lists a maximum of 14 long, the improvement gained in using a Shell's Sort rather than a Straight Insertion Sort is minimal.

Q6.16   Probably not, any of the $O(n^2)$ or $O(n \cdot \lg n)$ sorts would be fine.

Q6.23 Copy the contents to another list first.

E6.5 $h_s = (3^s - 1)/2$

P6.1 See answer for P5.1.

chapter 7

Q7.1 No, the way one typically eats then by cutting a vertical byte out of all of them at once.

Q7.5 O(1)

Q7.7 `#define increment(x) (((x)==MAX-1) ? 0 : (x)+1)`

Q7.8 ii=di

Q7.10 V = XPOP
TPUSH V

Q7.11 We do not have to worry about arbitrary order of operations. In particular, the queue does not have to implemented as a circular structure.

Q7.13 Insertion would be unchanged. After deleting a value, then examine the next location to see if contains an EMPTY, if so move the *di* forward until an non-EMPTY value is found or the queue is empty.

Q7.17 ... = array[++i];

Q7.19 Societal customs suggest a queue.

E7.6 a.   3 5 4 * +

E7.7 For 3, may obtain: ABC ACB BCA BAC CBA; 5 patterns out 6 possible ones. For n=4, get 14 out of 24.

P7.2 Last dump:

0	1	2	3	4	5	6	7
16	54	61	85	18	19	16	15

insert at 3, delete at 3

P7.4   b.   A B C D E * F + − * G H / / +

chapter 8

Q8.1   131,072

Q8.4   a.   127

Q8.5   An address

Q8.7   C stores arrays as row-major, the formula for computing the address does not need the left-most size
                    FORTRAN stores arrays as column-major, the formula for computing the address does not need the right-most size

Q8.9

vector	1
table	2
box	6
hyperbox	24

The general case is $N!$ where N is the number of dimensions.

Q8.11   A cube implies that all three sides are equal in length. A box can be any rectangular shape.

Q8.13   Seven multiplications and seven additions.

Q8.15   Only the values of the coefficients and constant term.

Q8.17   hbox[b,p,r,c]   column-major

          b most rapidly, p next most rapidly, c least rapidly

Q8.23   For entire matrix multiplication, $O(n^3)$; that is, compute n^2 values, each taking n multiplications.

E8.1   b.   address(i,j) = 3984 + 12i + 4j

E8.7   "wasted space" = (M + 1)*(N + 1) − M*N

E8.8   There are 80 lines and 80 squares in a hyperhypercube.

P8.2   c.   9666

P8.4   b.   address(i,j) = 1242 + 9i + 3j

chapter 9

Q9.3   There must be sufficient storage allocated to hold the catenated string.

Q9.4   c.   "Zebra"

Q9.5   C stores tables in row-major form, left-most size is not need to compute the address.

Q9.7
```
char states[50][15];
```
"North Carolina" has 14 letters

Q9.9   More robust, handles newline characters consistently, takes the entire string.

Q9.11   "3 out of 4 girls like C\n"

Q9.13   The compiler tries to implement it as if it were returning an int—strange results!

Q9.19   Wastes time in computing the length of the string twice. It is also rather obscure.

E9.7   Change the multiplier in step AI5 from 10 to 16. We would need to change the digit equivalent to something like:

```
((isdigit(ch)) ? ch-'0': ch-'A'+10)
```

P9.7   An interesting solution to displaying a palindrome is the following C program originally found on the INTERNET, author unknown, with modifications.

```
#include <stdio.h>/*\<h.oidts> edulcni#
                  \*/
             char rahc
               [ ]
                =
             "\n/"
               ,
            redivider
               [ ]
                =
    "Able was I ere I saw elbA"
```

```
                    *
                 top,pot
                    =
                   1+1
                    '
                niam ; main
                   ( )
                 {/*\}
                  \*/
                int tni
                   =
                  0x0
                    '
          rahctup/*\putchar
                  \*/
          ,LACEDx0 = 0xDECAL,
                rof ; for
              (;(int) (tni);)
                (int) (tni)
              = pot ; top =
                redivider
                    ;
for ((int) (tni)++,++pot;pot* *top;top++,++(int) (tni)) rof
                    =
              (int) -1- (tni)
               ;pot--;--top;
               (tni) = (int)
            - 0xDECAL + LACEDx0 -
                rof ; for
      (live--,(int)--(tni);(int) (tni);(int)--(tni),--evil)
              rahctup - putchar
                (pot* *top)
                    ;
              rahctup * putchar
              ((char) * (rahc))
                    ;
                  /*\
                 {\*/}
```

chapter 10

Q10.1   a.   expr = 5   x = 6   p = 34210

Q10.4   At the point strcat() is invoked, date[] is not NULL terminated.

Q10.6   *stack* is a pointer constant.

Q10.10   *x* is a pointer constant, *y* is a pointer variable.

Q10.11   Both are pointer variables.

Q10.13   The struct *person* is not included in the struct *person*, only a single item that can point to such a record.

Q10.21   Less arithmetic needed at execution time to change from an index to an address; hence faster.

Q10.25   c.   declares

Q10.27   The address of the array.

E10.1
```
date[3] = mon[3*m-3];
date[4] = mon[3*m-2];
date[5] = mon[3*m-1];
```

E10.2
```
struct phone {int area_code;
              int prefix;
              int number;
              }
```

or

```
struct phone {char area_code[4];
              char prefix[4];
              char number[5];
              }
```

E10.9   b.   472 bytes (including NULL) + 100 bytes for pointers = 572 bytes

chapter 11

Q11.1   All but *birthday* are arbitrary identifiers—it is possible to perform arithmetic on dates.

Q11.4   fgets() requires, in addition to the file pointer, a length and it does not replace any trailing newline characters with a NULL.

Q11.13   none

Q11.14   20*8 = 160

Q12.18   RF6. [read back]   Perform step RF7 for j=9,8,...,0.

Q11.20   It does not matter the number of initial records processed; however, all initial pieces must contain the same number; after the first pass, the size of the sorted pieces double with each pass.

Q11.21   No extra storage required for the Quick Sort.

Q11.22   The Enumeration Sort does leave the original list intact. For the others that sort in-place, we could make a copy of the original list before sorting.

Q11.25   The number of operations is independent of the initial order. The algorithm performs the same operations regardless.

Q11.27   Internal sorts: random access
External sorts: serial access only

chapter 12

Q12.1   Record consists of $20 + 2 + 4 = 26$ bytes; $2/26 = 0.077$

Q12.4   Advantages: can move forward and backwards—do not need to keep track of the predecessor record when inserting or deleting

Disadvantages: must update both links when inserting or deleting and the two takes extra space

Q12.5   No, linked list requires physical random access.

Q12.7   With one *tol* for each list—need only one empty list.

Q12.10   Including an explicit link for the empty list wastes space, when a record is on the empty list all the normal fields are unused, therefore, use an ordinary link field.

Q12.13   All the external sorts could be used because of their serial access; of the internal sorts, Shell's requires jumping large distances in the list and random access.

Q12.15   No, as long as it can be accessed with having to search the record.

Q12.17   Faster and allows the use of C library functions to manage memory.

Q12.21   a.   1

Q12.25   The rest of list is already linked o the current record.

E12.1   e.

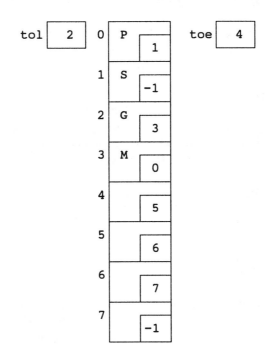

E12.4   Some link fields are: Mercury 8, Venus -1, Earth 3, Mars 0

P12.1   See answer for P2.3.

chapter 13

Q13.2
```
A          A          B          C          C
    B          C          A C        B          A
        C          B                     A          B
```

Q13.4   They are both linked structures, but a linked list is basically linear, whereas a binary tree has branching.

Q13.5   a. 5   b. 3   d. no

Q13.8   32

Q13.7   No, random access is required.

Q13.9   c.   IRHMTSASC

Q13.11   O(n · lg n)

Q13.17   We have a list of all the locations of the records.

Q13.18   Three values requires 2 bits (3 out of 4 possible values).

Q13.20   3

Q13.27   For all nodes that were not the last, we were adding more nodes and hence changing the right child link. For the last node, its right child link was already END.

Q13.32   Generally reduces the number of levels by one.

E13.9   For n = 10, P(n) = 16,796

P13.1   See answer for P2.3.

chapter 14

Q14.1   Insertion at one end, deletion at the other.

Q14.2   Yes, it has both the heap properties; i.e. no "holes" and each item is greater than or equal to its children.

Q14.4   Four distinct items, three distinct heaps.

```
        4                    4                    4
      3   2                3   1                2   3
    1                    2                    1
```

Q14.9   The descending order was already a heap, therefore the make heap part did not have to move any items.

Q14.11   By treating it as a binary tree; however, we would need parent links so we could move up the tree.

Q14.13   The resultant might not be a heap, as an example:

```
        1                           4
      4   5   would become:       3   5
    3   2                        1   2
```

which does not have heap order.

Q14.15   For 10,000 items, 5,700,000 seconds $\approx$ 66 days.

Q14.22   Worst case for Heap Sort is easy to find: already sorted list!

E14.4   Yes, adding a constant does not affect the shape property and adding a constant does not change the order of any of the items.

E14.10   Simple Swap, random 10,100 sec

P14.1   Jobs are executed in order:

1	priority 5
4	priority 8
3	priority 8
6	priority 9
5	priority 8
2	priority 7
9	priority 7
7	priority 8
8	priority 8
11	priority 8
10	priority 8

P14.2   See answer for P5.1

chapter 15

Q15.1   Two keys hash to the same address or location.

Q15.2   67—the next largest prime after $50/.8 = 62.5$.

Q15.3   From the table with $\alpha = .8$, we get 2.01.

Q15.5   M!

Q15.7   So all possible locations are included in the probe sequence.

Q15.9   1, 1,2,3,...,M-1 (the 0 is replaced with a 1).

Q15.11   No, consider the number of Smith's as compared to the number Faura's in the United States.

Q15.13   Without checking for a full list or for a probe address to become equal to the original hash address, we get an infinite loop!

Q15.15   O(1)

Q15.21   No, some will be stored in **their** original hash location.

Q15.24   Test and assignment may be faster to execute than a modulo operation.

E15.3   For h = 0, p = 4; sequence: 0, 4, 8, 12, 3, 7, 11, 2, 6, 10, 1, 5, 9

E15.5   a.   110

E15.7   c.   Similar to p=p(h) since probe sequence depends only upon *h*.

P15.2   Largest prime less then 1,000,000 is 999,983.

P15.4   b.   42

chapter 16

Q16.1   sizeof is an operator and is part of the basic C specification, the others are "add on" functions.

Q16.3   It is a generic pointer, without type.

Q16.6   b.   compilation

Q16.7   Test if the pointer value returned by malloc() is a NULL.

Q16.10   The algorithms are really independent upon the language implementation.

Q16.17   `int *(*fun)()`

Q16.21   *tolptr* is a pointer to a pointer
                     arrpts is a pointer to an array of pointers

Index

"Of course you know your A B C?" said the Red Queen.

"To be sure I do," said Alice.

"So do I," the White Queen whispered: We'll often say it over together, dear. And I'll tell you a secret--I can read words of one letter! Isn't that grand? However, don't be discouraged. You'll come to it in time."

Here the Red Queen began again. "Can you answer useful questions?" she said. "How is bread made?"

"I know that!" Alice cried eagerly. "You take some flour—"

"Where do you pick the flower?" the White Queen asked. "In a garden or in the hedges?"

"Well, it isn't picked at all," Alice explained: "it's ground—"

"How many acres of ground?" said the White Queen. "You mustn't leave out so many things."

V

W